The Politics of the New Welfare State

Edited by
Giuliano Bonoli and David Natali

OXFORD
UNIVERSITY PRESS

OXFORD

UNIVERSITY PRESS

Great Clarendon Street, Oxford OX2 6DP
United Kingdom

Oxford University Press is a department of the University of Oxford.
It furthers the University's objective of excellence in research, scholarship,
and education by publishing worldwide. Oxford is a registered trade mark of
Oxford University Press in the UK and in certain other countries

First edition published in 2012
Reprinted 2013

British Library Cataloguing in Publication Data
Data available

Library of Congress Cataloging in Publication Data
Data available

ISBN 978-0-19-964525-1

Acknowledgments

This book has its origin in the strong interest of both editors and contributors in the analysis of the political dimension of the process of welfare state transformation. Interest alone, however, would not have allowed us to complete such an ambitious book project. In order to do this, we were able to count on the support of several people and institutions.

Many of the ideas that are put forward in the volume were developed in the context of the RECWOWE project (Reconciling Work and Welfare), a European network of excellence financed through the 6th Framework Program between 2006 and 2011. The editors and many of the volume's contributors were part of this network and within it, they had the opportunity to engage in research and discussions on the future of the welfare state in Europe.

A key role in initiating this project was played by the European University Institute (EUI) and its former President, Yves Mény. He convinced us that the time was ripe for a new comprehensive contribution to the study of welfare state transformation, since policy change was occurring so rapidly. In December 2009, on the occasion of the end of Yves Mény's EUI Presidency, we had the opportunity to organize a conference in his honour at the Badia Fiesolana. As sometimes happens, the shared sentiment of gratitude and friendship allowed us to organize a truly exceptional event: three generations of leading scholars and social policy analysts came to the EUI to exchange on the future of the welfare state. The list of participants looks like a 'dream team': Tito Boeri, Dorothe Bohle, Giliberto Capano, Jochen Clasen, Daniel Clegg, Colin Crouch, Maurizio Ferrera, Anton Hemerijck, Silja Häusermann, Jane Jenson, Martin Kohli, Trudie Knijn, Maarten Keune, Ingela Naumann, Bruno Palier, Philippe Pochet, Martin Rhodes, David Rueda, Sven Steinmo, Tiziano Treu and Frank Vandenbroucke. The event—financed by the EUI, RECWOWE, IDHEAP (Institut d'hautes études en administration publique de Lausanne) and the University of Bologna—was thus a first step towards a more accurate analysis of the changes that we had recently observed in European welfare states. We want here to thank all the conference participants who largely helped us develop the idea of this book.

After the first conference, the need for a comprehensive study of recent social policy change was clear to everyone. The original idea of a large summary of the literature produced so far on welfare reforms left room to a more accurate and precise reconstruction of the theoretical debate on the 'new' welfare state (or at least what is new in the realm of welfare provision), the analysis of the main institutional innovations in the field of social and employment policies, and the reconsideration of the main analytical tools proposed some 10 to 15 years ago by political scientists and sociologists for the study of welfare politics.

A second event was held at the EUI in October 2010. This time, we were able to count on the support of the Robert Schuman Centre and of its Director, Stefano Bartolini. Thanks to them, a new round of debate and exchange focused on draft chapters was possible. Many friends—Pepper Culpepper, Sven Steinmo, and Valeria Fargion—came to provide their input to the project. The workshop represented in fact an opportunity to finalize the project and to improve the coordination among the different chapters. It became increasingly evident that the first light we saw on the 'new' welfare state and its political dynamics was more than an intuition. Increased evidence of new institutions, new 'boundaries' of social rights and new political trends was collected at that time.

For the production of the book, we were also able to rely on the support of a number of people. At Oxford University Press we would like to thank Dominic Byatt for his support and efficient handling of our book proposal, and Sarah Parker, for sorting out administrative issues. Kimberly Way has done a terrific job in transforming our not-always-so-elegant English into a decent text. Finally, Aurélien Abrassart and Nicolas Turtschi assisted us in the preparation of the manuscript.

Giuliano Bonoli,
David Natali
Lausanne and Bologna, December 2011

Contents

List of Figures

List of Tables

List of Abbreviations

ALMP	active labour market policy
ATP	Swedish supplementary pension scheme
CDU	German Christian Democratic party)
CNPF	Conseil national du patronnat français (French employers confederation)
DIRECCTE	regional agencies of the French Ministry of the economy
ECJ	European court of Justice
ENCAs	Emplois nouveaux à contraintes allégés, (French low regulated jobs)
ESA	Employment Support Allowance
FDP	German liberal party
IPR	institutional power resources
LO	Swedish blue collar union
NSR	New Social Risks
OECD	Organisation of Economic Co-operation and Development
PES	Public Employment Services
RMI	Revenu minimum d'insertion (French social assistance scheme)
RSA	Revenu de solidarité active (replaced RMI in 2009)
SAP	Swedish Social Democratic party
SPD	German Social Democratic party
TAG	Childcare Expansion Act or Tageseinrichtungsausbaugesetz
TCNs	third country nationals
UNEDIC	French administration of unemployment benefits
WAO	Dutch disability insurance scheme
WIW	Jobseekers Employment Act
WWB	Dutch social assistance scheme

List of Contributors

Giuliano Bonoli is Professor of social policy at the Swiss Graduate School of Public Administration at the University of Lausanne, Switzerland. He has published some 50 articles and chapters in edited books, as well as a few books. Among these: Bonoli, G. (2000) *The Politics of Pension Reform: Institutions and Policy Change in Western Europe*, (Cambridge University Press); and Bonoli, G. (2013) *The Origins of Active Social Policies*. (Oxford University Press).

Jochen Clasen is Professor of Comparative Social Policy in the School of Social and Political Science at the University of Edinburgh. He has published widely on social security policy, comparative welfare state analysis, labour market policy and unemployment mainly in European context. Recent publications include: Clasen, J. (ed.) (2011) *Converging Worlds of Welfare? British and German Social Policy in the 21st Century* (Oxford University Press); Clasen, J. and Clegg, D. (eds) (2011) *Regulating the Risk of Unemployment: National Adaptations to Post-industrial Labour Markets in Europe*, (Oxford University Press); 'Exit Bismarck, enter dualism? Assessing contemporary German labour market policy' (with A. Goerne), *Journal of Social Policy*, 4/2011.

Daniel Clegg is Senior Lecturer in Social Policy at the University of Edinburgh, UK. He has published widely on unemployment benefit and labour market policy, and is co-editor (with Jochen Clasen) of *Regulating the Risk of Unemployment: National Adaptations to Post-Industrial Labour Markets in Europe* (Oxford University Press, 2011).

Colin Crouch is Emeritus Professor of Governance and Public Management at the Business School of Warwick University. He is also an External Scientific member of the Max Planck Institute for the Study of Societies at Cologne. He has published within the fields of comparative European sociology and industrial relations, on economic sociology, and on contemporary issues in British and European politics. His most recent books include: *Social Change in Western Europe* (1999); *Postdemocrazia* (2003); *Capitalist Diversity and Change: Recombinant Governance and Institutional Entrepreneurs* (2005); and *The Strange Non-death of Neoliberalism* (2011).

Johan B. Davidsson is Post-doctoral Fellow at Lund University. Before he was a PhD student at the European University Institute, where he wrote his thesis on the politics of labour market policy reform in France, Sweden and the UK, and a researcher at the University of Southern Denmark. He has articles forthcoming in, for example, Political Studies.

Bernhard Ebbinghaus is Professor of Sociology at the University of Mannheim, and former Director of the Mannheim Centre for European Social Research (MZES). He has published widely on welfare states and industrial relations. Among these, he has authored *Reforming Early Retirement in Europe, Japan and the USA* (2006) and edited *The Varieties of Pension Governance: Pension Privatization in Europe* (2011). Both titles were published with Oxford University Press.

Patrick Emmenegger is Professor of Comparative Political Economy and Public Policy at the University of St. Gallen. He has published some 30 articles and chapters in edited books, among others in the *European Journal of Political Research, Comparative Political Studies*, and *Comparative Politics*. His latest book, entitled *The Age of Dualization: The Changing Face of Inequality in Deindustrializing Societies* and co-edited with Silja Häusermann, Bruno Palier and Martin Seeleib-Kaiser, has been published by Oxford University Press.

Maurizio Ferrera is Professor of Political Science and President of the Graduate School in Social and Political Studies of the University of Milan. He is a member of the Board of Directors of the Collegio Carlo Alberto and of the Centro di Ricerca e Documentazione Luigi Einaudi, both in Turin. He has served on many High-level Advisory Groups and commissions at national and EU levels. He has published extensively in the fields of comparative welfare states and European integration on international journals, including *Comparative Political Studies, West European Politics*, the *Journal of Common Market Studies*, the *Journal of European Social Policy*. His last book in English is *The Boundaries of Welfare* (Oxford University Press, 2005).

Silja Häusermann is Professor of Political Science at the University of Zurich, Switzerland. Her current work focuses on comparative welfare policy, political parties, representation and dualization. Her articles have appeared in journals such as the *European Journal of Political Research, British Journal of Political Research, Journal of European Public Policy and Socio-Economic Review*. She is also the author of *The Politics of Welfare Reform in Continental Europe. Modernization in Hard Times*, published in 2010 by Cambridge University Press.

Anton Hemerijck is the Dean of the Faculty of the Social Sciences at the VU University Amsterdam and Vice Rector. Between 2001 and 2009 he was Director of the Netherlands Council for Government Policy (WRR). He obtained his doctorate from Oxford University in 1993. He publishes widely on issues comparative social and economic policy and institutional policy analysis. Between 1997 and 2000 he was a senior researcher at the Max Planck Institute for the Study of Societies, working on the large comparative project on welfare and work in the open economy, directed by Fritz W. Scharpf and Vivien A. Schmidt. He has also been involved in drafting reports on social policy for Portuguese (2000), Belgian (2001), Greek (2003), Finnish (2006), German (2007) and Portuguese (2007) presidencies of the EU. Important publications include *A Dutch Miracle* with Jelle Visser (Amsterdam University Press, 1997) and *Why We Need a New Welfare State* with Gosta Esping-Andersen, Duncan Gallie, and John Myles (Oxford University Press, 2002), and *Changing Welfare States* (Oxford University Press, 2012)

Jane Jenson In 2001, Jane Jenson was awarded the Canada Research Chair in Citizenship and Governance at the Université de Montréal, where she is Professor of Political Science. She is also Member of the Successful Societies programme of the Canadian Institute for Advanced Research. Her research interests and publications include social policy and social citizenship in Canada and the European Union. She has published numerous books and articles, including most recently in *Global Social Policy*, *Social Politics*, and *Comparative European Politics*.

Maarten Keune is Professor of Social Security and Labour Relations at the Amsterdam Institute of Advanced Labour Studies, University of Amsterdam. He has published widely on industrial relations, employment policy, and the welfare state. Recent publications include Burroni, L., Keune, M., and Meardi, G. (eds.) (2012) *Economy and Society in Europe: A Relationship in Crisis* (Edward Elgar); Pochet, P., Keune, M., and Natali D. (eds.) (2010) *After the Euro and Enlargement: Social Pacts in the EU* (ETUI); Burroni, L. and Keune, M. (2011) 'Flexicurity: a Conceptual Critique', *European Journal of Industrial Relations*; Glasner, V., Keune, M., and Marginson, P. (2011) 'Collective Bargaining in a Time of Crisis: Developments in the Private Sector in Europe', *Transfer European Review of Labour and Research*.

David Natali is Associate Professor of Public Policy Analysis at the University of Bologna, R. Ruffilli faculty of Political Sciences in Forlì and Research Director of the European Social Observatory (OSE). He has published widely on social policy and industrial relations, among these: Natali, D. (2008), *Pensions in Europe, European Pensions* (PIE-Peter Lang, Brussels) Pochet, P., Keune, M. and Natali D. (eds.) (2010), *After Euro and Enlargement: Social Pacts in the EU* (ETUI/OSE, Brussels).

Ingela Naumann is Lecturer in Social Policy at the University of Edinburgh and Member of the international research networks RECWOWE—Reconciling Work and Welfare in Europe, and NordWel—the Nordic welfare state: historical foundations and future challenges. She has published several articles and book chapters on international childcare and education policy and on gender and religious cleavages in welfare state politics, among these 'Child care and feminism in West Germany and Sweden in the 1960s and 1970s', Young Researcher Prize Essay, Journal of European Social Policy, 2005, 15(1):43–63.

Bruno Palier is CNRS Research Director at Sciences Po, Centre d'études européennes. His main research topic is welfare reforms in Europe. He was the Scientific Coordinator of the European Network of excellence RECWOWE. He has published numerous articles on welfare reforms in France and in Europe in different academic journals and has co-edited various books. In 2010, he edited *A Long Good Bye to Bismarck? The Politics of Welfare Reforms in Continental Europe* (Amsterdam University Press). In 2012, he co-edited *The Age of Dualization: The Changing Face of Inequality in Deindustrializing Societies* (with Patrick Emmenegger, Silja Häusermann, and Martin Seeleib-Kaiser) (Oxford University Press); and *Towards a Social Investment Welfare State? Ideas, Policies and Challenges* (with Nathalie Morel and Joakim Palme) (Policy Press).

Introduction

1

The Politics of the 'New' Welfare States

Analysing Reforms in Western Europe

Giuliano Bonoli and David Natali

Since the early 1990s, European welfare states have undergone substantial changes, in terms of objectives, areas of intervention, and instruments. Traditional programmes, such as old age pensions have been curtailed throughout the continent. Funded pensions have been introduced and expanded in several countries. Cost-containment measures have been adopted also in other parts of the welfare state, ranging from health care services to invalidity benefits. At the same time, today's welfare states have taken up some new functions. They are expected to help and/or push non-working people back into employment, to complement work income for the working poor, to help parents reconcile work and family life, to promote gender equality, to support child development, and to provide social services for an ageing society. These are big changes. Today's welfare states are very different from those we have inherited from the postwar years, and focused their efforts in securing an income stream to male breadwinners.

Sure, the traditional functions of the welfare state have not lost relevance, and remain important. Old age pensions, for instance, still make up the bulk of social spending. However, the impression that some profound changes are taking place in this field is widespread among experts. This is probably why, over the last few years, many scholars have used the adjective 'new' to describe the orientation taken by social and employment policies (see e.g. Esping-Andersen 2002; Hemerijck 2012). Moreover, in recent times, notions aiming to signal a qualitative shift in social policymaking have mushroomed. These include 'social investment' (see for instance Jenson, Chapter 2), 'new social risk policies' (Taylor-Gooby 2004; Bonoli 2005), 'flexicurity' (Wilthagen and Tros 2004) to name a few. Each of these labels emphasizes a different aspect of welfare state transformation, but they all understand recent changes are substantial.

With this book, we would like to move beyond a simple description of this emerging settlement in terms of 'newness' and focus on two sets of questions. First, we want to gain a better understanding of the welfare settlement that is emerging in early 21st century Europe. What role is the welfare state playing in today's post-industrial societies? To what extent are welfare states shifting away from the provision of income protection and towards the promotion of employment? What may the distributional consequences of this shift be? Second, we are interested in the factors that have shaped the recent transformation. Our focus is on finding out what are the mechanisms and trajectories that lead to the current welfare settlement. What role are the key political actors playing? How do they position themselves in the social policy arena?

The notion of a 'new welfare state' must be understood as a putative statement. We are not interested in claiming that the emerging settlement is qualitatively different from the one developed during the postwar years. Instead, we simply use the notion of a new welfare state to denote the current arrangement. We present and discuss possible interpretations of it, but leave it up to our readers to decide whether or not change has been so substantial that the result is a qualitatively different set of institutions. This is because the latter question is necessarily a subjective one.

We decided to limit the focus of the book to Western Europe because the intellectual issue at stake, how welfare states that were built during the postwar years are now being transformed, makes sense only in countries that have followed a specific trajectory: construction of an encompassing welfare state in the 1950s and 1960s, crisis in the 1980s and early 1990s, and transformation in the late 1990s and 2000s. This condition is not fulfilled by North America (where the welfare state has remained residual) and Eastern Europe (which has not experienced the first two phases in a democratic context).

In this introductory chapter we begin by reviewing, in a brief and stylized manner, the main changes that have taken place over the last decade or two in advanced welfare states. We start from the mid-1990s, a period characterized by a general reorientation of social policy in many OECD countries. Second, we consider two different interpretations of the changes that have been observed. These are present throughout the book, and pay attention to different elements of the transformation. Third, we ask whether the observed changes are well accounted for by existing theories of social policymaking. We argue that, in many respects, the current transformation represents a challenge for theory. In this introduction, we only highlight what we believe to be the key challenges for theory. Our own take on the factors that are driving the process of welfare state transformation is presented in Chapter 13.

What Has Changed?

Over the last 20 years, and perhaps even more during the last decade, change in social policies has been substantial. Pension systems have been reformed a number of times in virtually all European countries, with the term 'reform' being usually a synonym for cutbacks. Unemployment compensation systems have been transformed from passive providers of replacement income into activation tools. New policies have emerged too, such as parental leave, childcare, and in-work benefits. Finally, the field of social policy is increasingly considered as part of a broader politico-economic settlement that can impact significantly on the functioning of a country's economy. This new understanding of social policy has resulted in a stronger connection between economic, fiscal, education and social policy. In this section, we briefly sketch the main trends that have taken place in most countries over the last two decades.

Development of new functions and policies

One of the most salient developments in social policy over the last two decades is the assignment of a new set of functions to the welfare state and the development of the tools that go with them. Most of these new functions can be seen as part of a broader reorientation of social policy from income protection to the promotion of labour market participation. The new functions and tools developed include:

- Policies aiming at moving non-working people into employment. Such policies concern increasingly large groups of welfare state beneficiaries. In the past, only unemployment insurance recipients were expected by policy to seek employment (see Clasen and Clegg, Chapter 7). Increasingly efforts to (re-) enter the labour market are expected by other types of beneficiaries as well, including disabled people, social assistance recipients, lone parents, etc.;
- Policies that provide an income supplement to the working poor. Changes in labour market and family structures have resulted in the emergence of the working poor as a social policy problem, especially in liberal welfare states. Several countries have responded to this problem by introducing negative income tax types of programmes;
- Policies aimed facilitating the conciliation of work and family life. These include subsidized childcare and parental leave, as well as work regulations such as the right to part-time employment for parents of small children (Naumann, Chapter 8);

- Provision of services to older people. This is an area of development of the welfare state that is often seen as related to population ageing. However, value change may also be an important explanatory factor and relate to the fact that current generations of children are less inclined to provide informal care than previous ones;

- Policies aiming at investing in human capital. These include lifelong learning efforts in vocational training, but also an increased focus on child development as a key priority of social intervention. Social policy in the 2000s has been characterized by an emphasis on social investment, through programmes like lifelong learning and concerns for child development (Jenson, Chapter 2);

- In some countries, the improvement of social protection for non-standard workers, i.e. part-time employees or workers on time-limited contracts. This has been the case above all in the Netherlands (Visser 2002), and to a lesser extent in other continental European countries.

These developments clearly go under the rubric of social policy expansion. Western European welfare states, while performing retrenchment in some traditional areas were also expanding provision in these new fields. Indeed, the extent of development of these policies varies considerably across countries and in some cases (especially investment in human capital), emphasis is much stronger in discourse than in actual policies. They nevertheless constitute instances of expansion and need to be taken into account in our discussion of the new welfare state.

Continued retrenchment

Retrenchment and cost-containment have been important themes of social policymaking throughout the 2000s. Efforts at containing and reducing social expenditure have concerned, above all, the Bismarckian welfare states of Continental Europe. Old age pensions, as the biggest spending programme, have been mostly affected. Most continental European countries had adopted retrenchment-oriented pension reforms earlier on (in most countries since the early 1990s), but the cuts adopted were generally regarded as insufficient to guarantee the long-term sustainability of these generous schemes. As a result, throughout the 2000s we see the continuation of the trends set in motion in the previous decade. Above all, these consist of a reduction in the replacement rate of pay-as-you-go public pensions and the expansion of private-funded schemes (at the company or at the individual level). The combined effect of these changes is unlikely to be neutral. The development of supplementary funded provision in fact remains patchy, which suggests that retirement will be characterized by bigger inequalities once the cuts introduced during the various waves of reform will begin to bite. In addition, the last decade has witnessed an increase of the effective age of retirement, sometimes resulting from the phasing out of incentives for early retirement that had been put in place a in the 1980s (Ebbinghaus, Chapter 9). These reforms have tended to have relatively long phasing in periods, which arguably made them politically more acceptable (Bonoli and Palier 2008).

Retrenchment and cost containment have been applied to other policy areas as well, such as unemployment compensation. Germany, with the Hartz IV reform of unemployment policy, has cut the unemployment benefit for large numbers of long-term jobless people, who have seen their earnings-related benefit being downgraded to the equivalent of social assistance. Cost containment measures have been adopted also in other continental European countries (Clegg 2008).

Retrenchment was less of a dominant theme in policymaking, both in the Nordic countries and in Liberal welfare states. In the former, a good macro-economic performance since the mid-1990s has meant that retrenchment was unnecessary (Kangas and Palme 2009). In the UK, the financial sustainability of social policies had been addressed during the previous decades, and policy, until the financial crisis of 2008, was geared more towards addressing uncovered social needs and alleviating poverty, for example, in the field of pensions (Clasen 2005).

Retrenchment initiatives have often been characterized by the fact of producing an uneven impact on actual or future beneficiaries. This is reminiscent of one of the strategies identified by Pierson as used by governments to make retrenchment politically feasible: division. According to this strategy, rather than adopt across the board cuts that affect large sections of the electorate, governments will prefer, where possible, reforms that concern only a smaller group. Division is a strong dimension of the pension reforms adopted in the Bismarckian countries. Given the long phasing-in periods, reforms have predominantly affected voters who are rather young and unlikely to mobilize against pension cuts. Current retirees and older workers have generally been spared the negative consequences of reform.

Labour market deregulation 'at the margin'

The last two decades have also seen in many continental European countries (but to some extent also in Sweden) a new form of labour market deregulation, consisting of the introduction of new forms of employment contracts that are considerably more flexible than standard ones. These include time-limited contracts, short part-time contracts (such as Germany's mini-jobs) or contracts for young workers. In addition, access to self-employed status has been facilitated, so that tasks that had traditionally been performed by employees are now increasingly outsourced to self-employed. These developments have important social consequences in terms of economic security. First, by definition, flexible contracts provide less employment security than standard ones. Second, these new contracts tend to be associated with reduced social protection coverage, which means that in the event of unemployment, sickness or old age, workers on flexible contracts may find themselves under-protected.

It is important to point out that these developments have not been accompanied by a weakening of employment protection for core workers, i.e. those covered by standard employment contracts. This pattern can be observed in most continental European countries, but also in Sweden, as pointed out by Davidsson and Emmenegger (Chapter 10). The result of this trend is an increasingly dualized labour market, where insiders continue to enjoy employment and social protection at levels close to those provided in postwar welfare states, and outsiders are instead exposed to considerably higher levels of insecurity (Crouch and Keune, Chapter 3; Palier, Chapter 11).

Towards stronger integration of employment, fiscal, education and social policy

The new welfare state understands social policies as part of a broader settlement that can have a decisive impact on the functioning of a country's economy. This new understanding goes hand-in-hand with the reorientation of social policies towards the promotion of labour market participation. It translates a new imperative for social policies: that of being a productive factor. This is very different from the view of social policy that informed the development of postwar welfare states. At that time, social policies were seen as responses to market failures in the allocation of resources.

One result of this reorientation is the fact that more actors are involved in designing social policies. Ministries of finance, even before the public finance crisis of 2010–2011, were already playing an increasingly important role in social policymaking (see Jenson, Chapter 2). The fiscal dimension of social policy has certainly gained much importance over the last few years. The link between social and employment policies have been stressed with the aim of increasing labour market opportunities for women while raising fertility rates through comprehensive social services. Finally, education is increasingly seen as a function that must be promoted by the welfare state. Unequal educational outcomes are the cause of many social problems (Esping-Andersen 2009) and social policy can also play a preventive role by investing in people's skills. This view, reflected in what Jenson has termed the social investment perspective, has gained influence over the last decade.

It is undeniable that the welfare state has changed over the last two decades. What is less certain are questions such as: What are the most salient developments? What do such changes amount to? What are their distributional consequences? In short, what does the new welfare state look like? Of course, these are largely questions of interpretation. Next we discuss some possible answers to them which are more fully explored in the book's chapters.

How Do We Interpret Change?

Together with profound transformations in social policies, the last decade has also witnessed the development of numerous interpretations of current change. In this book we consider two ways of understanding the new welfare settlement. First, some authors have emphasized the functional reorientation of welfare states towards the promotion of labour market participation and investment in skills as a tool to deal with social problems. This view is well summed up by Jenson's notion of a social investment perspective (Jenson, Chapter 2, and Hemerijck, Chapter 4. See also Morel et al. 2012). There are a number of basic ideas behind the notion of social investment. These include dealing with disadvantage, not so much by providing cash transfers, but instead by promoting success in the labour market and in education. The social investment perspective takes a life-course view of social problems, and as a result favours efforts targeted on children, as they have been shown to be particularly effective in breaking the inheritance of disadvantage (Esping-Andersen 2009).

A second, more pessimistic view of where the welfare states are headed, is found in studies emphasizing dualization trends in modern welfare states (Palier, Chapter 11; Emmenegger et al. 2012). In this view, the new welfare settlement is characterized by the preservation of postwar like levels of economic security for insiders and by the development of a new societal segment, outsiders, who are exposed to much higher levels of economic insecurity (Crouch and Keune, Chapter 3). This perspective takes a rather sceptical view of active social policies. Unlike the social investment strand, which sees them as an effort to reduce social problems by facilitating access to employment, dualization believers view activation as a tool to push disadvantaged people into bad quality jobs (Palier and Thelen 2010).

The two perspectives are not mutually exclusive at the conceptual level. It is perfectly conceivable that a general social investment push be combined with, for example, labour market deregulation at the margin. In reality, however, most scholars tend to emphasize one or the other interpretation, which is viewed as the most salient.

Interpretations of recent and current change cannot ignore the economic turmoil that has followed the financial crisis of 2008 (see Hemerijck,

Chapter 4). Of course, the type of analysis that we make in this book requires hindsight. As a result, it is impossible to fully integrate the consequences of the crisis in our account of the new welfare state. We can nonetheless identify a number of likely developments. First of all, as pointed out above, the last decade had seen expansion on pro-employment social policies. The budgetary context that has emerged in the aftermath of the crisis clearly leaves little room for continuing in the development of such policies. The Great Recession was first addressed through Keynesian fiscal stimulus, but then the financial and budgetary crisis have led European policymakers to introduce more effective cost containment measures. The latter risks putting welfare programmes under huge constraints, while pushing decisionmakers to abandon more ambitious strategies for social investment. Second, the current crisis seems to have a rather asymmetric impact in Europe. Retrenchment has been strongest in Southern European and Anglo-Saxon countries. Other countries have safeguarded their welfare programmes, because of more favourable economic conditions (Germany) and a deliberate strategy of defending social entitlements (Scandinavian countries). Third, because of budgetary constraints and a change in prevailing policy ideas, a rerun of the 'labour supply reduction' strategy seen in the 1970s and early 1980s is unlikely.

What remains unclear is what overall impact the crisis will have on the trends observed up to 2008 and discussed in this book. Hemerijck's overview of reforms adopted since 2008 (Chapter 4) shows that policies with a 'social investment' flavour have been more resistant to retrenchment than purely protective ones. This suggests that the notion of an investment oriented or an active social policy remains attractive to policymakers, though its further development is clearly impaired by the unprecedented budgetary problems many European countries are facing.

Challenges for Theory

Throughout this project, we decided to build on existing scholarship. Our starting point are the theories developed in the 1990s by authors like Kent Weaver and Paul Pierson, who developed a clear, theoretical framework for the analysis of welfare state transformation (see Bonoli, Chapter 5, for a review of this literature). In these analyses, a key mechanism explaining policy change is found in electoral politics, with policymaking seen as being driven mostly by politicians' need to avoid blame for unpopular decisions. A corollary to this proposition, is that in the ageing democracies of Western Europe, the welfare state is expected to be an extremely resilient institution.

Second, our understanding of social policy has been very strongly influenced by the notion of welfare regimes, developed by Esping-Andersen in his seminal book *The Three Worlds of Welfare Capitalism* (1990). Welfare regime theory expects countries belonging to different 'worlds' of the welfare state to react differently to similar challenges. As a result, regime theory expects persistent diversity or even divergence among welfare regimes. This view is strongly present in many contributions made in the early 2000s (Kuhnle 2000; Scharpf and Schmidt 2000; Huber and Stephens 2001).

In this book, we ask to what extent this understanding of social policy-making helps us make sense of the developments observed over the last decade. The evidence provided in the chapters suggests these traditional theoretical approaches to comparative social polices are only partially success-ful when it comes to account for observed developments. In other words, by looking at policy trajectories in Western Europe, we can identify a number of challenges to these views. These are discussed next.

More radical retrenchment

The number and the content of recent reforms have proven the ability of policymakers to react to socio-economic challenges and modernize welfare programmes. If we look back at the last wave of social policy reforms, we see a 'story of change' (rather than stability). It is clear that the significance of welfare reform has increased over time. Reforms that looked unfeasible in the 1990s are now being adopted in many countries. Radical departure from the past has occurred in labour market policy, family, and childcare policies. As stressed by Clasen and Clegg (Chapter 7), labour market policy has seen major transformations consistent with the objective of employment promotion.

Some of these reforms have meant substantial retrenchment. The field of old age pensions provides a good example of the mechanism described above. As shown by Ebbinghaus (Chapter 9), old age pensions were expected to be one of the most resilient areas of the welfare state, given their universal character and the strong value attached by workers to the notion of retirement. Yet old age pensions have seen some of the most radical cuts over the last two decades. Countries like Germany, France and Italy have reduced the replacement rate of their old age insurance schemes from around 70 per cent of earnings in the early 1990s to somewhere between 40 and 50 per cent, to be effective in a few decades. Retrenchment and cost containment have been applied to other policy areas as well, such as unemployment compensation (in Germany, with the Hartz IV reform of unemployment policy, and elsewhere in Europe) (Clegg 2008).

Expansion of new social policies

Over the last two decades, together with some undeniable instances of retrench-ment, we have also seen the expansion of some social policies, mostly in the fields of active labour market policies, publicly subsidized childcare and paid parental leave. This expansion movement is visible in expenditure data and through qualitative analysis of the reforms adopted. In the case of family and childcare policies (see Häusermann, Chapter 6 and Naumann, Chapter 8), policymakers have progressively abandoned the male breadwinner model and shifted towards the dual-earner model. At different times and through different paths, many Western European countries have shifted their family policy model. The expansion of childcare services and the development of new facilities and opportunities for the combination of work and care activities are part of a radical shift.

The emergence of policy objectives unrelated to austerity

As stressed by Häusermann (Chapter 6), the 'retrenchment-literature' (e.g. Clayton and Pontusson 1998; Pierson 2001) focused on the conditions under which existing levels of welfare benefits are reduced. The basic idea was that austerity generates a need for cutbacks on social policy, because existing benefits have become unsustainable.

While pressures to contain cost have been strong throughout the period covered in this book, the intense political debate on recasting the welfare state focused also on different challenges (see Natali and Rhodes 2008). These have included the issue of economic competitiveness (financial problems have been related to general economic difficulties, including a low GDP growth and relatively low levels of employment). Social adequacy and equity have represented further dimensions of the debate. As to the former, part of the dilemma for policymakers has been how to reorganize welfare programmes to reduce financial imbalances while also improving their protection against old—and new—risks. As for the equity problems, these derive both from the uneven distribution of protection and costs between social and occupational groups, and differences in funding resources between the various social programmes. This complex set of challenges has often resulted in multi-dimensional reform packages, i.e. reforms simultaneously pursuing several objectives.

The role of ideas beyond neo-liberalism

As stressed by some of the following chapters (see Jenson, Chapter 2), a new set of ideas, that we can label 'social investment' suddenly found a fertile political ground and policy has been shaped by this new way of seeing things. Other contributions have started putting more emphasis on the ideational aspects of social policy change (Culpepper 2008; Stiller 2010). As Seeleib-Kaiser and Flekenstein (2007) put it, beyond any structural and/or functional interpretation of reforms, what has shifted the most in the last decades of welfare policies are the interpretative patterns decisionmakers have proposed and debated. Policy themes, preferences, values and symbols are all elements of these patterns.

Recent reforms have proven that ideational perspectives have changed remarkably. New paradigms and ideas have gained momentum and shaped both the interpretation of problems and the definition of solutions. Permanent austerity has not been characterized by the dominance of neo-liberalism. By contrast, new perspectives have redefined social and employment policies to be decisive for the fate of Western countries and also for the competitiveness of their economies in the global context.

All this is very much related to the role of puzzling in social policymaking. As argued by Heclo, in fact, 'Governments not only "power" (...) they also puzzle. Policymaking is a form of collective puzzlement on society's behalf' (Heclo 1974: 305). While the early reading of welfare retrenchment assumed socio-economic challenges to be self-evident, discourse analysis has shown the role of learning dynamics in shaping the way both policy problems and solutions are defined (see Schmidt 2008; Hoppe 2011). Evidence provided by the present volume suggests that Western European policymakers have framed problems and solutions well beyond the traditional neo-liberal narrative. The identification of new social risks and the interpretation of welfare spending in terms of an investment on the future have clearly shaped the reform process and has contributed to the more open room for combining blame avoidance with credit-claiming strategies (see Bonoli, Chapter 5).

Rediscovering the role of ideas also means to assess the role of different actors. As stressed by Jenson (echoing Marshall), civil servants have played a key role in framing welfare and labour market policy reforms, while international organizations have been crucial in promoting new ideas and norms. This is particularly the case of Europe, where the EU has proven to be an agent of the redrawing of welfare boundaries.

Converging trends

The further limit of existing theory we want to emphasize here concerns the supposed persistent divergence of welfare models across Western Europe. A long process of innovation has characterized Western European countries. The number and the content of recent reforms introduced between the end of the 20th and the beginning of the 21st century has proven the ability of national policymakers to react to socio-economic challenges and modernize welfare programmes. As stressed by Palier and Thelen (2010), in the case of Bismarckian welfare systems, transformative change has resulted from the interaction of institutions inherited from the past and new programmes initially introduced at the margin. Yet, these marginal changes lead to new complex arrangements based on a new logic (see also Steinmo 2010).

As shown by the evidence presented in the following chapters, some convergence can be detected as far as public policy goals, institutional designs and mechanisms of risk-pooling are concerned. In the words of Hemerijck (2006), we observe a process of 'contingent convergence'. Countries have adopted policies that broadly go in the same direction, but maintain substantial differences. Innovations have been consistent with the adoption of similar policy measures (related to the European Union integration process), with a transition (at least in normative terms) from a corrective and passive welfare state to a more active social investment strategy (see Ferrera, Chapter 12).

The Structure of the Book

Besides the introduction and conclusion, the book is organized into four different parts. In the first part, three chapters provide different interpretations of the welfare settlement that has emerged in the late 2000s. Together, they help us make sense of the new emerging settlement. Jenson (Chapter 2) first defines the 'social investment perspective' in social policymaking, and then provides an account of why it emerged, based on both ideational and bureaucratic power arguments. Crouch and Keune (Chapter 3) provide an encompassing approach to the welfare state in post-industrial societies. They critically depart from the literature on new social risks, while proposing the term uncertainty to shed light on opportunities and risks related to the emergence of new social and employment policies. In Chapter 4, Hemerijck focuses on the first effects of the Great recession on welfare policies, and the new constraints under which welfare states must now operate.

Part two provides some theoretical propositions capable of accounting for at least part of the changes occurred. Bonoli (Chapter 5) provides a discussion of the limits of the credit claiming/blame avoidance perspective that has influenced much of the literature on welfare reforms over the last decade. Starting from the most evident anomalies to this perspective, he suggests some amendments to the theory. In Chapter 6, Häusermann sheds light on the political dynamics related to the new multidimensional social policy space. Increased opportunities for compromises are consistent with more fragile political coalitions that in Western Europe are engaged in modernizing the welfare state, or alternatively in welfare protectionism.

Part three contains empirical accounts of policy developments in key policy fields. Clasen and Clegg (Chapter 7) identify a movement of triple integration in labour market policy. By this they mean that distinctions among working age beneficiaries of social programmes are slowly fading away, whether in terms of expectations to work, access to services, or benefit levels. Naumann (Chapter 8) shows how two apparently very different countries, Sweden and

Germany, followed surprisingly similar trajectories in the field of childcare policy, only with a 20 to 25 year time lag. She shows how important electoral politics have been in both countries. Ebbinghaus (Chapter 9) confirms that while pension reforms have led to the apparent 'retreat' of the State from old-age protection, they have also entailed policy innovation in terms of active ageing (postponing exit from the labour market) and the full implementation of the 'actuarial' logic through the more direct link between contributions and benefits. All this could lead to the re-emergence of old age poverty across Europe with the consequence of a growing pressure on public authorities to re-enter this policy area. Finally, Davidsson and Emmenegger (Chapter 10) provide an account of the process of labour market deregulation at the margin, concerning only non-standard employment. They show that strong unions tend to favour reforms that do not endanger their institutional position in the system. In many countries, this means making concessions only on non-standard employment.

Part four concludes with two more ample reconstructions of the main trends in Western European welfare change. They focus on two different aspects of the redrawing of welfare boundaries (who has access to what form of protection). In Chapter 11, Palier looks at the long term evolution of continental European welfare states that represent in many respects the hard test for the hypothesis of radical change. The long path of reforms proves consistent with the departure from the old Bismarckian logic of an encompassing welfare state, through the definition of a new cleavage between insiders and outsiders (each belonging to different welfare settlements). Ferrera (Chapter 12) refers to the progressive interplay between national and supranational authorities for the governance of social rights. The growing role of the EU has had an evident impact on the territorial demarcation of social rights for EU citizens and third country nationals.

Finally, the concluding chapter focuses on the question of how to explain the developments observed at the empirical level. It develops an analytical framework based on a multidimensional understanding of social policymaking. Considering change on different dimensions, it is argued, helps make sense of apparent anomalies, and reconcile what we knew about the determinants of social policymaking and the transformations that we have observed during the last decade.

Bibliography

Bonoli, G. (2005) The Politics of the New Social Policies. Providing Coverage Against New Social Risks in Mature Welfare States. *Policy and Politics*, 33, 431–49.

15

Bonoli, G. & Palier, B. (2008) When Past Reforms Open New Opportunities: Comparing Old-age Insurance Reforms in Bismarckian Welfare Systems. *Social Policy and Administration*, 41, 21–39.

Clasen, J. (2005) *Reforming European Welfare States. Germany and the United Kingdom Compared*, Oxford, Oxford University Press.

Clayton, R. & Pontusson, J. (1998) Welfare-State Retrenchment Revisited: Entitlement Cuts, Public Sector Restructuring, and Inegalitarian Trends in Advanced Capitalist Societies. *World Politics*, 51, 67–98.

Clegg, D. (2008) Continental Drift: On Unemployment Policy Change in Bismarckian Welfare States. *Social Policy and Administration*, 41, 62–81.

Culpepper, P. (2008) The Politics of Common Knowledge: Ideas and Institutional Change in Wage Bargaining. *International Organisation*, 62, 1–33.

Emmenegger, P., Häusermann, S., Palier, B. & Seeleib-Kaiser, M. (2012) *The Age of Dualization. The Changing Face of Inequality in Deindustrializing Societies*, New York, Oxford University Press.

Esping-Andersen, G. (1990) *The Three Worlds of Welfare Capitalism*, Cambridge, Polity Press.

Esping-Andersen, G. (Ed.) (2002) *Why We Need a New Welfare State*, Oxford, Oxford University Press.

Esping-Andersen, G. (2009) *The Incomplete Revolution. Adapting to Women's New Roles*, Cambridge, Polity Press.

Heclo, H. (1974) *Modern Social Politics in Britain and Sweden: From Relief to Income Maintenance*, New Haven, Yale University Press.

Hemerijck, A. (2006) Recalibrating Europe's Semi-Sovereign Welfare States, Berlin, WZB Discussion paper, No. 2006/103.

Hemerijck, A. (2012) *Changing Welfare States*, Oxford, Oxford University Press.

Hoppe, R. (2011) *The Governance of Problems: Puzzling, Powering and Participation*, Bristol, Policy Press.

Huber, E. & Stephens, J. D. (2001) *Development and Crisis of the Welfare State. Parties and Policies in the Global Markets*, Chicago, University of Chicago Press.

Kangas, O. & Palme, J. (2009) Making Social Policy Work for Economic Development: the Nordic Experience. *International Journal of Social Welfare*, 18, 62–72.

Kuhnle, S. (Ed.) (2000) *Survival of the European Welfare State*, London, Routledge.

Morel, N., Palier, B. & Palme, J. (2012) *Towards a Social Investment Welfare State?* Bristol, Policy Press.

Natali, D. (2009) Pension Reforms in Italy and US: Policy Change Through Political and Institutionalized Policy 'Gates'. In Capano, G. & Howlett, M. (Eds.) *European and North American Experiences in Policy Change: Policy Drivers and Policy Dynamics*, London, Routledge.

Natali, D. & Rhodes, M. (2008) The New Politics of Pension Reforms in Continental Europe. In Arza, C. & Kohli, M. (Eds.) *The Political Economy of Pensions: Politics, Policy Models and Outcomes in Europe*, London, Routledge.

Palier, B. & Thelen, K. (2010) Institutionalizing Dualism: Complementarities and Change in France and Germany. *Politics & Society*, 38, 119–48.

Pierson, P. (1994) *Dismantling the Welfare State? Reagan, Thatcher, and the Politics of Retrenchment,* Cambridge, Cambridge University Press.

Pierson, P. (Ed.) (2001) *The New Politics of the Welfare State,* Oxford, Oxford University Press.

Scharpf, F. W. & Schmidt, V. A. (Eds.) (2000) *Welfare and Work in the Open Economy,* Oxford, Oxford University Press.

Schmidt, V. A. (2008) Discursive Institutionalism: The Explanatory Power of Ideas and Discourse. *Annual Review of Political Science,* 11, 303–26.

Seeleib-Kaiser, M. & Fleckenstein, T. (2007) Discourse, Learning and Welfare State Change: The Case of German Labour Market Reforms. *Social Policy & Administration,* 41, 427–48.

Steinmo, S. (2010) *The Evolution of Modern States: Sweden, Japan and the United States,* Cambridge, Cambridge University Press.

Stiller, S. (2010) *Ideational Leadership in German Welfare State Reform,* Amsterdam, Amsterdam University Press.

Taylor-Gooby, P. (2004) *New Risks, New Welfare. The Transformation of the European Welfare State,* Oxford, Oxford University Press.

Visser, J. (2002) The First Part-time Economy in the World: A Model to be Followed? *Journal of European Social Policy,* 12, 23–42.

Wilthagen, T. & Tros, F. (2004) The Concept of 'Flexicurity': A New Approach to Regulating Employment and Labour Markets. *Transfer—European Review of Labour and Research,* 10, 166–87.

Part I
Perspectives on the New Welfare State

2

A New Politics for the Social Investment Perspective

Objectives, Instruments, and Areas of Intervention in Welfare Regimes

Jane Jenson

Introduction

Even as some political scientists were promoting the concept of 'permanent austerity' and arguing that the new politics of the welfare state could bring only retrenchment if it brought any change at all, policy communities within international organisations and national governments, and including university-based policy experts, were designing and promoting significant reforms to 'modernise' their welfare regimes.[1] The years at the middle of the last decade of the 20th century were marked by activity that we can now, with hindsight, label significant innovation, involving a move away from *both* the Keynesian welfare state of the *trente glorieuses* and the standard neo-liberalism of the 1980s.

- The Organisation of Economic Co-operation and Development (OECD), a fervent proponent of neo-liberal style labour-market interventions in the 1980s and early 1990s, had by mid-decade begun to be concerned about social cohesion, instability and the social as well as political costs of its so-called structural adjustments. The 1996 high-level conference, Beyond 2000: The New Social Policy Agenda, concluded with a call for what it termed a new framework for social policy reform, labelled a 'social investment approach,' in which 'the challenge is to ensure that return to social expenditures are maximised, in the form of social cohesion and active participation in society and the labour market' (OECD 1997: 5–6).

- The European Union supplemented its commitment to economic and monetary union with the key notion that social spending is not a burden but an investment in economic growth. As the conclusions of the Dutch Presidency of 1997 said: 'Economic and social policies are mutually reinforcing.' In what became the build-up to the 2000 Lisbon Agenda, the presidency called for social protection systems to be modernised, strengthening 'their functioning in order to contribute to competitiveness, employment and growth', as well as establishing a durable basis for social cohesion.[2]

- In post-Thatcher Great Britain, as the Labour Party moved toward electoral victory, it significantly re-jigged its programme, following on the 1994 report of its *Commission on Social Justice* (explicitly intended to up-date the *Beveridge Report* on its 50th anniversary). The Commission wrote, 'the first and most important task for government is to set in place the opportunities for children and adults to learn their personal best. By investing in skills, we raise people's capacity to add value to the economy, to take charge of their own lives, and to contribute to their families and communities' (CSJ 1994: 119–20) while its Chair made the point that social justice—that is, a modernised welfare state—is 'an economic not merely a social necessity' (Borrie 1996).

- The World Bank's 1997 World Development Report refocused the Bank's attention, being 'the first report to make a systematic and comprehensive attempt to show that an effective—not minimal—state was vital for economic development. An effective state was needed to enable markets to develop and to address social issues.'[3]

These are only four examples of important innovations that date from the mid-1990s. By that time numerous countries and international bodies had begun to alter their assessment of the objectives of social policy, of where interventions should be targeted and of the instruments to do so. With the arrival of the new millennium, these significant adjustments continued, re-forming the welfare state rather than simply retrenching it.

As this book testifies, there has been a growing recognition that it is no more possible, as it may have been in the 1980s, to analysis welfare states only in terms of neo-liberal ideas and commitments to retrenchment than it is to believe that the male breadwinner model continues to inform policy design.[4] New ideas have replaced both those about containing social risks by supporting male breadwinners, which underpinned the Keynesian welfare state, and the commitment to cost containment, which drove neo-liberals' efforts to roll back the state.

The label of the 'social investment perspective' has been used to capture this congeries of ideas about the objectives, areas of intervention and instruments. At first, the term seemed to fit best with processes of change in liberal welfare regimes (Jenson and Saint-Martin 2003; Lister 2003; Lunt 2009), in large part no doubt because of early references to a 'social investment state' by, among others, one of New Labour's gurus (Giddens 1998). However, versions of a social investment perspective have been identified in European social-democratic welfare regimes and even more recently in some Bismarckian ones (Esping-Andersen et al. 2002; Delors and Dollé 2009). The social investment perspective captures a way of framing problems and solutions that is now quite widely shared across regions of the world as well as across welfare regime types (Dobrowolsky and Saint-Martin 2002; Esping-Andersen et al. 2002; Jenson and Saint-Martin 2006; Jenson 2010; Morel, Palier and Palme 2011). There is now some consensus around descriptions of a shared package of policy design that is child-centred as well as employment friendly, and focused on investments in human capital as well as on breaking the intergenerational cycle of disadvantage.

This chapter asks how this policy perspective was set in motion. It argues that, as in previous eras, innovations emerged and were promoted within the public administration, by particular actors within that bureaucracy. Therefore, after a brief theoretical and historical discussion of bureaucratic politics, the chapter proceeds in two steps. First, it presents in a stylised and schematic way a comparison of the main objectives, areas of intervention and instruments of previous 'moments' of the welfare state. Then it turns to an examination of how this policy perspective was developed and put into place.

Bureaucratic politics in welfare states

As Fiona Ross (2000: 17) reminds us, 'the new politics tends to envisage policy as formulated by electorally driven politicians with the ballot box at the forefront of their minds. Yet unelected civil servants have played a critical role in retrenchment politics,' and, we would add, in the development of the social investment perspective that superseded neoliberalism. This chapter focuses on the bureaucratic processes that reconfigured the universe of political discourse in the second half of the 1990s.

This reconfiguration of the universe of political discourse could anchor new ideas and policy practices in institutions, precisely because this universe is the terrain upon which actors struggle for recognition and representation (Jenson 1989). It is a space in which socially-constructed meaning systems and practices jostle each other for social attention and legitimacy, a political terrain structured by power relations. It is also one on which, among other things, practices of 'puzzling' about public policies occur, particularly in moments of uncertainty about the effectiveness of interventions and instruments.[5] The configuration of political discourse as well as institutional position and power provides greater representative legitimacy to some actors and their ideas than to others (Jenson 1989: 238ff; Hall 1993: 289).

Numerous empirical studies of public policy have documented that the universe of discourse of public policy as well as state action is often structured as much by bureaucratic politics as by electorally-driven reasoning (Heclo 1974: 308 and *passim*; Weir and Skocpol 1985; Carpenter 2001; Dahlström 2009). As Max Weber taught us, 'bureaucratization and increased governmental use of social knowledge [were] twin aspects of a more comprehensive process of "rationalization"' (Rueschemeyer and Skocpol 1996: 6). Bureaucrats' universe of political discourse is populated by the ideas and analyses of officials and experts located inside and outside the state. Their stock-in-trade is social knowledge about public policies, knowledge based on theories or evidence about the reasons for 'social problems' generated in the academy and transferred to policymakers in the various networks linking the policy and research worlds. This knowledge allows bureaucrats to identify needs and assess whether public policy can—and should—address them.

Operating in this universe of sometimes arcane and certainly complicated social knowledge, bureaucrats have been able for decades to achieve significant autonomy, thereby not only resisting political control but even making is costly for politicians to ignore the ideas developed within administrative settings (Carpenter 2001: chapter 1 and *passim*). This capacity to establish 'leverage' in part follows from bureaucrats' participation in networks with experts outside the state, at the interface of state and civil society. This has been as much the case in liberal regimes as in corporatist or social-democratic ones, although in the latter the social partners have formal roles to play (see the historical cases in Rueschemeyer and Skocpol 1996 for example). In addition, bureaucratic actors maintain networks in broad institutional settings, such as international organisations or transnational movements, that may serve as transmission belts for ideas about how to respond to puzzles as well as providing legitimacy to certain discursive formulations (for an overview, see Dobbin, Simmons and Garrett 2007: 460–62).

Starting from such claims about the importance of the universe of discourse of bureaucratic policy puzzling, this chapter describes the development of the social investment perspective as one characterised by the pre-eminence of ministries of finance and the extension of their instruments directly into the broad social policy domain. Two examples drawn from widely differing welfare regimes illustrate this point; in Britain and Sweden ministries of finance built on their authority acquired during the neo-liberal decades to promote social investment. These actors puzzled through the design of tax-based and income-contingent policy instruments that partially replaced longstanding ones such as unemployment insurance and family allowances. They often learned from international organisations that were promoting particular objectives and instruments.

While the bureaucratic politics that made ministries of finance key actors in social policy are not the only politics of the new welfare state worth considering, they cannot be ignored.[6] Quite simply, if the years of standard neo-liberalism had not already empowered ministries of finance within the universe of political discourse and internal politics of many states and if their instruments had not already been honed, it would be difficult to understand why the social investment perspective took on the characteristics it did, as quickly as it did.

From Keynes to the Social Investment Perspective

In the decades after 1945 Keynesian welfare regimes, simultaneously conjugating capitalist economies and democratic politics, were solidly institutionalised across Europe. While recognising that there were many key differences among them, the universe of political discourse of each was characterised by a variable structuring of the six moral values identified by Goodin et al. (1999: 22–23). These key ideas are: promoting economic efficiency, reducing poverty, promoting social equality, promoting social integration and avoiding social exclusion, promoting social stability, and promoting autonomy.

Innumerable studies have documented, mapped, and confirmed that these values were advanced by parties of the Left and many centrist Christian Democrats, often with the support of organised labour. But the lack of a perfect correlation between the power resources of the partisan Left and policy outcomes—much debated in the scholarly literature (summarised in Quadagno 1987 for example)—confirms that other actors, their ideas and institutional locales were also important for the translation of these values into policy and service provision. In particular, an array of state employees in a variety of ministries and other agencies not only implemented decisions taken by the legislature or decreed by the executive. They also designed policy, through processes of social and policy learning.

The emerging role of public administrations in innovation was well-recognised decades ago, even as modern social policy was taking form. Contemporary observers, such as the expert on Britain's interwar public service, understood that: 'the official is less concerned to administer the law then to promote energetic and far-reaching projects based on plans which he himself must create' (Robson 1937: 19). Moreover, in these same years the resort to commissions of inquiry and outside expertise became common, often producing 'a piece of big-scale social research' (Marshall 1939: 335).[7] Later studies by historical institutionalists mapped the generality of these observations, in cross-national comparisons across all regime types. Dietrich Rueschemeyer and Theda Skocpol conclude their assessment of the pre-1945 relationship among states, social knowledge and social policy this way:

> The desire of public officials to act in 'the national interest' in increasingly complex socioeconomic settings created growing demands both for general theories of how economies or societies functioned and for reliable information on particular issues that seemed problematic – such as the living conditions and the likely responses of the lower classes. (Rueschemeyer and Skocpol 1996: 297)

The various chapters in their edited book traced this demand as well as the interests of middle-class reformers and advocates that gave rise to a vast array of increasingly systemised social knowledge carrying names such as statistics, policy science, and *Staatswissenschaften*.

These practices and patterns were only reinforced after 1945, as welfare regimes were consolidated and expanded. Keynesian economics in its multiple manifestations provided a 'general theory' of the relationship between the economy and policy, while vast bureaucracies housed in social ministries puzzled over, designed and implemented new social services in the domains of pensions, health, family and so on. And, as observers and analysts had noted, the emphasis on social research and knowledge put the agencies involved in service delivery in a direct relationship with outside experts as well as with their 'political masters'.

Welfare regimes of the golden age

In the universe of political discourse of *liberal welfare regimes* after 1945, as John Myles summarises, the predominant social knowledge had generated 'a preference for market solutions to welfare problems' (1998: 342). Thus labour markets were responsible for the initial distribution of income. Additional or alternative sources of income (family benefits or unemployment insurance, for example) were provided either out of general revenues or, less frequently, contributory regimes. Social policy was organised with the objective of avoiding the supposed moral hazard of discouraging employment among those deemed able to work, and instruments relied on strict targeting, low cut-offs, and a clear distinction between having a job or being out-of-work. These ideas and practices generated social programmes that were not very generous, whose benefits were conditional on having demonstrated the legitimacy of a claim, and that tended to be 'passive' rather than actively helping with labour force participation (Goodin et al. 1999: 40–45).[8] Lower-level state employees' task was to police eligibility and control access to benefits, whether transfers or services. The design of policy interventions was the task of social ministries, and their senior employees trained in social statistics, social work, political economy, and so on.

In *social-democratic welfare regimes* of the Keynesian era, in contrast, significant 'decommodification' was the approach to achieving the primary goal of promoting social equality (Esping-Andersen 1990: 27). In other words, services were removed from the market, universally available and provided almost exclusively by the public sector, in the name of equality (Blomqvist 2004: 142–4).[9] Indeed, the social-democratic regimes were characterised by the direct provision of public services (Clayton and Pontusson 1998: 70). In contrast to liberal regimes, social assistance was a very minor part of the welfare economy, with other programmes carrying the weight of income support. Because many social programmes were defined as social rights, state employees were not only more numerous but also more likely to be involved in service delivery than in patrolling eligibility, as was so important in liberal regimes. This design also brought a supply of good and well-paid jobs for women in the—public— service sector (Myles and Clement 1994: 84–6). In these social-democratic welfare regimes, the universe of policy discourse was constituted in networks of social knowledge that traversed the social ministries, the unions (who were identified as social partners), business and social policy experts in the academic world, often also linked to the labour movement.

Finally in *corporatist welfare regimes* of the Keynesian period, equality was trumped by the objective of maintaining status differences. This goal generated 'a labyrinth of status-specific insurance funds' (Esping-Andersen 1990: 24). In addition, the institutionalisation within social policy design of the commitment to a traditional family division of labour not only often implied women gained access to benefits only via their relationship to a male-breadwinner but that services to support women's employment, particularly child and elder care, were in short supply.[10] They were organised neither in nor by government departments or ministries (Palier 2010: 24). Instead, their policy communities were officially constituted by representatives of the social partners (unions and employers) as well as the state and often civil society, particularly the churches, both Catholic and Protestant.

The emerging social investment perspective

The universe of political discourse of the neoliberal era (approximately that is the 15 years from 1980 to 1995), was dominated by criticism and intellectual assaults on the welfare regimes of the so-called golden age that had opened in 1945. Economist after economist stepped up to accuse welfare regimes of fostering rather than ending dependency. Neo-liberal public intellectuals described the ways social benefits undermined the work ethic as well family values, and so on. In less ideological terms, welfare regimes were simply accused of being unsustainable and sowing the seeds of their own demise. In ministries of labour, officials responsible for managing public pensions worried about the solvency of the regime while policymakers puzzled over what to do about the long-term unemployed, massive resort to disability pensions, or rising rates of in-work poverty. This ideological attack and bureaucratic puzzling structured Swedish politics, for example, in this way:

> A main target of the political attacks was the provision of social services. Echoing ideas that were influential in, for example, the USA and UK at the time... the public welfare service sector was described as wasteful, overly bureaucratic, and, above all, depriving the Swedish people of their right to choose freely what services they preferred.... The critical public debate about the organization of the welfare services sector during the 1980s also reflected the growing problems of local governments in delivering services as their own financial situations deteriorated. (Blomqvist 2004: 144)

These widespread criticisms and concerns are summarised in Chapter 1 as well as most of the other chapters of this book. So too, however, is the growing consensus, to which this volume subscribes, that descriptors such as 'permanent austerity' or 'frozen' welfare regimes poorly characterise the situation of European social policy since the mid-1990s. Policy puzzling and innovation have generated new instruments as well as different types of interventions.

Alternatives to the social knowledge of the Keynesians and neoliberals are proffered by public officials as well as outside experts and political parties. These actors mobilise their new ideas to push for reform, and this in a variety of institutionalised settings, ranging from national governments to the European Union and international organisations.

One direction of change is toward a social investment perspective. Just as with Keynesianism after 1945,[11] the perspective takes on different coloration depending on the political circumstances and particular intellectual influences that shape it in each case. It is possible however, to extract the essential components of this perspective and to construct an ideal-type, in the Weberian sense.

There are a number of shared premises that underpin this perspective. Within the universe of political discourse, the emphasis is on policies for children and their families, on the future more than the present, and on the societal as well as individual advantages of social investments. A key idea of the social investment perspective is the notion that there should be less emphasis on 'social protection' than on being preventive and proactive. Its announced goals can be identified as being to increase social inclusion and minimise the intergenerational transfer of poverty as well as to ensure that the population is well-prepared for the likely employment conditions (less job security; more precarious forms of employment) of contemporary economies. Policymakers claim that moving towards this perspective will allow individuals and families to maintain responsibility for their well-being via market incomes and intrafamily exchanges, as well as lessen the threats to welfare regimes coming from ageing societies and high dependency ratios. The state's role is to define its interventions and social citizenship practices so that these conditions will be met. In terms of policy instruments this implies increased attention to and investment in children, human capital and making work pay.[12]

Three key building blocks can be identified.[13] First is the notion of *constant learning*. The claim is that individuals' security no longer follows from protection when markets fail. Security has come to mean the capacity to confront challenges and adapt, via life-long learning to acquire new or up-date old skills as well as via early childhood learning. The objective of social policy is captured by its dominant metaphor. It is of a trampoline rather than a protective shield or a safety net; policy instruments should be designed to bounce people back into the labour market if for one reason or another they fall out of it. Having an adequate stock of human capital is promoted as the way to ensure continued connection to a rapidly changing labour market. Acquisition of human capital is usually proposed as a response to the changes associated with de-industrialisation, the growth of services and, particularly, the emergence of a knowledge-based economy. State services will both help ensure successful acquisition, for example via successful early childhood education or job training, and provide support for job seeking, via job centres attuned to local labour markets.

Second is an *orientation to the future*. The metaphor of investment is most obviously linked to this dimension. Investing implies adopting a particular notion of time. Investments generate dividends in the future, whereas spending is something that occurs in the present. These notions reframe state spending from 'passive expenditures' towards proactive and preventive 'investments,' and re-legitimate the role of the state intervening, among other things, to overcome new social risks, as we saw above with respect to the OECD's policy turn in 1996 as well as that of the World Bank at the same time. They also legitimate a policy stance that pays less attention to poverty in the here-and-now as long as it is 'only' short-term and does not undermine the future well-being of today's children. But in this discourse child poverty is acknowledged as more dangerous than adult poverty. With this orientation to time, fighting intergenerational transmission of disadvantage as well as relying on a life-course perspective for social analysis take on all their meaning.

And finally, as in any social policy framework, there is a link between individuals' circumstances and the collective well-being. The social investment perspective promotes the notion that *investments in individuals enrich our common future* and ensuring success in the present is beneficial for the community as a whole, both now and into the future. Rather than stressing promotion of equality as a basis for social justice, claims for the social investment perspective are framed such that policy instruments providing some measure of income security now (via state spending on activation measures and in-work benefits) will break the intergenerational cycle of poverty, thereby leading to children's school success, less crime and positive school-work transitions. These policies and instruments benefit everyone less by limiting expenditures now than by promising to limit those of the future.

Each of these building blocks—or dimensions—of the ideal type can usually be found in each welfare regime but some jurisdictions usually emphasise some dimensions more than others. For example, social-democratic Nordic welfare regimes have concentrated on human capital, and thus Sweden provides a good example of how the institutions and instruments of a policy domain have been reformed so as to bring it into conformity with the social investment perspective. If Sweden has been a leader in providing childcare services since the 1970s, the goals and instruments have not been the same over the four decades. In the early 1970s, 'the aim...was to bring about a powerful democratisation of activities for children, and introduce a progressive pedagogy for creating equivalent conditions for growing up' (Korpi 2007: 24). In other words the goals focused on the individual child's development and on Swedish society's equality goals, including to ensure 'the opportunity of [children] developing their social competence in democratic processes' (Korpi 2007: 24). Then, in the mid-1990s as the social investment perspective began to emerge, Sweden worked a major realignment both in the organisation of childcare and its philosophical grounding. Prime Minister and leader of the Social Democrats, Göran Persson, announced 'a major change' and did so using the classic language of the social investment perspective:

> Lifelong learning should be a foundation stone in Government policy for combating unemployment. Sweden should be able to compete with high competence, and the prerequisites for this are to be provided through high-quality in all school forms, from pre-school to higher education. The pre-school should contribute to improving the important early years of the compulsory school. (Korpi 2007: 61)

With this turn towards a human capital approach, responsibility for childcare was transferred from the National Board of Health and Welfare to the Ministry of Education, to ensure that the transition to the new approach was fully institutionalised. By 1998 the national pre-school curriculum that was newly developed focused on the skills the child should have in order to enter and succeed in school rather than equality and democratic citizenship (Korpi 2007: 63). And finally, greater space had been introduced into the system so as to allow for parental 'choice' (Jenson and Sineau 2001: chapter 6; Blomqvist 2004: 149ff).

For liberal welfare regimes the second dimension was important because within their own universe of political discourse poverty, worklessness and social exclusion were identified as the key policy challenge. Addressing child poverty was one of the big policy ideas of the New Labour government after

1997; Tony Blair in his 1999 Beveridge Lecture pledged to end it in 20 years.[14] Investments for the future and breaking the intergenerational cycle of poverty translated into specific policy instruments. The Prime Minister contextualised his commitment to end child poverty by promising to implement 'good spending' on programmes such as the Child Benefit and to cut back 'bad spending on the bills of economic failure', by which he meant social assistance and other forms of income support (full quote in Dobrowolsky and Jenson 2005: 208). This policy stance was also promoted by Blair's Chancellor of the Exchequer, Gordon Brown, who made standard claims drawn from a social investment perspective:

> Tackling child poverty will both improve individuals' life chances and contribute to the development of an educated and highly-skilled workforce. The Government has an ambitious, long-term goal to eradicate child poverty by 2020. The Government's strategy is to provide financial support for families, with work for those who can and support for those who cannot; and to deliver high quality public services, which are key to improving poor children's life chances and breaking cycles of deprivation. (Brown, quoted in Dobrowolsky and Jenson 2005: 207–8)

The other European liberal welfare regime is Ireland. In the last decade it too was called on to put greater effort into becoming a 'developmental welfare state' by placing its priorities on 'key services which support people in employment' (such as childcare), 'greater and more effective investment in tackling child poverty and educational disadvantage' in order to prepare for the 'knowledge economy and information economy,' as well as making 'the investments that reduce social exclusion' (NESC 2005: 136). Indeed, 'children receive priority because of the greater awareness of the later problems that result from a poor start in life and from birth rates maintained at a low level for society' (NESC 2005: xx). This second argument aligned the second and third dimensions of the social investment perspective.

The third dimension—the idea that the social investment perspective benefits not only individuals but all society—is a favourite theme in corporatist welfare regimes as they inch toward making social investments by moving away from the anchor of the male breadwinner model. In Germany's universe of political discourse, the future of its welfare regime and indeed the country as a whole was understood to depend on a convincing policy combination that would raise employment rates but even more importantly keep fertility rates up. Policymakers puzzled about how to do so and by the mid-1990s the need for improved provision of childcare was finally accepted politically; 'the driving factor behind the new interest in childcare provision was the sharp drop in fertility rates' (Morel 2007: 631). Parental leaves followed the expansion of childcare services. But so too did policies that would increase the employment rate, and these drew from the social investment style experiments of the British welfare regime under New Labour. As such, they focused on those excluded from the labour market. As in Britain, Germany combines in one benefit support for many social assistance recipients and long-term unemployed, the goal being to transfer as many as possible of both into employment (Seeleib-Kaiser and Fleckenstein 2007: 432–3). As the German policy-makers puzzled through the challenges of high unemployment plaguing the economy they explicitly mimicked the UK model.

Stressing one dimension over another has consequences for the policy instruments via which investments are made. Some jurisdictions rely more on child-centred policy instruments to alter practices in early childhood education and care (Sweden, for example) while others put the accent on supplementing income so as to 'make work pay' for the parents of children at-risk of poverty (Britain and France, for example).[15] Still others rely on this perspective in order to better anchor the levels of social contributions, by encouraging higher employment rates (Germany and the Netherlands, for example).

Despite this variation, however, in the universes of political discourse across all regime types there is an agreement about instrument choice. The strategy of 'triple integration' described by Clasen and Clegg (Chapter 7) uses in-work benefits (earning supplements) to foster activation. If parents are supported to remain in any job, including very low-income employment, the same lack of attention to 'quality' is not meant to characterise services for their children. There is consensus on the human-capital approach to childcare, with an early start to schooling being linked explicitly to the need to address issues of intergenerational disadvantage as well as learning. One result is that educational authorities are given new responsibility for increasing childcare (that is, pre-school) services whether within their institutions (the schools) or in other types of settings. As part of the EU's 2020 strategy, for example, education ministers set a target of placing at least 95 per cent of children from age 4 into pre-school settings in the next decade.[16] In setting this benchmark, schools are getting into the business of pre-school childcare; compulsory schooling starts after age 4 in all countries.[17] This benchmark is an explicit recognition that more than non-parental 'childcare' is needed in the pre-school years and is a classic stance in the political discourse of social investment. The social investment perspective has also brought enthusiasm for a particular instrument—public provision of initial capital assets. New Labour's Child Trust Fund began in 2002, the OECD promoted asset-building as an investment, and the Commission of the European Union has explored the instrument of *Bambini Bonds* (bonuses paid to newborns and young children rather than their parents) (Hubert 2010: 119ff; Jenson 2011). They are all presented as investments in childhood that will provide a nest egg when the child becomes an adult.

The Politics of Social Knowledge in the Social Investment Perspective

T. H. Marshall, that astute observer of the history of social policy, noticed an important change in the role of public administrations as modern social policy took shape. As the politics of the welfare state was taking early shape, he wrote of change under way:

> Civil servants are not commercially minded and politically they are passive. In the past it was said that this left them spiritually eviscerated; they were reduced to a collection of type-writers, calculating machines, and rubber stamps actuated by a plausible imitation of human vitality. This is not, and could not, any longer be true because the Civil Service is *no longer* merely an administrative body. (Marshall 1939: 335, emphasis added)

Yet, to observe that the public administration is a developer as well as utiliser of social knowledge, engaged in puzzling over policy problems, does not tell us much about which of the myriad institutional locales within a modern state will engage in social policymaking. Indeed, as Carl Dahlström (2009: 217) puts it, 'the bureaucratic influence in what has been called an era of 'permanent austerity' is yet to be explored' and the same is true of its successor, that of social investment.

More is needed, then, to understand the institutionalisation of the ideas and instruments of the social investment perspective. We have already noted some of institutional locales for service provision in the Keynesian welfare regimes, and described some changes as social investment emerged. Institutions charged with ensuring a measure of income security to those outside the labour force (for example lone mothers or those with disability pensions), have been merged with institutions addressing the unemployed, to create job centres and other agencies for translating active labour market policy into services (Clasen and Clegg, Chapter 7; Bonoli 2011). Childcare, now most often labelled early childhood education and care, has been relocated from social to education ministries, an objective the OECD promoted with its *Starting Strong* studies that were the product of the education directorate of that organisation. Policy instruments such as asset-endowments for children and in-work benefits have been consolidated into significant tools for promoting social investment goals.

In all their variation and divergence, these instruments and institutions do share a common characteristic. They often reflect the policy discourse of economists and they have often been promoted by finance ministries more than social ministries, relying on the tools most familiar to them, such as fiscally-based incentives and credits. One example is in-work benefits such as Britain's Working Tax Credit, France's *Revenu de solidarité active,* or Finland's

Earned Income Allowance. These instruments all reflect efforts not only to encourage employment but also to recognise that in current labour market situations employment income is often inadequate to avoid working poverty. They are all also benefits delivered through the tax system or wage package to individuals or families with some earnings but nonetheless low income.[18] They rely on having reliable information about earnings and tax status.

New technologies have been particularly helpful in the development of such instruments, but technology alone cannot account for the migration of social policy analysis to finance ministries. Two national examples, drawn from different welfare regime types, illustrate this transfer of policy puzzling and instrument design from social to finance ministries. In both cases the ministries acquired new authority in the neoliberal era and this predominance allowed them to advance into the years of social investment from a position of power.

Britain's Treasury and the social investment perspective

One example comes from Britain, where New Labour replaced the neoliberal Conservatives in 1997. Peter Hall (1993: 285ff) has recounted in detail the way in which the British Treasury was discredited in the last years of Labour government before 1979, many of its key bureaucrats left or were let go, and monetarism was brought in by a coterie of advisors to Margaret Thatcher. But, 'over time, an aggressive policy of promoting civil servants who were highly pliable or sympathetic to monetarist views implanted the new paradigm even more firmly. By 1982, the operating routines at the Treasury and the Bank of England as well as the terms of policy discourse had shifted decisively toward monetarism' (Hall 1993: 287) and the universe of political discourse had been altered. Neo-liberal practices institutionalised the 'antiservice bias of the ongoing restructuring of the welfare state' (Clayton and Pontusson 1998: 71). These included a turn to privatisation, quasi-markets for provision, decentralisation to local authorities of decisions about provision but with centralised budgetary control, and creation of means-tested instruments such as the Family Credit, usually in the name of choice for consumers (Clayton and Pontusson 1998: 93).

Wrapped in the discourse of 'new public management' these reforms of state institutions shook up bureaucratic routines and institutional arrangements, and also gave central economic agencies, particularly the Treasury, greater control over policy design, even if that design was one in which the institution was more interested in cost containment than social policy objectives. Without their service functions, other ministries saw their influence and power wane.

This was the institutional authority structure that Tony Blair and Gordon Brown inherited in 1997, and which they could infuse with the social investment perspective. Instead of turning to the 'social' ministries and reinstating their service mandate, New Labour continued to use the policy instruments familiar from the Conservative years, such as tax credits, and to rely on financial incentives. And, as numerous observers have documented, most of the key social initiatives were developed in the Treasury, under Gordon Brown. The objectives were less classically neoliberal but the instruments of tax-based delivery, quasi-markets, and decentralisation were frequently deployed as Treasury policy thinkers puzzled over how to address child poverty, social inclusion, worklessness and so on. As part of this puzzling, New Labour policy thinkers engaged with examples and policy intellectuals from abroad, whether US welfare reformers during the Clinton years or at the OECD.

This gave rise to Treasury publications such as *Tackling Poverty and Extending Opportunity* (1999), *Tackling Child Poverty: Giving Every Child the Best Possible Start in Life* (2001), *Saving and Assets for All* (2001) *Balancing Work and Family Life: Enhancing Choice and Support for Parents* (2003), *Choice for Parents, the Best Start for Children: A Ten Year Strategy for Childcare* (2004). Their titles indicate not only the significant social policy content of Treasury's thinking but also the focus on the key concepts of the social investment perspective and the coherence of the analysis (Dobrowolsky and Saint-Martin 2002; Millar 2008). For her part Ruth Lister parses the roles of the Prime Minister and Chancellor of the Exchequer in promoting a child-centred policy this way: 'Although the pledge to end child poverty was made by Blair, much of the policy impetus on children has come from the Treasury, which under Brown has become a key actor in the development of social policy' (2003: 431). Whereas the budgets in the last years of Conservative government had concentrated on controlling spending and reducing taxes, starting in 1997 the first Brown budget announced the New Deals, and the trend towards Treasury announcing new social spending continued.[19]

The analyses generated within the Treasury also relied on the familiar instruments of the social investment perspective, and displaced those of the social ministries. For Gordon Brown, as Lister (2003: 431) puts it, his reforms marked '"one of the biggest single investments in children and families since the welfare state was formed in the 1940s." He was referring primarily to additional investment in an evolving tax credits system. . . . ' These were the Working Families Tax Credit, later the Working Tax Credit, a Childcare Tax Credit, and so on. They mark 'various innovations in the design, coverage and level of tax credits compared with the UK's traditional means-tested social security support. Tax credits highlight the way that the UK income maintenance system is increasingly focused on wage supplementation rather than on wage replacement, which was the rationale for the Beveridge welfare state' (Millar 2008: 27).

The idea of tax credits was not new to the UK. Indeed the Working Family Tax Credit was the direct heir of the Family Credit, familiar from the Thatcher years. Different, however, was its form of delivery. Instead of coming from the Department of Social Security it came via Inland Revenue, with a direct tie made to income earned (Millar 2008: 22). Indeed this tie-in to earnings was explicitly emphasised by its designers, as part of the stress of making work pay so key to New Labour's political discourse.

> Delivery through the tax system, rather than through the social security system, was central to the design from the start, not least because the government was keen to associate tax credits with participation in employment. As an early Treasury paper put it, 'A tax credit will associate the payment in the recipient's mind with the fact of working, a potentially valuable psychological change'... It was also argued that association with the tax system would make this transfer more popular with the public at large, because it would be seen as a positive reward for work, rather than as a handout for dependency. A tax credit rather than a social security benefit would 'reduce the stigma associated with claiming in-work support, and encourage higher take-up'... as Treasury documents claimed. (Millar 2008: 25)

The British case illustrates the ways that it followed prescriptions circulating in policy networks, both international and domestic, to develop social policy practices that concentrated on making work pay and homogenising benefits (see Clasen and Clegg, Chapter 7). It also tells a story about increasing reliance on tax credits as policy instruments to achieve human capital ends and, more broadly, to ensure the consolidation of the lead in policy development to the Treasury. Was this case unique, perhaps because Tony Blair's political rival was the Chancellor of the Exchequer? The next case suggests that this simple answer is too simple.

Sweden's finance ministry and social investment

The consolidation of the social investment perspective in Sweden, with its classic social-democratic welfare regime, happened differently than in post-Thatcher Britain, to be sure. Nonetheless, it too is a story led by a finance ministry, involving tax reform and the introduction of new fiscal instruments. Already in the 1980s, the Swedish welfare regime was under pressure and a 'third way' was being touted as offering a middle route between Thatcherism and Keynesianism (Steinmo 2003: 35ff). In the process, the Social Democrat, Kjell-Olof Feldt, Minister of Finance between 1982 and 1990, and the economists surrounding him within the ministry and outside, became convinced that significant reform was necessary.[20] Among other things, and 'in contrast to other Social Democrats, Feldt's prime concern was not the lack of consumer orientation within the public sector, but this sector's size and productivity. During the following years, virtually all publications from the ministry of finance came to advocate the introduction of various types of so-called "quasi-markets" in the social services sector' (Blomqvist 2004: 145).

In the 1980s ideas about tax policy changed the universe of political discourse. 'During the 1980s it became virtually "conventional wisdom" amongst the economic elite both inside and outside government that the structure of the tax system was by now creating far too many problems for the economy' (Steinmo 2003: 37–38).[21] However, despite all his work on guiding research and debate, Feldt did not get to implement his major reform; the Centre-Right defeated the Social Democrats. This electoral defeat meant that it was the Centre-Right that actually brought in tax reform in 1991.

But the Centre-Right also came to power just in time to preside over the huge recession of the early 1990s. Unemployment shot up and stayed high, as it became clear that macroeconomic recovery was not going to bring back all the jobs that had been lost. Poverty began to rise among young people and lone-parent families as well as immigrants (Palme et al. 2002). Thus, just as other right-wing governments under the influence of neoliberal ideas (Pierson 1996), the Swedish Centre-Right failed to make the cuts in social spending that it had promised.

The Social Democrats were returned to power in 1994. In office, they never completely repudiated either their own positions from the 1980s or those of the Centre-Right. This appearance of consensus has been attributed to a political system that depends heavily on social knowledge and has institutional mechanisms for developing and deploying it.[22] The result has been an expansion of fiscal incentives, in the form of subsidies, including for private childcare, schooling, and private services in the health system.

Tax policy has been one of the areas of debate about how to respond to globalisation and about how much Sweden can afford to spend in the social area. While for some on the Centre-Right the primary problem was the role of the state, for Social Democratic economists there was a widespread belief that low growth was 'the' problem (Korpi 1996: 1729). In the first half of the 1990s, as Carl Dahlström (2009) has documented, cuts to budgets and new forms of service delivery like tax reform were orchestrated within the state, and in particular under the influence of the ministry of finance. His in-depth analysis of the bureaucratic politics of the *Crisis Package* period of 1991–1994 documents the ways in which that ministry had the initiative, making lists for budget cuts to which other departments and agencies had to respond (Dahlström 2009: 226–227). But 'lists' are not neutral; they shape the decisions about where to cut services and for whom. Such bureaucratic practices, in a universe of political discourse that valued 'choice' as well as social investment had consequences as the economic situation improved.

After 1994 the finance ministry continued its role as key player in policy puzzling and learning. It commissioned a number of new analyses, including several by tax experts assessing the consequences of the 1991 reform legislated by the Centre-Right. With these reports in hand, the ministry of finance decided on further tightening of tax expenditures for, among other things, capital income, which brought a substantial increase in revenues. Faced with new spending possibilities, the Social-Democratic Finance Minister decided to pay down the public debt but also to increase spending on child support (Steinmo 2003: 40). This child-focus was easily justifiable within the terms of the social investment perspective. In 2007 the ministry added another standard instrument of the social investment perspective when it created an in-work benefit, designed by the tax experts to create an incentive for labour force participation.

These reforms, alongside other instruments to promote activation, meant that it was hard to find the 'decommodification' emphasis that had characterised the Swedish universe of political discourse in the Golden Age of the welfare state (Esping-Andersen 1990). Social knowledge in networks linking economists and the ministry of finance took the lead, even sidelining at times the social partners who had played such key roles in implementing the social-democratic regime from the 1930s on.

Concluding Remarks

The take-up of the ideas informing the social investment perspective in liberal and social democratic welfare regimes has had consequences for instruments but also for institutional arrangements. Clayton and Pontusson (1998: 90), in a direct critique of Paul Pierson's insistence on welfare state's 'resilience,' identified transformations in policy and instruments: 'In the Swedish and British cases alike, we observe two important changes: first, a shift of social spending from services to transfer payments and, second, a shift of spending on transfers from social insurance schemes to social assistance.' Less attention has gone, however, to the institutional champions of the instruments of these policies, which stress fiscal incentives and transfers more than services, and indeed root social assistance in tax credits and transfers designed as in-work benefits.

These champions, and therefore those who propose to resolve the 'puzzles' of social policy, are located in ministries of finance rather than the traditional social agencies that T. H. Marshall and others described as the great producers as well as consumers of social knowledge about social structures and relations when welfare regimes were being built from the 1930s to 1960s (Marshall

1939; Rueschemeyer and Skocpol 1996). They use social knowledge to be sure, but it is more often the theories of economists and others concerned about supposedly getting the incentives right and attentive to marginal tax rates as well as negative income tax tools (Myles and Pierson 1997).

It was in the years of neo-liberalism that such analytic tools displaced the social statistics and social surveys that had been the mainstay of post-1945 welfare regimes. Monetarists told Keynesians their paradigm had failed. Discredited by association were the policy communities within state bureaucracies and outside the state that had hitched their wagon to the instruments and institutions of Keynesian welfare regimes. Alternative analyses, focused on 'choice' as well deficit and debt reduction, gained greater legitimacy.

Of course, neo-liberalism never produced the social benefits that were promised. 'Trickle-down' did not reach the poor, growth did not raise all boats, and poverty intensified as did concerns about social cohesion and inclusion. Promoters of the social investment perspective could then begin to make headway against the notion of TINA (there is no alternative) (Jenson 2010: 67ff). But in contrast to the great wars pitting neoliberal monetarists against Keynesians, social investment was presented as a series of adjustments, a way of getting the incentives right or smoothing out the negative consequences of the interactions between markets and states. It was, in other words, an approach that retained much that was familiar from neoliberalism's universe of political discourse while returning to some of the social objectives of equity and even equality that underpinned Keynesian welfare regimes (Jenson 2011). Social policy gurus might have had to adapt their conceptual apparatus in order to be heard, but little dramatic partisan debate or political conflict within the state or international organisations was required.[23] The OECD and other international agencies as well as national ministries of finance, all surrounded by their social policy experts, could begin to pay more attention to the social, without being forced to give up their preferred world views or policy instruments. The social investment perspective arrived more on the economistic 'little cat feet' of fiscally-based reform than with the *Strum und Drang* of neoliberalism's 'new politics'.

Notes

1. In addition, the basic proposition of resilience rather than change had quickly generated opposition. See for example, Clayton and Pontusson (1998).
2. See Annex 1 of the Amsterdam European Council, June 1997 at <http://www.europarl.europa.eu/summits/ams2_en.htm#1>.
3. <http://siteresources.worldbank.org/INTWDRS/Resources/WDR_Summaries_4DC3.pdf>, p. 4.

4. Jane Lewis (1992) provided a systematic overview of the male breadwinner model in Keynesian welfare states. Her important article a decade ago (Lewis 2001) then identified the decline of this model following the move toward new welfare policies, particularly those of activation.

5. The notions of puzzling and powering are obviously a reference to Hugh Heclo's (1974: 305) argument in his seminal study of social policy learning in Britain and Sweden: 'Tradition teaches that politics is about conflict and power. This is a blinkered view of politics.... Politics finds its sources not only in power but also in uncertainty ... Policy making is a form of collective puzzlement on society's behalf.'

6. Both Bonoli and Häusermann (this volume) examine the role of partisan conflict in the new politics of the welfare state.

7. Bradford (1998) has traced the role of royal commissions as institutions for creating social knowledge.

8. There was, however, one significant exception; liberal welfare regimes were almost as concerned about maintaining traditional gender roles and relations as were the familialist corporatist regimes (Lewis 1992).

9. This design was explicitly chosen by post-1945 social-democratic reformers, who could build on a well-staffed and professional public administration. 'Historians have repeatedly pointed to the early development of a strong and professionalized state bureaucracy, which preceded democratic political institutions by several hundred years and which provided early social modernizers with an effective instrument for reform.... They [reformers] argued that only by producing services *itself* could the state guarantee access to high-quality social services for all citizens. In this way, a large public sector became intrinsic to the Swedish Social Democratic notion of freedom, which meant freedom from reliance on the market' (Blomqvist 2004: 143).

10. Here of course there were exceptions, as in certain liberal regimes. If Britain's liberal welfare regime actively discouraged women's employment via its benefit structure, France's corporatist-style regime has been long characterised by relatively generous childcare provision (Jenson and Sineau 2001: chapter 4).

11. As Peter Hall wrote of the adoption of Keynesianism: 'To be Keynesian bespoke a general posture rather than a specific creed. Indeed the very ambiguity of Keynesian ideas enhanced their power in the political sphere. By reading slightly different emphases into these ideas, an otherwise disparate set of groups could unite under the same banner' (Hall in Hall 1989: 367).

12. The works cited in section 1 of this chapter present these elements of the social investment perspective.

13. The three building blocks were identified in Jenson and Saint-Martin (2006), which provides examples of their various expressions in policy discourse and design. See also Jenson (2010).

14. Blair announced: 'Our historic aim will be for ours to be the first generation to end child poverty, and it will take a generation. It is a 20-year mission, but I believe it can be done.'

15. France's *Revenu de solidarité active* (rSa) implemented in 2009 is a programme intended 'to make work pay'.

16. <http://ec.europa.eu/education/school-education/doc2266_en.htm>.

17. Some examples show the extent to which schools and ministries of education are being called on to serve a new 'clientele.' The compulsory school age is 5 in Britain and the Netherlands, 6 in Austria, Belgium and France, and 7 in Sweden and Finland.

18. As the OECD summarised its study of in-work benefits as of 2002, 'the nature, method and frequency of payment are related and important aspects in the design of in-work benefits. In several countries, in-work benefits take the form of tax credits, moving away from the idea of a benefit paid by social security offices towards a system where eligibility determination and payments fall within the competence of the tax offices' (OECD 2005: 156 and chapter 3 *passim*).

19. For the budgets see <http://archive.treasury.gov.uk>. At <http://archive.treasury. gov.uk/docs/2001/child_poverty/index.html> there is the record of the international conference on child poverty, opened by the Chancellor of the Exchequer and at which he made a major speech full of social investment rhetoric.

20. A finance minister was not necessarily previously surrounded by economists. Perhaps following from his own Master's degree in economics, Feldt 'trebled the number of academically trained economists among the top advisors within the Ministry of Finance' (Korpi: 1996: 1729).

21. Belfrage and Ryner (2009: 272) recount a similar consensus emerging, this time around pension reform. 'In the 1980s, in social democratic circles, it was only a small group of senior personnel in the Central Bank and the Ministry of Finance that advocated reform in a neoliberal direction. Their policy decisions in the financial and macroeconomic sphere involved such small circles and had such a lack of transparency that they had the quality of a palace coup. These factors severely limited the legitimacy of the reforms within the labor movement, especially since the trade unions and their economists provided a counter discourse. However, at the time of the formulation of the pension reform, key intellectuals at the apex of the trade unions and the social welfare complex were very much on their side . . . the entire weight of corporatist intellectual representation and authorization has come down on the side of the reform.'

22. As Bergh and Erlingsson (2009: 81) put it: 'Taken together, the influence of social science on policy making and the commission system have helped to produce a culture of political consensus. First, Swedish politics has traditionally been connected intimately to social science research, especially concerning economic and social policy.'

23. Examples of adaptations of intellectual discourse are numerous. One suffices to make the point. Esping-Andersen (in Palier 2010) develops his argument for reform in corporatist regimes by appealing to the concept of Pareto-optimality.

Bibliography

Belfrage, C. & Ryner, M. (2009) Renegotiating the Swedish Social Democratic Settlement. From Pension Fund Socialism to Neoliberalization. *Politics & Society*, 37, 557–88.

Bergh, A. & Erlingsson, G. (2009) Liberalization without Retrenchment: Understanding the Consensus on Swedish Welfare State Reforms. *Scandinavian Political Studies*, 31, 71–93.

Blomqvist, P. (2004) The Choice Revolution. Privatization of Swedish Welfare Services in the 1990s. *Social Policy and Administration*, 38, 139–55.

Bonoli, G. (2011) Active Labour Market and Social Investment: A Changing Relationship. In Morel, N., Palier, B. & Palme, J. (Eds.) *Towards a Social Investment Welfare State? Ideas, Policies and Challenge.* Bristol, Policy Press, 181–204.

Borrie, L. (1996) Is Social Justice Affordable? Speech to the Centre for the Understanding of Society and Politics, Kingston University, 20 March. Available at: <www.kingston.ac.uk/cusp/Lectures/Borrie.htm.> Consulted March 2005.

Bradford, N. (1998) *Commissioning Ideas. Canadian National Policy Innovation in Comparative Perspective,* Toronto, Oxford University Press.

Carpenter, D. (2001) *The Forging of Bureaucratic Autonomy,* Princeton, Princeton University Press.

Clayton, R. & Pontusson, J. (1998) Welfare-State Retrenchment Revisited: Entitlement Cuts, Public Sector Restructuring, and Inegalitarian Trends in Advanced Capitalist Societies. *World Politics,* 51, 67–98.

Commission on Social Justice (1994) *Social Justice: Strategies for National Renewal. Report of the Commission on Social Justice.* London, Vintage.

Dahlström, C. (2009) The Bureaucratic Politics of Welfare State Crisis. Sweden in the 1990s. *Governance: An International Journal of Policy, Administration, and Institutions,* 22, 217–38.

Delors, J. & Dollé, M. (2009) *Investir dans le social.* Paris, Odile Jacob.

Dobbin, F., Simmons, B. & Garrett, G. (2007) The Global Diffusion of Public Policies: Social Construction, Coercion, Competition, or Learning? *Annual Review of Sociology,* 33, 449–72.

Dobrowolsky, A. & Jenson, J. (2005) Social Investment Perspectives and Practices: A Decade in British Politics. In Powell, M., Bauld, L. & Clarke, K. (Eds.) *Social Policy Review, 17. Analysis and Debate in Social Policy, 2005.* Bristol, Policy Press, 203–30.

Dobrowolsky, A. & Saint-Martin, D. (2002) Agency, Actors and Change in a Child-Focused Future: 'Path-Dependency' Problematised. *Commonwealth and Comparative Politics,* 43, 1–33.

Esping-Andersen, G. (1990) *The Three Worlds of Welfare Capitalism.* Princeton, Princeton University Press.

Esping-Andersen, G., Gallie, D., Hemerijck, A. & Myles, J. (2002) *Why We Need a New Welfare State,* Oxford, Oxford University Press.

Giddens, A. (1998) *The Third Way. The Renewal of Social Democracy,* Cambridge, Polity Press.

Goodin, R. E., Headey, B., Muffels, R. & Driven, H.-J. (1999) *The Real Worlds of Welfare Capitalism,* Cambridge, Cambridge University Press.

Hall, P. A. (1993) Policy Paradigms, Social Learning, and the State: The Case of Economic Policymaking in Britain. *Comparative Politics,* 25, 275–96.

Hall, P. A. (Ed.) (1989) *The Political Power of Economic Ideas. Keynesianism across Nations,* Princeton, N.J.: Princeton University Press.

Heclo, H. (1974) *Modern Social Policy in Britain and Sweden. From Relief to Income Maintenance,* Essex, ECPR Press.

Hubert, A. (2010) Empowering People, Driving Change: Social Innovation in the European Union. Brussels, BEPE Report. Available on <http://ec.europa.eu/bepa/pdf/publications_pdf/social_innovation.pdf>.

Jenson, J. (1989) Paradigms and Political Discourse: Protective Legislation in France and the United States before 1914. *Canadian Journal of Political Science,* XXII, 235–58.

Jenson, J. (2010) Diffusing Ideas After Neo-liberalism: The Social Investment Perspective in Europe and Latin America. *Global Social Policy,* 10, 59–84.

Jenson, J. (2011) Redesigning Citizenship Regimes After Neoliberalism. Moving Towards Social Investment. In Morel, N., Palier, B. & Palme, J. (Eds.) *Towards a Social Investment Welfare State? Ideas, Policies and Challenges,* Bristol, Policy Press, 61–90.

Jenson, J. & Saint-Martin, D. (2003) New Routes to Social Cohesion? Citizenship and the Social Investment State. *Canadian Journal of Sociology,* 28, 77–99.

Jenson, J. & Saint-Martin, D. (2006) Building Blocks for a New Social Architecture: The LEGO™ Paradigm of an Active Society. *Policy & Politics,* 34, 429–51.

Jenson, J. & Sineau, M. (2001) *Who Cares? Women's Work, Childcare and Welfare State Redesign,* Toronto, University of Toronto Press.

Korpi, B. M. (2007) *The Politics of Pre-school—Intentions and Decisions Underlying the Emergence and Growth of the Swedish Pre-school,* Stockholm, Ministry of Education, 3rd edition.

Korpi, W. (1996) Eurosclerosis and the Sclerosis of Objectivity: On the Role of Values Among Economic Policy Experts. *The Economic Journal,* 106, 1727–46.

Lewis, J. (1992) Gender and the Development of Welfare Regimes. *Journal of European Social Policy,* 2, 159–73.

Lewis, J. (2001) The Decline of the Male Breadwinner Model. Implications for Work and Care. *Social Politics,* 8, 158–69.

Lister, R. (2003) Investing in the Citizen-workers of the Future: Transformations in Citizenship and the State under New Labour. *Social Policy and Administration,* 37, 427–43.

Lunt, N. (2009) The Rise of a 'Social Development' Agenda in New Zealand. *International Journal of Social Welfare,* 18, 3–12.

Marshall, T. H. (1939) The Recent History of Professionalism in Relation to Social Structure and Social Policy. *Canadian Journal of Economics and Political Science,* 5, 325–40.

Millar, J. (2008) Making Work Pay, Making Tax Credits Work: An Assessment with Specific Reference to Lone-parent Employment. *International Social Security Review.* 61, 21–38.

Morel, N. (2007) From Subsidiarity to 'Free Choice': Child- and Elder-care Policy Reforms in France, Belgium, Germany and the Netherlands. *Social Policy & Administration,* 41, 618–37.

Morel, N., Palier, B. & Palme, J. (Eds.) (2011) *Towards a Social Investment Welfare State? Ideas, Policies and Challenges,* Bristol, Policy Press.

Myles, J. (1998) How to Design a 'Liberal' Welfare State: A Comparison of Canada and the United States. *Social Policy & Administration,* 32, 341–64.

Myles, J. & Clement, W. (1994) *Relations of Ruling. Class and Gender in Postindustrial Societies*, Montreal & Kingston, McGill-Queen's University Press.

Myles, J. & Pierson, P. (1997) Friedman's Revenge: The Reform of 'Liberal' Welfare States in Canada and the United States. *Politics and Society*, 25, 443–72.

NESC (National Economic and Social Council) (2005) *The Developmental Welfare State*, Dublin, NESC.

OECD (1997) Beyond 2000: The New Social Policy Agenda. *OECD Working Papers*, V, Paris: OECD.

OECD (2005) *Employment Outlook*. OECD, Paris.

Palier, B. (Ed.) (2010) *A Long Goodbye to Bismarck? The Politics of Welfare Reform in Continental Europe*, Amsterdam, Amsterdam University Press.

Palme, J., Bergmark Å., Bäckman O., Estrada, F., Fritzell J., Lundberg, O., Sjöberg, O. & Szebehely, M. (2002) Welfare Trends in Sweden: Balancing the Books for the 1990s. *Journal of European Social Policy*, 12, 329–46.

Pierson, P. (1996) The New Politics of the Welfare State. *World Politics*, 48, 143–79.

Quadagno, J. (1987) Theories of the Welfare States. *Annual Review of Sociology*, 13, 109–28.

Robson, W. A. (Ed.) (1937) *The British Civil Servant*, London, George Allen & Unwin.

Ross, F. (2000) Interests and Choice in the 'Not Quite So New' Politics of Welfare. *West European Politics*, 23, 11–34.

Rueschemeyer, D. & Skocpol, T. (1996) *States, Social Knowledge and the Origins of Modern Social Policy*, Princeton and New York, Princeton University Press and Russell Sage Foundation.

Seeleib-Kaiser, M. & Fleckenstein, T. (2007) Discourse, Learning and Welfare State Change: The Case of German Labour Market Reforms. *Social Policy & Administration*, 41, 427–48.

Steinmo, S. (2003) Bucking the Trend? The Welfare State and the Global Economy: The Swedish Case Up Close. *New Political Economy*, 8, 31–48.

Weir, M. & Skocpol, T. (1985) State Structures and the Possibilities for 'Keynesian' Responses to the Great Depression in Sweden, Britain, and the United States. In Evans, P., Rueschemeyer, D. & Skocpol, T. (Eds.), *Bringing the State Back In*. New York, Cambridge University Press.

3

The Governance of Economic Uncertainty

Beyond the 'New Social Risks' Analysis

Colin Crouch and Maarten Keune

Introduction[1]

The New Social Risks (NSR) school of social policy analysis has enabled scholars and policymakers alike to reshape their approach to take account of the main relevant changes that have affected advanced societies since the major reformulation of welfare state arrangements that took place, in most cases, after World War II (Taylor-Gooby 2004; Bonoli 2007). Major examples of these changes are deindustrialization, female labour-force participation, ageing, flexibilization, and an increased variety in employment relationships. It shows how these changes have created new vulnerable groups; and it also shows that welfare policies have changed, bringing increasing diversity rather than convergence across Europe. Perhaps its most important contribution has been to identify the intricate set of relationships that link care policies (for children, the elderly and other vulnerable groups) to women's labour-force participation, and to family structures, breaking down the divisions that led to these being viewed as separate areas during the heyday of male-breadwinner, industrial economies.

However, now that approaches to social policy have been reoriented in response to the NSR agenda, it is time to point to certain deficiencies in it, or to problems that it has either overlooked or discounted as unimportant. These can be grouped under the headings of scope, market dominance, interests, and governance.

Scope. The NSR school argues that welfare states have to be reoriented in a way that *reflects* changed socio-economic circumstances that are themselves taken for granted. There is no consideration for the possibility of changing these circumstances through state policy, conflict, collective bargaining, corporatist practices, transnational regulations or other means. Hence, certain socioeconomic circumstances remain outside the political sphere; their definitions are not questioned, and no inquiry is made into the sources of those definitions. Politics and policy are restricted to social and educational policy that merely reacts to changes. From the outset, this limits the scope of intervention, and the range of possible policies available to influence welfare is reduced to a restricted set of labour market, welfare and educational policies. This is problematic, since it may well be possible that certain welfare problems are best addressed through, for example, a different regulation of international finance, changes in dismissal protection systems and the range of possible employment contracts, or alternative minimum wage policies. This is particularly relevant today, when policymakers in several countries are insisting that social spending must bear the brunt of the consequences of the crisis that has been caused by the malfunctioning of the Anglo-American neo-liberal financial model.

Market dominance. Further, the NSR perspective concentrates on adapting people to the market rather than reducing their dependency on it. The welfare state needs to prepare the labour supply in demand (both qualitatively and quantitatively), stimulate female participation and reduce welfare dependency. There is a risk that this leads to a situation in which people in low wage employment or working poverty become defined as social problems, and issues relating to them are removed from the labour relations and labour standards agenda. Also, the individual is seen as responsible for ensuring her own employment and can choose from the jobs offered, become self-employed, or seek forms of education that will improve her employability. Unemployment is thus an individual problem to be addressed through active labour market policies and education. The most obvious weak point in this reasoning is that it assumes that ordinary individuals have the capacity to predict and identify the kinds of jobs for which they should prepare themselves in the future, while even specialist job-research institutions have difficulty making such predictions.

Interests. The NSR approach also fails to take account of the fact that it is to an important extent employers, managers and financial capital that drive and manage the uncertainties that emerge in the new circumstances, which are rarely 'natural' phenomena (Crouch 2009a; Keune and Schmidt 2009). Their strategies have important effects on welfare and uncertainty, but the NSR approach tends to take these for granted as facts of life. The questions whether these strategies are acceptable, or whether there are alternatives to them, are not on the table. A conflict of interests between classes is therefore obscured by the NSR approach.

Governance. Although NSR pays attention to governance, and has clear links to research on 'new modes of governance', another school that tries to define the changed institutions of post-industrial society, it does not do so systematically. In particular, while claiming a new diversity of governance following a perceived decline in the role of government, it in reality concentrates only on the resurgence of the market and questionable claims for the importance of networks. In its concern to describe a shift from vertical (state) to horizontal (market and network) governance, it tends not to notice the growing role of the vertical governance of individual large corporations, for example in setting the terms of new forms of labour contracts and supply chains, or in replacing defined benefits pension schemes (for employees) with less advantageous defined contribution schemes. It also fails to notice the reduction in governance diversity involved in the decline in associational governance. The NSR approach risks to reduce this to macro-level participation in public policy through such devices as social pacts. It misses out on the role of collective bargaining, which has important direct and indirect welfare effects, and which is giving way in several industries and countries to autonomous governance by corporate managements. Collective bargaining operates directly on the welfare mix through such schemes as those for pensions, early retirement, work-life balance, or the implementation of state policies (Trampusch 2007). (For example, during the current crisis many short-time work schemes have been implemented through collective bargaining.) Indirectly, collective bargaining affects welfare through such devices as complementary dismissal regulations which influence if or when a person comes into contact with social security provisions.

Towards a New Approach

The NSR school is rooted in certain premises about the mainly benign character of the forces at work in post-industrial economies. In trying to go beyond the achievements of the school, we need to rebalance that assumption of benignity. Rapid change and globalization, as well as the move away from Keynesian demand management, have together brought new vulnerabilities to working people's lives, uncertainties which are in the first instance defined and managed by employers and the owners of finance capital. They have considerable scope to decide how uncertainties, experienced initially as exogenous shocks, will impact on different parts of the population, both within and beyond the labour force. Social policy, in the expanded sense of all interventions (positive and negative) that come between economic shocks and the lives of working people, has to be studied primarily in terms of this process. It should not be assumed that the crude old risks associated with labour's helplessness in the face of major market forces have disappeared. This is clearly demonstrated by the global crisis that emerged in the late 2000s, which resulted in rapidly growing unemployment and the decline of the real value of pensions in many countries. Indeed, distinctions such as that between old and new risks are of secondary importance in this respect. This then leads us to examine various phenomena that go beyond the scope of the new social risks agenda.

The economic uncertainty of people with limited personal wealth and dependent on their place in the labour market for their security, the heart of the 'old' social risks, has in fact re-emerged as the central theme of labour policy through the dialectic over flexibility and security emerging from international, and particularly European, policy debates over the past two decades, with the European Commission's White Paper *Growth, Competitiveness and Employment* (1993) and the OECD's *Jobs Study* (1994) standing as crucial documents. (But see the OECD's reassessment of its strong liberalization stance in 2006 (OECD 2006)). Globalization and associated sectoral changes in employment, as well as rising costs of social policy, have been presented as challenging an earlier approach to work and welfare based on guaranteeing security to the working population, as well as to those remaining outside the labour force on grounds of age, disability, inability to find work, or motherhood. The new approach, of which the NSR school is a part, is based on maximizing labour force participation in order to reduce dependency rates and increase the tax base, and on increasing work flexibility both among those within the existing workforce and those considered to be outside it.

While these new priorities bring some distinct gains to many parts of the work force, they have had the unfortunate indirect consequence of turning attention away from the guarantee of protection from uncertainty. The one word that embodied the new priority was, and remains, 'flexibility'. This has brought a total reorientation of perspectives on all policies associated with labour. Davies and Freedland (1993), who in 1993 were able to remark that employment law is primarily about protecting workers from insecurity, have more recently (2007) declared that, at least in the UK, this has changed: employment law is now about fitting workers to the exigencies of the market and maximizing labour force participation. They point out, in particular, how legislation that seems to be giving workers new rights (such as law for the promotion of employment among women or elderly people) is actually about increasing the supply of labour. Policy for skills is about improving potential employees' quality and therefore their employability. One might summarize by saying that, if earlier labour law was concerned with human rights, today's law is concerned with human resources.

But flexibility clearly stands in a relationship of some tension, not only with the demand of working people for stability in their lives, but also with the dependence on consumer confidence of an economy based on mass consumption. Some forms of labour flexibility are unwelcome to employers themselves, if it becomes difficult to sustain continuity of employment among skilled and well-trained staff, or where firms are trying to develop strong corporate cultures. Policymakers, including senior managements of large corporations, have not been presented with the simple possibility of tearing down protections that they had come to see as inhibiting economic performance, but have been required simultaneously to provide alternative forms of assurance to at least sections of the working population that, barring natural disasters and the unforeseen, should be able to plan their lives with reasonable confidence. This includes consideration of the different forms of labour flexibility, which can have very different implications for security. There has been particular interest in policies and practices that claim to combine flexibility and security, leading policymakers to developed such hybrids as the primarily Danish and Dutch concept of 'flexicurity' (Wilthagen and Tros 2004; Madsen 2006), but the overall range of policies and practices involved in the reformulation of the balance between flexibility and security is considerably more extensive than this (Burroni and Keune 2011).

It is clear that new approaches are needed for bringing together analysis of the full ensemble of issues affecting labour market policies, related social policies, and industrial relations regimes in this changed situation, in terms of collective action games around the distribution of uncertainty. This can be tackled as a collective problem, in various ways, or it can be one of 'dumping' the uncertainty burden on different sections of the population. This is not because economic life today is more uncertain than in the past; the very reverse is likely to be true. Rather, people in modern democratic societies have high expectations that they will find protection from economic uncertainty; but after the collapse of the post-war model, they experience greater difficulty in meeting those expectations; and there is some diversity in the possible answers to their problems.

To replace the narrow focus of current public policy concerns on flexibility and security, and to remedy some of the distortions of the NSR approach, we need to construct an analytical scheme to accommodate the wide empirical diversity of both policies and practices, and modes of governance, as there can be no exhaustive or theoretically defined empirical list of these. Creative actors are constantly seeking, and often finding, new means to achieve security in fluctuating world markets, or bending to that purpose policies that were initially introduced for other reasons. It is also important to recognize, particularly in a neo-liberal economy, that concern should not be limited to public policy; we must also embrace the practices of firms and other employing organizations.

We can move to a more analytical level by applying the 'grammar of uncertainty management', the four main interrogatives, the questions: How? Where? When? Among whom? The first of these relates to the modes of governance. The other three concern the distribution of protection against uncertainty.

The Grammar of Uncertainty Management

How? The means (governance) of distributing uncertainty

The theory of governance (Hollingsworth and Boyer 1997; Hollingsworth, Müller and Hollingsworth 2002) has identified a number of key governance modes. It should be noted that in practice these often operate jointly within an area:

Law. The first field to which we look for governance is to government, or the state. In the case of states under the rule of law it is necessary to separate government and law as two separate components of the state, as government itself is subject to law. There may be a distinction, even a conflict, between current government preferences and the existing state of the law. This will be particularly important in fields subject to change and controversy, as is the case with sustainable security. Law is essential for the definition of employment statuses and their associated rights, and including the various forms of 'soft law' that are emerging, particularly at the European level through the Open Method of Coordination.

Government. Government is clearly a central form of governance in the whole field of employment and social policy, including some of its more extended aspects. When combined with law and some other institutions as the state, it is also the modern institution most commonly identified as a public collectivity. We also include here, in addition to national governments, regional and local levels and the European Union.

Market. If law and government together constitute the forms of governance provided by the polity, there are also two forms of governance provided from within the economy. The first is the market, a public space in which virtually everyone participates. Its main form of uncertainty management is to convert uncertainties into tradable risks. Individuals participate in the market with very unequal resources. Not only does the strength in the labour market of workers with different kinds of skill and capacity determine their ability to demand different levels of security guarantees from their employers, but the market (combined with corporate hierarchy and redistributed by government through fiscal means), determines income levels, capacity to save from income being a major form of uncertainty protection. By themselves, market forces do not categorize individuals into groups, but they may combine with other forms of governance (government, corporate hierarchy) to do so, as for example in employers' classifications of manual and non-manual workers, frequently with different arrangements for pensions, sick leave, etc.

Corporate hierarchies. Following on from this, individual firms establish different packages of entitlements for different kinds of worker, extending not only to direct employees, but also to contract labour and to the firms in their supply chains and their workers. Many items in these packages have direct and major implications for the degree of protection from uncertainty that individuals can expect. Employing organizations are important determinants of life chances for individuals. Although they are directly concerned only with working life, the income and status derived from that area affect most other areas of life too.

It is as important to distinguish between markets and corporate hierarchies as it is to do so between law and government. The distinction has been important in economic theory ever since the theory of the firm (Coase 1937) identified a difference between the firm as a simple nexus of markets and as an organization with the capacity to shape its use of markets, as in the distinction between external and internal labour markets. In more recent years the works of Oliver Williamson (1975, 1985) have firmly established markets and hierarchies as different forms of economic governance.

Associations. While, in modern societies, the polity and the economy are the principal sources of governance, other institutions in the wider society also regulate and manage areas of economic life. The most formal of these are associations, particularly important in the labour field through agreements reached between trade unions and employers' associations, or sometimes individual firms (Schmitter and Streeck 1985). This governance operates at a number of levels, defining collectivities from local groups of firms to cross-national arrangements.

Networks and communities. Networks, as loose, informal forms of association, play an important role in modern economies, while the far tighter, but still informal units that we call communities, are more characteristic of traditional economies. Communities can be differentiated from networks by their tighter controls over the members, extending across many areas of their lives, and their development of moral codes and norms. However, in the study of the governance of security and flexibility, communities of various kinds, particularly the family, are of considerable importance, and networks relatively weak. The only kinds of network sometimes relevant are those among firms that regulate employment relations and local supply chains in a more informal way than is found in associational governance.

Where, when and among whom? The distribution of uncertainty

The study of inflation in the 1970s and 1980s made considerable use of the theory of collective action (Olson 1965). In particular, it used Olson's (1982) analysis of how business associations and trade unions would tend to solve problems affecting them by dumping them (technically, externalizing) onto groups outside their own boundaries. In Olson's limiting case, groups whose members constituted the greater part of a defined whole could not externalize, and therefore developed means for resolving problems without burdening others. While the dynamics of the distribution of uncertainty are different from those surrounding inflation, the issue of externalization is central to both, as both define insiders and outsiders. Inflation research took it for granted that the associations at the heart of its analysis existed within nation states, and that the nation state constituted a universe within which the proportion of a wider community represented by a particular associational relationship could be assessed. Once we relativize the nation state, this analysis becomes more complex.

Four different approaches may be taken to the management of uncertainty in relation to an insider/outsider divide. First, members of a collectivity may try to externalize the insecurity that their members bear in the same way as was attempted with inflation, externalizing onto other communities, separate from them in place. Second, a similar process may take place in relation to time: a society of people living in a particular period may postpone resolution of various issues, leaving a later generation to face the burden. These processes are of considerable importance, and elsewhere we have discussed them (Crouch 2010). Here, however, we shall restrict our attention to approaches that exist on the level of analysis at which most discussion of new social risks concentrates: distribution of risk-bearing within a collectivity, whose members may have to accept that they must internalize the uncertainty, minimizing it by sharing it through various collective measures. Simple universal sharing constitutes the third approach, but in the fourth, collectivities are internally stratified, and externalization may take the form of more powerful members requiring the less powerful to bear disproportionate shares of the burden of uncertainty—a kind of internal externalization. This may not necessarily occur as a result of conscious policy, but by repeated practice. In effect, sub-collectivities emerge within what seemed at first to be a single one.

Different policies and practices for the governance of economic uncertainty and the balancing of security and flexibility can therefore be analyzed in terms of the main forms of governance involved and the forms of externalization, internalization or internal externalization at work.

Policies and Practices Concerning the Governance of Uncertainty

There can be no exhaustive list of policies and practices, as they are empirical, and capable of considerable multiplication as human beings tackle issues in new ways and find creative and innovative solutions, sometimes not even aware that they are doing so. The following discussion will embrace what appear to be the major examples of these that are relevant to the task of moving beyond the NSR agenda and developing an extended concept of the social policy environment. Research would do well to look for them, and in particular to look for typical combinations in which they seem to appear. But it will also need to look out for policies and practices not covered here, but which are relevant to how the balance between security and flexibility is achieved in any given society at any point in time.

Table 3.1 summarizes the principal terms of the following discussion. They are organized according to their principal modes of governance, though subsidiary modes are often at work too. In order to better perceive the implications of our account for the NSR school, we arrange the various components in three groups: those that would be considered to constitute 'old' social risks, but which we consider as still highly relevant to the experience of contemporary populations; those that form part of NSR analysis; and those that lie 'beyond' usual accounts of both old and new risks. By this we do not necessarily mean phenomena that are new or recently arrived on the scene, but those that are usually neglected by all schools of social policy analysis, but which we consider need to be introduced onto the scene, as they are often central in setting the context in which more obviously 'public policy' elements operate.

Employment law. First, employment law provides frameworks of employment rights and limits to them. As noted above, during at least democratic periods, the main purpose of labour law has been to protect the rights of employees against employers who are regarded as being *prime facie* more powerful than they are (Davies and Freedland 2007; Knegt 2008). Labour law has therefore reinforced security, in some cases at the expense of flexibility. As such, it has come under sustained criticism from economists and others during recent years when employment sustainability has been seen to depend on increasing flexibility. The aim of much of this criticism has been to encourage labour law to accept a role in achieving a balance between security and flexibility. This is sometimes expressed in terms of degrees of deregulation, but deregulation nearly always requires some re-regulation, as maintenance of the market order itself requires a framework of rules (Majone 1990). A key development here (in at least some countries) has been the introduction of 'reflexive regulation', or legally induced 'voluntary' regulation to induce reductions in standards of protection, matching attempts in collective bargaining for derogations from sector standards by company-level negotiators.

Social policies. Prominent within the realm of formal public policy is the delivery of various services. These have a wide variety of implications for security, not all of them obvious. In the first instance, directly provided services remove certain important areas of activity from the market, providing security of continuing access to them during times of economic difficulty.

Table 3.1. Potential analytical scheme for regimes of uncertainty distribution

Principal governance modes	Policies and practices, by analytical framework			Characteristics
	'Old'—but still real—social risks	'New' social risks	Beyond scope of NSR analysis	
Law	Employment law			I: none II: internal distribution III: ranging from sharing to internally externalizing
Mainly government		Social policies directly delivering services		I: family II: internal distribution III: sharing
		Advancement of population's skill and employability level		I: family, market II: place; internal distribution III: externalizing on to economies without advancing skills; internally externalizing at point of input on to families with difficulties in access; at output on to workforce with lower education achievements
Government, market, corporate hierarchy	Government demand management			I: market II: time; internal distribution III: sharing
	Insurance and pensions			I: associations II: internal distribution; time III: shared within insured community; internal externalization through inequalities in access to schemes
Mainly market			Credit to sustain mass consumption	I: possibly government II: time; internal distribution III: externalizing on to future if confidence collapses

Mainly corporate hierarchy	Managerial organization of activities offering varying degrees of security among different countries and regions; supply chains	I: market II: place; internal distribution III: externalizing or internally externalizing on to economies/regions on margins of corporate strategy
	Internal labour markets and organization of work	I: market, associations, communities II: internal distribution III: internally externalizing on to marginal employee groups/contract workers
Associations	Collective bargaining	
	'New' collective bargaining	I: market II: internal distribution; place III: ranging from sharing to internally externalizing, depending on inclusiveness and arrangements; can be externalizing on to other countries (competitive corporatism)
Mainly community (including family)	Inter-generational transfers and support	I: family; possibly assisted by government via social insurance II: time; internal distribution III: shared within family; internally externalizing on to families with low resources

Key: I Subsidiary forms of governance involved; II Relationship to issues of place, time and internal distribution; III Form of externalization, internalization or internal externalization involved.

Especially among lower-paid workers, this can relieve the strain of labour-market insecurity, possibly enabling them to accept more uncertainty in that market than counterparts in societies where social service provision is much lower.

From this has flowed a secondary, originally accidental consequence, which has its own implications for economic uncertainty, appreciation of the importance of which constitutes one of the main achievements of the NSR school. Public services offered in kind include a range of care services: child care, sickness care, elderly care. Where these services are provided by the market, they tend to be too expensive for people on modest incomes, so there is under-provision. They are often provided within the family, primarily by women. In that case the provision exists, but not as part of the labour market. Where government provides or subsidizes services, they are still primarily provided by women, but within the labour force, generating jobs, incomes, and therefore purchasing power. Further, other women relieved of family caring roles by the availability of the public services, enter other parts of the labour force. This leads to a kind of femino-multiplier of job creation. At least within Europe, those economies that provide high levels of publicly funded direct services have higher levels of female and aggregate employment (Esping-Andersen 1999). To the extent that populations live in male/female partnerships, the increase in female participation has brought the stability of two separate employment incomes to households. In such cases, given the differences in the sectors in which men and women are likely to work (with women less likely to work in the exposed sectors), the dependence of individual households on individual industries and on the private market will often be reduced. Most important, the femino-multiplier has both created employment and, as a consequence, taxation revenues, which make possible further public-service provision.

Improving skill levels and employability. A form of security provision that is fully compatible with the free market is when individuals insure against future labour-market risk by investing in their own educational opportunities, including when they engage in mid-career education and training in order to anticipate future adverse labour-market change affecting their current employment. While wealthy individuals might do this unaided, this is a field with considerable government involvement; there is considered to be a collective interest in workforce upskilling, which extends beyond individuals' perceptions of their own interests; it is very difficult for individuals to anticipate future labour-market skill changes. Given that most education involves young people, it is also a form of future investment that requires a major contribution from the family. An exception may be training provided to employees by the employer. Here the issues are the amount of training employers provide and the type of training, i.e. if it equips employees only with firm-specific skills or also with skills that increase their employability and mobility beyond the firm. The time-related nature of the distributions involved here is relatively short-term, and they are therefore turned into distributions among contemporaries. Whether, and among whom, they externalize depends on the identity of the collectivities managing them. If implemented by families, it is likely to reproduce and enhance existing social inequalities; if by the state, the outcome depends on the characteristics of the scheme adopted.

Social policy measures to stimulate labour-force participation, or active labour market policy (ALMP), another central theme of NSR analysis, also need to be considered here (for a recent survey of different labour market policy measures being implemented in Europe, see Eurostat 2009: 269–72). In many countries many transfer payments are increasingly being linked to active labour market policy (ALMP) measures which are in turn often linked to official encouragement of training and education. These are responses to fears about the sustainability of social transfer regimes alone. There is an important triangle linking social insurance and social security, ALMP and personal investment in education. To the extent that ALMP policies are linked to transfers, they take the form of 'workfare', threatening loss of benefit if advantage is not taken of activation opportunities. If they are more linked to improved access to investment in personal futures, we may speak of Danish and Dutch 'flexicurity' measures (Wilthagen 2002; Wilthagen and Tros 2004; Muffels et al. 2008; Rogowski 2008), though the distinction is far from clear. These systems are all based on sharing within a community, but with possible inegalitarian effects where ability to benefit from schemes is unevenly distributed.

Demand management. In Keynesian demand management government acts alongside the market. It uses its own spending to boost the economy to avert recession and to cool the economy during inflation. By damping the impact of the trade cycle it seeks to reduce the degree of insecurity in the labour market. This was the main macro-economic strategy pursued in the USA, the UK and the Nordic countries for the first three decades after World War II. The approach fell into relative disuse after it was considered to have worsened the inflationary crises of the 1970s. This change precipitated the chain of developments that led eventually to the questioning of employment security regimes that emerged during that same post-war period, but it remains among the policy devices that governments still use. It operates over time, using government's own spending to smooth trade cycles, and its impact within a society tends to be egalitarian. But these characteristics depend on governments being willing to act counter-cyclically during both parts of the trade cycle, and not only to encourage demand during potential recessions.

Insurance. As already noted, within markets it is possible to assign probabilities to uncertainties and then to turn them into tradable risks; this is a form of distribution of the costs of uncertainty over time. In a pure market economy, workers and others would insure themselves against risks that might affect their security. But, important though the insurance model is for many purposes, it is not common for the mass of a workforce to insure privately against labour market risk. Such behaviour is vulnerable to three market failures. First, the costs of such insurance are likely to take the poor to very low levels of subsistence, leading them to place a small improvement in comforts today over provision for the future. Second, more generally than this, individuals are myopic in relation to likely major economic developments and would find it hard to make rational calculations concerning their insurance needs. Third, the classic reasons for breakdown of insurance markets—adverse selection and moral hazard—are likely to be a severe problem, particularly for insurance against sickness and unemployment. Finally, given that the collective interest in achieving sustainable security is greater than that of any individual, individuals must be expected to take precautions below the level needed for this collective purpose.

This is therefore an area where governments have intervened. The most direct form of government intervention to seek to reduce economic uncertainty is the provision of social insurance systems, usually reinforced by social security measures. In the former, management of schemes is often shared with associational governance. These systems are limited to distribution within the risk community identified, though they also operate across the time dimension as does all insurance. In principle they are relatively egalitarian, but systems comprising schemes for different occupational groups have certain inegalitarian effects. For example, workers on flexible contracts often build up fewer entitlements than their colleagues on open-ended contracts. Also, many workers may be left outside the scope of all insurance schemes, in particular workers in the informal sector or workers active as dependent self-employed.

The market has been more active in the pensions part of social insurance. In fact, within pensions we see four strong governance modes: government, in the form of public social insurance; associational governance, in those countries and sectors where pension funds are typically managed by unions and associations of employers; the corporate hierarchy, in the case of company and occupational pension schemes not subject to associational governance; and the market in the personal pensions sector.

Credit-based economies. A market-driven practice that has developed in some countries in recent years has been to separate individuals' consumption behaviour from their labour market income through extensive unsecured credit, usually mortgage debt but also credit cards. Although these practices developed solely for reasons associated with the financial sector's search for profits, it had the unanticipated effect of reducing the stress placed on individuals' concern for labour-market security as such. It required three conditions to grow. The first was a general rise in home ownership funded by mortgages, giving individuals on moderate and even low incomes forms of collateral partly independent of labour market position. The second was the growth of secondary financial markets that enabled the risks associated with housing and other forms of debt (such as credit cards, which were growing during the same period) to be shared among an increasing number of players in the financial markets. The third was the global deregulation of financial markets, which enabled more and more players and holders of different kinds of funds to enter these markets. Eventually, risks were being shared so widely that collateral requirements on mortgages, credit cards and other forms of debt became nugatory. The sums that people could borrow both rose strongly and became detached from their labour market positions.

The system can be seen as a market-generated functional equivalent of government demand management—a form of 'house price Keynesianism' (Hay et al. 2008), or 'privatized Keynesianism' (Bellofiore and Halevi 2009; Crouch 2009b). Whereas under straight Keynesianism, mass demand is sustained through government's own borrowing, here the borrowing is undertaken by individuals themselves, incurring mass individual debt. Financial irresponsibility curiously became a collective good. This element—the maintenance of consumer confidence—has meant that public policy eventually became involved in sustaining it. The model depends on continued housing market buoyancy, and governments may intervene to ensure this situation. This regime is vulnerable to eventual questioning of the value of the risks being traded, as was demonstrated in 2007–2008 in the global financial crisis.

Managerial organization of activities. The corporate hierarchies of major companies, acting alongside the market, have an impact on the spatial distribution of security when they devise a strategy for locating jobs with different levels of security in different parts of the world, or perhaps regions of a large nation state. Individual corporate practice, alongside other governance forms, is also important in structuring different security outcomes for different parts of the work force within a society through the way in which it defines different work categories and their attendant privileges. Both international and internal practices extend from a firm's own employees to its supply chains.

Management strategy is concerned to maximize the interests of the firm; the geographical distribution of degrees of security and insecurity within different societies that flow from its actions is just a by-product, but the social implications and resulting inequalities of this can be extensive. Complications are introduced if firms use their geographical flexibility to create labour insecurity in all countries in which they operate, in the stereotypical 'race to the bottom' in labour standards. From a European perspective there are differences between geographical flexibility that extends to other parts of the world, and that contained within the basic rules of EU social and labour policy. This has, of course, become particularly important since the entry of the new member states in central and eastern Europe. This has led, not merely to competition between Europe and the rest of the world, but—at least as importantly—competition within Europe between different member states, different regions, and, by implication, different social models.

Within internal markets explicit or implicit guarantees of employment and/ or stable incomes are offered to parts of the work force, often combined with having other parts within the firms on flexible contracts or in the external market through sub-contracting and supply-chains. The protection offered to privileged groups or, more generally, to insiders is partly dependent on outsiders bearing the brunt of any difficulty encountered in maintaining the stability guarantee given major market fluctuations. In explicit cases, employers distinguish between categories of workers who enjoy guarantees and those who are regarded as temporary or casual. This has been a central feature of large Japanese corporations, and also of German firms distinguishing between *Stamm-* (core) and *Randbelegshaften* (marginal workforces). The general theme has long been recognized by students of the labour market as 'segmentation' (Berger and Piore 1979; Loveridge and Mok 1979) or more recently as dualization and insider-outsider divides (e.g. Häusermann 2010; Emmenegger et al. 2012; Davidsson and Emmenegger, Chapter 10).

More implicit policies take the form of widespread understandings that certain principles will be followed in cases of redundancy or short-time working, such as tacit understandings that women, or immigrants, or very old workers will have the weakest claims to tenure. Anti-discrimination and equal opportunities legislation has often restricted the scope for such explicit practices. Nevertheless, demographic distinctions might produce implicit distinctions. For example, workers of different ages, ethnicities, genders might be typically found working for sub-contractors rather than in leading firms themselves. Use can also be made of illegal workers (usually illegal immigrants) in order to concentrate insecurity in particular groups and provide reassurance to others. All such cases of distinction between secure and insecure workers enable core workers to remain confident consumers while labour markets become flexible, but at the expense of potentially low confidence among the outsiders.

Collective bargaining. Associational governance, here collective bargaining between trade unions and either individual firms or groups of employers, is normally associated with reinforcing labour-market security, and is often criticized for doing so at the expense of flexibility and therefore in unsustainable ways. Alternatively, it may achieve a balance between security and flexibility by enforcing distinctions between insiders and outsiders. However, because collective bargaining involves negotiation and is capable of operating at a strategic level, it is possible for the participants in bargaining to trade flexibility and security. This can happen under a variety of contexts, but not all. For example, when bargaining takes place at the level of the individual firm, workers' representatives may have to trade the short-term protection of their members' security against possible needs for flexibility if the firm is to survive and thrive. This is generally known as concession bargaining. Alternatively, unions may protect the positions of current insiders at the expense of outsiders, through such formulae as 'first in, last out' (which tends to discriminate against young workers, as discussed above), or discriminating between a permanent core work force and one on temporary contracts (see Davidsson and Emmenegger, Chapter 10). Economists' theories of trade unions regard these practices as axiomatic to how unions operate (e.g. Blanchard and Summers 1986; Rueda 2005, 2007). This is because they assume a model of company-level bargaining (as in the US and Japanese cases). But a union with members across an entire industry or other generally defined labour market is likely to see such arrangements as leading eventually to employers' preferring the creation of temporary and insecure contracts over stable ones. For example, in Spain, the European country where most use is made of temporary contracts, unions oppose the strategy (Talani and Cerviño 2003).

Above individual firm level, collective bargaining may be involved in explicit flexibility/security trade-offs, but only where bargaining takes a co-ordinated form, with unions and employers associations being so structured that they cannot easily avoid taking responsibility for macro-economic consequences of their actions, including a significant role for unions and associations representing the exposed sector of the economy (Traxler, Blaschke and Kittel 2001; Traxler 2003; Traxler, Brandl, and Glassner 2008). This takes us back to something similar to the politics of counter-inflation strategies in the 1970s. Different forms of coordination will have different implications for different patterns of flexibility and security: for example, the difference between vertical and horizontal coordination and the role of sectoral or company-level negotiations. Some forms are more consistent than others with the maintenance of security traditionally associated with multi-employer, sector (or inter-sector) bargaining.

A different attempt at a kind of 'collective privatized Keynesianism' has been made by German unions. They have sought to use collective bargaining counter-cyclically, accepting restraint and the priority of competitiveness during periods of rising costs, but seeking to boost consumption through high wages during recessions (Erne 2008).

Inter-generational transfers and support. Family also appears prominently as an institution for managing security balances among individuals and over time, outside the scope of the market. It is an important channel for inter-generational financial transfers, for example in housing finance. While elements of its role can be seen in most societies, there is considerable diversity. There is also a considerable difference in mean ages for young people leaving the parental home—ranging from the early 20s in north-west Europe to over 30 in the south-west. This is relevant to different ways in which young people are helped through difficult labour-market situations in different societies. Social norms about family obligations play a part in determining these differences, but they are sometimes supported by social and fiscal policy (Jurado Guerrero 1999). Again, as this becomes a form of governance among contemporaries its impact depends on differences in access to the relevant resources among different families.

Family has particular implications for the labour market position of women. They often occupy insecure places in the labour market, but may be deemed to have a primary identity as working within the family, with security provided by a husband or other male 'bread-winner'. Studies of social policy and redistribution usually concentrate on relations between markets and state provision, leaving out these activities of the family. While its welfare role was historically considerably reduced by the rise of the welfare state, it remains fundamental for the living standards and security of persons not participating in the labour market, whether because of age, disability, household responsibilities or unemployment. There is also considerable diversity in the relationship between families, welfare states and commercial activities and the provision of care services. Family members both provide and receive care, in both cases affecting the labour market. This kind of role for the family perpetuates inequalities across generations, and there may be doubts about its sustainability. It depends today on certain incentives from social policy and transfer payments (mainly pensions), and certain forms of gender relations. In some countries the family's capacity to support its members through insecurity depends on the house price phenomenon discussed above, with older generations being able to stand by younger ones because of the security of their property assets.

Applying the Framework

There is no space here to present detailed applications of the above outlined framework to specific empirical cases. Rather, we want to give one key illustration of how existing research can be broadened by factoring in some of the above discussed dimensions, with the aim of strengthening the analysis. This example concerns the segmentation of the labour market, resulting in growing differences between insiders and outsiders as well as a growth in low quality or precarious jobs. This issue is high upon the European social policy research agenda and on the political agenda across the EU. At present, the analysis focuses largely on (i) mapping differences between groups active on the labour market in terms of flexibility, wages and welfare entitlements; (ii) the role of legislation in terms of dismissal protection and non-standard forms of employment in fostering or reducing segmentation (e.g. Davidsson and Emennegger, Chapter 10; Esping Andersen and Regini 2000); (iii) the extent to which reforms of the welfare state and labour market policies can exacerbate or limit insider-outsider differences (Wilthagen and Tros 2004); and (iv) the role of political actors (political parties of various colours, trade unions) in developing public policy that cements or reduces segmentation (Rueda 2007; Häusermann, Chapter 6). In this way, a number of the elements of the above developed framework are present.

However, with some exceptions, two of them are almost invariably absent, one being the role of corporate hierarchies and managerial strategies and the other being the role of associational actors through collective agreements. Indeed, the main part of the literature limits itself to the study of regulations and politics at the macro level. In our view, this leads to only a partial understanding of the emergence and development over time of segmentation and low quality jobs. We shall here confine ourselves to some examples of managerial strategies. But when considering associational actors, it would also be important to perceive the role of managerial strategies; the outcomes of collective bargaining are at least in part shaped by managerial preferences, not just by those of trade unions.

Corporate hierarchies and managerial strategies are largely treated as a black box in the social policy literature. The employers' need for flexibility is often accepted as a given, but little attention is given to the question whether this need really exists, what alternatives are open to firms to create flexibility, and what factors determine their choices in this respect. This is surprising, since it is first and foremost through managerial strategies that low quality or precarious jobs are created and segmentation or dualization is shaped. And as indicated above, multinational firms can also allocate outsider jobs in specific geographical locations or stages of their supply chain. Of course, the legal and social policy context sets boundaries to such strategies, but within these boundaries firms have a range of options, while they also explore how the boundaries themselves can be stretched. Within the same framework not all firms behave in the same way, not even within the same sector, emphasizing the importance of understanding their strategies when studying segmentation.

A good example of this is the recent growth of dependent self-employment, which formally is self-employment but where the conditions of work are similar to those of employees (one client, hierarchical relationships, etc.).

These jobs are, especially in the case of lower educated jobs, often considered outsider jobs since they lack in many cases any form of dismissal protection, lead to no or only limited accumulation of social security entitlements, and impose high levels of working time flexibility. They emerge first of all because firms, out of a mix of cost, flexibility and control considerations, convert standard jobs into dependent self-employment through 'hierarchical outsourcing' (Muehlberger 2007). It is only after firms start creating such jobs that a political debate emerges on the need for legal reforms and targeted social policy to deal with the phenomenon, or that trade unions start considering their role in representing such quasi employees (e.g. Supiot 2001; Pernicka 2006). Similar arguments can be developed for temporary contracts, low wage jobs or other low quality jobs. Hence studying the process, mechanisms and motives of the creation of such jobs by firm can broaden our understanding of segmentation processes.

And of course the reverse mechanism can also be at work. In particular, large firms have the resources and instruments to develop their own way of internally combining flexibility and security at firm level, in order to, for example, reduce uncertainty for workers and to increase their motivation, participation and productivity (Burroni and Keune 2011). This may well mean that they increase security for (some of) their workers to above the level set by the regulatory framework with the aim of tying them to the firm and/or strengthening their performance, a process that may again lead to segmentation, both within the firm and in the more general labour market.

Studying managerial strategies and their consequences is vital to understanding both processes of segmentation and ways of remedying it. Appropriate interventions do not necessarily have to be limited to redressing the effects of firm strategies (e.g. by providing more social rights to outsiders), but can be addressed to these strategies themselves (e.g. by limiting the strategic options of firms where the use of certain atypical forms of employment are concerned).

Conclusion

We offer the above approach as an overall framework of analysis for an extended concept of the social policy environment. It incorporates the insights of the NSR school, without making any claims that the newly identified risks have somehow eclipsed the importance of the older ones. In expanding the range of study to include corporate practices as well as formal public policy, it partly recognizes the degree of privatization that has taken place in several social policy fields—for example, pensions—and the role of autonomous decisionmaking by corporate managements that has dominated decisionmaking. However, we also take the opportunity to include a regard for the role of private corporate welfare practice that should really have been included by all approaches many years ago.

Finally, and with particular regard for this role of autonomous corporate decisionmaking, our approach does not make the implicit functionalist assumptions of much NSR accounts. We do not necessarily always assume conflict and a lack of shared interests, but we present an account that can recognize inequalities of both power and distribution. Our approach does not assume that all is for the best in a best of all possible worlds.

Note

1. This chapter draws on our work for European Union Framework Programme 7 project 'The Governance of Uncertainty and Sustainability: Tensions and Opportunities' (GUSTO) (grant no. 225301). We are very grateful to our colleagues within this program for many of the ideas contained within it, though they do not necessarily share the views that we have expressed here.

Bibliography

Bellofiore, R. & Halevi, J. (2009) Deconstructing Labor. A Marxian-Kaleckian Perspective on What is 'New' in Contemporary Capitalism and Economic. In Gnos, C. & Rochon, L.-P. (Eds.) *Employment, Growth and Development. A Post-Keynesian Approach.* Cheltenham, Elgar.

Berger, S. & Piore, M. (1979) *Dualism and Discontinuity in Industrial Societies*, Cambridge, Cambridge University Press.

Blanchard, O. J. & Summers, L. H. (1986) *Hysteresis and the European Unemployment Problem*, Cambridge, MA, NBER Macroeconomic Annual.

Bonoli, G. (2007) Time Matters: Postindustrialization, New Social Risks, and Welfare State Adaptation in Advanced Industrial Democracies. *Comparative Political Studies,* 40, 495–520.

Burroni, L. & Keune, M. (2011) Flexicurity: A Conceptual Critique. *European Journal of Industrial Relations,* 17, 75–91.

Coase, R. (1937) The Nature of the Firm. *Economica,* 4, 386–405.

Crouch, C. (2009a) Collective Bargaining and Transnational Corporations in the Global Economy: Some Theoretical Considerations. *International Journal for Labour Research,* 1, 43–60.

Crouch, C. (2009b) Privatized Keynesianism: An Unacknowledged Policy Regime. *British Journal of Politics and International Relations,* 11, 382–99.

Crouch, C. (2010) Flexibility and Security on the Labour Market: An Analysis of the Governance of Inequality, *Zeitschrift für ArbeitsmarktForschung,* 43, 17–38.

Davies, P. & Freedland, M. (1993) *Labour Legislation and Public Policy*, Oxford, Clarendon Press.

Davies, P. & Freedland, M. (2007) *Towards a Flexible Labour Market: Labour Legislation and Regulation since the 1990s*, Oxford, Oxford University Press.

Emmenegger, P., Häusermann, S., Palier, B. & Seeleib-Kaiser, M. (Eds.) (2012) *The Age of Dualization. The Changing Face of Inequality in Deindustrializing Societies*. New York, Oxford University Press.

Erne, R. (2008) *European Unions: Labor's Quest for a Transnational Democracy*, Ithaca, NY, Cornell University Press.

Esping-Andersen, G. (1999) *The Social Foundations of Post-Industrial Economies*, Oxford, Oxford University Press.

Esping-Andersen, G. & Regini, M. (2000) *Why Deregulate Labour Markets?* New York, Oxford University Press.

European Commission (1993) *Growth, Competitiveness and Employment*, Luxembourg, Office for Official Publication of the European Communities.

Eurostat (2009) *Employment in Europe 2009*. Luxembourg, Office for Official Publication of the European Communities.

Häusermann, S. (2010) *The Politics of Welfare State Reform in Continental Europe: Modernization in Hard Times*, Cambridge, Cambridge University Press.

Hay, C., Riiheläinen, J. M., Smith, N. J., & Watson, M. (2008) Ireland: The Outside Inside. In Dyson, K. (Ed.) *The Euro at 10*. Oxford, Oxford University Press.

Hollingsworth, J. R. & Boyer, R. (Eds.) (1997) *Contemporary Capitalism: The Embeddedness of Institutions*, Cambridge, Cambridge University Press.

Hollingsworth, J. R., Müller, K. H. & Hollingsworth, E. J. (2002) *Advancing Socio-Economics: An Institutionalist Perspective*, Lanham, Rowman and Littlefield.

Jurado Guerrero, T. (1999) Why Do Spanish Young People Stay Longer at Home than the French? The Role of Employment, Housing and Social Policies, unpublished PhD thesis, Florence, European University Institute.

Keune, M. & Schmidt, V. (2009) Global Capital Strategies and Trade Union Responses: Towards Transnational Collective Bargaining? *International Journal for Labour Research*, 1, 9–26.

Knegt, R. (Ed.) (2008) *The Employment Contract as an Exclusionary Device. An Analysis on the Basis of 25 Years of Developments in The Netherlands*, Antwerp, Intersentia.

Loveridge, R. and Mok, A. L. (1979) *Theories of Labour Market Segmentation: A Critique*, The Hague, Nijhoff.

Madsen, P. K. (2006) How Can It Possibly Fly? The Paradox of a Dynamic Labour Market in a Scandinavian Welfare State. In Campbell, J., Hall, J. & Pedersen, O. (Eds.) *National Identity and the Varieties of Capitalism: The Danish Experience*. Montreal, McGill-Queen's University Press, 321–55.

Majone, G. (1990) *Deregulation or Re-regulation? Regulatory Reform in Europe and the United States*, London, Pinter.

Muehlberger, U. (2007) Hierarchical Forms of Outsourcing and the Creation of Dependency, *Organizational Studies*, 28, 709–27.

Muffels, R., Chung, H., Fouarge, D., Klammer, U., Luijkx, R., Manzoni, A., Thiel, A. & Wilthagen, T. (2008) *Flexibility and Security Over the Life Course*, Dublin, European Foundation for the Improvement of Working and Living Conditions.

Olson, M. (1965) *The Logic of Collective Action*, Cambridge, MA, Harvard University Press.

Olson, M. (1982) *The Rise and Decline of Nations*, New Haven, Yale University Press.

OECD (1994) *The Jobs Study*, Paris, OECD.

OECD (2006) *Boosting Jobs and Incomes. Policy Lessons from Reassessing the OECD Jobs Study*, Paris, OECD.

Pernicka, S. (2006) Organizing the Self-Employed: Theoretical Considerations and Empirical Findings. *European Journal of Industrial Relations*, 12, 125–42.

Rogowski, R. (Ed.) (2008) *The European Social Model and Transitional Labour Markets: Law and Policy*, Aldershot, Ashgate.

Rueda, D. (2005) Insider-Outsider Politics in Industrialized Democracies: The Challenge to Social Democratic Parties. *American Political Science Review*, 99, 61–74.

Rueda, D. (2007) *Social Democracy Inside Out: Partisanship and Labour Market Policy in Industrialized Democracies*, Oxford, Oxford University Press.

Schmitter, P. C. and Streeck, W. (Eds.) (1985) *Private Interest Government: Beyond Market and State*, London, Sage.

Supiot, A. (2001) *Beyond Employment. Changes in Work and the Future of Labour Law in Europe*, Oxford, Oxford University Press.

Talani, L. S. & Cerviño, E. (2003) Mediterranean Labour and the Impact of Economic and Monetary Union: Mass Unemployment or Labour Market Flexibility? In Overbeek, H. (Ed.) *The Political Economy of European Employment*. London, Routledge.

Taylor-Gooby, P. (Ed.) (2004) *New Risks, New Welfare: The Transformation of the European Welfare State*, Oxford, Oxford University Press.

Trampusch, C. (2007) Industrial Relations as a Source of Social Policy: A Typology of the Institutional Conditions for Industrial Agreements on Social Benefits. *Social Policy & Administration*, 41, 251–70.

Traxler, F. (2003) Bargaining, (De)centralization, Macroeconomic Performance and Control Over the Employment Relationship. *British Journal of Industrial Relations*, 41, 1–27.

Traxler, F., Blaschke, S. & Kittel, B. (2001) *National Labour Relations in Internationalized Markets*, Oxford, Oxford University Press.

Traxler, F., Brandl, B. & Glassner, V. (2008) Pattern Bargaining: An Investigation into its Agency, Context and Evidence. *British Journal of Industrial Relations*, 46, 33–58.

Williamson, O. E. (1975) *Markets and Hierarchies: Analysis and Antitrust Implications. A Study in the Economics of Internal Organization*, New York, Free Press.

Williamson, O. E. (1985) *The Economic Institutions of* Capitalism, New York, Free Press.

Wilthagen, T. (2002) Managing Social Risks with Transitional Labour Markets. In Mosley, H., O'Reilly, J. & Schömann, K. (Eds.) *Labour Markets, Gender and Institutional Change: Essays in Honour of Günther Schmid*. Cheltenham, UK, Edward Elgar, 264–89.

Wilthagen, T. & Tros, F. (2004) The Concept of 'Flexicurity': A New Approach to Regulating Employment and Labour Markets. *Transfer—European Review of Labour and Research*, 10, 166–87.

4

Stress-testing the New Welfare State

Anton Hemerijck

Stress-testing the Welfare State

The aftermath of the global financial crisis of 2008 inevitably marks a 'stress test' for the welfare state. Can the welfare state weather the storm, once again, as it did in the 1980s and 1990s? Or are recalibrated welfare systems running the danger of becoming a *crisis casualty* and of reverting to marginality in the cascade of violent economic, social, and political aftershocks unleashed by the collapse of finance-driven global capitalism? The long-term social repercussions of the crisis are severe. Considerable employment growth across the EU, achieved through intelligent social reforms over the past decades, has been wiped out as a consequence of the banking crisis. Massive increases in fiscal deficits and public debt, required to pre-empt a more dramatic economic meltdown, have since forced policymakers to consider cuts in welfare services, including health, education, and social transfers to the poor, the unemployed and pensioners, in order to support public finance solvency and economic stability. What are the consequences of these developments on the trajectory social policy had embarked upon in the run-up to the 2008 crisis? Is the social investment perspective discussed by Jenson (Chapter 2) one of the casualties of the crisis?

Answering these questions is not easy. As this book goes to press, the fiscal crises in the smaller economies on the European periphery of Greece, Ireland, and Portugal, with contagion fears rapidly spreading to the large economies of Spain, Italy, Belgium, and even France, has transfigured into a fully-fledged currency crisis of the euro. Uncertainty dominates the economic developments that are crucial in determining the course of policy. The challenges that prompted many to turn towards the promotion of an investment-oriented social policy, however, have not gone away with the crisis. If anything, they have become more pressing.

In this chapter, I review the sequence of policy responses that have been implemented in various European countries, since the outbreak of the crisis in 2008, focusing mostly on employment and social policies. Following this introduction, Sections 2 and 3 survey two sequences of crisis management over the period of 2008 to 2011, each triggered by different, but complementary, sets of economic problems and related political challenges. The 2008 financial crisis has brought the welfare state to a new political crossroads. The years ahead, in any event, will differ markedly from the past decennium of reasonable—but in part illusory—growth, when the social investment paradigm across Europe, partly inspired by the Lisbon Agenda, gained currency. Section 4, therefore, concludes on the prospects of social investment in the aftermath of eurozone sovereign debt and currency crisis.

Aftershocks

The global financial crisis has brought advanced European welfare states into unchartered territory. Europe went through three interconnected crises: a banking crisis in 2008, followed by a severe economic recession in 2009, which in turn invoked a fiscal crisis of the state, most dramatically exemplified by the sovereign debt crises in Greece, Ireland, and Portugal. A monetary crisis followed after 2011, which potentially threatens the long-term viability of the euro. What has made the aftermath of the Wall Street crash of 2008 so uncomfortable for policymakers is that they have since been hard pressed to act almost instantly to a cascade of rapidly unfolding economic, social and political aftershocks. The magnitude of these aftershocks and their interaction effects not only potentially jeopardize economic recovery, they have also changed the range of social policy choices available to national governments and supranational institutions, sometimes overnight. I distinguish six of these crisis aftershocks (Hemerijck 2009).

First, there was the aftershock of de-globalization. The forces of financial de-globalization, such as bank bailouts and elements of re-nationalization of financial sectors, are not dangerous per se, as unfettered financial globalization through capital market deregulation was the root cause of the global downturn. That banks are being placed under stricter supervision by national authorities is the price to pay for greater financial stability. What is dangerous, however, is the risk of the banking crisis cascading into falling demand, as happened in 2009. More worrisome is the prospect of real economy protectionism with shrinking trade and overall declines in wealth.

The second aftershock concerned the crisis of unemployment caused by the severe 2009 recession. The crisis has highlighted the vulnerability of the low-skilled. Most worrisome is the surge in youth employment: in Latvia, Italy,

Greece, Sweden, Estonia, Hungary, Lithuania, France, Ireland, and Belgium, youth unemployment has crossed the 20 per cent threshold, and in Spain it is over 40 per cent.

Third, there is the aftershock of the pension crisis, beyond the difficulties already caused by significant ageing of the population. PAYG systems have suffered losses of financing and contributions, due to the effect if the crisis of employment, while funded systems have been more vulnerable to the sharp fall in equity markets, which have adversely affected the value of pension fund assets. A painful combination of lower benefits and higher contributions are inevitable if the steep rise in old-age dependency ratios is not coupled with measures to promote longer working lives.

The fourth aftershock has been the fiscal crisis of the state since 2010. Costly bank bailouts, stimulus packages have drained the public purse, resulting in a 'double bind' of rising social benefit expenditures combined with declining government revenues. Elevated public debt-to-GDP ratios will make fiscal consolidation imperative; requiring painful cuts also in welfare programmes. As social benefits and services, including health and education, add up to over 50 per cent of government spending, cuts in public expenditures will have to come from significant welfare retrenchment.

By mid-2010, the Greek sovereign debt crisis and the Irish banking crisis set the scene for the fifth aftershock of a currency crisis threatening the long-term viability of the euro. As contagion spread to Spain and Italy by mid-2011, eurozone leadership hastily enlarged the available rescue funds, while the ECB resumed buying besieged government bonds. These interventions did not, however, restore confidence to capital markets. Also the 2011 proposal of German Chancellor Merkel and French President Sarkozy to establish a real 'economic government' of the eurozone, under the helm of the president of the European Council, Herman van Rompuy, failed to impress markets.

The sixth and final aftershock is not really a shock in the conventional sense of a sharp and violent change in external conditions. Rather, it pertains to the realistic expectation of a protracted period of low growth resulting from crisis. The magnitude of systemic debt, the sum of private and public indebtedness, is very likely to delay recovery from the current crisis across advanced economies. The crisis has surely dismantled the most important growth driver of the recent decade: easy credit and private consumption. A burning question is what growth driver can put in place beyond buoyant growth in the emerging economies China, Brazil and India. There is real danger of the crisis persisting for more than just a few bad years conjures up the realistic antecedent of Japan's 'lost decade' following the crisis in the early 1990s.

At some point, no doubt, the recession is likely to recede. Before that happens, moreover, European welfare states will face long-run societal changes not adequately dealt with before crisis, such as population ageing, the incomplete revolution of women's roles and family structures, and associated shifts in labour supply and demand.

Although stable resolutions to the crisis aftershocks, listed above, may call for specific economic and social policies, whether these policies are enacted or not depend to a large extent on the political context of current era. Across Europe, citizens continue to hold high expectations of social protection from economic uncertainty. To the extent that the cascade aftershocks results in high unemployment, strained pensions, social benefits and public finances, this will put enormous pressure on elected politicians.

Revisiting the Keynesian Moment

Faced with an exceptionally deep crisis, immediately after the fall of Lehman Brothers, most advanced economy governments showed no inhibition in pursuing bold strategies of Keynesian fiscal stimulus, on a scale unthinkable before the credit crunch. Public authorities—especially governments and central banks—took on a hyperactive role in response to the credit freeze panic. Suddenly, the state (re-)emerged as key strategic economic actor. Activist public intervention in the economy was very successful in forestalling the darkest scenario—a rerun of the Great Depression. Following the economic teachings of John Maynard Keynes, the majority of the European countries chose to temporarily relax budget restrictions prescribed by the 1997 Stability and Growth Pact (SGP), with the support of the European Commission. On 26 November 2008, the European Commission proposed the European Economic Recovery Plan (EERP), adopted by the European Council in December 2008. The purpose of the plan was to boost public spending by 3.3 per cent of GDP, at both Member State and European level, with a financial contribution from the European Union of about 0.3 per cent of GDP. The scale of the fiscal expansion varied greatly among member states, depending also on the fiscal room to maneuver (Mandl and Salvatore 2009). The early responses to the crisis revolved, by and large, around two urgent priorities. On the one hand, governments responded to the credit crunch by increasing expenditures in support of financial institutions. On the other hand, social and employment programmes were expanded to help to cushion the fall in demand while aiming to keep people in employment, or at least upkeep their skills.

Fiscal expansion, including banking bailout support, were effectively supported by monetary policy, especially on the part of the European Central Bank, with massive provision of liquidity by the ECB at near-zero interest rates, helping banks to rebuild their capital stock. Given its strong competition policy mandate, the EU played the vital role in ensuring that protectionist responses among the Member States were avoided. Prior to the crisis, there were worries that the rigidity of the Stability and Growth Pact and European monetary union would prevent the EU from responding swiftly to the financial crisis (Eichengreen 2007). In fact, despite the initial delay in cutting interest rates, the ECB responded very quickly, by providing essentially unlimited amounts of liquidity to the euro-area financial systems. At the same time, the Stability and Growth Pact was relaxed in order to increase governments' capacities to borrow in the interests of recapitalizing their banks. These EU measures may have helped to offset the relative weakness of national stimulus plans.

The second imperative was to mitigate and forestall the rise in unemployment as a consequence of falling demand and export decline. Figure 4.1 displays the development of the harmonized unemployment rates in twelve European from January 2007 to January 2010. Despite the differences between the countries, this figure reveals an increase in unemployment in all EU Member States across 2009. The smallest increases were observed in Belgium (7.5 per cent to 7.9 per cent) and Germany (7.2 per cent to 7.7 per cent). The highest increases were registered in Latvia (7.4 per cent to 18.3 per cent) and

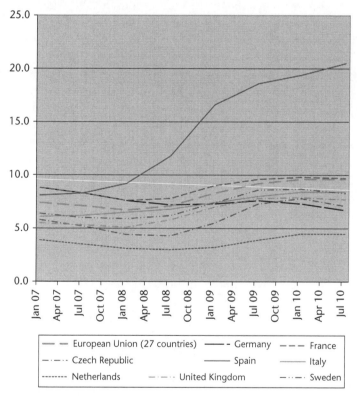

Figure 4.1. Harmonized unemployment rates for all persons
Source: Eurostat

Spain (9.1 per cent to 18.3 per cent) between the second quarters of 2008 and 2009 (see Figure 4.1). Despite overall country differences, there is quite a clear pattern in terms of age and gender in most member states. In most countries, unemployment has hit young people, and particularly men, disproportionately hard. It is striking to note how employment rates for women, also older women, held firm. Probably the most striking impact is the massive increase in the unemployment of the younger members of the labour force in most member states.

Unemployment rose mainly as a result of falling exports, among other things caused by lower consumer confidence. The highest reduction in exports took place in Sweden (minus 15.9 per cent), trailed by the UK (minus 15 per cent), and, at some distance, the Netherlands (minus 12.9), Germany (minus 10.7 per cent), and Denmark (minus 8.7 per cent). As the immediate threat of financial collapse receded, employment reached the top of the policy agenda. At the Employment Summit held on 7 May 2009 in Prague, the President of the European Commission, José Manuel Barroso, raised employment as Europe's number one priority. Due to falling demand, many European companies have had to reduce their production level, especially in manufacturing. The majority of the measures developed in the period between late 2008 and 2010 across the Member States of the EU are characterized by a 'preventive' character, aiming to keep people in employment. Many European companies have put their employees on short-term working or temporary lay-off. For this purpose, many countries have adapted already existing public support instruments in order to support companies and workers who have agreed to reduce working hours. In Germany, there was already a partial unemployment scheme in place—in the form of structurally lower working time—which has been extended from 6 to 18 months ('stimulus package 1'). Similar policies were developed in Austria, Belgium and Denmark, France, Italy, Lithuania, Luxembourg and the Netherlands, often based on tripartite agreements with the social partners at sector or company level, approved by government authorities. In addition, other preventive measures include further training initiatives while employed, with the aim of increasing the adaptability of workers and thereby the competitiveness of enterprises through skill development. Financial support for training may be provided to employers, as for example in Belgium, or directly to employees, as is the case in Austria, where the general provisions for unpaid training leave have been amended during the initial phase of the recession. In the Czech Republic, training support is in part funded by the European Social Fund (ESF). In Germany, Poland, and the Czech Republic, public training support is linked to short-term working programmes. In France, a social investment fund has been established to provide training for workers in partial unemployment and for jobseekers. Temporary reductions in social security contributions (including health and pension insurance) have been agreed to in Germany, Slovenia, Finland, Czech Republic, Hungary, and Portugal. In Ireland, direct subsidies to enterprises are paid out to avoid redundancies. Some companies have offered career breaks or sabbaticals, while still receiving a percentage of their salary.

Measures to promote (re-)integration into the labour market for the unemployed, including job matching, active labour market policy, mobility grants and tax incentives for companies employing additional workers, through reduction or exemption from non-wage labour costs, wage subsidies, have taken effect in many countries. In the UK, a wage subsidy is given to employers who hire people who have been unemployed for more than six months, funded by the public employment office (Jobcentre Plus) (Clegg 2010). Reductions in the non-wage labour costs for employers have been enacted in France, Germany and Poland or through wage subsidies, as in Belgium, Greece, and Slovakia. Training access for the unemployed has been enlarged in France and the Netherlands, based on tripartite agreements, and in Italy on the basis of special funds for underdeveloped areas. The Dutch mobility centres have been characterized by cooperation between local governments, companies, schools, trade unions, and job-searching organizations. The Swedish job security councils are established and regulated by social partners on a bipartite basis through collective agreements and management and administration is also divided equally among the social partners. In the UK, unemployed persons under the age of 25 years who have been out of work for 12 months will receive additional money on top of their benefits if they participate in training. Similar arrangements have been enacted in Bulgaria and Portugal. A few EU member states, such as Belgium, Slovakia, and the Czech Republic, have introduced or strengthened incentive for workers to relocate—either temporarily by daily commuting or permanently by changing their place of residence.

Finally, passive social insurance arrangements to support individuals in case of redundancy with income support for unemployed people and those who are outside the labour market are of critical importance as 'automatic stabilizers'. In the wake of the crisis, several governments have made amendments to the prevailing programmes. In France, as of 1 April 2009, the government has relaxed the rules for entitlement to unemployment benefits. In Italy, the government has extended the possibility to benefit from the unemployment allowance to a maximum of 90 days. In addition to widening the eligibility criteria, several countries have made unemployment benefits more favorable to beneficiaries, such as the Czech Republic, Estonia, and Romania. In Poland, the government has extended the unemployment benefit from 12 to 18 months. There have been temporary extensions of early retirement, in Ireland, Hungary, Latvia, Luxembourg, Romania, and Italy for the banking sector. However, and in contrast to the experience of the 1980s and 1990s, on the European continent, early exit is the exception to the general rule of 'preventive' policy measures (Palier 2010).

In terms of process, social partnership agreements have a played a critical role in the development and implementation of social and employment policy recession measures in many countries. In some cases, the impact of the crisis also significantly changed the content of collective agreements in several countries. In order to avoid redundancies, in a number of cases, the social partners have agreed over pay freezes or even cuts with their employees. In the Swedish metal sector, a central agreement opened up the possibility for local-level negotiation on the reduction of working time, with corresponding reduction in wages up to 20 per cent. Also in Continental countries, various kinds of 'opening clauses' were seen in collective agreements; including rotating lay-offs and short-term work at the sectoral and company level. In Germany, at the Daimler, a newly renegotiated company agreement called for a delay of bonuses and general pay increases for six months.

The combined impact of social insurance automatic stabilizers, low interest rates, fiscal stimulus, contributed to stabilizing demand across Europe's more generous Nordic and Continental welfare states. Many jobs have thus far been maintained. In Germany, where GDP fell by 6 per cent, employment loss up to the second quarter of 2009 was marginal. Production of motor vehicles fell by 27 per cent; employment, however, dropped by only 2.5 per cent over the same period.

Towards Pre-emptive Austerity

By the end 2009, it became increasingly evident that the aftermath of the global financial crisis had proven to be a far more serious 'stress test' for Europe's welfare systems than initially recognized. The cumulative effects of costly bank bailouts, tax cuts, rising social expenditures, lower revenue from social contributions, and other stimulus measures, drained the public purse, and in turn raised the stakes for social reform. Public debt increased significantly in many countries (see Figure 4.2).

Below I survey the main characteristics of domestic fiscal consolidation strategies since 2010 by paying special attention to the more emblematic social reforms, including cuts in social transfers and subsidies, pensions and public sector pay, employment and services, together with measures to increase revenue. I start with the Mediterranean welfare regimes, two of which—Greece and Portugal—have had to seek assistance from the newly created European Financial Stabilization Facility (EFSF). Next, I assess the adjustment packages two Anglo-Irish economies, which both have been heavily implicated in global financial deregulation, after which I review fiscal

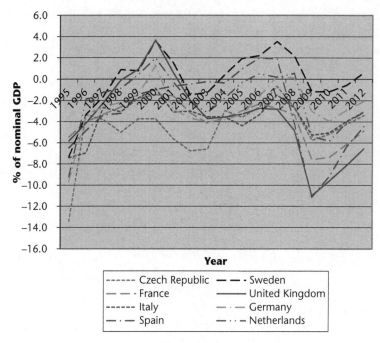

Figure 4.2. General government financial balances, surplus (+) or deficit (−) as a per cent of nominal GDP
Source: Eurostat

consolidation and social reforms in the Continental welfare regimes of Germany, France and the Netherland. Finally, I compare Nordic crisis management in Sweden, Denmark and Finland.

Delayed Mediterranean pension and labour market reform

Although *Greece* experienced exceptional growth rates, reaching almost 4 per cent of GDP between 1999 and 2008, growth failed to translate into improved competitiveness and healthy public finance. Since the largest overruns in the state budget concerned the social security funds, and given the projected increase in public pension spending between, cuts were imperative after 2008. The Greek *Pasok* government, led by Georges Papandreou, pledged to make truly draconic spending cuts and boost tax revenue in return for a €110 billion bailout form the EU and the IMF approved in mid-2010, when unemployment was reaching 15 per cent. In the area of pension, Papandreou set out to curb widespread early retirement schemes (Greek Government 2010a). The average retirement age is set to rise from 61.4 to 63.5 and all pensions were frozen over a three year period. In July 2010, the Greek parliament agreed to a new architecture of the pension system, whereby assistance and insurance functions are separated (Greek Government 2010b). The statutory retirement age will be raised to 65 years, voluntary exit plans will be abolished and pension benefits will be linked more closely to lifetime contributions (Greek Government 2011). From 2015, pension benefits will be made up of the newly introduced basic (flat rate) component, amounting to €360 in 2010 prices and granted on a 12 month basis, and a PAYG element based on life-time earnings (Angelaki and Natali 2011). The era of retiring at 50 on full pension has come to pass; people will need to work until 65, with 40 years' full contributions. Social insurance transfers have been cut and more means-testing introduced (Greek Government 2010a). The Greek government hopes to collect more social security contributions by cracking down on evasion and undeclared work. Labour market reform has primarily been directed at enhancing labour market flexibility, including more scope for temporary work, and the liberalization of services and closed professions. In a new round of austerity measures adopted in early 2011, the Greek government cut nominal wages in the public sector by 15 per cent and public and private pension in the order of 10 per cent (Greek Government 2011). Cuts in public sector employment will add up to €82,400. One-in-10 civil servants retiring in 2011 will be replaced and only one-in-5 in coming years. In the area of education, 2000 schools were closed and had to merge. On the revenue side, excise taxes were raised by 33 per cent on fuel, cigarettes and alcohol. Moreover VAT rose from 19 per cent to 23 per cent. Finally, the government aims to raise €50 billion from a large privatizations strategy by 2015: selling stakes in banks, port operators, state land, airports and mining rights.

In *Portugal*, by the end of 2010, the public deficit stood at an estimated 7.3 per cent of GDP and the debt-to-GDP ratio has risen to 84.6 per cent, while unemployment hovered around 12 per cent. Public services were paralyzed by a general strike in November 2010. By the early spring of 2011, borrowing costs rose precipitously, and it became clear that after Greece, also Portugal also required EFSF assistance. In May 2011 Portugal became the third eurozone country to receive EU-IMF bailout support of €78 billion. The social-democratic government of José Socrates, next, announced a range of austerity measures aimed at cutting the 2011 deficit to 4.6 per cent with the view of accelerating budget reduction to below 3 per cent by 2013 (Portuguese Government 2010). In the austerity drive top earners in the public sector, including politicians, have seen a 5 per cent pay cut. VAT will rise by 1 per cent and there will be income tax hikes for those earning more than €150,000. By 2013 they will face a 45 per cent tax rate. Military spending is to be cut by 40 per cent and the launch of two high-speed rail links—the Lisbon-Porto and Porto-Vigo routes was delayed. Like Greece, in education, teacher staff is to be reduced by €5,000 through more efficient class formation, teaching allocation, the closures of small schools, and reductions in scholarship support. Pensions were frozen, family allowances cut, indexation in social benefit suspended. Moreover, social transfers became subject to means-testing. On the other hand, employment services expanded with a strong focus on active labour market policies and training programmes. New programmes for young job-seekers include the launch of 50,000 apprenticeships and financial support to hiring young people. In addition, employment services will be improved by professionalizing account management, job placement sector agreements between employment agencies and business associations, and more focus on the improvement of basic skills of the unemployed on social assistance. With respect to labour market regulation, new legislation of 2011 serves to decentralize collective bargaining and establish a new model severance pay, aimed at reducing the costs of corporate restructuring. It will become easier to shift to temporary reductions of working hours. A new centre-right coalition government took office after elections in June that is able to rely on a large enough majority in parliament to enact additional austerity measures under the EFSF bailout conditions. The new government now aims to bring the budget deficit down to 5.9 per cent of GDP by the end of 2011.

In *Spain*, unemployment has more than doubled, to about 20 per cent of the workforce, since 2007 by the end of 2010. Meanwhile, the Spanish budget deficit rose to over 9 per cent of GDP. By mid-2010, the Spanish government, led by the social-democrat José Luis Rodriguez Zapatero approved an austerity budget for 2011 which include a tax rise for the rich and 8 per cent spending cuts, amounting to €27 billion in 2010–2011. Cuts mainly focused on physical infrastructure and certain items of current spending. Civil servants pay has been cut by 5 per cent for 2010 and salaries will be frozen for 2011.

The tax on tobacco rose to 28 per cent. In addition, the Spanish government plans to sell 30 per cent of the Spanish lottery and a minority stake in the country's airport authority. A tax rise of 1 per cent will be applied to personal income above €120.000. Smaller savings include an end to new-born child benefits. Madrid will also stop paying a monthly subsidy of €426 to the long-term unemployed who are no longer eligible. Finally, the Zapatero government pledged to reform the pension system, including a rise in the retirement age from 65 to 67. The Spanish government has also agreed with the social partners to suspend the revalorization of pensions in 2011, excluding minimum and non-contributory pensions. What is strikingly different from the austerity packages of Greece and Portugal is that Spain has tried very hard to preserve social protection and investment in human capital. Emergency measures include special benefits for the long-term unemployed reaching the end of their entitlement to regular benefits, minimum and non-contributory pensions, extra assistance and benefits for the dependent groups in society and child tax deductions. Expenditure on education has doubled in absolute terms in the last seven years. Access to the lowest income groups has been granted, with an overall increase in scholarships of 107 per cent in value and 30 per cent in the number of beneficiaries since 2004. The Spanish Government has also kept the pace in the expansion of education for 0–3 year old children, with a 101 per cent increase since 2004. Finally, the Spanish Government has continued to place strong emphasis on activation, mainly through a special focus on the re-skilling and re-employment of people losing their jobs as a consequence of the crisis. In area of labour market regulation, the government approved to give employers more control over how they deploy workers, while making it cheaper to fire—and therefore easier to hire—permanent employees. But excessive use of temporary workers is restricted. The objective was to cut the deficit from 11.5 per cent to 3 per cent in only four years, which would be one of the strongest adjustments undertaken by any advanced economies in recent decades.

In *Italy*, the budget deficit was estimated at 5 per cent of GDP in 2010. The Italian government approved austerity measures in the order of €24 billion for the years 2011–2012, amounting to about 1.6 per cent of GDP (Italian Government 2010). The government decided to cut public sector pay and freeze new recruitment, replacing only one employee for every five who leave. Progressive pay cuts of up to 10 per cent are planned for high earners in the public sector, including ministers and parliamentarians. Retirement will be delayed by up to six months for those who reach the retirement age in 2011. Pressed by the ECB, the Berlusconi government had to step up its austerity ambition by August 2011. The new 2011 austerity package is intended to cut the fiscal deficit by €48 billion and balance the budget in 2014. The new package therefore adds only marginally to deficit cuts worth €25 billion the government approved in 2010 year to rein in public finance in 2011 and 2012. Most of the measures will take effect in 2013 and 2014. The consolidation measures include cuts to the budgets of central government ministries (worth a total of €1 billion in 2012, €3.5 billion in 2013, and €5 billion in 2014), a salary hike freeze for public workers, to be extended to 2014, important cuts in subsidies of provinces and towns (worth €3.2 billion in 2013 and €6.4 billion in 2014), cuts to health spending (worth €2.5 billion in 2013 and €5 billion in 2014), savings from state pensions, including delaying retirement and a tax on pensions over €90,000 annually. At the same time, the retirement age for women working in the private sector jumps to 65 years from 60, starting only in 2032. The introduction of automatic increases to the retirement age on the basis of regular assessments of life expectancy will be brought forward to 2013 from 2015. On the revenue side, higher taxes on banks, insurance companies, management stock options and bonuses, together with private contributions to certain hospital and medical visits, savings from retrenching early retirement, and privatization of state-controlled firms, feature prominently.

Anglo-Irish retrenchment

Ireland, having shown budgetary surpluses until 2008 and a level of public debt among the lowest in the eurozone, suddenly experienced a debt explosion resulting from a severe banking crisis, followed by a deep recession. The collapse of the housing bubble in 2007 led the government to underwrite the entire banking system and thereby greatly increased its own indebtedness. Self-imposed spending cuts contributed to an estimated 9 per cent annual fall in GDP in 2009. A new bank rescue plan announced in October 2010 provided another cash injection to the banks of around €50 billion from public funds, thus raising the public deficit for 2010, from 12 per cent to 32 per cent of GDP. Meanwhile unemployment soared to 14 per cent. Stringent bailout conditions imposed by the EFSF rescue package required this figure to fall to 2.9 per cent by 2015. To this end, Ireland has pledged to make €15 billion worth of savings by 2014 of which €6 billion in cuts are frontloaded (Irish Government 2010).

Public servants have their salaries cut by at least 5 per cent, social welfare is reduced, and nearly 25,000 public sector jobs are being cut. €1.9 billion will come from rising income taxes, a reduction of the minimum wage and a VAT rise from 21 per cent to 23 per cent in 2013 and 24 per cent in 2014. Cuts in social insurance are about 4.2 per cent, including job seeker allowance and child benefits. The government has cut the unemployment assistance rate for young unemployed people unless they undertake training and education. In addition, the minimum wage was reduced by €1 to €7.65. The Irish government has decided to raise the minimum pension age to 66 years in 2014, 67 in 2021, and 68 in 2028, for which career average earnings rather than final salary will be used to calculate pension benefits. Additional reforms include the development of a rebalanced and integrated child income support payment system. This would provide for a universal component to replace Child Benefit with one single payment rate per child. Furthermore, a single social assistance payment is to replace the different means-tested working age payments, including some secondary and supplementary payments, as part of a more active labour activation strategy which will involve work placement programmes, skill development and internship programmes to ensure that unemployed people can make a swift return to work. Finally, students are to contribute more from private funds to the costs of tertiary education.

In *Britain*, the public deficit stood over 11 per cent of GDP in 2010 and public sector net debt (excluding financial interventions) was equivalent to only 58 per cent of GDP. The coalition government (Conservatives and Liberal Democrats) adopted a plan for €20.3 billion spending cuts. Proposed measures include an increase in the VAT tax by 2.5 per cent (to 20) and a spending reduction of 25 per cent over the next four years for all civil service departments, except health and overseas aid. Welfare spending will be cut by £11 billion (about €13 billion) over the next five years. Child benefits will be frozen, family tax credit will be reduced, housing benefits will be capped, medicals for disability benefits will be stricter, and the increase of the state pension age from 65 to 66 will be accelerated (European Institute 2010; United Kingdom Government 2010). Savings of about €100 billion are to be made over four years, which amount to the largest public expenditure cut in the United Kingdom since World War II. Close to 500,000 public sector jobs will be lost. It is predicted that a similar number of jobs will disappear in the private sector. Ministries face budget retrenchments in the order of 20 per cent on average, exempting the defense budget which will be cut by 8 per cent. In terms of the composition of retrenchment, social protection and education are among the hardest hit sectors. First, as a result of the adjustment the UK social spending will decrease by 1.3 per cent of the GDP in the coming years, profoundly altering the British welfare system. The cuts in social policies amount to over 30 per cent of the total, more than €22,000 billion in the period 2010–2014, with a particular effect on lower income families, including unemployed and retired people. The UK Government cuts affected incapacity benefits, housing support, child benefits, tax credits, tax subsidies, and rebates to low income households. The retirement age is to rise from 65 to 66 by 2020. Second, access to the British higher level educational system is also being distorted, with an average increase in university fees of around 143 per cent. The reasoning behind social retrenchment of the Cameron cabinet is that the UK has inherited from the New Labour government before them a welfare system that has trapped the poorest families and children in welfare dependency cultures. The coalition government does hope to extend childcare for disadvantaged 2 year olds to support children from the lowest income households. The extension of childcare services also plays an important role in facilitating women's access to employment opportunities.

Continental modernizing consolidation

The total government deficit of *Germany* in 2010 was estimated 3.7 per cent, lower than originally forecast because of the country's relatively strong growth performance over that year. In July 2010, the *German* government agreed on significant cutbacks in a savings plan (*Sparprogramm*), amounting to approximately €80 billion, 3 per cent of GDP, between 2011 and 2014 to achieve a fully balanced budget by January 2016 (German Government 2010). At the heart of the deficit reduction plan is the so-called 'debt-brake' law, agreed to by the former CDU-SPD coalition, which commits Germany constitutionally to a permanently balanced annual budget after 2016, exempting deep recessions and natural disasters, provided there is a two-third majority in parliament. In addition to cutting 10,000 government jobs over four years, the German *Sparprogramm* is a mixture of cancellation of existing subsidies, higher taxation (on nuclear power), a major reform of the army, public administration reforms, reform of the financial sector, and several—taken on their own— relatively minor benefit cuts and entitlement restrictions (German Government 2010). Housing benefits will be cut, parental allowance and subsidies for statutory health insurance curtailed, all intended to achieve the objectives of higher employment, lower welfare spending, and rising tax revenue, and to restore the balance between personal responsibility and solidarity. Some reforms include reducing the rate of parental allowance from 67 per cent to 65 per cent of the income eligible for replacement, where recipients' relevant attributable net income is more than €1,200 per month, removing the heating cost supplement under housing benefit legislation. At the second stage of unemployment benefit, the limited-term supplementary payment (during the transition from stage one to stage two) and the compulsory contributions to the state old age pension insurance scheme (and thus the contributions of the government to the scheme) are to be discontinued. Expenditure incurred by old age pension schemes resulting from German unification will no longer be reimbursed from the national budget. The pension system remains untouched, as the decision to raise the pension age to 67 was already made in 2007. In addition to the savings, the government at the same time is investing €12 billion in education, research, and development, i.e. in the forces of growth and in new jobs. With its relatively strong recovery, the German *Sparprogramm* conjures up an excellent opportunity to set a European example for other countries to follow.

President Sarkozy was under pressure to follow Ms Merkel's lead for *France*. In order to meet the target of reducing the budget deficit from 7.7 per cent of GDP (2010) to 3 per cent, France announced plans to cut spending by €45 billion by the end of 2013 (French Government 2010). Some of the cuts were to be saved through closing tax loopholes, the withdrawing of temporary economic stimulus measures and a 1 per cent increase in tax on the highest income band. In addition, some 97,000 public sector jobs will be discontinued in the period 2011–2013. The most politically controversial measure has been President Starkozy's plans to raise the French retirement age. The key elements of the law entail an increase in the retirement age from 60 to 62 years between 2011 and 2018, an increase in the contributions required for the award of a full pension from 40 in 2008 to 41 in 2010 and 41.5 by 2020, while the age at which workers who have not made full contributions can receive a pension without penalties will be raised to 67 years. Despite significant social protest, the bill was voted through by the French Parliament and approved by the National Assembly in late October 2010. The reform also foresees changes in the amount of income tax payable on certain levels and types of income (e.g.

the highest band of income tax, the levies of stock options, the supplementary pension schemes, the capital income, and inheritance income). While it introduces measures that promote the employment of older workers, it also includes solidarity elements targeted at young people in precarious situations, farmers and women. Pension reform was deemed essential as it would erase the growing deficit in the PAYG system, curb rising public debt and preserve the country's coveted AAA credit rating, enabling it to borrow at the lowest market rates. The reform is expected to bring the system back into balance by 2018. Finally, it must also be said, that beyond pension reform, France has done little to further restructure public spending. As a share of GDP, the French state now spends more than Sweden.

In the *Netherlands*, the centre-right coalition that came to power on 8 October 2010 said it wanted to cut the 2010 budget deficit, estimated at 5.8 per cent of GDP, by €18 billion between 2011 and 2015 (Dutch Government 2010). Expenditure cuts hit both the child allowance and the tax relief for the upkeep of children, by lowering the age limit from 30 to 21. Families in high income brackets are no longer entitled to child support, while the allowance rate per child will be reduced to a maximum hourly rate of €5. The largest spending reduction, saving a structural amount of €9 billion, is the overhaul family tax allowances. At present, families with young children (up to 5 years old) and families with a non-working partner born before 1 January 1972 can transfer the general tax allowance in full. This will be restricted over 13 years: the exception for families with young children will be abolished in full. The age limit for non-working partners will be changed to 1 January 1963. With respect to healthcare there are basically two measures. First, the healthcare benefits will be frozen, resulting in a structural saving of €2.9 billion. Second, means-testing for healthcare benefits are introduced; people earning in excess of €80,000 will no longer be entitled to public healthcare benefits. With respect to education, an age limit of 30 is introduced to be eligible for funding. Furthermore, not only is the annual public transport pass abolished for students taking more than one extra year to complete their studies, those students will also see their tuition fee increase by €3,000. Additionally, a loan system is introduced for a Master's degree. Also, there is an efficiency cutback for institutions: €3,000 per student. Other measures include a tightening of the eligibility criteria of the incapacity insurance for young people, and a reduction of the partial benefit to 70 per cent of the statutory minimum wage and an increase of the state pension age to 66 as from 1 January 2020. The will be no indexation of social insurance benefits to wages between 2012 and 2015. It needs to be emphasized that the liberal-Christian democratic minority coalition relies on parliamentary support from the xenophobic right-populist Freedom Party to enact the proposed cuts. This casts some doubts about the long-term viability of the coalition.

Upkeeping Nordic social investment

In *Sweden*, the center-right government has proposed a fiscal consolidation package for 2011 of about SEK 13 billion, but no new initiatives are taken for the labour market and the welfare security system, both of which have been reformed in the previous term in the office of the ruling coalition. The explicit aim of the Swedish government is to 'nurture' the reforms that have been implemented before and ensure that they have the intended effects of replacing passive schemes by active measures (Swedish Government 2010). If anything, the social expenditures in the 2011 budget are likely to rise. For example, the Budget Bill includes proposals for further reductions in the income tax for pensioners (by increasing their allowance) and higher housing allowances for families with children. The local government sector will be allocated an extra central government grant in 2011 of SEK 3 billion to promote welfare and jobs. Moreover, a number of new measures are proposed to improve health care and elderly care. Concerning the labour market, the Swedish government aims at providing more job opportunities resulting from a work-first principle. Furthermore, the government aims to introduce a general unemployment benefit to prevent that people in the labour market are without income-related protection in the event of unemployment. In spring 2010, the government appointed a cross-party inquiry to consider ways of improving the sickness and unemployment insurance systems in the long term so as to make them coherent, balanced and sustainable, and to contribute to higher employment in the long term.

Also in *Denmark*, the center-right government has not seen the need for deep cuts in the 2011 budget, but did proposed a shift in spending priorities for a total of DKK 10 billion (€3.2 billion)(Danish Government 2010). While the budget for welfare services in the municipalities is kept unchanged at 2010-budget levels in real terms, in the central government a general savings operation over the ministries of ½ per cent per year in 2011–2013 is implemented, resulting in a loss of 20,000 jobs in the public sector. Moreover, a series of more targeted central government savings are implemented, which do including cuts in education and a 5 per cent reduction in child benefits. These savings are redirected notably towards health and training initiatives for more vulnerable groups. A more politically contentious measure was the (further) reduction in the duration of the unemployment benefit from four to two years, which has been adopted in 2011. Additionally, an annual ceiling of DKK 3,000 on tax deductions of union fees and limitations on tax deductions of certain employer contributions are introduced. Concerning the revenue side, the automatic adjustment (wage indexation) of the thresholds for income taxes is suspended for the 2011–2013 period. The suspension is neutral for the income distribution and provides revenue of approximately DKK 6.5 billion in 2013. The planned increase in the income threshold for top-bracket tax in 2011 agreed in the Spring Package 2.0 is deferred for three years until 2014. This is to result in a gross revenue of around DKK 2 billion per annum. Finally, a fully financed tax reform was also implemented in 2010 aimed to strengthen household incomes.

In November 2010, the government of *Finland* proposed a reform package of measures explicitly aimed a lengthening working careers and investment in education to support full-time studying through student grants (Finnish Government 2010). Specifically, the measures consist of an increase of 60 million euro per year to promote youth employment, i.e. people under 25 and graduated people under 30 are given the guarantee of a job or training no later than three months after they became unemployed. Moreover, basic education is improved by reducing class sizes, establishing after-school club activities, and promoting the supplementary training of teachers. On the other hand, the government also saves on education, for example by restricting the maximum period of student benefits in upper secondary education and reducing the number of general upper secondary schools. Also, an experiment is launched to tackle long-term unemployment. Furthermore, the Finnish government proposed to increase the unemployment security basic allowance by €100 per month. Concerning social affairs, the government aims to save on expenditure by a review of the system of adult education allowances and reduce the state's share on the benefit of job alternation leave. The government is using income taxation as a means of promoting employment, better household purchasing power and domestic demand; there are plans to ease the tax bases on earned income altogether by €400 million in 2011. Moreover, the taxation of pension income would be eased by about €30 million to ensure that the tax ratio for pension income stays in the same range as that for earned income. The basic deduction in local government taxation would be increased by around €16 million to secure purchasing power for those in the very lowest income brackets. In addition, the hole left in central government finances by the 2010 abolition of the employer's national pension contribution will be filled by net increases in energy taxes totaling around €730 million. An index adjustment of 1.6 per cent will be introduced to the central government transfers for basic public services in local government, which will increase transfers to local government by nearly €120 million in 2011. Altogether, central government transfers to local government will grow by €286 million relative to 2010. In June 2011, a new government was installed, which pledged to reinforce the former cabinets emphasis on youth and education (Finnish Government 2011).

Conclusion

Over the past four years, the welfare states of the European Union have gone through two phases of crisis management. In the immediate aftermath of the Lehman Brother's bankruptcy in the fall of 2008, the first wave of crisis management was critically inspired by the return of Keynesian policy solutions to economic instability in response to a deep liquidity strain and a rapid fall in global demand. Public authorities acted swiftly. National governments and central banks acted by supporting financial institutions, and the European Central Bank by providing ample liquidity and the European Commission by enforcing competition discipline flexibly. Between 2008 and 2010, many EU Member States responded to the crisis by extending short-term working arrangements, training and activation, gender equality in labour markets, and later retirement, fairly consistent with the social investment perspective, which gained prominence in the decade before the onslaught of the crisis. Some of the most generous welfare states, with large public sectors devoted to human capital formation and family services, clearly outperformed many of the most liberal political economies in the wake of the crisis. In other words, an ambitious, generous, and active welfare state, with a strong social investment impetus, proved to be an asset rather than a liability after the onslaught of the early 21st century Great Recession. Moreover, the strong focus on maintaining employment and expanding training, with extensive public support, reveals a learning experience from the 1990s, when many continental welfare states opted for early-exit as the main policy response to the recession. In this respect, the 1990s and 1980s temptation of labour supply reduction through early retirement really is history!

After December 2009 a second wave, based on a more conservative macroeconomic problem definition of the crisis took root, punctuated by the Greek sovereign debt predicament. After governments had been forced to bail out banks taxpayers' money, the new crisis diagnosis became one of state failure. In the shadow of a looming fiscal crisis of the state, countries like Greece, Ireland, Portugal, and Spain, but also France and Italy, have since pushed through bold, austerity-oriented social reforms, including labour market deregulation, cuts in civil servant salaries, pension benefit freezes, retirement age rises, and retrenchment of social transfers and services. In conclusion, it needs to be said that the kind of pension and labour market reforms in Greece, Spain, Portugal, and also Italy and France, had already been enacted in most other European countries over the past two decades, and this in a far more incremental and negotiated fashion and under less dire economic conditions. Before the crisis, labour market deregulation and pension reform with the intent to raise levels of employment, in Southern Europe, except for Spain, were undermined by the legacies of clientelism and patronage and a high inefficient bureaucracy. The Zapatero government tried to save the social investment turn as much as possible within his fiscal adjustment packages. Similarly, the Irish government remains committed to activation. Nowhere, except for the United Kingdom, was fiscal consolidation precipitated on the neo-liberal narrative of welfare dependency cultures. On the other end of the welfare regime spectrum, the Scandinavian countries remained more than ever before committed to the service intensity of their family friendly and education and skills promoting social policy regimes. To a certain degree, Germany also moved in this direction, however, with much leaner social protection and active labour market supports for vulnerable groups. Rather surprisingly is that the Netherlands, hailed in the 1990s as the first continental welfare state that explicitly moved in the direction of social investment, is now cutting child benefits and disinvesting in education, while preserving passive social insurance and insider-biased labour market regulation by the liberal-conservative government, backed by the populist right Freedom Party (PVV).

If recent European, particularly Scandinavian but also German, experiences testify to broadly supported Pareto-optimal solutions to the final crisis and socioeconomic restructuring more generally, the recent US experience represents something of a mirror image. In the many attempts to decipher lessons from the Great Recession of early 21st century global capitalism, leading economists, including Eichengreen (2009), Stiglitz (2009), Rajan (2010), Roubini (2010), and Rodrik (2011), have come to the conclusion that the US economy is in dire need of stronger safety nets. The former IMF economist Raghuram Rajan reasons that as workers have to be flexible, switch jobs and careers frequently, workers and families need to receive more public support to navigate them through the water of their increasingly uncertain employment careers, while improving their resilience to economic adversity. This implies greater investments in education, jobs skills, and more generous and portable unemployment insurance, health care plans, and pension benefits. A more progressive tax system is in order, not only to pay for these benefits, but also to smooth the business cycle. Stronger and active welfare provision would take the pressure off governments and central banks to keep injecting stimulus in times of slow job growth.

In conclusion, the fundamental societal trends that necessitated a social investment perspective are as relevant and important today as they were ten years ago. Perhaps even more so because of adverse demography. Many of the jobs lost in the 2008–2009 shock will not come back. Skill mismatches will continue to grow, despite significant unemployment. For these reasons, the case for social investment social policy is as strong, if not stronger, than before 2008. With fewer active persons supporting ever more dependents, low labour market participation is simply no longer affordable with the demographic changes now taking effect across the EU. Social investments, especially in older workers, that allow for combinations of flexible retirement while continuing to work, together with investments in life-long learning and continuous training, incur positive macroeconomic effects far beyond the current crisis. There is no denying that a social investment strategy generates tensions and trade-offs between various social policy goals in the short term, but most important to emphasize is that social investment is a long-term strategy par excellence with high rates of economic returns and social rewards, in an era where human capital is swiftly becoming a scarce resource. There is great potential for employment growth, if people are skilled for the new jobs and families can get the quality child services they need. Population ageing will also surely raise employment opportunities in the form of rising demand for care services. The key policy challenge in the current crisis, therefore, is to make *long-term* social investments and *short-term* fiscal consolidation mutually supportive (Vandenbroucke et al. 2011). The erosion of the tax base and the imperative of budgetary austerity in the wake of the economic crisis of 2008–2010 is a dangerous threat to the social investment strategy. Saving social investment from ill-conceived pre-emptive retrenchment will continue to be an uphill political battle of injecting common sense into the current conservative political climate across Europe. Time here is perhaps the scarcest resource. Policymakers and larger publics need time to see the aftershock repercussions of the crisis and appropriate policy responses in a different light and to adapt their ideas and measures accordingly. We are also aware that democratic decision-making time is slow, compared to the volatile cascade of crisis aftershocks. Hopefully not too slow.

Bibliography

Angelaki, M. & Natali, D. (2011) Pension Policy in Europe Since the Crisis: EU Developments and National Reforms. In Degryse, C. & Natali, D. (Eds.) *Social Developments in the European Union 2010*, Brussels, Ose/etui.

Clegg, D. (2010) Labour Market Policy in the Crisis: The UK in Comparative Perspective. *Journal of Poverty and Social Justice*, 18, 5–17.

Danish Government (2010) *Fiscal Consolidation Agreement*, available at: <http://uk.fm.dk/Publications/2010/~/media/Publikationer/Imported/2010/Fiscal%20Consolidation%20Agreement/Fiscal_Consolidation_Agreement_Summary.ashx>.

Dutch Government (2010) *Budgetary Framework*, available at: <http://www.kabinetsformatie2010.nl/dsc?c=getobject&s=obj&objectid=127751>.

Eichengreen, B. J. (2007) The Breakup of the Euro Area, NBER Working Paper no. 13393.

Eichengreen, B. J. (2009) A Tale of Two Crises. In Hemerijck, A., Knapen, B. & van Doorne, E. (Eds.) *Aftershocks, Economic Crisis and Institutional Choice*, Amsterdam, Amsterdam University Press, 55–66.

European Institute (2010) EU *Austerity: A Country-By-Country Table*, available at: <http://www.europeaninstitute.org/June-2010/eu-austerity-a-country-by-country-table.html>.

Finnish Government (2010) *Budget Review 2011: November 2010*, Helsinki, Ministry of Finance.

Finnish Government (2011) *Programme of the Finnish Government*, Helsinki, Prime Minister's Office.

French Government (2010) Loi de finances 2011, no. 201–1657, available at: <http://www. legifrance.gouv.fr/affichTexte.do;jsessionid=?cidTexte=JORFTEXT00002331 4376& dateTexte=&oldAction=rechJO&categorieLien=id>.

German government (2010) *Government Draft of the 2011 Budget and Financial Plan to 2014*, available at: <http://www.bundesfinanzministerium.de/nn_103388/EN/Topics/Fiscal-policy/Articles/20100816-Government-draft-2011-budget.html?__nnn=true>.

Greek Government (2010a) Budget 2011. Draft Law, available at: <http://www.minfin.gr/content-api/f/binaryChannel/minfin/datastore/b1/62/3a/b1623a6c1b61846-f144e5337988f0d69daa6ea00/application/pdf/20101118_budget+2011_EN.pdf>.

Greek Government (2010b) Greek Parliament adopts 2011 Budget, *Hellenic Economic Policy Programme Newsletter*.

Greek Government (2011) From May 2010 to May 2011, *Hellenic Economic Policy Programme Newsletter*, 19 May.

Hemerijck, A. (2009) The Institutional Legacy of the Crisis of Global Capitalism. In Hemerijck, A., Knapen, B. & van Doorne, E. (Eds.) *Aftershocks, Economic Crisis and Institutional Choice*, Amsterdam, Amsterdam University Press, 13–52.

Irish Government (2010) *The National Recovery Plan 2011–2014*, Dublin, Stationery Office.

Italian Government (2010) *Public Finance Decision 2011–2013*, Italy, Ministry of Economy and Finance.

Mandl, I. & Salvatore, L. (2009) *Tackling the Recession: Employment-related Public Initiatives in the Member States and Norway*, European Monitoring Centre on Change, available at: <www.eurofound.europa.eu/docs/erm/tn0907020s/tn0907020s.html>.

Palier, B. (2010) *A Long Goodbye to Bismarck? The Politics of Welfare Reforms in Continental Europe*, Amsterdam, Amsterdam University Press.

Portuguese Government (2010) *Fiscal Consolidation, Competitiveness and Structural Reforms*, available at: <http://www.portugal.gov.pt/pt/GC18/Governo/Ministerios/MF/Documentos/Pages/20101220_MFAP_Com_Decisoes_Recentes.aspx>.

Rajan, R. (2010) *Fault Lines. How Hidden Fractures Still Threaten the World Economy*, Princeton, NJ, Princeton University Press.

Rodrik, D. (2011) *The Globalization Paradox. Why Global Markets, States, and Democracy Can't Coexist*, Oxford, Oxford University Press.

Roubini, N. (2010) *Crisis Economics. A Crash Course in the Future of Finance*, London, Penguin Books.

Stiglitz, J. (2009) The Global Crisis, Social Protection and Jobs. *International Labour Review*, 148, 1–13.

Swedish Government (2010) *Budget Statement*, available at: <http://www.sweden.gov.se/content/1/c6/15/38/32/91bbec67.pdf>.

United Kingdom Government (2010) *Spending Review 2010*, London, The Stationery Office.

Vandenbroucke, F., Hemerijck, A. & Palier, B. (2011) *The EU Needs a Social Investment Pact*, available at: <www.ose.be/EN>.

Part II

The Theoretical Underpinnings of the New Welfare State

5

Blame Avoidance and Credit Claiming Revisited

Giuliano Bonoli

Introduction

The study of welfare state reform has been strongly influenced by the twin concepts of credit claiming and blame avoidance, popularized in an article published by R. Kent Weaver and then widely used in the seminal work of Paul Pierson on welfare retrenchment (Weaver 1986b; Pierson 1994,1996, 2001). These two concepts provide a framework for thinking about policies that impact on large sections of electorates in competitive democracies. Decisions taken in these areas are likely to have electoral consequences, and governments are likely to consider the expected electoral consequence when designing policies.

Of the two concepts, 'blame avoidance' has clearly received the most attention in the recent literature on welfare state transformation. The reason is that given the persistent context of budgetary restrictions faced by advanced democracies, or of 'permanent austerity' (Pierson 1998), reforms have tended to entail widely unpopular cuts and cost containment measures. It is precisely in these types of reforms that a blame avoidance strategy becomes important.

This framework has proven to be tremendously useful in the study of the processes of retrenchment of mature welfare states. It predicts that retrenchment will be a politically difficult exercise, and that governments will adopt strategies that minimize the political risks involved in it. Most of the time, these strategies entail reducing the visibility of reform, dividing electorates between winners and losers, making retrenchment 'automatic', or delaying the effects of reform (Weaver 1986a; Pierson 1994).

The predictions of the framework have often proven to be accurate. Entitlement-reducing reforms have been adopted across OECD countries, most of the time through obscure changes in benefit formulas (such as demographic factors); with long delays and targeted on different groups. On some occasions, governments or politicians who have ignored the implicit advice the framework gives them, and have tried to cut benefits in an explicit fashion, have been voted out of office. Well known examples are the failed pension reforms in Italy (1994) and in France (1995) that have resulted in a change of majority some months later.

While the framework has been largely successful, some have identified a number of anomalies, or unexpected developments over the last two decades or so. For example, there have been instances where retrenchment has been used by the parties in government for credit claiming. There are also examples of quite radical reforms, above all in the field of pensions, which are difficult to reconcile with the view of strong popular support behind benefits that one finds in this strand of literature. Finally, since the mid-1990s we have seen the expansion of some policies, above all active labour market policy and childcare, something unexpected given the context of permanent austerity.

This chapter deals with these anomalies. It discusses them and suggests some ways to adapt the way we think about parties in government acting in the social policy field.

The Blame Avoidance/Credit Claiming Framework

The framework was put forward in a seminal article published in 1986, placing most emphasis on the first of the two notions: blame avoidance. It argued that 'politicians are motivated primarily by the desire to avoid blame for unpopular actions rather than by seeking to claim credit for popular ones' (Weaver 1986a: 371). The main reason for this is found in the so called 'negativity bias' of voters, a notion that refers to an asymmetry in the behaviour of the winners and the losers of a governmental policy. Voters who perceive to be on the loosing side of a reform are more likely to react and adapt their voting behaviour than those who believe to be on the winning side. As a result, a zero-sum reform that creates as many winners as losers will turn out to have an overall negative impact on a government's electoral fortunes. For this reason, parties in governments will be more inclined to care about how to avoid the potential blame than how to claim credit (Weaver 1986b; Pierson 1994: 18–19).

Applied to the field of welfare state reform, the salience of blame avoidance over credit claiming is likely to be reinforced by two factors.

First, the current climate of 'permanent austerity' leaves little room for popular 'give away' policies that could be exploited in order to claim credit.

The situation was of course different during the postwar expansion of Western welfare states. At that time, strong economic growth and a favourable demographic situation allowed the development of ever more generous social protection systems. Their costs, covered by the 'growth dividend' were not visible. Those who were net contributors saw their post-tax income rise anyway. Credit claiming was further encouraged by the financing structure of old age pension schemes. Pay-as-you-go (PAYG) financing in the context of a favourable demographic context meant that generous promises for future benefits could be made at very little cost, given the small size of pensioners' cohorts. As Myles and Pierson put it:

> PAYG systems offered enormous 'front-end' political benefits during the initial phase-in period. Since there was no preceding generation of entitled pensioners, politicians could immediately offer a potent combination of modest payroll taxes, generous promises of future pensions, and 'unearned' benefits for those near retirement age. (Myles and Pierson 2001: 310)

In the current context of permanent austerity there is no 'growth dividend' to share, and every improvement in benefits must be financed by highly visible and painful contribution or tax increases. Of course, governments can also use debt to expand their social programmes and many clearly turned to this technique in the 1980s (Manow and Plümper 2005). However, the debt tensions experienced since 2011 by several EU members have shown that this avenue is also largely closed.

Second, the process of welfare state retrenchment is such that in a zero-sum reform, the losses are likely to be concentrated on a relatively small group of current beneficiaries. The gains, instead, are likely to be diffused across a large and unstructured tax-payer community. Beneficiaries also tend to be organized through ad hoc outfits (e.g. pensioners organizations) or within the labour movement. As a result, the process of welfare state retrenchment is characterized by a powerful asymmetry between the losers (concentrated and organized) and the winners (diffused and unstructured). The result is an additional incentive for governments to avoid retrenchment, and if they are forced to retrench, to resort to blame avoidance strategies.

Anomalies

The framework presented above has been extremely influential during the past two decades. It has been proven to be right on many occasions. Often, governments that have succeeded in reforming social programmes have applied the blame avoidance strategies identified by Weaver and Pierson of obfuscation, delay, automatic government and so forth. In addition, there are also some well known failed attempts at explicit retrenchment that have cost the responsible government major electoral losses, such as the Italian 1994 and the French 1995 failed pension reform (Natali 2002). All this supports the hypotheses formulated on the basis of the blame avoidance/credit claiming framework.

However, together with these events that tend to confirm the centrality of blame avoidance in successful welfare reform, we also find other developments that do not conform to expectations based on this framework. Following Thomas Kuhn (1962), these can be considered to be anomalies, or empirical observations that are not accounted for by existing theories. These are discussed next.

Retrenchment as credit claiming

Successful retrenchment has not always been accompanied by blame avoidance strategies. Since the 1990s, there have been a few examples of governments presiding over reductions in entitlements that have quite clearly claimed credit for their achievement, by highlighting fiscal responsibility, the ability to take unpopular but necessary measures and so on. There are a few examples of credit claiming in retrenchment. The Italian 1995 pension reform, adopted by a non-partisan government supported by the centre-left is one such example. The sponsors of this law claimed that it was a necessary step to take given the budgetary conditions at the time, especially given Italy's aspiration to be part of the single European currency from the beginning.

The adopted cuts were quite substantial. The key modification was a shift from a defined-benefit system, where benefits are expressed as a proportion of earnings over a given number of years, to a defined-contribution system. Benefits now depend on the total amount of contributions paid by workers, which upon retirement is converted into an annuity whose value depends on the age of the person, on how the country's economy is performing and on the number of pensioners. The last two parameters are meant to allow the government to keep pension expenditure under control. The reform will result in lower benefits for the vast majority of retirees (Natali 2002; Ferrera and Jessoula 2005).

From the first stages of the preparatory work for the 1995 reform, it was clear that it was going to be essential for the government to obtain the support—or at least the acquiescence—of the labour movement. Berlusconi's previous failure to retrench pensions unilaterally, coupled with the weakness of the 'technical' government (which did not have its own majority in parliament, but was supported externally by a small number of centre-left parties), provided powerful incentives to seek consensus. The starting point for the negotiations was even a document drafted by trade union experts.

The 1995 reform was adopted with the support of the trade unions who, in return for their approval, obtained a fairly long phasing-in period for the new system, which affects people retiring from 2013 onwards. The key constituencies of the Italian trades union movement—current pensioners and older workers—were not affected by this reform. The unions also obtained equalization of treatment between the different occupational groups. (Under the previous legislation, some groups—civil servants, but also some self-employed—had been entitled to more generous treatment.) More specifically, contribution rates for public sector workers were increased to the same level as those paid by private sector employees (20 per cent of earnings). Those paid by the self-employed were also increased, though to the lower rate of 15 per cent of earnings. In addition, the reform increased the incentives for saving into a pension fund, first introduced in the previous reform.

In subsequent years, the 1995 reform was used as a credit-claiming device, most particularly in relation to the key role it may have played in allowing Italy to be among the first group of countries entering the Euro, something which the political leaders behind the 1995 reform (and other retrenchment efforts) celebrated in May 1998 (Ferrera and Gualmini 2000: 393).

The Swedish benefit cuts of the early 1990s provide another example. The centre-right government in power at the time obtained the support of the Social democrats for a series of measures that were unpopular in principle. Such an attitude is completely at odds with the expectations of the blame avoidance framework. In opposition, the Social democrats could easily have avoided the blame for the cuts. Instead, they chose to share it with their competitors (Dahlström 2006).

The cuts were substantial. In 1992, as part of two so-called 'crisis packages', the government adopted highly visible benefit cuts. The basic pension was reduced by 98 per cent of the standard amount (known as the base amount). Sickness and work accident insurance benefits were cut from 90 per cent to 80 per cent during the first year, and 70 per cent thereafter. In addition, waiting days were introduced in sickness insurance and various other benefits were cut (subsidies to housing, child allowances). The most visible cut, however, was the reduction of the replacement rate for unemployment insurance and parental leave, from 90 per cent to 80 per cent (Benner and Vad 2000; Dahlström 2006).

As in the Italian case, cuts were not hidden. Instead, government and opposition shared the responsibility for what were widely regarded as harsh but inevitable measures. It is noteworthy that during the same period (1990–1994) the bourgeois government also adopted other retrenchment measures, but outside the scope of the two crisis packages. These were not supported by the Social democrats ((Benner and Vad 2000; Dahlström 2006).

Major reforms have taken place

The corollary of the 'retrenchment through blame avoidance' view is that radical retrenchment is unlikely. Even though governments can rely on a range of strategies to diminish the political risks associated with retrenchment initiatives, these have limitations. In Pierson's account, the key strategies of obfuscation, division and compensation are presented as mixed blessings for government. If, on the one hand, they might reduce the risk of electoral punishment, on the other they pose a range of problems, such as 'restricted ranges of application', or the 'weakening of governmental control over policy' (Pierson 1994: 24–5). In sum, blame avoidance strategies may allow governments to push through unpopular reforms, but there is a limit to how big these reforms can be. This is the reason why the radical retrenchment and privatization plans of Thatcher and Reagan were not successful, and the welfare state is considered to be an area of relative stability (Pierson 1994: 4–5).

Some developments over the last two decades may be interpreted otherwise. Of course, part of the question refers to how we assess the significance of given policy reforms, or the size of retrenchment (Alber 1996; Clayton and Pontusson 1998; Green-Pedersen 2000). How big must retrenchment be to be substantial? This is a question that has probably not yet been answered in a satisfactory fashion, as most assessments of the significance of retrenchment tend to contain a large subjective component. Without entering into this complex debate, it is clear that the significance of welfare reform has increased over time. Reforms that looked unfeasible in the 1990s, such as highly visible increases in the age of retirement, are now being adopted in many countries.

The field of old age pensions provides a good example of the mechanism described above. Old age pensions can be expected to be one of the most resilient areas of the welfare state, given their universal character and the strong value attached by workers to the notion of retirement. Yet old age pensions have seen some of the most radical cuts over the last two decades. Countries like Germany, France and Italy have reduced the replacement rate of their old age insurance schemes from around 70 per cent of earnings in the early 1990s to somewhere between 40 and 50 per cent, to be effective in a few decades. The exact figures are not known, because the new pension formulas tend to include links to demographic and economic developments. However, the most likely projections confirm a clear reduction in benefit levels.

That retrenchment has been radical in this field is also shown by the projections made by the EU concerning the expected funding gap in pension scheme finances. For France, Germany, and Italy, pension spending as a proportion of GDP is now expected to increase only marginally until 2060 (two percentage point of GDP at the most). Reforms have contributed to this outcome. The EU estimates that changes in benefit rules adopted since the

1990s will, by 2060, produce savings equal to 2.2 per cent of GDP in Germany, 4.0 per cent in France, and 5.5 per cent of GDP in Italy (European Commission 2009: 91).

These outcomes are the result of several reforms adopted in more or less rapid succession since the early 1990s. They have tended to be characterized by long phasing-in periods (Palier, Chapter 11; Bonoli and Palier 2008). Delay, of course, was one of the strategies identified by Pierson (1994: 21–2). In this case, however, this blame avoidance strategy seems to have had a larger impact than what would be expected in the original credit claiming/blame avoidance framework. In Pierson's view, blame avoidance strategies have only limited potential. In fact, taken together, the various reforms have rather fundamentally transformed pension policy. A replacement rate of 40–50 per cent is insufficient to provide an acceptable living standard in retirement for most current middle class workers. They will need to make up the difference through other channels (company pensions, private savings, work).

Some expansion has taken place

Over the last two decades, together with some undeniable instances of retrenchment, we have also seen the expansion of some social polices, mostly in the fields of active labour market policies, publicly subsidized childcare and paid parental leave. As documented in many of the contributions included in this book, expansion has taken place in childcare services (Naumann, this volume), in active labour market policies (Clasen and Clegg, Chapter 7), in general in relation to policies targeting new social risks such as working poverty, job insecurity or family related risks (Häusermann, Chapter 6).

This expansion movement is also visible in expenditure data (Castles 2005). Spending on active labour market policies as a per cent of GDP increased from 0.66 to 0.73 between 1985 and 2005 among OECD countries (unweighted average of the traditional members). The increase is more substantial if one excludes Sweden, where ALMPs were introduced much earlier (0.58 to 0.70). Spending on family services has also increased constantly over the last few decades. Comparable data is available only since 1998,[1] but even within a short time span (1998–2005) one can see a substantial increase in spending on this function, from 0.43 to 0.60 per cent of GDP on average among OECD countries (OECD.Stat, available at www.oecd.org).

This is the third anomaly in the credit claiming/blame avoidance framework. From this perspective, given voters negativity bias, if, in spite of the context of permanent austerity, some spare cash is available to policymakers, they are more likely to invest it fruitfully by limiting retrenchment rather than by distributing it, since the losers are more likely than the winners to punish/ reward parties in government at the ballot box.

True, sometimes expansion was part of policy packages that contained substantial retrenchment measures (Häusermann 2010; and Chapter 6 this volume). This is a result that is perfectly compatible with the credit claiming/blame avoidance framework. The expansion measures can be seen as a strategy to minimize the negative consequences of retrenchment. However there are many instances of expansion measures unrelated to the retrenchment measures that where going on at the same time, in other parts of the welfare state.

Governments have used some of the spare cash they had to expand some new policies. According to the credit claiming/blame avoidance framework, and given voters' negativity bias, they would have made better use of these monies by using them to soften the retrenchment they were performing in other areas during the same years.

Revisiting the Credit Claiming/Blame Avoidance Framework

Seeking retrenchment and votes

The credit claiming/blame avoidance framework understands governments' actions as driven by both a policy-seeking and a vote-seeking logic. In this respect, the framework offers a balanced and possibly realistic view of how parties in government operate. Governments are assumed to be policy seekers, i.e. they want to retrench the welfare state; but they are at the same time seen as worrying about the electoral consequences of their actions. In this respect they also operate within a vote-seeking logic.

As pointed out in the literature on party objectives (Müller and Strøm 1999), policy- and vote-seeking goals may or may not be compatible. In the case of welfare retrenchment they clearly are not. The unpopularity of welfare retrenchment across social groups makes it unlikely that a government will be rewarded electorally for cutting benefits.

In the standard situation the policy objective of retrenchment is incompatible with vote seeking. However, in some particular circumstances we can expect the two objectives to be pursued simultaneously. This can be the case when the economic and budget situation of a country is considered to be disastrous by a large majority of actors and the public. The Swedish situation of the early 1990s may illustrate this point. Sweden went through an unprecedented crisis in the early 1990s, and even though in opposition, the Social democrats decided to support the bourgeois government in its austerity measures, which entailed quite visible cuts in benefits. The replacement rate of most benefits was simply cut from 90 per cent to 75 per cent. According to

Dahlström, who relies on interview data and published statements of the then Social democratic leader, it was the severity of the recession and budget situation that prompted the Social democrats to support the cuts.

> To understand why they [the Social democrats] made an agreement, one must recall the depth of the economic crisis and the hard currency policy. The Social Democratic leader Ingvar Carlsson says that 'it was an extraordinary situation. It trembled in a way that is not common in Sweden'. In his memoirs, Mr. Carlsson writes about their motives. He points to the three arguments important to the Social Democrats: they worried about how Sweden would look when the Social Democrats once again came into office if they did not solve the crisis in a 'reasonable' way; they were concerned about where they could seek support once in office, if they denied their own support now; and, they worried about the public reactions if the crisis was not solved as efficient as possible. (Dahlström 2006: 14)

Under particularly harsh economic conditions, retrenchment as a policy objective becomes compatible with vote seeking, and it is perfectly rational for an opposition party to share the image of a responsible party capable of making tough decisions when these are needed. The fact that the Social democrat did not support all the cuts adopted by the bourgeois government on 1990–1994, but only those that were part of the emergency 'crisis packages' suggests that it is really the perception of a major crisis situation that makes retrenchment politically attractive.

This is arguably also what happened in the Italian 1995 pension reform. The reform introduced a new benefit formula which, with a very long phasing-in period, would deliver dramatically lower benefits. The long phasing-in period meant, in clear blame avoidance logic, that those who were near retirement as well as those who were already retired were not affected by the changes. The success of the reform can thus be explained by the credit claiming/blame avoidance framework. What the framework fails to account for, however, is the fact that in subsequent years the supporters of the reform clearly used their ability to push it through as a credit claiming opportunity. The centre-left coalition (behind the reform) claimed to have succeeded in modernizing the pension system, making it sustainable, in spite of the political difficulties involved. The credit claiming exercise was reinforced with mentions of the link between the reform and participation in the single currency. Italian elites and the public cared about remaining a core country in the process of European integration, and being part of the single currency from the outset was a broadly shared priority (Ferrera and Gualmini 2000).

A severe economic crisis or a superior goal (being part of the single currency) may reduce the incompatibility of policy- and vote-seeking objectives for governments wishing to retrench social programmes. Under such circumstances parties in government can pursue the two goals simultaneously. This is not to say that a major crisis makes life easier for government. In a game-theoretical perspective, a situation of major crises probably reduces the payoffs associated with inaction rather then increasing those associated with retrenchment. In other words, I am not arguing that retrenchment becomes popular when the economy is in a severe crisis. Rather, my point is that in a severe crisis, inaction may become more unpopular than retrenchment.

Reform through the 'path of least resistance'

The blame avoidance perspective is about how to reconcile the policy- and vote-seeking logic when the policy sought entails retrenchment. As seen above, in a situation of major crisis, the incompatibility between these two objectives may be reduced. Governments may as a result be more determined in their retrenchment initiatives, but are still likely to face formidable obstacles. Retrenchment remains unpopular and the losers are likely to use the room for manoeuvre granted to them to try and prevent the adoption of austerity measures, both on a formal and an informal level.

Some of the losers may turn out to be veto players. Examples are well organized trade unions, such as in the French rail workers who have managed to force a government in 1995 to withdraw plans to cut their pensions (Bonoli 1997; Natali 2002; Palier 2002). Under such circumstances, rather than by 'blame avoidance', government actions are likely to be guided by the search for politically feasible options. Governments under pressure from the markets and supranational actors to contain social spending and to liberalize labour markets, are likely to look for the 'path of least resistance', or the politically safest way to obtain this type of result. In many cases this means to concentrate the consequences of retrenchment on groups of people that are less likely to become veto players: younger people in the field of pensions; younger people and marginal workers in the field of labour market deregulation.

According to this view, governments expect to be punished by voters more severely if they fail to reform than if they do reform. However, given the political obstacles retrenchment faces, it may be difficult to carry a reform all the way through. As a result, they will look for reforms that they are confident they will be able to push through. Pension reforms adopted with extremely long phasing in periods and labour market deregulation at the margin are examples of reforms adopted through a 'path of least resistance' approach. In both fields the 'path of least resistance' logic consists in concentrating the losses on groups that are less likely to mobilize effectively. In both fields it is mostly younger people, those who have in insecure labour market position, immigrants and so forth, in other words those who tend to be identified as outsiders. In this respect, the path of least resistance hypothesis is helpful in accounting for the emergence of a dualization trend in continental European (or Bismarckian) welfare states (Palier, Chapter 11).

The 'path of least resistance' hypothesis is helpful in accounting for many observed developments, but some of the transformations described above do not fit within this interpretation. Some governments have invested in child-care subsidies; they have turned social security systems into activation tools; they have improved benefits for working people; they are transforming the institutional structure of social security systems so as to make them more suited to the objective of promoting labour market participation. These changes cannot be interpreted as blame avoidance under pressure from markets and supra-/inter- national organizations.

Affordable credit claiming

The notion of credit claiming seems more helpful when it comes to developments such as the reorientation of welfare states toward employment promotion and social investment. Being able to avoid blame may be a difficult enough target in the current context of permanent austerity. However, re-election-seeking governments can be expected to be on the look out for credit claiming opportunities: actions that are broadly popular and can be expected to impact favourably on a government's re-election chances. In the past, during the postwar years, the expansion of social rights provided precisely a much appreciated opportunity for such credit claiming, and many have explained the expansion of social programmes during the '*trente glorieuses*' with reference to political competition in the context of well functioning mass democracies (Alber and Flora 1981; Wilensky 1981; Ferrera 1993).

In the current context of permanent austerity, such opportunities have become increasingly rare. For most governments, increases in the generosity of transfer programmes are off limits for budgetary reasons. In this context, the new ideas popularized by Third Way thinkers and international organizations may constitute opportunities for 'affordable credit claiming'. Most of these policy ideas: to help parents reconcile work and family life, help work-less people re-enter the labour market, or more generally the social investment perspective described by Jane Jenson in Chapter 2,[2] can be presented as win-win solutions to the social problems they are meant to address, and as a result generate broad support. Pro-welfare groups and parties may welcome a bigger effort in this field; employers and right-of-centre parties may like the positive impact on labour supply of these policies, and perhaps, their promise to be cost-effective, at least in the medium term, by reducing reliance on transfer programmes. Employment promoting social policies, as well as notions like activation and social investment, facilitate the sort of 'ambiguous agreement' that has proven instrumental in making difficult reforms possible (Palier

2005). Different actors support certain measures, but do so for very different reasons.

In addition, many of these policies have acquired a connotation of 'modern social policy' in current debates, and are as a result difficult to oppose for political parties. Take the example of the German CDU-CSU, a Christian democratic party that has historically favoured policies supporting the male-breadwinner model (van Kersbergen 1995; Seeleib-Kaiser et al. 2008), abstaining in the parliamentary vote on the Red-Green sponsored 2004 bill providing federal subsidies for childcare, for fear that a vote against could be exploited politically by the Social democrats (Zylka 2004).

In addition, the relatively low level of development of pro-employment and social investment social polices guarantees a high visibility even when only limited funds are assigned to new programmes. In practical terms, one additional euro spent on childcare is arguably going to be considerably more visible than the same amount spent to increase (or to avoid a reduction in) old age pensions. High profile reforms of labour market policy such as the New Deals introduced by the first New Labour government (1997–2001) in the UK have not resulted in an overall increase in spending on ALMPs (ALMP spending in the UK remained stable between 1997 and 2000 at 0.4 per cent of GDP (OECD *Statistic*). The 2004 German law on childcare, meant to create 200,000 new subsidized childcare places, was priced at €1.5 billion (Zylka 2004), or 0.006 per cent of annual pension expenditure. The new policies, probably because they are developed in a context of absence of provision, offer credit claiming opportunities that are more affordable than is the case in the field of the mature policies inherited from the postwar years.

Affordable credit claiming can be based on the traditional mechanism, whereby the state grants advantages to citizen-voters, who in turn respond with electoral support. This may be the case in the field of policies aiming at helping parents reconcile work and family life, particularly childcare and leave policies. Affordable credit claiming can also take a different shape, by targeting not so much the beneficiaries of a policy, but the middle classes. This is likely to be the case with activation, especially its most recommodification-based variants. Here credit can be expected not necessarily from those who are targeted by the measures but by those who are in employment, and see themselves as net contributors to the social security system. In their analysis of public support for activation in labour market policy, Kananen et al. (2006) show that between a third and half of German, British, and Swedish electorates think that '*The unemployed should be forced to take a job quickly, even if it is not as good as their previous one*'.[3] Support for 'enabling activation' is even stronger. Considering the pro-altruism bias one tends to find in these surveys (Epstein 2006), these figures suggest that there is some potential for credit claiming in activation.

While there is potential for credit claiming in the new policies, there are also some dangers. These new policies may run against deeply held normative perceptions among sections of the electorate, in relation to the proper roles of the state and the family with regard to the care of children or in relation to prevailing notions of appropriate social citizenship rights. In the end, the German Hartz IV reforms turned out to be a major blow in terms of support for the Red-Green coalition government, and probably one of the main causes of its fall in 2006. However, this seems to be the exception rather than the rule. Other governments and political leaders who have championed activation have taken credit for it and won subsequent elections. Here examples abound: the British Labour Party and Tony Blair in 2001 and in 2005; Denmark's Poul Nyrup Rasmussen, who presided over the 1994 activation oriented reform of unemployment policy and stayed on as prime Minister until 2001; or the Netherlands's Wim Kok who was instrumental in promoting the reorientation of the Dutch welfare state towards activation and stayed in power between 1994 and 2002.

The selective expansion of the welfare state through the development of a pro-employment orientation seems to occur more frequently when Social democrats are in power. Often a high visibility re-orientation exercise takes place soon after a return to power of a left-of-centre government (e.g. Denmark in 1994, the Netherlands 1996, the UK in 1997, Germany 1998). Activation and pro-employment policies are not necessarily left-wing polices. Two hypotheses can be made to account for this fact. First, Social democrats returning to power after a prolonged period in opposition are expected by their supporters to go for policies that are qualitatively different from those adopted by their right-of-centre predecessors. Traditional Social democratic pro-welfare policies are nonetheless off the menu, because of the overall context of permanent austerity. Under such circumstances, a high profile re-orientation exercise based on affordable credit claiming may offer an opportunity to Social democrats to distinguish themselves from their competitors without endangering public finances.

There is also a second factor that may help to explain why high profile reorientation exercises have been performed most often by Social democrats. Re-orienting social policies toward employment promotion is a highly ambiguous exercise from the point of view of the policy-takers. These exercises generally combine re-commodification with enabling measures, but where most of the emphasis will fall, can often only be seen during the implementation phase. For this reasons, it may be easier to exploit the credit claiming potential of these measures for the Social democrats, who are less likely to be suspected than their right-wing counterparts to hide retrenchment and recommodification under the activation discourse. This mechanism is akin the Nixon-goes-to-China explanation of why often, Social democrats have been more successful at retrenching welfare states than right-wing parties (Green-Pedersen 2000; Ross 2000).

The British trajectory in active labour market policy well illustrates these two hypotheses. It is difficult to appropriately time the activation turn in the UK, as many elements of the new orientation were put in place by the Conservative governments since the early 1990s. In fact, New Labour's flagship programme, know as the New Deals, resembled the Conservative 'Project work' (Clegg 2005): 192. With the Labour party's accession to power in 1997, however, active labour market policy became a high profile, highly publicized area of government policy. Already in the 1997 election manifesto, the Labour party emphasized the mix of duties and responsibilities that was to become a trademark of the Third Way: 'The best way to tackle poverty is to help people into jobs—real jobs. The unemployed have a responsibility to take up the opportunity of training places or work, but these must be real opportunities' (British Labour Party 1997: 15).

The Left seems both more interested and better able to exploit the mechanism of affordable credit claiming. The need to distinguish itself from their predecessors and the image of pro-welfare party have encouraged and allowed Social democrats to play a key role in the reorientation of social security towards employment promotion. Whether the types of policies they developed were qualitatively different from those pursued by they right-wing competitors is an open question. What is certain is that once the path to employment oriented policy was opened, subsequent right-of-centre government have clearly pursued policy along the same lines.

Conclusion

The twin notions of credit claiming and blame avoidance provide a very powerful framework for analysing welfare state reform, or more generally, policy change that is likely to impact in large sections of the electorate. On the basis of the observation of recent reform processes, however, these two notions need to be somewhat adapted. Three elements need to be taken into account.

First, the overall economic and budgetary context can impact on public perceptions of the adequacy of reform. The notion that we live in a context of permanent austerity is insufficiently precise to characterize this economic and budgetary context. At least, one should distinguish between 'normal permanent austerity' and 'major crisis situation'. In the former, the expectations of the credit claiming/blame avoidance framework tend to be confirmed. In the latter, inaction may become more unpopular, or politically dangerous, than retrenchment. Under such circumstances, retrenchment does not need to be performed by stealth, and can of course be more substantial. On occasions, it has also been used for credit claiming, emphasizing the image of a responsible government capable of taking tough decisions when needed. Of course, for this to happen, the majority of the public must be convinced that the economic and budgetary situation constitutes a 'major crisis situation'.

Second, the credit claiming/blame avoidance framework emphasizes the fact that governments try to minimize the risk of electoral punishment when adopting a potentially unpopular reform. This is a reasonable assumption, but downplays the question of the political feasibility of a reform. In veto-point dense political systems or in countries where the labour movement has a strong mobilizing capacity, governmental decisions are not automatically translated into law. On the contrary, opportunities to prevent the adoption of a new law abound. Under such circumstances, governments that are seeking retrenchment are likely to give much consideration to the question of political feasibility. They are likely to look for solutions that they believe will make it through parliament and won't generate too strong a public outcry. This idea is picked up by the notion of reform through 'the path of least resistance', or the targeting of saving measures on those groups who are least likely to mobilize effectively and prevent the adoption of a new law.

Third, over the last few years we have seen the expansion of some areas of the welfare state: active labour market policy and policies that help parents reconcile work and family life (mostly childcare). This development is clearly an anomaly for the credit claiming/blame avoidance framework, which would expect a re-election-seeking government to prefer to use any spare cash for softening retrenchment rather than for expanding other policies. In fact, the expansion of these new policies has been quite clearly driven by credit claiming. Credit claiming seems to remain an essential activity for governments, in spite of the limitations that budget constraints impose on this exercise. For this reason, credit claiming is performed in areas of the welfare state which allow high visibility reforms at a relatively low cost, what I have termed 'affordable credit claiming'.

Notes

1. The OECD does provide data for the period of 1980–1998, but prior to 1998 preschool programmes are only included in some countries, providing a biased picture of countries' efforts in this field.
2. Jane Jenson explains the development of the social investment perspective as a result of the involvement of Finance ministries in social policy, something that was rather unusual before the mid-1990s. Here, instead, I focus more on electoral politics. The two accounts can be seen as complementary, highlighting different

mechanisms that together have contributed to the reorientation of Western welfare states.

3. The authors used Eurobarometer data collected in 2001 (Eurobarometer 56.1)

Bibliography

Alber, J. (1996) Selectivity, Universalism, and the Politics of Welfare Retrenchment, Paper presented at the annual meeting of the American Political Science Association, San Francisco.

Alber, J. & Flora, P. (1981) Modernization, Democratization and the Development of Welfare States in Europe. In Flora, P. & Heidenheimer, A. J. (Eds.) *The Development of Welfare States in Europe and America*, New Brunswick, Transaction Books.

Benner, M. & Vad, T. (2000) Sweden and Denmark: Defending the Welfare State. In Scharpf, F. W. & Schmid, V. (Eds.) *Welfare and Work in the Open Economy*, Oxford, Oxford University Press.

Bonoli, G. (1997) Pension Politics in France: Patterns of Co-operation and Conflict in Two Recent Reforms. *West European Politics, 20,* 111–24.

Bonoli, G. & Palier, B. (2008) When Past Reforms Open New Opportunities: Comparing Old-age Insurance Reforms in Bismarckian Welfare Systems. *Social Policy and Administration, 41,* 21–39.

British Labour Party (1997) *New Labour because Britain Desrves Better,* London, Labour Party.

Castles, F. G. (2005) Social Expenditures in the 1990s: Data and Determinants. *Policy and Politics, 33,* 411–30.

Clayton, R. & Pontusson, J. (1998) Welfare-state Retrenchment Revisited: Entitlement Cuts, Public Sector Restructuring, and Inegalitarian Trends in Advanced Capitalist Societies. *World Politics, 51,* 67–98.

Clegg, D. (2005) Activating the Multi-tiered Welfare State: Social Governance, Welfare Politics and Unemployment Policies in France and the United Kingdom, Florence, PhD thesis, European University Institute.

Dahlström, C. (2006) Big Cuts, Little Time: Welfare State Retrenchment in Sweden, Center for European Studies Working Paper No.128, Cambridge, MA, Harvard University.

Epstein, W. M. (2006) Response Bias in Opinion Polls and American Social Welfare. *The Social Science Journal, 43,* 99–110.

European Commission (2009) *The 2009 Ageing Report: Economic and Budgetary Projections for the EU-27 Member States (2008–2060),* Brussels, European Commission (DG ECFIN) and the Economic Policy Committee (AWG).

Ferrera, M. (1993) *Modelli di solidarietà. Politica e riforme sociali nelle democrazie,* Bologna, Il Mulino.

Ferrera, M. & Gualmini, E. (2000) Italy: Rescue From Without? In Scharpf, F. W. & Schmidt, V. A. (Eds.) *Welfare and Work in the Open Economy,* Oxford, Oxford University Press.

Ferrera, M. & Jessoula, M. (2005) Reconfiguring Italian Pensions. From Policy Stalemate to Comprehensive Reforms. In Bonoli, G. & Shinkawa, T. (Eds.) *Ageing and Pension Reform Around the World*, Chelthenam, Edward Elgar.

Green-Pedersen, C. (2000) How Politics Still Matters. Retrenchment of Old-age Pensions, Unemployment Benefits, and Disability Pensions/Early Retirement Benefits in Denmark and in the Netherlands from 1982 to 1998. Department of Political Science Paper, Aarhus, University of Aarhus.

Häusermann, S. (2010) *The Politics of Welfare State Reform in Continental Europe*, Cambridge, Cambridge University Press.

Kananen, J., Taylor-Gooby, P. & Larsen, T. (2006) Public Attitudes and New Social Risk Reform. In Armingeon, K. & Bonoli, G. (Eds.) *The Politics of Postindustrial Welfare States*, London, Routledge.

Kuhn, T. (1962) *The Structure of Scientific Revolutions*, Chicago, University of Chicago Press.

Manow, P. & Plümper, T. (2005) The Relative Costs of Fiscal Policy Instruments. Fiscal Adjustment in the OECD, 1973–1995', Paper presented at the project meeting 'The Politics of Bismarckian Reforms', 9–11 December, CEVIPOF, Paris.

Müller, W. & Strøm, K. (Eds.) (1999) *Policy, Office or Votes? How Political Parties in Western Europe Make Hard Decisions*, Cambridge, Cambridge University Press.

Myles, J. & Pierson, P. (2001) The Comparative Political Economy of Pension Reform. In Pierson, P. (Ed.) *The New Politics of the Welfare State*, Oxford, Oxford University Press.

Natali, D. (2002) La ridefinizione del welfare state contemporaneo: la riforma delle pensioni in Francia e in Italia. Phd thesis, Department of Political and Social Sciences, Florence, European University Institute.

Palier, B. (2002) *Gouverner la sécurité sociale. Les réformes du système français de protection sociale depuis 1945*, Paris, Presses Universitaires de France.

Palier, B. (2005) Ambiguous Agreement, Cumulative Change: French Social Policy in the 1990s. In Streeck, W. & Thelen, K. (Eds.) *Beyond Continuity. Institutional Change in Advanced Political Economies*, Oxford, Oxford University Press.

Pierson, P. (1994) *Dismantling the Welfare State? Reagan, Thatcher, and the Politics of Retrenchment*, Cambridge, Cambridge University Press.

Pierson, P. (1996) The New Politics of the Welfare State. *World Politics*, 48, 143–79.

Pierson, P. (1998) Irresistible Forces, Immovable Objects: Post-industrial Welfare States Confront Permanent Austerity. *Journal of European Public Policy*, 5, 539–60.

Pierson, P. (Ed.) (2001) *The New Politics of the Welfare State*, Oxford, Oxford University Press.

Ross, F. (2000) 'Beyond Left and Right': The New Partisan Politics of Welfare. *Governance: An International Journal of Policy and Administration*, 13, 155–83.

Seeleib-Kaiser, M., Van Dyk, S. & Roggenkamp, M. (2008) *Party Politics and Social Welfare. Comparing Christian and Social Democracy in Austria, Germany and the Netherlands*, Chelthenam, Edward Elgar.

van Kersbergen, K. (1995) *Social Capitalism. A Study of Christian Democracy and the Welfare State*, London, Routledge.

Weaver, K. (1986a) *Automatic Government. The Politics of Indexation,* Washington, DC, Brookings.

Weaver, K. (1986b) The Politics of Blame Avoidance. *Journal of Public Policy,* 6, 371–98.

Wilensky, H. (1981) Leftism, Catholicism and Democratic Corporatism. The Role of Political Parties in the Recent Development of the Welfare State. In Flora, P. & Heidenheimer, A. J. (Eds.) *The Developemnt of Welfare States in Europe and America,* New Brunswick, Transaction Books.

Zylka, R. (2004) Unionsfraktion lehnt Kita-Gesetz nicht mehr ab. *Berliner Zeitung,* 28 October.

6

The Politics of Old and New Social Policies

Silja Häusermann

Introduction

After a decade in which research on the welfare state first focused on explaining institutional stability and then progressively started acknowledging a somewhat surprising amount of change and reform, there is today a certain consensus with regard to the observation that welfare states are not 'frozen landscapes' as some argued in the 1990s (see e.g. Esping-Andersen 1996: 2). Instead, welfare states have changed in diverse ways, both cutting back existing benefits as well as expanding and developing new ones. While the reform capacity was less of a surprise in the case of liberal and Nordic welfare states (given both their accent on tax-financed, egalitarian, and means-tested benefit on the one hand and the lower number of veto players on the other hand), it is particularly intriguing to see that even continental welfare states are changing profoundly:[1] a range of recent studies evidence systemic reforms in all major social policy areas (see Vail 2009; Häusermann 2010a; Palier 2010).

However, the literature has not come to a consensus yet, neither with regard to the forces that are driving this change, nor with its actual direction. With regard to the driving forces and mechanisms, institutionalist (e.g. Bonoli and Palier 2007; Palier and Martin 2007), quasi-functionalist (e.g. Hering 2004; Vis and van Kersbergen 2007) and actor-centred explanations (e.g. Levy 1999; Vail 2009; Häusermann 2010a) co-exist, and with regard to the direction, the literature has identified a range of very different reforms. Some studies emphasize retrenchment of the 'old' industrial welfare state, while others stress changes in the direction of 'new' policies, such as activation, social investment, work-care conciliation or needs-based social security for outsiders.

In this chapter, I will start by arguing that these reforms can be classified into 'new' vs. 'old' social policy instruments, depending on whether they deal with and operate within the frontiers of the inherited institutions of income and job protection, or whether they enact alternative approaches to welfare provision, namely activation or needs-based social benefits (section 1). Second, I will develop how these different types of policy instruments can be combined in a variety of ways that define specific directions of welfare reform: both old and new social policy instruments can be either cut back or expanded, which implies that welfare reforms can go into a range of different directions: on the one hand, they can be expansive in all directions (*expansion*) or restrictive in all directions (*retrenchment*). On the other hand, however, post-industrial welfare reforms may involve particular packages and 'mixtures' of policy instruments: they can, e.g. expand activation and social safety nets at the expense of income and job protection (*flexicurity*); they can also re-allocate spending from generous income protection towards more outsider-oriented needs-tested benefits (*welfare readjustment*). Alternatively, however, they can also preserve and shield old social rights and privileges against outsiders and new risk groups (*welfare protectionism*).

After sketching the policy space of current welfare reform in Europe, I will explore an actor-centred approach to the *politics* of new and old social policies by discussing the conflict lines and actor configurations typical of post-industrial welfare reform and by discussing the determinants of actor preferences (section 3). The original 'new politics literature' (see e.g. the contributions in Pierson 2001) assumed that actors, i.e. political parties, unions and employer organizations, will tend to matter less in post-industrial welfare reform than in the industrial era of welfare state growth, because institutional dynamics have become predominant. Theoretically, this argument is based on institutional feedback mechanisms, and empirically, it is closely tied to the fact that we observe different, 'unexpected' actor configurations for or against recent reforms, with e.g. left-wing parties supporting retrenchment or certain employer associations supporting expansion. Building on this literature, I would like to rephrase this point in a somewhat different way: actors, their preferences and ideas, may not matter less, but they may matter differently than in the industrial era, because different issues are at stake. How actors position themselves with regard to the new social policies increasingly depends on their interests and also the ideational values they defend. Given the fact that such new issues and new motivations become relevant, it is perfectly sensible that actor alignments and coalitions have changed accordingly. However, once we take the multidimensionality of the new welfare policy space and the realignment of actors into account, it becomes clear that post-industrial welfare reform relies on variable and highly contingent actor coalitions. Hence, there is not one single new actor or actor alliance that drives welfare reform. Rather, the reconfiguration of actors can orient policies in different directions and it may both enable or prevent reforms, depending on the overall structure of the policy space.

In the empirical part of this chapter (section 4), I will present three illustrative examples taken from family policy reform in Switzerland and Germany (as two veto-point dense continental welfare regimes). These case studies are not intended to provide a conclusive and systematic test of my arguments, but to illustrate, underline and substantiate three main points of this chapter: first, old and new social policy reform generate distinctive actor configurations; second, the combination of these different reform elements can both enable and prevent reform-success, which makes welfare reform increasingly difficult to predict; and third, political majorities for 'narrow' reforms that deal with old or new policies exclusively (i.e. without linking them to other issues in a package deal) rely on fragile and highly contingent actor coalitions.

New vs. Old Social Policy Instruments

The main point of this section is that we can and should distinguish between 'old' and 'new' social policies. Old social policies refer to those measures typical for addressing the needs of an industrial society, whereas new social policies target social risks and demands characteristic of the post-industrial era. However, it would be wrong to classify entire policy fields in the categories of old and new. Rather, we can identify old and new policy instruments *within* the main social policy fields. There is old and new family policy, old and new labour market policy, old and new pension policy, etc. Following the literature in this field and the overall framework of this volume (Pierson 2001; Bonoli 2005; Armingeon and Bonoli 2006; Häusermann 2006; Bonoli and Natali 2009), I define *old social policies* as those which deal with the welfare coverage of the typical risks of income and job loss that were prevalent in the industrial era. Income loss by the male breadwinner due to old age, unemployment, sickness or disability are key in this respect. Old social policies deal with these risks by means of income protection, i.e. passive transfers and job protection regulation. *New social policies*, by contrast, are those policies aimed at covering welfare risks that are typical of the post-industrial society (either because they are 'new', more widespread or newly politicized), such as atypical employment, long-term unemployment, working poverty, family instability and lacking opportunities for labour market participation (due to care obligations or obsolete skills). New social policies can be divided in two groups, depending on the policy strategy (ex ante vs. ex post) they pursue: a first group of new social policy measures focuses on employability and activation, rather than passive income replacement. The goal here is to bring recipients back into gainful employment (ex ante protection). A second group of typically new or post-industrial social policies focuses on the coverage of new risk groups (labour market outsiders, single parents, etc.), which were neglected by the old male breadwinner welfare state and which are unable to secure their own social protection via employment. The objective of this second type of policy measures is to provide needs-based social protection which is less dependent on labour market participation and previous income than the old, industrial social insurance schemes (ex post). These measures have become increasingly important, because post-industrial labour markets have become unable to provide stable employment trajectories, and because indirect protection for outsiders via marriage and family has also become unstable (what Esping-Andersen 1999 refers to as 'family and labour market failures').

In determining which issues should be considered and classified into the different groups of new and old social policy instruments, three strands of welfare literature are important, because they have turned the spotlight on distinct sets of policy reforms. We need to take into account works on retrenchment, new social risk policies and social investment/activation policies. The 'retrenchment-literature' (e.g. Clayton and Pontusson 1998; Pierson 2001; see Starke 2006 for a review of this literature) focuses on the conditions under which and the extent to which existing levels of welfare benefits are reduced. The basic idea is that the 'era of austerity' (Pierson 2001) generates an overwhelming (quasi-functionalist) need for cutbacks in all realms of social policy, because existing benefits and privileges have become unsustainable. In this context, governments are expected to aim at reducing benefit levels and tightening eligibility criteria in all major policy fields. Since it deals with the generosity of existing policy schemes, this literature focuses on the reforms of *old* social policies.

In parallel to the retrenchment literature, some studies (Bonoli 2005; Armingeon and Bonoli 2006) have focused on a quite different challenge to mature welfare states, namely the rise of new social risks, stemming from labour market and family failure (Esping-Andersen 1999). Bonoli (2005) focuses on labour market activation and family policy, but new social risk policies have appeared in other fields, such as pensions, too (Häusermann 2010a). They become relevant wherever the income- and employment-related insurance schemes of the industrial welfare state fail to ensure adequate social protection, because individuals have become unable to contribute sufficiently to insurance schemes.

Finally, the literature on social investment and activation (Lister 2004; Jenson and Saint-Martin 2006; Bonoli 2010; Morel et al. 2012) is empirically related to the concept of new social risks, but starts from a top-down instead of a bottom-up angle. Contrary to the new social risk literature, the question is not what new needs and demands have emerged in the post-industrial society. Rather, the social investment model conceptualizes a new approach of welfare

Table 6.1. 'Old' and 'new' social policy instruments

	'Old' social policies	'New' social policies	
	Income and job protection policies	Activation/Social Investment policies	Needs-based social protection policies
Family policy	Family and child allowances (transfers)	Child and elderly care services Parental leave schemes	Subsidized childcare services for low-income earners
Labour market/ unemployment policy	Passive benefits (income replacement) for insiders Employment protection	Active labour market policies Investment in training and human capital formation	Needs-based income support for the (long-term) unemployed
Pension policy	Income replacement for labour market insiders	Pension insurance coverage of labour market outsiders	Pension credits for child rearing Universal minimum pensions
Disability insurance	Income replacement (transfers)	Integration policies (re-commodification)	
Social assistance	Poverty relief (transfers)	Activation and re-integration programs	Income supplement to working poor (negative income tax etc.)

provision, inspired by the idea of welfare as investment in the employability of risk bearers (i.e. an ex ante prevention of poverty), rather than as compensation of welfare losses (i.e. an ex post coverage of risks and needs). Hence, social investment policies focus on access to education, training and work.

Table 6.1 provides a—non exhaustive—list of policy instruments, which can be categorized as corresponding to the different old and new logics of welfare reforms: income and job protection as typical of the industrial welfare state, activation and social investment policies, and needs-based social protection. As outlined above, large parts of the literature have analyzed these reform trends separately, and tried to identify the distinctive driving forces for each trend. As I try to argue in the next section, this is a mistake. All three groups of old and new social policies are raised and politicized in one and the same policy reform space. Hence, if we want to understand the politics of the post-industrial welfare state, we need to look at them simultaneously (Häusermann 2010a).

Mapping the Policy Space of Welfare State Reform in Europe

Governments can, of course, attempt to implement *either* old social policy reforms *or* new social policies separately. Part of the literature even argues that we can explain the adoption of rejection of both types of reform with the same variables (Armingeon and Bonoli 2006). These studies remain in a rather linear logic of welfare reform analysis, which tries to identify the factors driving welfare state change in specific directions. Both theoretically and empirically, however, things have become considerably more complex: in many instances, governments may combine old and new social policies in reform packages. The literature on political exchange and social pacts (e.g. Levy 1999; Rhodes 2001; Häusermann 2006, 2010b; Natali and Rhodes 2008) has argued that these package deals have become a pattern in post-industrial welfare reform, and as I have shown elsewhere, they have even become a necessary condition for successful retrenchment in continental pension politics (Häusermann 2010a). Hence, we need to look at the *combined* reforms, if we want to understand the dynamics of post-industrial welfare reform (see Vail 2009 for a similar argument).

The important point here is that both old and new social policies can be reformed in either expansive or restrictive ways, even though from very different starting points. Old social policies start at the 'mature' level, which implies that reforms of social insurance and job protection can either implement cutbacks or leave these benefits and privileges untouched. New social policies, by contrast, are typically underdeveloped, precisely because they are 'new'. Hence, both activation and needs-based social protection may be either expanded or kept at very low levels (if not cut back). Now governments can either propose and implement reforms, which go in a similar direction (expanding or restricting the overall level of benefits and rights), or they can propose packages of measures that go in opposite directions, meaning that they expand or restrict one type of measures at the expense or to the benefit of the other. Consequently, we need to take into account all four possibilities of reform. By combining the two dimensions of old and new social policies, we arrive at a schematic and aggregated representation of the 'new' policy space of welfare reform in Europe. The direction the reforms in a particular field or country take can be located anywhere in this space, and one can also imagine that reforms in different fields go in different directions. But identifying these four possibilities of welfare reform may be useful to identify patterns as well as cross-sectional and cross-national differences.

The two fields of expansion and retrenchment are obviously straightforward, but probably less likely and less analytically interesting. *Expansion* could historically be observed mostly in the era of welfare state growth in countries that expanded early in new social risk coverage (such as the Nordic countries, Bonoli 2007). In the 1960s and early 1970s, the overall direction of welfare reform was expansive in all respects. Today, the reforms taking place most plausibly in this quadrant would probably preserve existing levels of welfare, while at the same time expanding additional measures and benefits for new risk groups. *Retrenchment*, by contrast, can be identified when governments

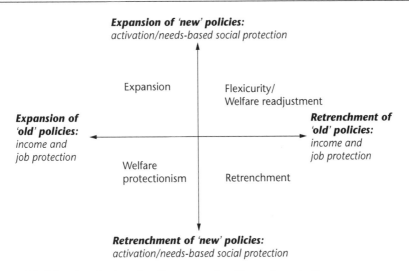

Figure 6.1. Mapping the 'new' policy space of welfare reform in Europe

cut back on existing rights without compensating the losers of the reforms and without reallocating the savings to new social needs and policies. Formerly privileged groups lose their benefits and new risk groups do not see their coverage improved. This is precisely the type of reform Pierson probably had in mind when he argued that retrenchment was very unlikely to be implemented in democratic polities, since it involved no credit-claiming at all and entails—at least among welfare beneficiaries—reform losers only. We can also relate Streeck's (2009) concept of 'liberalization' to this quadrant: job and income protection are being eroded for the core workforce, which eventually makes all workers rely on minimum poverty protection only, similar to the well-known pattern in liberal countries.

The two remaining quadrants—flexicurity/welfare readjustment and welfare protectionism—involve trade-offs: in the case of *flexicurity and welfare readjustment*, governments cut back on existing levels of old benefits, while at the same time expanding new social policies. Flexicurity denotes a strategy of liberalizing and deregulating job protection, while in turn providing more adequate support for job seekers (through activation) and the unemployed (through generous income support). Welfare readjustment, by contrast, is less tightly linked to job protection: it denotes the idea that old privileges of the core workforce in terms of income security are somewhat restrained to the benefit of new risk groups, which are unable to meet the tight eligibility criteria of the social insurance welfare state. Thereby, welfare readjustment comes very close to what Levy (1999) had in mind when he described some reforms in terms of turning 'vice into virtue': welfare reforms that cut back on generous benefit levels to reallocate spending to more acute and insufficiently covered social needs. Finally, *welfare protectionism* denotes reforms that shield the privileges of old beneficiaries against the claims, needs and demands of new risk groups. Eligibility is tightened in the main social insurance schemes at the expense of growing groups of outsiders who have no access to decent social protection.

Welfare readjustment and welfare protectionism can also be linked to the growing literature on increasingly *dualized* welfare states. The concept of dualized welfare (Bleses and Seeleib-Kaiser 2004; Palier and Thelen 2010; Emmenegger et al. 2012) means that post-industrial welfare states move in the direction of two distinct sorts of welfare benefits: the old schemes of earnings- and work-related social insurance are largely maintained for the core workforce, i.e. the insiders, while reforms introduce a different type of welfare state for the marginally, atypically and unemployed, i.e. the outsiders (based on tax-financed and needs-based benefits and new social risk policies more generally). Thereby, the distinction between welfare readjustment and welfare protectionism helps distinguishing the two ways in which the term 'dualization' is being used: some authors use it to denote that increasing numbers of outsiders are ejected from the 'real' and 'good' social protection into a secondary, residual and more fragile kind of welfare (see Clegg 2007; Palier and Thelen 2010). Others, however, use the word in a less negative way, meaning that welfare states re-balance the insider-focus of their social insurance schemes towards a second type of welfare provision that is more adequate and adapted to the needs and work biographies of outsiders (see to some extent Levy 1999; Bleses and Seeleib-Kaiser 2004; Häusermann 2010a). The introduction of needs-based social protection via pension minima or more generous social assistance levels (think, e.g., of the RSA in France) goes in this direction. While welfare protectionism refers to the first type of dualization, welfare readjustment is linked to the second type. The result is structurally similar: two types of welfare provision instead of the formerly coherent social insurance state. The distributional implications, however, are very different: In the case of welfare readjustment, outsiders gain increased protection while insiders lose some of their privileges. In the case of welfare protectionism, outsiders lose at the expense of an (ever shrinking) proportion of insiders.

The Location and Configurations of Actors in the Policy Space

If political parties, trade unions, and employer organizations aligned identically on income protection-, activation-, and needs-based social protection reforms, the distinction of these three groups of old and new policy instruments would not matter for the analysis of welfare *politics*, i.e. actors, interests and alliances. However, they do not. A whole range of studies have evidenced new and atypical reform coalitions when it comes to new social policies, with e.g. employers supporting activation and family policy expansion (Ballestri and Bonoli 2003; Bleses and Seeleib-Kaiser 2004; Daguerre 2006), left-wing parties cutting back existing benefit levels (Ross 2000; Kitschelt 2001) or increasing heterogeneity among trade unions with regard to pension reform (Häusermann 2010b). I argue here that these coalitions stop being unexpected or surprising once we take into account the *multidimensionality of post-industrial reform politics*. Political parties, trade unions and employer organizations align differently on the three dimensions illustrated in Table 6.1, depending on the interests and values they represent. Hence, if we want to understand why an actor advocates or opposes a particular reform, we need to look at the material interests and the values of this actor's constituency. Figure 6.2 presents schematic hypotheses on the idea-typical location of the main political forces with regard to the three dimensions of policy reform. The important message in Figure 6.2 is that the alignment of actors is very likely to be different across these dimensions. In the following, I briefly explain why.

With regard to income and job protection, the policies typical of the industrial era welfare state, we would expect employers and market-liberal political parties to advocate retrenchment, because they increase the cost of labour and account for the bulk of social spending in the mature welfare state. At the opposite end of the conflict line, we would expect the industrial 'working class'—i.e. blue-collar insider workers—to advocate expansion/maintenance of benefit levels, because the social insurance welfare state was built precisely for these workers. The old working class is the main constituency of the 'old', workerist left, which is why we might expect the major trade unions and old left parties to defend their material interests. In between employers and the old left, the new left—defending women's, outsiders and the new middle

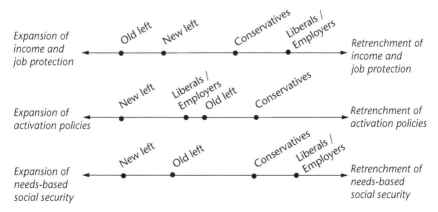

Figure 6.2. Hypotheses on ideal-typical actor positions with regard to 'old' and 'new' social policies

classes' interests (Kitschelt 1994)—should support old welfare policies, but less clearly so than the old left, since the new left's constituencies are not the main beneficiaries of the old welfare state. Finally, the conservatives—mainly Christian Democrats—should be more sceptical against state intervention in general, but they traditionally have a left-wing, interventionist part of their electorate which makes them more open for social insurance than employers and market-liberal parties (van Kersbergen 1995).

The new left's voters, including many outsiders—i.e. those members of the workforce particularly affected by atypical employment and unemployment (Häusermann and Schwander 2012), as well as new risk groups more generally (mostly young and female risk bearers, Bonoli 2005)—have lower stakes in these old social insurance schemes than insiders, because they do not have full contribution records anyway. By contrast, outsiders and new risk groups have a very strong interest in the development of new social policies (both activation and needs-based social security), in contrast to insiders. Hence, the new left is expected to be the strongest supporter of the new social policies. The difference between activation and needs-based social protection is to be found on the right, rather than on the left: employers may favour activation, because activation and social investment reforms are oriented towards a commodification of the workforce. They may even have more favourable stances on activation than the old left who traditionally was the main opponent of commodification. Conservative forces, by contrast, may see activation and social investment (including notably the commodification of women and early schooling for children) as a threat the traditional family and gender roles,[2] which may increase their scepticism against such policies. Things are different with needs-based social security measures for labour market outsiders. Again, we expect the new left to be the main advocate of these measures, because they benefit most directly to their electorate and members.[3] Market-liberal parties and employers, by contrast, may have less of an interest in these—clearly redistributive and de-commodifying—policies than in activation, which is why I would expect them to oppose such reforms most clearly. Given the profiles of their electorates, we would expect the old left and conservative parties between these two poles. The old left supports redistribution, but privileges social insurance and job protection, and the conservatives may tend to refrain from the more equalizing and non-stratifying character of these policies.

Figure 6.2 shows that the reform of the post-industrial welfare state can go in very different directions, which divide the relevant actors in distinct ways. This divergence of actor alignments holds a clear potential of varying coalitions ad alliances of actors driving such reforms. It also evidences why reform packages are so important. Indeed, governments can combine different reform elements, thereby facilitating political exchange and actor coalitions.

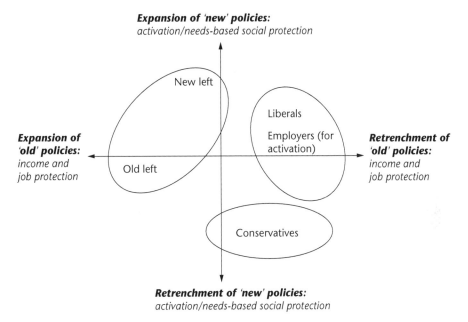

Figure 6.3. Ideal-typical actor positions in the multidimensional policy space of welfare reform in Europe

Liberals alone, e.g. may not have a sufficient majority to implement retrench-ment, their main priority, just as the new left alone cannot achieve activation and more needs-based social security, and the old left alone fails in 'saving' welfare protection. Each of them, however, can find allies if a reform package includes more than one type of measure, i.e. if it makes concessions and side-payments along other reform dimensions. I illustrate this logic in Figure 6.3, which shows a hypothetical policy space identical to the one shown in Figure 6.1. If governments combine new and old policy instruments, they may create potentials for actor coalitions.

The ellipses in Figure 6.3 represent the approximative location of the different political forces in the policy space. While the left is split and/or oscillating—depending on the country—between their support for old and new social policies, conservatives clearly oppose the 'new' policies, while they have a rather wide margin with regard to the old welfare state. Employers and mar-ket-liberal parties, by contrast, may side with the new left when it comes to activation policies, or with the conservatives when it comes to enacting retrenchment or preventing needs-based social protection. The precise condi-tions and dynamics of coalition-formation in different policy fields and countries are beyond the aim and scope of this chapter, and their analysis would require that we integrate institutional and strategic variables to this model (Häusermann 2010a). The point I would like to emphasize here is that the actor configurations in the new policy space of the European welfare state are characterized by complex multidimensionality, which makes the result of reform processes highly contingent. Looking at the power resources of e.g. the old left or of capital is insufficient to evaluate the chances of reforms in a particular direction. Alliances depend strongly on the issues that are on the table, on the dimensionality of the policy space and on the positions and power balances of all actors in a policy subsystem. The three case studies I will briefly present in the empirical part of this chapter demonstrate this contingency of the new politics of the welfare state.

Reforming Family Policy: The Contingency of Actor Configurations and Reform Success

This section presents three illustrative examples of reforms taken from family policy reform in Switzerland and Germany (as two veto-point dense continental welfare regimes). These short case studies illustrate, underline and substantiate three main points of this chapter: (1) welfare states can be reformed, because complex package deals of different reform dimensions allow for successful reform coalitions. (2) The complexity of coalition formation in multidimensional policy spaces, however, makes reform outcomes highly unstable and difficult to predict, since they can both assemble and divide reform supporters. And (3), political majorities for 'narrow' reforms that deal with a single dimension of reform exclusively (i.e. without linking it to other issues in a package deal) rely on fragile and highly contingent actor coalitions.

The choice of family policy for illustrating these reform dynamics results from the fact that other fields, such as labour market or pension policy have been widely researched over the past decade. Recent studies have emphasized the importance of package deals, trade-offs and issue-linkage in reforming unemployment policies towards more narrow insider protection and new forms of poverty relief for the (long-term) unemployed (see e.g. Vail 2009; Palier and Thelen 2010; Clegg 2012). Similarly, it has been shown that pension modernization in many European countries relied on complex dynamics of political exchange and compensation between advocates of pension cutbacks and new trends of expanding specific aspects and new 'pillars' of pension reform (see e.g. Bonoli 2000; Schludi 2005; Natali and Rhodes 2008; Vail 2009; Häusermann 2010a).

Family policy is considered to be a typical field of 'new' welfare policies, both with regard to new social risk-policies and with regard to social investment and activation. The saliency of family policy reform is particularly high in continental Europe, where all countries—except France—have been relying on the 'old' male breadwinner model of family policy (mainly based on child benefits, i.e. financial transfers) way into the 1990s. With increasing societal modernization and secularization on the one hand (weakening the Christian Democratic imprint of continental family policy), and structural pressure towards the commodification of women on the other hand (in particular the EU Lisbon agenda, as well as a need to boost employment ratios in continental Europe (Iversen and Wren 1998)), however, claims for a more interventionist, individualized and work-care related family policy have generally become stronger (e.g. Jenson and Sineau 2001; Morgan 2009). At the same time, new poverty risks and declining earnings power of families put (or keep) family policy as a means of poverty alleviation on the agenda. Hence, both old and new policy instruments are at stake.

The first example discussed here shows how the interplay of different reform dimensions enabled family policy modernization in Germany, through a reform of the federal law on educational benefits in 2000 by the red-green coalition government (see also Leitner et al. 2004). The reform included five main elements, two of which could be subsumed under the heading of 'old' measures of job and income protection (the expansion of educational benefits and the strengthening of parent's rights at the workplace) and three under the heading of a 'new' logic of activation. The first two elements can be considered expanding on 'old policies', because they increase transfers and strengthen workers rights to withdraw (partially) from the labour market. At the same time, however, the bill proposed to introduce incentives for parents to shorten their parental leave to six months instead of a full year, to encourage them to take up part-time work early during their parental leave and to combine work and care. For the purpose of this empirical analysis, I have coded actor positions on all reform issues, in order to locate actors in the policy space formed by these two types of measures. I will not go into the details of measurement and methods here, because the aim is only to sketch the policy space in relation to the theoretical expectations developed in the theoretical sections above (more details are given in the Appendix). Figure 6.4 shows the positioning of actors in the two-dimensional policy space.

Trade unions, family organizations, and the Green party strongly advocated the expansion of benefits and workers rights (horizontal dimension), while the employers' organizations and the all three other parties (SPD, FDP, CDU/ CSU) were more reluctant with regard to this orientation of reform.[4] On the vertical axis, things look, however, very different: trade unions, employer organizations, the market-liberal FDP, the Social Democrats SPD and the Greens all clearly advocated activation, against the more conservative posi- tions of the Christian Democrats CDU/CSU and family associations. Thus in this reform, the red-green government developed a 'welfare expansion' pack- age that contained elements, which could appeal to advocates of both the traditional model of family policy and a more activation-oriented model of

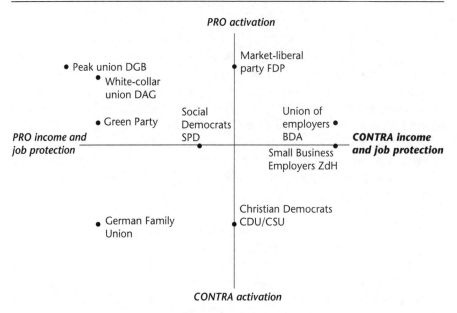

Figure 6.4. Actor configuration in the reform of the German law on educational benefits 2000

work-care conciliation. In that sense, this reform can be seen as a typical example of successful new politics of welfare reform.

When welfare reforms involve some sort of retrenchment, a compensation to part of the losers of the reform has turned out to be necessary to allow for policy change (Häusermann 2010a). When it comes to purely expansive reforms, however, they may also rely on a single reform dimension. This strategy, however, is very fragile and contingent, as the second example shows, taken from the Swiss 2003 reform of public subsidies for childcare infrastructure.

Family policy in Switzerland works quite differently from that of Germany. Indeed, the traditional male breadwinner family policy is not only very limited in scope, and it is also a 'victim' of federalist fragmentation (Bonoli and Häusermann 2011). The level of child benefits lies in the competence of cantons and the responsibility for work-care infrastructure is shared between the local, cantonal and federal levels. This implies that issue-linkage and package building are more constrained than in the German case: the national government has only very limited leverage over 'old' transfers in exchange for new policies. The case of the introduction of public subsidies for childcare facilities illustrates a reform under these constraints (see also Ballestri and Bonoli 2003 on this reform). The bill proposed that the federal government grants subsidies for newly founded childcare facilities, in order to improve the very poor coverage of childcare infrastructure in Switzerland. This is a typical

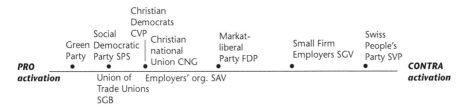

Figure 6.5. Actor configuration in the Swiss law on public subsidies for child care facilities

'new' policy reform, which appeals to political actors who represent (working) women and who advocate progressive values of gender equality, as well as to actors with an interest in activation and the commodification of women. Hence, the reform gave rise to an alignment of actors (Figure 6.5, for data, see again the Appendix), which included the parties of the new left, trade unions, as well as certain employer organizations and liberal parties among the supporters, against the conservative Swiss People's party and small business employers on the side of the opponents.

The bill was eventually accepted in parliament, but only with the tenuous support of the employers and the market-liberal party FDP. Yet, the uni-dimensionality of this policy makes this winning coalition fragile. While in Germany, the government has the capacity to bolster 'modernizing' new policy reforms with some side-payments to the more conservative actors, the Swiss government has a much harder time to do so. Hence, as soon as the support of the employers towards care infrastructure weakens (e.g. in the wake of a recession), the support coalition vanishes. The upshot of this is that the diversification of the welfare agenda has led to heterogeneous reform coalitions, which are fragile and variable, because they do not rely on long-standing, traditional alliances (Häusermann and Kübler 2011).

The third example illustrates a final aspect of the 'new' politics of welfare reform, i.e. the risk of multidimensionality actually dividing the underlying coalition of a policy. In the German 2000 reform of educational benefits, multidimensionality contributed to assembling a successful coalition. Assembling different dimensions in a reform process, however, not necessarily guarantees successful reform outcomes. Indeed, raising a series of reform dimensions can also split the potential advocates of policy change. The Swiss decision-making process on means-tested child allowances provides an example of this dynamic. Already in the early 1990s, left-wing parliamentarians started a law proposal aiming at the introduction of means-tested supplementary child allowances, in particular for single mothers or low-income families. Indeed, general child allowances are granted universally, irrespective of the income of families. This proposal was thus a response to growing

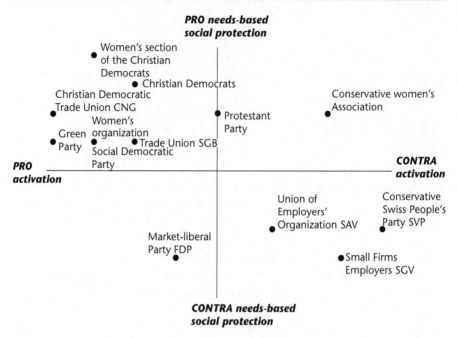

Figure 6.6. Actor configuration on the Swiss law proposal on means-tested child allowances

concerns about children being a source of poverty, especially for single mothers. The proposal, however, included also a second element, aimed at activation. In order to increase incentives for labour market participation even for low-income parents, the law would have provided tax cuts for low-income families combining work and external childcare. The parliamentarians behind the proposal were hoping to raise a broader support base for the reform with this combination of measures (Häusermann 2006). The decision-making process, however, was blocked repeatedly, because the market-liberal party FDP was too reluctant to support needs-based social protection as an activation tool.

As Figure 6.6 shows that the left-wing parties, trade unions, and Christian Democrats mostly supported the bill. The protestant party was inclined to support increased transfer to poor families, but was more reluctant towards work-care conciliation, as was the conservative women's association. On the other hand, the FDP supported activation, but not the increase in financial transfers. Eventually, the specific reservations of each camp prevented the formation of a sufficient coalition for support, which created a reform deadlock.

Conclusion

The main point I intend this chapter to make is that reforms of the 'new welfare state in Europe' can go in several distinct but interrelated directions. Not only can they be divided into three logics of welfare reform—an 'old' policy logic based on transfers, passive income replacement and de-commodification, and two 'new' logics based on activation/social invest-ment and needs-based social security—but moreover, these logics can be combined in various ways. Therefore, welfare reforms, and the development of the 'new welfare state' more generally may be classified with respect to at least four models or directions of change: *expansion*, i.e. the introduction of new social policies and the preservation or expansion of old ones, *retrench-ment*, i.e. cutbacks in old policies and a lacking development of new policies, *flexicurity* and *welfare readjustment*, i.e. the development of new policies instead of and at the expense of old policies of job and income support and, finally, *welfare protectionism*, i.e. the preservation of the old welfare rights for a shrinking proportion of insiders at the expense of largely unpro-tected and marginalized outsiders. The distinction of these three dimensions and four models may be useful for the analysis, measurement, and compari-son of actual policy change, but even more so, it is important to understand the *politics* of the new welfare state.

Indeed, the distinction of the three dimensions of post-industrial welfare reform matters, because actors align differently with regard to them. Old policies tend to oppose the representatives of labour market insiders (the 'old left' and trade unions) to employers and the right, while new policies are in the interest of outsiders and the new middle classes (and their repre-sentatives, i.e. the 'new left') as well as—when it comes to activation—employers and market-liberal actors. This is the reason why—in addition to the traditional distributional class conflict—insider/outsider divides and value divides become key for the understanding of the new welfare state politics. With three case studies of family policy reforms, I have tried to show empiri-cally that we cannot understand either the politics or the policies of the new welfare state unless we take into account the multidimensionality of the reform space and the ensuing contingency of reform coalitions.

A further implication of the multidimensionality of post-industrial reform politics is that outputs and outcomes—i.e. the actual substance of reforms—have become difficult to predict. Equilibria in a multidimensional space are per definition difficult to predict. A government, which actually favours a welfare expansion model, may join a coalition with either supporters of the welfare protectionist model or of the welfare readjustment model—the distri-butional outcome of which will obviously be very different. Hence, small coalitional realignments may have strong consequences for reform outputs. Therefore, the welfare state literature—15 years after the 'new politics'-turn— has two important tasks on its agenda: it must evaluate and measure the direction and extent of policy change in a comparable way, and it must theorize the dynamics that lead to one or the other outcome. Welfare reform outputs cannot be explained in simple linear models anymore. A leads to 'more' and B to 'less' welfare have become inadequate hypotheses, because 'more' and 'less' refer to multiple dimensions, and A and B must be combined. Hence, we need configurational theories of welfare development, which explain the patterns of alliances governments enter. These alliances depend on strategies, the institutional context and the 'political supply' (i.e. the country-specific actor configuration). All three factors can and should be theorized, in order to develop an understanding of the policies and politics of the new welfare state.

Appendix

Data and methods

In analysing actor configurations, I coded the position of each actor on every reform element on a scale ranging from 0 to 2. 1 means that the actor supports the governmental bill proposal, 0 means that the actor favours more generous and encompassing coverage, and 2 means that the actor favours less generous coverage. I coded the positions of each actor on four aspects of each reform element:

1) *intervention*: whether state intervention is required to resolve the problem or not;[5]
2) *scope*: who should be covered by the social policy measure;[6]
3) *level*: which level of benefits should be adopted;[7] and
4) *competence*: at what state level the intervention should take place.[8]

I used the average of the four positions in the subsequent empirical analyses, to locate actors in the policy space.

The coding relies on the following data sources: For Switzerland, the responses and official statements of political actors to the official pre-parliamentary consultation procedure ('Vernehmlassungsverfahren'), bill proposals and parliamentary debates, as well as press documents for the final positions. For Germany, the minutes of the meetings, and the official statements of actors in the public parliamentary hearings ('Anhörungen') and the positions of party groups in the parliamentary debates, as well as press documents and secondary literature.

Notes

1. The reform-capacity of continental Europe's social insurance-welfare states is surprising for a number of reasons: first, their institutional setup is supposed to prevent cutbacks because contribution-financing and earnings-related benefits create institutional feedbacks (Pierson 2001). Second, continental welfare states are insider-oriented male breadwinner systems, which tend to neglect new social risks (Armingeon and Bonoli 2006). And third, both retrenchment and new social risk pressures arise in a time of austerity supposed to sharpen conflict and increase polarization (Häusermann 2010a).

2. The value-dimension is important on the side of advocates of these policies, too: new social policies (both activation and needs-based support) are not only structured in a less stratifying and more egalitarian way, they also question the male breadwinner model by bringing more women into work and covering their social risks independently from the family. This is why progressives—the new left representing the new middle classes—agree to them.

3. The conceptualization and precise patterns of representation of electoral constituencies in relation to changing social structure is an empirical question that cannot be analysed thoroughly in the scope of this chapter (see to this end e.g. Kitschelt and Rehm 2005; Oesch 2006; Häusermann 2008; Kriesi et al. 2008; Häusermann 2010a). In addition, it is important to note that the actual parties and trade unions behind the labels of 'new and old left', 'conservatives' and 'liberals' vary between countries. Social Democratic parties, for instance, have kept a more old left profile in some countries, whereas they have shifted to the 'new left' in others (see e.g. Kriesi et al. 2008). These are empirical questions analysts of welfare reform have to take into account.

4. The position of the SPD is particularly intriguing here. Under the leadership of the Social Democratic family minister, the SPD was keen on reorienting family policy away from the male breadwinner model towards activation and work-care conciliation, which may explain its reluctant position on the old policy expansion.

5. 0 meaning that the actor favours more modest state intervention than the government bill proposes and 2 meaning that the actor wants a faster or more far-reaching reform.

6. 0 meaning that the circle of beneficiaries should be smaller than is proposed by the government and 2 meaning that the reform should benefit more people (and vice versa in case of retrenchment).

7. 0 meaning that the actor wants lower benefits than the government proposes and 2 meaning that the actor votes for higher benefits.

8. 0 meaning that the actor favours a more subsidiary approach than the government proposes (e.g. a reform at substate-, sector-, or firm-level) and 2 meaning that the actor favours a more homogenous and centralized policy.

Bibliography

Armingeon, K. & Bonoli, G. (2006) *The Politics of Post-Industrial Welfare States*, London, Routledge.

Ballestri, Y. & Bonoli, G. (2003) L'Etat social suisse face aux nouveaux risques sociaux: Genèse et déterminants de l'adoption du programme de subventions pour les crèches. *Swiss Political Science Review*, 9, 35–58.

Bleses, P. & Seeleib-Kaiser, M. (2004) *The Dual Transformation of the German Welfare State*, Basingstoke, Palgrave Macmillan.

Bonoli, G. (2000) *The Politics of Pension Reform. Institutions and Policy Change in Western Europe*, Cambridge, Cambridge University Press.

Bonoli, G. (2005) The Politics of the New Social Policies: Providing Coverage Against New Social Risks in Mature Welfare States. *Policy and Politics*, 33, 431–49.

Bonoli, G. (2006) New Social Risks and the Politics of Post-Industrial Social Policies. In Armingeon, K. & Bonoli, G. (Eds.) *The Politics of Post-Industrial Welfare States: Adapting Post-War Social Policies to New Social Risks*, London, Routledge.

Bonoli, G. (2007) Time Matters. Postindustrialisation, New Social Risks and Welfare State Adaptation in Advanced Industrial Democracies. *Comparative Political Studies*, 40, 495–520.

Bonoli, G. (2010) The Political Economy of Active Labour Market Policies. *Politics & Society*, 38, 435–57.

Bonoli, G. & Häusermann, S. (2011) The Swiss Welfare State: Between Expansion and Retrenchment in Hard Times. In Mach, A. & Trampusch, C. (Eds.) *Switzerland in Europe, Europe in Switzerland*, London, Routledge.

Bonoli, G. & Natali, D. (2009) The Politics of the New Welfare State, Background paper for the Conference 'The New Welfare State in Europe', Florence, 10–11th December.

Bonoli, G. & Palier, B. (2007) When Past Reforms Open New Opportunities: Comparing Old Age Insurance Reforms in Bismarckian Welfare Systems. *Social Policy and Administration*, 41, 555–73.

Clayton, R. & Pontusson, J. (1998) Welfare-State Retrenchment Revisited: Entitlement Cuts, Public Sector Restructuring and Inegalitarian Trends in Advanced Capitalist Societies. *World Politics*, 51, 67–98.

Clegg, D. (2007) Continental Drift: On Unemployment Policy Change in Bismarckian Welfare States. *Social Policy & Administration*, 41, 597–617.

Clegg, D. (2012) Solidarity or Dualization? Social Governance, Union Preferences, and Unemployment Benefit Adjustment in Belgium and France. In Emmenegger, P., Häusermann, S., Palier, B. & Seeleib-Kaiser, M. (Eds.) *The Age of Dualization. The Changing Face of Inequality In De-industrializing Societies*, New York, Oxford University Press.

Daguerre, A. (2006) Child Care Policies in Diverse European Welfare States: Switzerland, Sweden, France and Britain. In Armingeon, K. & Bonoli, G. (Eds.) *The Politics of Post-Industrial Welfare States. Adapting Post-war Social Policies to New Social Risks*, London, Routledge.

Emmenegger, P., Häusermann, S., Palier, B. & Seeleib-Kaiser, M. (2012) *The Age of Dualization. The Changing Face of Inequality In De-Industrializing Societies*, New York, Oxford University Press.

Esping-Andersen, G. (1996) After the Golden Age? Welfare State Dilemmas in a Global Economy. In Esping-Andersen, G. (Ed.) *Welfare States in Transition: National Adaptations in Global Economies*, London, Sage.

Esping-Andersen, G. (1999) *Social Foundations of Postindustrial Economies*, Oxford, Oxford University Press.

Häusermann, S. (2006) Changing Coalitions in Social Policy Reforms: The Politics of New Social Needs and Demands. *Journal of European Social Policy*, 16, 5–21.

Häusermann, S. (2008) What Explains the 'Unfreezing' of Continental European Welfare States? Paper presented at the annual conference of the American Political Science Association, Boston, MA, 28–31 August.

Häusermann, S. (2010a) *The Politics of Welfare State Reform in Continental Europe: Modernization in Hard Times*, Cambridge, Cambridge University Press.

Häusermann, S. (2010b) Solidarity with Whom? Why Organized Labour Is Losing Ground in Continental Pension Politics. *European Journal of Political Research*, 49, 233–56.

Häusermann, S. & Kübler, D. (2011) Policy Frames and Coalition Dynamics in the Recent Reforms of Swiss Family Policy. *German Policy Studies*, 6, 163–94.

Häusermann, S. & Schwander, H. (2012) Varieties of Dualisation? Labour Market Segmentation and Insider–Outsider Divides across Regimes. In Emmenegger, P., Häusermann S., Palier, B. & Seeleib-Kaiser, M. (Eds.) *The Age of Dualisation. The Changing Face of Inequality in Europe,* New York, Oxford University Press.

Hering, M. (2004) Turning Ideas into Policies: Implementing Modern Social Democratic Thinking in Germany's Pension Policy. In Bonoli, G. & Powell, M. (Eds.) *Social Democratic Party Policies in Contemporary Europe*, London, Routledge, 102–22.

Iversen, T. & Wren, A. (1998) Equality, Employment and Budgetary Restraint: The Trilemma of the Service Economy. *World Politics*, 50, 507–46.

Jenson, J. & Saint-Martin, D. (2006) Building Blocks for a New Social Architecture: The LEGO Paradigm of an Active Society. *Policy and Politics*, 34, 429–51.

Jenson, J. & Sineau, M. (2001) *Who Cares? Women's Work, Childcare, and Welfare State Redesign*, Toronto, University of Toronto Press.

Kitschelt, H. (1994) *The Transformation of European Social Democracy*, Cambridge, Cambridge University Press.

Kitschelt, H. (2001) When do Governments Implement Unpopular Reforms? In Pierson, P. (Ed.) *The New Politics of the Welfare State*, Oxford, Oxford University Press.

Kitschelt, H. & Rehm, P. (2005) Work, Family, and Politics. Foundations of Electoral Partisan Alignments in Postindustrial Democracies, Paper prepared for delivery at the 2005 Annual Meeting of the American Political Science Association, Washington, DC.

Kriesi, H., Grande, E., Lachat, R., Dolezal, M., Bornschier, S. & Frey, T. (2008) *West European Politics in the Age of Globalization*, Cambridge, Cambridge University Press.

Leitner, S., Ostner, I. & Schratzenstaller, M. (2004) *Wohlfahrtsstaat und Geschlechterverhältnis im Umbruch. Was kommt nach dem Ernährermodell?* Wiesbaden, VS Verlag für Sozialwissenschaften.

Levy, J. (1999) Vice into Virtue? Progressive Politics and Welfare Reform in Continental Europe. *Politics and Society*, 27, 239–73.

Lister, R. (2004) The Third Way's Social Investment State. In Lewis, J. & Surender, R. (Eds.) *Welfare State Change: Towards a Third Way?* Oxford, Oxford University Press, 157–82.

Morel, N., Palier, B. & Palme, J. (Eds.) (2012) *Towards a Social Investment Welfare State? Ideas, Policies and Challenges*, Bristol, Policy Press.

Morgan, K. (2009) Child Care and the Social Investment Model: Political Conditions for Reform. In Morel, N., Palier, B. & Palme, J. (Eds.) *What Future for Social Investment?* Stockholm, Institute for Futures Studies, Research Report.

Natali, D. & Rhodes, M. (2008) The 'New Politics' of Pension Reforms in Continental Europe. In Arza, C. & Kohli, M. (Eds.) *Pension Reform in Europe*. London, Routledge, 55–75.

Oesch, D. (2006) *Redrawing the Class Map: Stratification and Institutions in Germany, Britain, Sweden and Switzerland*, London, Palgrave Macmillan.

Palier, B. (Ed.) (2010) *A Long Goodbye to Bismarck? The Politics of Welfare Reforms in Continental Europe*, Amsterdam, Amsterdam University Press.

Palier, B. & Martin, C. (2007) From a 'Frozen Landscape' to Structural Reforms: The Sequential Transformation of Bismarckian Welfare Systems. *Social Policy and Administration*, 41, 535–54.

Palier, B. & Thelen, K. (2010) Institutionalizing Dualism: Complementarities and Change in France and Germany. *Politics & Society*, 38, 119–48.

Pierson, P. (2001) Coping with Permanent Austerity: Welfare State Restructuring in Affluent Democracies. In Pierson, P. (Ed.) *The New Politics of the Welfare State*. Oxford and New York, Oxford University Press.

Rhodes, M. (2001) The Political Economy of Social Pacts: 'Competitive Corporatism' and European Welfare Reform. In Pierson, P. (Ed.) *The New Politics of the Welfare State*, Oxford, Oxford University Press, 165–94.

Ross, F. (2000) 'Beyond Left and Right': The New Partisan Politics of Welfare. *Governance*, 13, 155–83.

Schludi, M. (2005) *The Reform of Bismarckian Pension Systems. A Comparison of Pension Politics in Austria, France, Germany, Italy and Sweden*, Amsterdam, Amsterdam University Press.

Starke, P. (2006) The Politics of Welfare State Retrenchment: A Literature Review. *Social Policy and Administration*, 40, 104–20.

Streeck, W. (2009) *Re-Forming Capitalism: Institutional Change in the German Political Economy*, Oxford, Oxford University Press.

Vail, M. (2009) *Recasting Welfare Capitalism. Economic Adjustment in Contemporary France and Germany*, Philadelphia, Temple University Press.

Van Kersbergen, K. (1995) *Social Capitalism. A Study of Christian Democracy and the Welfare State*, London Routledge.

Vis, B. & van Kersbergen, K. (2007) Why and How do Political Actors Pursue Risky Reforms? *Journal of Theoretical Politics*, 19, 153–72.

Part III
Trajectories of Change

7

Adapting Labour Market Policy to a Transformed Employment Structure

The Politics of 'Triple Integration'

Jochen Clasen and Daniel Clegg

Introduction

Labour market policy has been prominent in debates concerning the transformation of developed welfare states in recent decades. Though the financial stakes are less high than in the fields of pensions or health care, effective labour market policies are seen as key instruments for providing working-age individuals with security in increasingly flexible labour markets and ensuring that the welfare state counteracts, rather than reinforces, the dualistic tendencies inherent in the transition to largely service-based economies (Bonoli 2005).

Despite the large number of comparative analyses of reform trends in this policy area in recent years (e.g. Barbier and Ludwig-Mayerhoffer 2004; Rueda 2007; Serrano Pascual and Magnusson 2007; Eichhorst, Kaufmann and Kohnle-Seidl 2008; Beer and Schills 2009), the magnitude of changes currently underway in the field of labour market policy has yet to be fully grasped. While analysis has to date focused mainly on the development of 'activation' strategies in cash benefit systems, in this chapter we argue that recent developments in labour market policies in fact point to a more fundamental and structural transformation of core foundational principles and institutional arrangements of the industrial-era welfare state. Perhaps more in this policy field than others, we see new welfare state logics and structures being developed in response to the changed risk structures of post-industrial economies.

Understood in this way, contemporary labour market policy change can be seen to involve a multi-faceted process of institutional realignment, which we refer to as 'triple integration'. As we detail below, adapting labour market policy to the transformed employment structure means challenging inherited 'divisions of institutional labour' between labour market and social security policy, between income maintenance and poverty relief programmes, and between provisions for different risk-groups in the working age population. In the literature on the 'new politics' of the welfare state (Pierson 1996, 1998, 2001), such thoroughgoing structural change has typically been seen as rather unlikely, as a result of the risk-aversion of political actors, the dense interest group networks that have grown up around existing institutional structures and the multiple veto-points that many political systems provide for vested interests to block change. As we will show below, these constraints have indeed slowed processes of labour market policy adaptation in many national contexts (Clasen and Clegg 2006; Clegg 2007). But we also identify some powerful political and institutional dynamics that are driving change forward, meaning policy development in this field is less bounded by historical legacies than might conventionally be assumed.

The chapter is organised in five parts. Section 1 presents a stylised reconstruction of the logic and structures of labour market policy in the 'old' welfare state, emphasising the fit between institutional arrangements in labour market policy and the profile of risks and problems in industrial labour markets. Section 2 then describes how socio-economic change—and the initial responses of governments to it in the 1970s and 1980s—undermined the efficiency of inherited divisions of institutional labour and created pressures for thoroughgoing reform. Section 3 introduces our multi-dimensional framework for analysing institutional developments in response to these pressures, while Section 4 draws on a recent comparative study (Clasen and Clegg 2011) to illustrate changes across these dimensions in different European countries since the early-to-mid 1990s. Section 5 turns finally to the politics of triple integration, showing how institutional dynamics and political interests have often worked to promote change in this policy area rather than merely impede it.

The Organisation and Functions of Labour Market Policy in the Old Welfare State

Though most contemporary policy instruments were already long established, labour market policy was not a major sector of state activity in the 'golden age' of the welfare state. In the context of an expanding industrial labour market regulated through an active macro-economic policy, unemployment was generally kept low and individuals—specifically men, in general—were assumed to be capable of managing their own transitions between jobs, and between employment and temporary periods of non-employment.

The core institution of labour market policy in the old welfare state was unemployment benefit, and notably contributory unemployment insurance. While the precise eligibility and entitlement parameters varied cross-nationally (Alber 1981; Esping-Andersen 1990; Schmid and Reissert 1996), unemployment insurance schemes everywhere shared a basic institutional logic. Payment of contributions while in work ensured that individuals were protected against risks of cyclical and frictional unemployment through benefits that replaced a part of their previous salary for a set period, usually long enough to find alternative work in a context of structurally favourable labour demand. In many countries secondary systems of unemployment assistance or social assistance also developed, paying benefits to those whose contribution records were inadequate to meet the eligibility criteria for unemployment insurance and/or who failed to find work before their regular benefit entitlement expired. These secondary systems paid benefits at a lower level, usually on a means-tested basis, and were often institutionally distinct from unemployment insurance as a result of different financing and governance structures. But even in the larger welfare states of Western Europe, in 1968 unemployment protection represented an average of only 5.25 per cent of all social insurance expenditure in the 11 countries for which historical data is available (cf. Huber et al. 1997).

As well as the institutional boundaries between insurance and assistance being clearly drawn in most countries, unemployment protection as a whole was also sharply distinguished from income maintenance provisions for other working-age groups, such as the long-term sick or disabled and, when these schemes developed later, single-parents. In part this was simply a result of the historically staggered process by which protections for different 'risk groups' were established (Flora and Heidenheimer 1981), and the inherent dynamic of 'sectoralisation' that characterised the expansion and rationalisation of state activities in the second half of the 20th century (Jobert and Muller 1987). But it also followed from a set of understandings about the severity of moral hazard problems and disincentive effects in the provision of replacement incomes for different risk groups in the working age population. In unemployment protection, tight contribution conditions ensured that benefits were restricted to *bona fide* workers with normally stable labour market attachment, while entitlements were calibrated with a close eye to preserving incentives to return to the labour market as early as possible (Van Langendonck 1996). By contrast, the risks faced by disabled people or single parents claiming benefits were more obviously exogenous, and as these groups were not expected to return to paid employment in the short term, economic incentives were considered less important. Accordingly, eligibility conditions were typically less strict and entitlements more generous for other working-age risk groups than they were for the unemployed.

Notwithstanding the emphasis on the need for unemployed people to return to work as early as possible, in most countries so-called active labour market policies (ALMPs)—such as training and job subsidy programmes or labour market intermediation services—were not a major concern of policy in the old welfare state either. Certainly, labour market offices or labour exchanges existed to provide labour market intermediation services such as the registration and publication of job offers, sometimes also serving as payment or registration offices for unemployment benefits (King 1995; Thuy et al. 2001). In the 1960s there was indeed a widespread concern to bolster the role of what had by then evolved into Public Employment Services (PES) in combating bottlenecks in a tight labour market. But this usually involved the work of the PES being detached from the central institutions of the welfare state as conventionally understood, out of a concern to rid the PES of its close association with benefit receipt—what was known as the 'dole queue image' in the UK context (Price 2000)—and to avoid the routine tasks of benefit administration crowding out the development of more efficient and professional placement services that all firms and workers would want to use (Thuy et al. 2001; Freedland et al. 2007).

Generally this was the full extent of ALMP effort. An exception to this rule was the case of Sweden, where ALMP—and especially retraining policies—was a core feature of the famed Rehn-Meidner model for the regulation of the labour market, where they helped the reallocation of workers made redundant by less competitive firms being deliberately priced out of the market through a solidaristic wage policy (Rothstein 1996; Sjöberg 2011). While it has been suggested that both the scale and effectiveness of ALMP in Sweden's 'golden age' model has been somewhat exaggerated (cf. Toft 2003), by the end of the 1960s their international reputation ensured that other countries, too, had begun timidly experimenting with the development of more comprehensive manpower training policies to encourage economic modernisation (Bonoli 2011). But these generally functioned as complements to the core labour market policies of the industrial-era welfare state, rather than being institutionally amalgamated with them (Bonoli 2011).

Even though expenditure on labour market policies was modest and ALMP was under-developed, labour market policy nonetheless played an 'active' role in the old welfare state, even from a micro-economic perspective. Insurance-based unemployment benefits in particular served a number of 'productive functions' (Clasen 1999) in a labour market dominated by industrial employment, where the development and maintenance of stable employment relationships was considered crucial. From its inception, unemployment insurance had been for many of its main proponents a crucial instrument for the 'organisation of the labour market' (Beveridge 1909). By providing better risk protection to those who had previously been in long-term employment relationships, unemployment insurance encouraged people to enter into such employment relationships in the first place (Atkinson and Micklewright 1991; Schmid and Reissert 1996). Further, by giving people the breathing space and resources necessary to find employment corresponding to their skills and interests if made redundant, unemployment insurance also improved job matching on the labour market, and militated against inefficient turnover (Clasen 1999). Finally, according to Estevez-Abe et al. (2001) the existence of relatively generous unemployment insurance, often accompanied with quite extensive possibilities for unemployed workers to restrict their job search in accordance with skills and/or prior income, helped prevent workers having disincentives from making what would otherwise be rather risky investments in the highly specific skill sets that many industrial employers required.

Socio-economic Changes, Political Reactions and the Unravelling of Established Policy Logics

The economic functionality of conventional labour market policies was however closely tied to a labour market structure that was destined to soon disappear. Initially largely masked by the more immediately obvious impacts of the mid-decade demand shocks that saw unemployment increase markedly, the 1970s also saw the acceleration of some secular economic trends that would completely change the context of labour market policymaking (Häusermann and Palier 2008). Industrial employment, having peaked in most countries sometime in the 1960s, began to rapidly shrink as a share of all employment, as developed economies became increasingly service based. In tandem, female labour market participation began to increase everywhere, as the male-breadwinner model crumbled under the impact of economic and social change.

Though there is some controversy over the extent of the effect (Kenworthy 2008), it is generally accepted that due to the scope for productivity increases being considerably lower in service-based economies, flexibility rather than stability becomes the key to profitable private sector production and the re-establishment of a virtuous cycle of falling prices, buoyant consumer demand and output expansion (Iversen and Wren 1998; Esping-Andersen 1999). While in high-skill segments of the labour market this flexibility can be secured thanks to highly polyvalent workers, in low-skill segments it is largely numerical and wage flexibility that tends to dominate, leading to downward pressure on wages and/or terms of employment at the bottom end of the labour market (Davidsson and Naczyk 2009). An increase in fixed-term and involuntary part-time employment is another common result (Kalleberg 2009). Due to the degradation in the employment norm, however, the risk of a 'collision' between the benefit system and the low end of the labour market increases. The danger is that there will be limited demand for low-skilled workers on the terms they expect, and limited supply on the terms that will be offered. In this context the risk of unemployment is no longer only cyclical or frictional, but at the bottom end of the labour market also increasingly structural.

The initial reaction of policymakers to this transformed risk profile, in a period broadly between the late 1970s and the early 1990s, differed in certain respects cross-nationally, but also shared some key similarities. Despite intense pressures on public budgets, in many countries unemployment benefit provision for the core workforce was largely spared from cuts, and often actually improved (Blöndal and Pearsson 1995). In most countries, the sharp increase in unemployment was in this period seen as a temporary and cyclical 'crisis', and the expansion of unemployment benefits understood as a useful way of cushioning its social consequences (Palier 2010). In this respect, the UK was an outlier in the European context. There, the level and duration of unemployment insurance benefit was limited in the name of reducing public expenditure and tackling disincentive effects, and people who remained unemployed and could not fall back on private savings were increasingly forced to rely on means-tested social assistance (Clasen 2011). But even in countries that maintained generous benefits for good contributors recourse to unemployment or social assistance often grew too, as a result of the tendentially lengthening duration of unemployment for certain groups and/or the increasing number of people employed on short contracts that did not allow entitlement to insurance-benefits to be built up (Van Oorschot and Schell 1991; Eardley et al. 1996).

Everywhere in this period social benefit schemes for other working age people were also explicitly or implicitly used to move unemployed people out of the labour market altogether. Many countries expanded early retirement schemes and sometimes—as in the case of France—also reduced the legal age of retirement, as a way of drawing older workers out of the labour market altogether (Ebbinghaus 2006). But less explicitly permanent exit-routes from the labour market were also opened up with the expansion of disability or incapacity benefits and specific family policies such as leave schemes or measures for single parents, including in countries such as the UK. Part of the expansion of the caseloads of these non-employment benefits—which was seen across most OECD countries during the 1980s (Clasen and De Deken 2011)—was the result of social changes such as the growing number of single parents, but part was also the result of such schemes coming to function as parallel systems of support for groups on the periphery of the labour market (Blöndal and Pearsson 1995; Erlinghagen and Knuth 2009). For claimants, these schemes often offered better benefit rates than formal unemployment protection, while for governments they served the useful function of masking the real level of the politically sensitive unemployment rate. Testifying to this last preoccupation, governments in countries such as Belgium, France and the UK even expanded the possibilities for the 'inactive' receipt of unemployment benefits, whereby agreeing to withdraw from the unemployment register allowed individuals to receive benefits without having to discharge job-search responsibilities and sometimes in return for slightly higher benefit levels (Clasen 2011; Clegg 2011; De Deken 2011). A further decoupling of functions of benefit payment and unemployment registration also occurred in a number of countries during the 1980s, largely for similar reasons.

Masking open unemployment was also the motive behind a final development in labour market policy in the 1980s; growing cross-national interest in the development of ALMPs. Unlike the human capital-enhancing policies of the earlier period, though, the new wave of ALMPs were mainly oriented to directly providing (usually temporary) employment to individuals, particularly in the public and para-public sector. Massive 'occupation' schemes (cf. Bonoli 2011) of this kind were established in most continental European countries, as well as in the UK. Even the once much-vaunted Swedish ALMP was largely turned into a vast public works programme (Sjöberg forthcoming). Young people were the main 'beneficiaries' of these schemes, though large programmes often also existed for the long-term unemployed.

Thus, as a result of changes in the labour market as well as initial political reactions to the new environment, the logic that had characterised the consolidation of the institutions of labour market policy in the old welfare state had by the late 1980s largely unravelled. While systems of unemployment insurance for core workers were often largely unchanged, some of their 'productive functions' had been undermined by the sharp reduction in stable employment opportunities for lower-skilled workers. Alongside them had grown up large systems of secondary support for those facing the greatest barriers to labour market (re-)integration, organised around unemployment or social assistance. The rationale for the continued disconnection of the work of the PES from the provision of benefits had become one of political expediency rather than efficiency, as the PES now devoted most of its resources to the provision of large employment programmes to occupy the unemployed rather than to counteracting skill shortages in the economy (Bonoli 2011). Finally, benefit schemes that had been designed for groups that were not expected to be active in the labour market had come increasingly to serve as 'pressure valves' for the challenges of managing the risk of unemployment in a transformed economic context, and served to draw people into inactivity and what more and more came to be seen as 'dependency'.

Triple Integration: Towards Policies for a Transformed Labour Market

Against the backdrop of this stylised reconstruction of the post-war history of labour market policy in developed welfare states, we argue that it is possible to identify a distinctively new phase of labour market policy development that has been taking shape across developed countries from around the middle of 1990s. While the thrust of labour market policy development in this phase has certainly been to reverse some of the consequences of political reactions to labour market change in the 1980s—the closure of exit routes from the labour market being probably the best example—we suggest that this is far more than a return to the *status quo ante*. Where labour market policy in the old welfare state was designed essentially to provide an institutional undergirding to an economy organised around stable labour market attachments, the common quest is today for policies that can help to enforce flexible labour relations, and thereby encourage service sector expansion. This, however, entails a fundamental reworking of the division of institutional labour around which labour market policy in the industrial-era welfare state was organised. We see this process of institutional change, which we call 'triple integration', as having three principal dimensions (see Table 7.1).

The first of these can be called *unemployment benefit homogenisation*, or alternatively standardisation. This refers to the process whereby social rights, expressed in terms of benefit generosity and entitlement, tend to become less dependent on previous labour market achievements and positions than in the past. In the service economy, the stable labour market attachment that rigidly contributory (and thus transparently 'acquired') rights to unemployment insurance encourage is no longer seen as something to be explicitly promoted,

Table 7.1. Triple integration in contemporary labour market policy

Process of integration	Possible policy implications
Benefit homogenisation	fewer tiers of unemployment protection emergence of dominant tier of provision diminishing differences between tiers
Risk re-categorisation	diminishing differences in entitlement and conditionality between unemployment and other benefit schemes transferring claimants to unemployment benefit systems merging some benefit programmes creating single benefit for working-age people
Activation	merging employment services (active LMP) and unemployment benefit provision (passive LMP) tightening requirements to engage in supported job search providing labour market advice and support systems for unemployed and other working-age benefit groups ('one stop shops')

while flexibility should not be penalised. The labour market rationale for rewarding good contributors with better benefits, and punishing those with unstable labour market attachments, thus disappears. Furthermore, calibrating an unemployed individuals' reservation wage—and job-search regime—on their previous employment is increasingly seen to generate disincentives for occupational mobility, which is perceived as necessary and desirable in a flexible labour market.

In concrete policy terms, unemployment benefit homogenisation can involve making insurance benefits less status confirming by lowering their generosity, weakening the earnings-relatedness of benefit provision or even substituting earnings-related with flat-rate benefits. It might also involve paying benefits at a similar level and duration irrespective of an individual's contribution record. Consequently, we would thus expect the 'gap' between insurance-based (primary) and other (secondary) benefits for the unemployed to diminish, which may in some circumstances lead to pressures for the introduction of a single scheme for all the unemployed. It should be pointed out that this does not necessarily mean the abolition of insurance-type protection, but merely reductions in the 'earnings-relatedness' of unemployment insurance, whether in terms of the diminishing relevance of the earnings relation within an encompassing unemployment insurance scheme or the restriction of generous earnings related benefits to a decreasing minority of the unemployed.

The second dimension of integration that we identify can be referred to as *risk re-categorisation*, and involves processes at the frontiers between (provisions for) the risk of unemployment and other groups in the working-age population. At a minimum, this dimension entails reversing the process of the narrowing of unemployment as an administrative risk category that characterised the 'labour shedding' policies of the 1990s, a process that is often driven by cost considerations. But more than simply returning the 'hidden' unemployed to their 'rightful' category, trends here also involve challenging the very distinctions between the long-established risk categories around which social provisions for working-age people have long been organised. Because of the limited productivity increases referred to earlier, the growth potential of a service-economy depends largely on its capacity to mobilise as much of the potentially active population as possible, including groups—such as those with young children, with health problems and with milder forms of disability—whose integration in the labour market would not previously have been a priority, and whose social support would not have been 'work-focused'.

In policy terms, this trend can again be manifested in several ways. Benefit levels across different risk categories might be harmonised, and obligations—particularly regarding job-search—might be built into programmes for working-age groups other than the unemployed, thereby blurring the boundaries between benefit programmes as the basis for logics of state intervention. A more extreme version of risk re-categorisation could involve the wholesale abolition of certain benefit schemes and the transfer of their recipients to unemployment support. Most radical of all would be the establishment of a single benefit scheme for all people of working age, in which benefit rights would be similar but obligations and access to additional support services calibrated on the particular needs of individual claimants.

A rather different but analytically related aspect of risk re-categorisation involves the frontiers between the risk of unemployment and the once 'non-risk' of employment. As being in work was usually a guarantee of a living wage and an indicator of social integration in the industrial labour market, the primary focus of benefit policies and other state interventions was logically on those who were out of work. Today, with the steep increase in in-work poverty in many countries (Bonoli 2005; Lohmann and Marx 2008), these assumptions seem less justified. While specific measures may be put in place to support the incomes of the working-poor through the benefit system or the tax system, another policy option might be to extend entitlement to out-of-work benefits, as well as some of the labour market support services that accompany them, to those in precarious positions in the labour market. In this way, employment status can be expected to become a less important operational category in the targeting of labour market policies of different kinds.

Thirdly, a process of so-called benefit *activation* has been witnessed across many welfare states since the early 1990s, in recognition of the greater difficulties that low-skilled people now have in making transitions from unemployment to work, as well as the disincentives they may face to do so. This last dimension of institutional change in labour market policy is by now very well-known, and requires less full elaboration here. ALMPs have undergone a further transformation in recent years, away from the 'occupation' policies of the 1970s and early 1980s and towards 'employment promotion' policies, based on some combination of employment subsidies and individualised job search support (cf. Bonoli 2011). From our perspective, the important issue is the articulation or even integration of these policies with the provision of benefits, whether through regulations concerning obligations for recipients of benefits to engage in activation measures, or through the creation of single administrative units ('one-stop shops') in charge of both 'active' and 'passive' labour market support. In line with the arguments developed above, these units could in principle be expected to be responsible for benefits and services not only for the unemployed, but also for other working-age benefit groups.

It should be emphasised that the notion of 'triple integration' is an analytical construct. We would not expect all instances of integration to be present in all developed welfare states, or to manifest themselves at similar periods of time. After all, national labour market policies are conducted within different institutional settings with varied socio-economic pressures, and will interact differently with areas such as family policy or industrial relations, which themselves differ substantially across countries. Significant cross-national variation is, thus, what we would expect, and to a large extent what we can observe. Nonetheless, the considerable cross-country evidence that these different processes of institutional integration *are* underway—albeit taking different forms and unfolding at different rhythms—supports the argument that all developed welfare states now find themselves within a distinctive and novel phase of labour market policy development.

Triple Integration Dynamics in European Labour Market Policies

Trends towards *activation* in developed welfare states have been extensively documented, making it unnecessary to recapitulate this evidence comprehensively here (for a thorough recent review, see Eichhorst et al. 2008). Suffice to say that reforms across many countries have both tightened the requirements for the unemployed—and often other working-age benefit claimants (cf. infra)—to participate in activities and measures organised by the PES, and restructured the articulation between benefit administrations and the PES. Regarding the latter point, it is noteworthy that even plans for institutional integration that until recently appeared impossible due to interests vested in the existing division of institutional labour have made considerable progress. The French case, where the organisational merger of the PES and the unemployment insurance institution UNEDIC was long blocked by opposition from the social partners who co-manage the latter, but was successfully achieved with the creation of *Pôle Emploi* in 2008, is telling in this respect (Clegg 2011). Likewise in Germany, the desire to provide more integrated services to the unemployed has helped overcome tensions between the local authorities and the federal state that had originally led to a rather complex and differentiated structure of delivery being adopted in the wake of the Hartz IV reforms (Dingledey 2011). The Belgian case represents in this respect something of an outlier, as the fuller integration of unemployment benefits and labour market services remains complicated by both the division of competence within the federal state and the role of the unions in the administration of unemployment insurance (De Deken 2011).

In many European countries we also find evidence of considerable *unemployment benefit homegenisation*. The UK represents perhaps the starkest example (Clasen 2011). British unemployment support has maintained an insurance element, but since the beginning of the 1980s this has been seriously diminished both in value and in relevance. The gulf between Unemployment Insurance and social assistance (Income Support) for the unemployed was gradually eroded, as was acknowledged in the re-branding of each as 'contributory' and 'income-related' Job Seekers Allowance (JSA). In the UK unemployment support has become a basic means-tested security for all but a very small minority of claimants, and most of the latter will rely on additional benefits due to the low value of the insurance-based JSA.

At the other extreme we find countries that have maintained an encompassing unemployment insurance scheme, but which has—also in line with the framework presented above—become increasingly flat-rate over time. This is the case in Denmark, where the non-uprating of the (already relatively low) benefit ceiling has resulted in a compression of benefit levels, which also tend more and more towards the level of social assistance. Along with across-the-board restrictions in maximum benefit duration, this has been the main way that costs have been contained in Danish unemployment benefit (Goul Andersen 2011). Belgium, where the unemployment insurance system was already rather encompassing and had only weak elements of earnings-relation, shows a similar development, with benefits having become if anything more flat-rate over time (De Deken 2011; Clegg 2012). The Swedish case is rather more complicated. As in Denmark, the erosion of the benefit ceiling has made benefits less earnings-related, but the recipiency rate of the once-encompassing unemployment insurance system has also fallen sharply, forcing growing numbers of the unemployed onto social assistance. Though benefit levels in the two tiers of Swedish unemployment protection are tending to become more similar, there is however little impetus or appetite to date for coordination between the two, including with respect to the application and organisation of activation measures. Furthermore, the strong growth in collectively bargained unemployment insurance arrangements is recasting a differentiated benefit structure, outside the strictly public schemes (Sjöberg 2011).

The 'Bismarckian' welfare states of continental Europe, with their strong normative orientation towards insurance and complex coupling of unemployment benefits with industrial relations systems, long appeared to be resistant to trends towards benefit homogenisation. Indeed, reforms up to at least the early 2000s were instead suggestive of greater differentiation—or even 'dualisation' (cf. Palier and Thelen 2010)—of social rights for the unemployed, with the maintenance of generous earnings related benefits for a bulk of 'insiders' and the rejection of more marginal workers onto much less generous and administratively very distinct assistance systems (Clasen and Clegg 2006; Clegg 2007; Palier 2010).

More recently, however, this situation has changed. In Germany, the merging of unemployment assistance and social assistance in the Hartz IV reform replaced the traditional three tiers of benefit support with a two-tier system for short-term and long-term unemployed people respectively. Though the level of benefits remained unchanged, because of changes to entitlement rules unemployment insurance claimants are now faced with a shorter period of insurance cover. As a whole the character of unemployment support has changed in Germany since 2005, with about 80 per cent of all claimants in receipt of means-tested assistance (ALG, II) rather than unemployment insurance (Dingledey 2011). If anything the Hartz reforms have led to less rather than more segmentation, because erstwhile divisions between previous unemployment assistance and social assistance claimants have been abolished and the latter are no longer excluded from participating in employment schemes at federal level (Clasen and Goerne 2011). A somewhat similar evolution can be seen in the Netherlands. With the abolition of unemployment assistance (RWW) in 1995, the social assistance system (WWB) now caters to large numbers of the unemployed. Social assistance might even be considered as the centrepiece of contemporary Dutch unemployment protection, as its caseload has grown to be far larger than that of earnings-related unemployment insurance (WW), in part as a result of cuts in the latter (Hoogenboom 2011). In expenditure terms unemployment insurance however remains important in Dutch labour market policy, particularly at times of rising unemployment.

In France, parametric unemployment benefit reforms long focused on maintaining generous benefits for better contributors, forcing those with broken contribution records onto unemployment assistance or more often the social assistance scheme (RMI), which despite a rhetorical activation (or *insertion*) emphasis was poorly articulated with mainstream labour market policy. In recent years, however, the thrust of policy development has altered in France too. The 2009 unemployment insurance agreement innovated by considerably improving benefit entitlements for those with short contribution histories, while reducing them for better contributors (Clegg 2011). Though this has improved recipiency rates for those with broken work histories somewhat, many of this group remain reliant on social assistance, and the overall system of unemployment protection remains marked by a strong divide between insurance and assistance. However, the recent transformation of the RMI into an 'active solidarity income' (RSA) has strengthened the articulation between minimum income support and labour market policy, RSA recipients now normally being obliged to register with the PES, and having access to a similar set of reintegration services as unemployment benefit recipients (Clegg and Palier forthcoming). Though the logic of dualisation remains clearly present in French labour market policy, it is being increasingly challenged by one of integration (Clegg 2011).

It is perhaps the UK case that once again represents the starkest example of *risk re-categorisation*. A merger of employment support with benefit provision for all working age groups has been gradually underway since the late 1990s, with first the extension of 'New Deal' activation programmes from the unemployed to people with disabilities and lone parents, and more recently the creation of a new, work-focused Employment Support Allowance (ESA) to replace the pre-existing Incapacity Benefit (Clasen 2011). The current government's stated ambition is to move the large system of tax credits that was developed under the New Labour governments to tackle in-work poverty out of the tax administration and into the Department for Work and Pensions, and ultimately to create a single working-age benefit both for those in low-paying work and for those seeking to move into it. If implemented these plans would thus 'remove the distinction between in- and out-of-work benefits', and apply 'conditionality in a way that pushes individuals to increase their work to levels that are appropriate to their own particular circumstances' (DWP 2010: 29). Concretely, this could involve requiring not only jobseekers to look for full-time work, but also 'push' those who have found a (subsidised) job to 'extend their working hours and/or increase their earnings until they were working full time or until they were off benefits altogether' (DWP 2010: 29).

Though the very limited place that insurance provision retains in the British system of income support means that the above initiative can be presented more easily as a 'system reform', and sound all-the-more radical for it, in fact similar innovations have already been introduced in other countries in the social assistance regime. In France, for example, the RSA replaced part of the pre-existing tax credit arrangement (*prime pour l'emploi*) with an extension of social assistance to working people. The RSA can be received not only as a non-employment benefit (RSA-*socle*), but also as an earnings supplement (RSA-*activité*), and theoretically at least recipients of the latter are expected to retain regular contacts with the PES to receive help for their further professional development (Clegg 2011). In Germany, too, the operational importance for the benefit system of the boundary between unemployment and employment has become considerably more blurred, with unemployment assistance (ALG II) now functioning as a wage subsidy for nearly a quarter of its beneficiaries (Bundesagentur 2010).

France and Germany also represent interesting cases for risk re-categorisation between non-employed working-age benefit claimant groups. The RSA replaced not only the RMI but also a previously separate means-tested scheme for single parents (API), who—although their benefits remain more generous—now have a more similar set of job-search requirements and supports as other social assistance claimants (Clegg 2011). In Germany, the creation of ALG II resulted in many former social assistance claimants being reclassified as 'able to work', where once they were inactive (Dingledey 2011).

In the Netherlands, once infamous for its high rate of disability benefit claimants, the eligibility conditions for WAO and other disability insurance schemes were tightened and as a result many former claimants now rely on WWB, where they are subject to the same activation regime as unemployed workers. Indeed, although the only last-resort social assistance scheme in existence, the WWB now treats all claimants as potential workers (Hoogenboom 2011).

Elsewhere, risk re-categorisation has often been limited to the extension of activation from unemployed to non-employed groups. In Switzerland, for example, the activation drive has gradually spread out from an original focus on claimants of unemployment insurance benefits in the 1990s to those receiving social assistance and other non-employment benefits, such as invalidity insurance, more recently (Champion 2011). It might be anticipated that such a process will tend to significantly increase pressures for harmonisation of activation regimes and administrative arrangements for different groups, as has latterly happened with respect to once distinctly treated claimants of unemployment and social assistance in Denmark (Goul Andersen 2011). It may even lead to calls for more thoroughgoing risk reconfiguration or benefit homogenisation, and come to counteract the institutional inertia that results from the horizontal and vertical divisions of policy competence in the Swiss federal system.

In summary, there is ample evidence from across European countries of substantial institutional change in the field of labour market policy since the early-to-mid 1990s. Furthermore, this change is not random. Rather, as the triple integration framework helps to illustrate, changes in contemporary labour market policies seem to push in some common directions across European countries, albeit at varying speeds and with different emphases. The direction of travel seems to be clearly towards a labour market policy that will increasingly provide combined packages of benefits and labour market support services in a relatively similar manner not only to all unemployed people, but more generally to all people of working age in precarious labour market positions. In this common development we possibly see the influence of the European Union's attempts to encourage countries to reorient their social security towards increased labour market participation (Ferrera, chapter 12).

Starting points do matter, however. Historically, there was of course far greater institutional diversity across the labour market policy arrangements of different developed countries than our stylised reconstruction of labour market policy in the old welfare state acknowledged. In some countries, the absence of any real institutional legacy in the field of labour market policy as conventionally defined has meant that the question of institutional reform has been posed in rather different terms in the current period. For this reason, recent labour market policy developments in countries such as the Czech

Republic (Sirovatka and Hora 2011), Hungary (Scharle and Duman 2011), and Italy (Jessoula and Vesan 2011) are difficult to understand with reference to triple integration, even if certain common policy orientations—notably activation—are evident there too. Elsewhere, for historical and political as much as socio-economic reasons, labour market policies were not necessarily that 'industrial' in the old welfare state, and this has facilitated these states embracing certain aspects of a 'post-industrial' policy mix, as the cases of Belgium, Denmark, and the UK all show in different ways. But a number of country cases discussed above are ones in which labour market policies were traditionally both heavily oriented to the risks of the industrial labour market and strongly institutionalised, and nonetheless reforms are being adopted that are fundamentally overhauling existing arrangements to bring them in line with new goals and policy logics.

The Politics of Triple Integration

One of the key lessons of welfare state scholarship in the last two decades is that social policy arrangements are highly resistant to change. As discussed more fully elsewhere in this volume, the literature on the 'new politics' of the welfare state focused mainly on the many political and institutional obstacles to thoroughgoing reform. For all that the pressures of socio-economic change and austerity are 'irresistible', and political parties of all stripes are obliged to formulate reform agendas with reference to them, existing welfare state arrangements are held to remain relatively 'immovable' (Pierson 1998). As a result of the desire of political actors to avoid blame for potentially unpopular structural reforms, institutional change is generally expected to be incremental and path dependent, with wholesale changes to established institutions and policy logics rare.

Labour market policy developments in developed welfare states since the 1990s tell a rather different story. Certainly, the labour market policy changes discussed above have encountered political resistance. Labour market 'insiders' (cf. Rueda 2007) stand to lose perhaps most from the changes currently unfolding, as activation policies increase competition in the labour market and the flattening of benefit structures deprives them of the guarantee of preserved living standards in the case of unemployment. For some large employers, too, the desire to maintain benefit systems that allow them to externalise the cost of workforce restructuring and preserve peaceful firm-level labour relations may considerably outstrip demands for policies that encourage thoroughgoing labour market flexibility. Particularly where the representatives of labour market insiders and large employers—trade unions and employers confederations—have institutionalised decision-making roles in labour market policy, policies that challenge the logic of industrial-era labour market policies risk encountering significant obstacles. This is borne out by the experience of the French and German cases, at least up to the early 2000s, and helps explain why policy adjustment followed a dualising logic that preserved institutional arrangements for the core while reforming arrangements, if at all, only on the margins of the unemployment protection system (Palier, Chapter 11; Clasen and Clegg 2006; Clegg 2007; Palier and Thelen 2010).

In addition to representing the interests of their members and constituents, corporate social actors involved in the governance of social policy arrangements sometimes also have an organisational interest in combating reforms that challenge existing divisions of institutional labour. In a similar dynamic as can be seen with employment protection (Davidsson and Emmenegger, Chapter 10), trade unions that have historically had strong roles in the governance of unemployment insurance have sometimes articulated substantive preferences—the defence of earnings-related benefits, or opposition to reforms that foster closer articulation with the work of the PES—mainly out of a concern for the preservation of their 'institutional power resources'. This for a long time complicated thoroughgoing reforms in countries such as Denmark, France and the Netherlands, for example (Clegg 2012; Goul Andersen 2011; Hoogenboom 2011).

The way that divisions of institutional labour in labour market policy are also often embedded in divisions of policy competence between different levels of government has been another constraint on labour market policy change in many contexts. While unemployment insurance is usually a national programme, and typically funded out of social contributions, social assistance is almost always a local or municipal programme, often with devolved or decentralised tax financing. While the different levels in such multi-tiered policy systems have strong incentives to try and shift costs onto the other (Schmid et al. 1992), it is rare that any level of government is willing to relinquish policy competence altogether. 'Turf wars' between different levels of government have characterised the politics of labour market policy in most of the cases discussed above, with the UK—where all social and labour market policy is the responsibility of central government—the only real exception. These problems have however proved particularly intractable in certain national contexts, whether because of their interaction with a federal political system characterised by multiple veto-points as in Switzerland (Champion 2011), or because they have been caught up in highly sensitive processes of state re-composition, as in Belgium (De Deken 2011).

Interests, institutions and interests vested in institutions have all impeded labour market reform in recent decades, then. But as we have emphasised, the politics of triple integration is more a story of institutional change than one of resistance to such change. In large part, this is because the dynamics of political competition appear rather different in contemporary labour market policy than would be suggested by the new politics literature. Certainly, partisan differences appear to matter little in explaining trajectories of reform—path-breaking advances in labour market policy have been made under governments of the right, as in France, and of the centre-left, as in the UK and Germany, and sometimes under both, as in the Netherlands and Denmark. What is apparent, though, is that political actors across Europe today see labour market policy reform as an opportunity for credit claiming, rather than something economically virtuous but politically risky (Bonoli, Chapter 5). Despite its benefits being diffuse and its costs concentrated, activation is a politically rather marketable policy idea. So too is the promise to tackle obvious anomalies inherited from the initial phase of adaptation to new labour market risks, such as 'unnaturally' high rates of disability or incapacity benefit claimants. A discourse of 'sorting this mess out' has been very prominent in recent labour market policy reforms in many countries. Finally, to the extent that interaction between the growth in new forms of flexible labour market attachment and old labour market policy institutions creates fairly visible inequities in terms of access to social rights and to labour market support, reforms that improve the situation of less-protected groups at the expense of more-protected ones can be—and have been—packaged in a language of 'fairness', and not merely efficiency (cf. Levy 1999).

The agenda of comprehensive labour market reform has probably been helped by at least two further factors. Firstly, the individuals that stand to lose most—labour market insiders without skills that would be marketable in high-end service employment—are a declining share of the electorate, meaning that the electoral risks of challenging their interests are declining too. Certainly, these workers are strongly represented by unions, but when governments have clear electoral mandates for reform—when they have boldly trumpeted their desire to 'sort this mess out', and won a handsome election victory—it becomes considerably more complicated for unions to block reforms. Even unions' institutionalised roles in labour market policy governance may not preserve their influence on decision-making in this context, as it itself becomes something governments feel empowered to challenge in the name of driving reforms through. In the Netherlands, the unions were thus evicted from their labour market policymaking roles (Hoogenboom 2011), while in France the threat of this happening encouraged them to moderate their opposition to activation and some benefit homogenisation (Clegg 2011; Clegg and van Wijnbergen 2011).

The second factor that has facilitated fundamental reform is rather different; the inter-dependence and 'spillovers' between the different processes of institutional change in labour market policy. As a result of these, even initially limited and rather timid reforms have tended to generate new policy problems and anomalies requiring resolution. More specifically, the common drive to activation has often initiated processes of risk re-categorisation and benefit homogenisation, as activation in one programme leads to increasing caseloads in another, and then 'competition' between activation measures for claimants in parallel benefit programmes generates pressures for their harmonisation. Thus, the gradual extension in the UK of the New Deal programmes from the unemployed to other groups of working-age benefit claimants posed the question first of their articulated administration, then of the harmonisation of conditionality regimes, and ultimately of the creation of an integrated benefit system for all working-age benefit claimants (Clasen 2011). A process that started with activation of only disability and unemployment benefit claimants in the Netherlands eventually led to the shift from a three- to a two-tier unemployment benefit system, and a standardised activation regime for all people of working age (Hoogenboom 2011). In France, an activation element initially introduced in social assistance essentially for rhetorical purposes gradually 'worked up' to unemployment insurance, resulting eventually in the merger of the social partner-run unemployment insurance institutions and the state-run PES, and there too the development of a unified activation regime for all job-seekers (Clegg 2011).

As these examples show, there is no standardised sequence through which processes of triple integration advance across different countries. But the advance of fundamental reform in labour market policy does have a self-reinforcing dynamic over time, of the sort that has been identified in the literature on incremental but transformative institutional change (cf. Streeck and Thelen 2005). This, allied to the opportunities for credit claiming that this policy area affords, suggests that yet further convergence on this new institutional template for labour market policy is likely in the years ahead.

Bibliography

Alber, J. (1981) Government Responses to the Challenge of Unemployment: The Development of Unemployment Insurance in Western Europe. In Flora, P. & Heidenheimer, A. (Eds.) *The Development of Welfare States in Europe and America*, New Brunswick, Transaction.

Atkinson, A. & Micklewright, J. (1991) Unemployment Compensation and Labour Market Transitions: A Critical Review. *Journal of Economic Literature*, 29, 1679–724.

Barbier, J-C. & Ludwig-Mayerhoffer, W. (2004) The Many Worlds of Activation. *European Societies*, 6, 423–36.

Beer, P. de & Schills, T. (Eds.) (2009) *The Labour Market Triangle*, Cheltenham, Edward Elgar.

Beveridge, W. (1909) *Unemployment: A Problem of Industry*, London, Longmans.

Blöndal, S. & Pearsson, M. (1995) Unemployment and Other Non-employment Benefits. *Oxford Review of Economic Policy*, 2, 136–69.

Bonoli, G. (2005) The Politics of the New Social Policies: Providing Coverage Against New Social Risks in Nature Welfare States. *Policy & Politics*, 33, 431–49.

Bonoli, G. (2011) Active Labour Market Policy in a Changing Economic Context. In Clasen, J. & Clegg, D. (2011) *Regulating the Risk of Unemployment: National Adaptations to Post-Industrial Labour Markets in Europe*, Oxford, Oxford University Press.

Bundesagentur (2010) *Analytikreport der Statistik. Arbeitslosigkeit nach Rechtskreisen im Vergleich*, Nürnberg, Bundesagentur für Arbeit, Statistik.

Champion, C. (2011) Switzerland: A Latecomer Catching Up? In Clasen, J. & Clegg, D. (Eds.) *Regulating the Risk of Unemployment: National Adaptations to Post-Industrial Labour Markets in Europe*, Oxford, Oxford University Press.

Clasen, J. (1999) Beyond Social Security: The Economic Value of Giving Money to Unemployed People. *European Journal of Social Security*, 1, 151–80.

Clasen, J. (2011) The United Kingdom: Towards a Single Working-age Benefit System. In Clasen, J. & Clegg, D. (Eds.) *Regulating the Risk of Unemployment: National Adaptations to Post-Industrial Labour Markets in Europe*, Oxford, Oxford University Press.

Clasen, J. & Clegg, D. (2006) Beyond Activation: Reforming European Unemployment Protection Systems in Post-industrial Labour Markets. *European Societies*, 8, 527–53.

Clasen, J. & Clegg, D. (2011) *Regulating the Risk of Unemployment: National Adaptations to Post-Industrial Labour Markets in Europe*, Oxford, Oxford University Press.

Clasen, J. & De Deken, J. (2011) Tracking Caseloads: The Changing Composition of Working-age Benefit Receipt in Europe. In Clasen, J. & Clegg, D. (Eds.) *Regulating the Risk of Unemployment: National Adaptations to Post-Industrial Labour Markets in Europe*, Oxford, Oxford University Press.

Clasen, J. & Goerne, A. (2011) Exit Bismarck, Enter Dualism? Assessing Contemporary German Labour Market Policy. *Journal of Social Policy*, 40, 795–810.

Clegg, D. (2007) Continental Drift: On Unemployment Policy Change in Bismarckian Welfare States. *Social Policy & Administration*, 49, 597–617.

Clegg, D. (2011) France: Intetgration Versus Dualization. In Clasen, J. & Clegg, D. (Eds.) *Regulating the Risk of Unemployment: National Adaptations to Post-Industrial Labour Markets in Europe*, Oxford, Oxford University Press.

Clegg, D. (2012) Solidarity or Dualization? Social Governance, Union Preferences and Unemployment Benefit Adjustment in Belgium and France. In Emmenegger, P., Häusermann, S., Palier, B. & Seeleib-Kaiser, M. (Eds.) *The Age of Dualization*, New York, Oxford University Press.

Clegg, D. & Palier, B. (forthcoming) Implementing a Myth: The Growth of Work Conditionality in French Minimum Income Provision. In Lodemel, I. & Moreira, A. (Eds.) *Workfare Revisited*, Oxford, Oxford University Press.

Clegg, D. & van Wijnbergen, C. (2011) Welfare Institutions and the Mobilisation of Consent: Union Responses to Labour Market Activation Policies in France and the Netherlands. *European Journal of Industrial Relations*, 17, 333–48.

Davidsson, J. & Naczyk, M. (2009) The Ins and Outs of Dualization, RECWOWE Working Paper REC-WP 02/09.

De Deken, J. (2011) Belgium: A Precursor Muddling Through? In Clasen, J. & Clegg, D. (2011) *Regulating the Risk of Unemployment: National Adaptations to Post-Industrial Labour Markets in Europe*, Oxford, Oxford University Press.

Department for Work and Pensions (2010) *21st Century Welfare*, London, HMSO

Dingledey, I. (2011) Germany: Moving Towards Integration Whilst Maintaining Segmentation. In Clasen, J. & Clegg, D. (2011) *Regulating the Risk of Unemployment: National Adaptations to Post-Industrial Labour Markets in Europe*, Oxford, Oxford University Press.

Eardley, T., Bradshaw, J., Ditch, J., Gough, I. & Whiteford, P. (1996) Social Assistance in OECD Countries, Department of Social Security Research report no. 46, London, HMSO.

Ebbinghaus, B. (2006) *Reforming Early Retirement in Europe, Japan and the USA*, Oxford, Oxford University Press.

Eichhorst, W., Kaufmann, O. & Kohnle-Seidl, R. (2008) *Bringing the Jobless Back into Work?* Berlin. Springer.

Erlinghagen, M. & Knuth, M. (2009) Unemployment as an Institutional Construct? Structural Differences in Non-employment Between Selected European Countries and the United States. *Journal of Social Policy*, 39, 71–94.

Esping-Andersen, G. (1990) *The Three Worlds of Welfare Capitalism*, Cambridge, Polity Press.

Esping-Andersen, G. (1999) *The Social Foundations of Post-industrial Economies*, Oxford, Oxford University Press.

Estevez-Abe, M., Iversen, T. & Soskice, D. (2001) Social Protection and the Formation of Skills: A Reinterpretation of the Welfare State. In Hall, P. & Soskice, D. (Eds.) *Varieties of Capitalism: The Institutional Foundations of Comparative Advantage*, Oxford, Oxford University Press.

Flora, P. & Heidenheimer, A. (1981) *The Development of Welfare States in Europe and America*, New Brunswick, Transaction.

Freedland, M., Freedland, M., Vraig, P., Jacqueson, C. & Kountouris, N. (2007) *Public Employment Services and European Law*, Oxford, Oxford University Press.

Goul Andersen, J. (2011) Denmark: Ambiguous Modernization of an Inclusive Unemployment Protection System. In Clasen, J. & Clegg, D. (2011) *Regulating the Risk of Unemployment: National Adaptations to Post-Industrial Labour Markets in Europe*, Oxford, Oxford University Press.

Häusermann, S. & Palier, B. (2008) The Politics of Employment-friendly Welfare Reforms in Post-industrial Economies. *Socio-Economic Review*, 6, 559–86.

Hoogenboom, M. (2011) The Netherlands: Two Tiers for All. In Clasen, J. & Clegg, D. (2011) *Regulating the Risk of Unemployment: National Adaptations to Post-Industrial Labour Markets in Europe*, Oxford, Oxford University Press.

Huber, E., Ragin, C. & Stephens, J. (1997) Comparative Welfare States Data Set, available at: <http://www.lisproject.org/publications/welfaredata/welfareaccess.htm>.

Iversen, T. & Wren, A. (1998) Employment, Equality and Budgetary Restraint: The Trilemma of the Service Economy. *World Politics*, 50, 507–46.

Jessoula, M. & Vesan, P. (2011) Italy: Limited Adaptation of an Atypical System. In Clasen, J. & Clegg, D. (2011) *Regulating the Risk of Unemployment: National Adaptations to Post-Industrial Labour Markets in Europe*, Oxford, Oxford University Press.

Jobert, B. & Muller, P. (1987) *L'Etat en action*, Paris, Presses Universitaires de France

Kalleberg, A. (2009) Precarious Work, Insecure Workers: Employment Relations in Transition. *American Sociological Review*, 74, 1–22.

Kenworthy, L. (2008) *Jobs with Equality*, Oxford, Oxford University Press.

King, D. (1995) *Actively Seeking Work?* Chicago, Chicago University Press.

Levy, J. (1999) Vice into Virtue? Progressive Politics and Welfare Reform in Continental Europe. *Politics & Society*, 27, 239–73.

Lohmann, H. & Marx, I. (2008) The Different Faces of In-work Poverty Across Welfare State Regimes. In Andreß, H.J. et al. (Eds.) *The Working Poor in Europe*, Cheltenham, Edward Elgar.

Palier, B. (2010) The Long Conservative-corporatist Road to Welfare Reforms. In Palier, B. (Ed.) *A Long Goodbye to Bismarck?* Amsterdam, Amsterdam University Press

Palier, B. & Thelen, K. (2010) Institutionalizing Dualism: Complementarities and Change in France and Germany. *Politics & Society*, 38, 119–48.

Pierson, P. (1996) The New Politics of the Welfare State. *World Politics*, 48, 143–79.

Pierson, P. (1998) Irresistible Forces, Immovable Objects: Post-industrial Welfare States Confront Permanent Austerity. *Journal of European Public Policy*, 5, 539–60.

Pierson, P. (2001) *The New Politics of the Welfare State*, Oxford, Oxford University Press.

Price, D. (2000) *Office of Hope: A History of the Employment Service*, London, Policy Studies Institute.

Rothstein, B. (1996) *The Social Democratic State: The Swedish Model and the Bureaucratic Problem of Social Reform*, Pittsburgh, University of Pittsburgh Press.

Rueda, D. (2007) *Social Democracy Inside-Out*, Cambridge, Cambridge University Press.

Scharle, A. & Duman, A. (2011) Hungary: Fiscal Pressures and a Rising Resentment Against the (Idle) Poor. In Clasen, J. & Clegg, D. (2011) *Regulating the Risk of Unemployment: National Adaptations to Post-Industrial Labour Markets in Europe*, Oxford, Oxford University Press.

Schmid, G. & Reissert, B. (1996) Unemployment Compensation and Labour Market Transitions. In Schmid, G. (Ed.) *International Handbook of Labour Market Policy*, Cheltenham, Edward Elgar.

Schmid, G., Reissert, B. & Bruche, G. (1992) *Unemployment Insurance and Active Labor Market Policy: An International Comparison of Financing Systems*, Detroit, Wayne State University Press.

Serrano Pascual, A. & Magnusson, L. (2007) *Reshaping Welfare States and Activation Regimes in Europe*, Brussels, PIE Peter Lang.

Sirovatka. T. & Hora, O. (2011) The Czech Republic: Activation, Diversification, and Marginalization. In Clasen, J. & Clegg, D. (2011) *Regulating the Risk of Unemployment: National Adaptations to Post-Industrial Labour Markets in Europe*, Oxford, Oxford University Press.

Sjöberg, O. (2011) Sweden: Ambivalent Adjustment. In Clasen, J. & Clegg, D. (2011) *Regulating the Risk of Unemployment: National Adaptations to Post-Industrial Labour Markets in Europe*, Oxford, Oxford University Press, 208–31.

Sjöberg, O. (forthcoming) A Flexicurity Model Goes South? The Politics of Flexicurity in Sweden. In Clegg, D., Jessoula, M. & Graziano, P. (Eds.) *The Politics of Flexicurity in Europe.*

Streeck, W. & Thelen, K. (2005) *Beyond Continuity: Institutional Change in Advanced Political Economies*, Oxford, Oxford University Press.

Thuy, P., Hansen, E. & Price, D. (2001) *The Public Employment Service in a Changing Labour Market*, Geneva, ILO.

Toft, C. (2003) Evidence-based Social Science and the Rehnist Interpretation of the Development of Active Labor Market Policy in Sweden During the Golden Age: A Critical Examination. *Politics & Society*, 31, 567–608.

Van Langendonck, J. (1996) The Social Protection of the Unemployed. *International Journal of Social Security*, 50, 29–41.

Van Oorschott, W. & Schell, J. (1991) Means Testing in Europe: A Growing Concern. In Adler, M. et al. (Eds.) *The Sociology of Social Security*, Edinburgh, Edinburgh University Press.

8

Childcare Politics in the 'New' Welfare State

Class, Religion, and Gender in the Shaping of Political Agendas

Ingela Naumann

Introduction

Childcare policy plays a prominent role in current discussions on the welfare state. Yet the provision of childcare services, by public or private agencies, is hardly something new. In virtually all European countries, fairly developed forms of formal childcare appeared during the second half of the 19th century. These interventions tended to have a pedagogical objective, providing early education and socialization, or were aimed at poor working class families where both parents needed to work. By the early 20th century countries as diverse as Sweden, Germany, the Netherlands, and Italy had developed some rudimentary forms of early childhood education and care systems. Some countries, such as France or Belgium, went even further by institutionalizing extensive pre-school systems.

Childcare policy is thus not a new policy per se. What has changed over the last few decades in the majority of Western European countries, however, is the salience of the policy within the welfare state, and the adoption of a pro-employment 'social investment' orientation. During the industrial period of the welfare state development, childcare provision, particularly for children under the age of three, was limited in most countries. Today, the most advanced welfare states aim at providing universal early childhood education and care, and also those countries with lower coverage are expanding their childcare services rapidly. Childcare has evolved from a marginal social policy field into a key pillar of modern welfare states. Second, the type of childcare policy that we have seen develop over the last decade in continental and in

English speaking Europe, and somewhat earlier in the Nordic countries, has a distinct orientation which can be summed up by the notion of 'social investment'. The investment dimension of childcare policy is at least twofold. First, it aims at bringing mothers into paid employment and is, in this respect, consistent with the ongoing re-orientation of Western welfare states towards the promotion of employment. Second, investment is supposed to take place in the development of young children. As Jenson (Chapter 2) notes, a focus on children is one of the defining features of the social investment perspective.

The expansion of childcare policy is further discussed in other contributions to this volume. Bonoli (Chapter 5) argues that this development can be explained by simple credit claiming mechanisms, as they play out in the current context of permanent austerity. Häusermann (Chapter 6) looks at the role played by shifting coalitions and identifies the actors' configurations that are most likely to be conducive to an expansion of an employment supporting family policy. In this chapter, I take a rather different perspective, and focus on developments that take place upstream of the political arena. My objective is to uncover the factors that bring childcare policy onto mainstream political agendas. In other words, what made childcare shift from being a marginal and largely neglected area of policy to a prominent component of modern welfare states?

Analytically, the chapter makes three claims: first, it argues for a multidimensional conceptualization of policies relating to family life and childcare. It will show how political conflict over childcare as policy issue has been shaped by the intersecting cleavages of religion, class and gender. As such, childcare politics have always comprised distributive conflict as well as contention over what norms and values should guide policymaking in this field. Welfare reform politics are complex and to some extent unpredictable, as political actors respond with a mixture of normative conviction, power play, and creative problem-solving to a range of interlaced internal and external pressures and constraints cleavages. Consequently, social and political do not determine social policy, but they delineate the field of politically viable policy solutions. Second, shifts in the national cleavage structures linked to socio-economic changes and contingent events created opportunities for new demands and ideas around childcare to enter political space. In particular, the weakening of religious influence and intensified and crosscutting conflict around gender led to new political alliances and party competition around working women's interests and demands. Thirdly, childcare policy has benefitted from the broader reorientation of Western welfare states towards the promotion of employment. The 'new' childcare policy has a distinct economic framing: only when perceived as economic policy that fit within the dominant economic paradigm did broad political alliances form that promoted the expansion of employment-oriented childcare service provision.

The chapter develops these arguments by presenting two different cases of childcare policy development in Sweden and in Germany. Sweden is an 'early mover' with respect to the transition from industrial, male-breadwinner-based family policy to postindustrial and employment-oriented family and childcare measures. Today, Sweden is among the countries with the most extensive childcare system: in 2008, 49 per cent of 1-year-olds and over 90 per cent of 2- to 5-year-olds attended extra-familial childcare, mostly in collective daycare centres (SCB 2009).[1] Formal childcare provision is flanked by generous parental leave policy and other social measures to support parents' gainful employment and children's upbringing. Germany is known for its conservative family policy, based on strong male breadwinner norms: generous monetary transfers such as child benefits and tax splitting support the male breadwinner/female housewife family, but services supporting mothers' employment have traditionally been scarce. At the end of the 1990s, less than 3 per cent of children under the age of 3 had a childcare place in West Germany. Meanwhile, preschool provision for 3- to 6-year-olds was extensive, covering around 90 per cent of this age group, yet mostly on a part-time basis that was not well suited to help parents combine work and family obligations. In the East German Länder, comprehensive daycare existed due to the very different policy legacy of the GDR (DJI 1998). A series of measures in the early 2000s signalled a new employment-orientation in German family policy, initiating a steady expansion of childcare services. By 2007, coverage for under-3s had expanded to 15.5 per cent (nationally), and around every second place for 3- to 6-year-olds was offered on a full-time basis (BMFSFJ 2008a: 37; DJI 2008: 26).

Differences in cleavage structures help account for the different development of childcare policy in the two countries. But the chapter also demonstrates, by employing a historical process-oriented approach, how a combination of similar factors led to the transition to an employment-oriented childcare policy in Sweden in the early 1970s and in Germany in the early 2000s. The chapter begins by highlighting what is new about childcare policy in the postindustrial age. It then moves on to consider the policy preference of key actors and constituencies in relation to childcare. These ideas are then illustrated by narrative accounts of childcare policy developments in Sweden and Germany. Finally, in conclusion, I identify the key factors that have allowed childcare to become mainstream social policy in both countries and those that explain the considerable difference in timing of this development between the two countries studied.

Childcare in the Postindustrial Welfare States

Childcare has been debated as a policy issue since the 19th century, albeit as a rather marginal one. In the industrial welfare state, formal childcare was generally conceived of as a social needs measure for poor families or as educational policy supporting the development and socialization of small children. In its first function, service provision for children of working mothers was a complementary measure to other family policies aimed at securing household income and supporting care within the family, and tended to be scarce. In its latter function it could be extensive, but was mostly provided on a part-time basis and not intended to support the gainful employment of mothers (Bahle 2009). Industrial welfare states were grounded on male breadwinner norms that defined childcare as a mother's natural duty. Accordingly, childcare policy was not designed to change gendered work-care arrangements in the family. But childcare policy has historically also been discussed as a means to women's emancipation by 'freeing' them from care obligations and supporting their labour market participation (see e.g. Myrdal 1945).

All of these functions persist in current policy debates, but a new dimension is brought to childcare policy through its economic framing. Postindustrial childcare programs share with historic social needs measures the concern to support families in difficulties, yet their aim is broader: by enabling parents to take up gainful employment, childcare services are meant to limit the risk of poverty and to allow welfare states to reduce passive cash-transfers to families. Also in its educational orientation, postindustrial childcare aims further than industrial early years provision: not only to foster small children's early development, but to improve their long-term educational achievements and future labour market prospects. On the other hand, the new policy-orientation is less ambitious than the gender equality vision of childcare: while breaking with traditional male breadwinner norms, it follows an adult-*worker* orientation rather than a 'work/life *balance*' model on gender-equal grounds (see also Ostner 2010; Daly 2011). It aims at making as many adults as possible economically active by outsourcing unpaid family care, but it does not concern itself with the gendered nature of care, that is, with the question of who is doing the care work, paid or unpaid. Ultimately, the goal of the 'new' childcare policy is to bolster the growth and competitiveness of a nation's knowledge-based economy. With this (human) 'capital generating' emphasis, childcare policy has moved from the fringes of welfare state activity to its centre. It now constitutes an integral part of the emerging new welfare state, alternatively labelled the 'social investment', 'activating', or 'enabling' state (see Jenson, Chapter 2; Taylor-Gooby 2008).

Mapping Cleavage-based Preferences Around the Politics of Childcare

A key point this chapter wishes to make is that political parties are not static or unified actors, but complex and dynamic organizations that harbour a variety of groups and factions with differing interests that compete with each other to influence the party's agenda. One reason for this is that party formation has not neatly followed socio-cultural divisions. Instead, cleavages intersect within and across parties (the preferences of a Catholic worker will differ from those of a non-religious one, a female academic will have a different perspective on work and family life than a female factory worker, and so on). This is particularly the case for large centre parties that aim to appeal to a wide range of interests. Accordingly, strong tensions may exist within a party over goals and policy solutions. Shifts in social cleavage structures may change political dynamics and bring previously marginalized interests and claims to the forefront. Party research has so far focused on changes in voter alignments and ensuing party competition, but changes in cleavages may also create new inner-party coalitions and cross-party alliances. This is important, for while party competition can provide a window of opportunity for certain interests and ideas, these need to be taken up by political actors and formulated into politically feasible policy solutions and programmatic strategies. Success of a policy not only depends on political pressure but on political actors finding a convincing narrative and framing of the policy issue.

Childcare and class politics

Class conflict is commonly understood to be the main driver of welfare state development, a thesis most prominently developed by the power resource theory. According to this approach, cross-national welfare state variations are the result of the differing capacity of labour movements to mobilize politically (see e.g. Korpi 1983). Welfare states with historically strong labour movements display extensive social service sectors reflecting the working class' consumption-oriented welfare state strategy and equality objectives. Childcare policy is often used as an example for this argument (Esping-Andersen 1990, 1999; Huber and Stephens 2000): the availability of childcare services is extensive in 'Social Democratic' welfare states such as Sweden or Denmark, but less so in countries dominated by centre-right parties, such as Germany or the UK. To interpret these national differences as a result of 'working class strength' is, however, problematic. The specific type of childcare we find in Sweden or Denmark—universal daycare provision—does not fit the core strategy of Social Democratic parties to 'decommodify' industrial workers, rather, it serves to 'commodify' parents, particularly mothers. Historical research has pointed out that labour movements—in their origins strongly male-dominated organizations—have been rather ambivalent, if not hostile, towards policies that help women combine family obligations with gainful employment: on the one hand, because female wage workers were perceived as unwanted 'cheap labour' competition; on the other, because it was considered inappropriate with respect to the traditional male breadwinner norm generally held in the working class (Curtin 1999).

Despite their historic ambivalence, trade unions and Social Democratic parties may still become promoters of employment-oriented childcare policy: as female membership increases, pressure mounts on these organizations to respond to the needs and demands of female workers in view of the labour movement's general equality and social justice principles (Bergqvist 1994). It has also been argued that Social Democratic parties have adapted to post-war conditions of de-industrialization by changing their political strategies to appeal to the growing class of white-collar workers (Bonoli and Reber 2010). Since women's entry into the labour market took place predominantly in the expanding service sector, addressing the interests of female employees becomes of particular importance to the new middle-class orientation of Social Democratic parties. But employers' organizations have also been shown, both in the past and present, to support childcare policy to encourage women's gainful employment, namely in situations of labour shortage (Hirdman 1998; Naumann 2006) or demand for specific skills (Fleckenstein and Seeleib-Kaiser 2011).

When it comes to party politics, Social Democratic parties may promote 'new' childcare policy if there is political pressure from within the labour movement. However, the initiative will most likely not come from their core constituency of male workers, but from female wage-earners. Centre-right/ conservative parties, due to their more traditional family values, can be expected to be more reluctant towards female employment than left political actors (see below), but partisan competition for middle-class votes and pressure from employers may also sway these parties to support employment-oriented childcare policy. As a consequence, it is likely that the promotion of 'new' childcare policy involves cross-class alliances.

Religion and the protection of traditional family values

The fundamental role of religion in the formation of welfare states has recently been emphasized by a number of scholars who draw on Stein Rokkan's seminal work on social cleavages and party systems (Bahle 1995; Morgan 2006; Manow and van Kersbergen 2009). These contributions remind us that, historically, the Churches were centrally involved in the provision of welfare, and were particularly concerned with the family and education. Religious influence is clearly manifest in countries with strong Christian Democratic parties that have upheld traditional family and gender norms and opposed state-intervention into the family on the grounds of Christian ethics. But religious cleavages have also shaped social policy in countries where religious conflict did not become part of modern party politics (Naumann 2006).

The extent to which religious cleavages have been influential in welfare states has been linked to the historic state–church relations and denominational composition of a country (see e.g. Morgan 2002; Bahle 2009). Strong tensions between the state and the Catholic church has led either to extensive state provision of childcare, such as in France (not just to support women's labour market participation, but to exert state control over children's socialization), or to minimal state provision and the dominance of the Church in family services, such as in the Southern European welfare states. In multi-denominational countries such as the Netherlands or Germany, state-church competition has led to various mixes of public/private welfare provision, with a strong role for religiously oriented welfare organizations. On the other hand, the non-conflictual relationship between state and Lutheran state churches in the Nordic countries has led to the absence of direct religious influence on social policy (Kaspersen and Lindvall 2008), which may explain the swifter modernization of family norms than in other countries (Naumann 2006).

Christian doctrine emphasizes an understanding of the family as an organic unit based on patriarchal gender norms, where women's role is defined as wife and mother. Religious actors will thus try to defend this 'natural order' against the economic framing, the individualization of family relations and the promotion of women's gainful employment, all of which form key elements of postindustrial childcare policy. There are, however, differences in religious doctrine and practice. Historical research suggests that Lutheran Churches tended to be more open to societal changes, such as women's increasing labour market participation, when compared with the Catholic Church (Markkola 2001; Naumann 2006). We can thus expect religiously affiliated political actors to be antagonistic to employment-oriented childcare policy and that such opposition will come most strongly from Catholic actors. Conversely, the processes of secularization and the weakening of religious cleavages in the form of electoral de-alignments are factors conducive to the development of postindustrial childcare policy.

Gendered preferences and conflicts around childcare

Women's political agency is generally acknowledged to play a positive role in social policy development, particularly with respect to policies around childcare and childrearing, but is rarely conceptualized systematically in welfare state analysis (for exception see Kulawik 1999).[2] Research on partisan politics usually conceives of political cleavages as the political articulation (via parties and voter alignments) of enduring conflicts based on social and cultural divides and accompanied by a high degree of social closure (see Bartolini and Mair 1990). It could be argued that this definition does not apply to gender as a political dimension: gender conflict has historically not played out on the same scale as religious or class conflict and women and men tend to live in intimate proximity and in peace with each other.[3] On the other hand, women and men's everyday life has traditionally taken place in distinctly different spheres, namely with women being barred from public and political life until some time into the 20th century; women display different preferences in their voting behaviour from men; and women have formed their own political organizations, albeit without impacting directly on modern party systems.

The extent and development of employment-oriented childcare policy and other measures supporting work/life balance has been found to correlate positively with the level of women's political representation irrespective of party affiliation (Huber and Stephens 2000; Bonoli and Reber 2010). This does not imply that preferences are uniformly gendered. Not all women automatically support reconciliation of family and work policies. In fact, women have traditionally been important voter segments for conservative parties who have opposed such policy development (Bösch 2002). An important factor shaping women's (and men's) normative orientations concerning care-related issues is the intersection of gender with religion and class: we can expect religiously oriented women to favour policies that support their care work in the family or, alternatively, the successive reconciliation of family life and work, based on ideas of gender difference. Women organized in the labour movement will be more likely to hold gender equality ideals that focus on the immediate reconciliation of family and work and support claims for employment-oriented childcare policy. Of course, men also hold different gender norms and differ in their support of (or opposition to) gender equality claims and related policies.

A number of scholars argue that a new value cleavage has emerged since the 1960s around new 'post-material' values and life-styles, including a reorientation to more gender-equal norms, creating conflict lines that cut across the historic religious and class cleavages (Kriesi 2011). There are similarities between the gender cleavage suggested here as analytical dimension and Kriesi's 'new value cleavage'. However, to understand the post-war gender conflict merely as an aspect of general value-change eclipses the gendered nature of power, and the gendered processes of interest formation based on structural divisions. Simply put, as long as women were predominantly housewives, political parties perceived to protect their family situation were likely to receive their support. Now, as more and more women are involved in paid work while having to care for young children, their political preferences seem to shift toward parties that are able to provide support for their double role.

Drawing on this discussion, we can expect politically active women ('femocrats') to be more likely than men to promote employment-oriented childcare policy due to women's greater involvement in familial care work, but their political engagement depends on the way their political identities and interests are shaped by the cross-cutting lines of religion and class. In the absence of strong political women's organizations, the success of women's claims for employment-oriented childcare policy depends on their ability to forge political alliances within and across existing parties.

The Transition from Industrial to Postindustrial Childcare Policy in Sweden and Germany

Sweden

Fundamental to the development of childcare policy in Sweden is the historic absence of a religious cleavage in welfare state politics. Consensual state-church relations are commonly ascribed to European nations with Protestant state churches (Morgan 2006; Bahle 2009); however, this is not self-evident with respect to Social Democratic welfare states. The Lutheran Church, for a long time the only legitimate post-Reformation religion in Sweden, was a powerful force in Swedish society and a central actor in the provision of welfare and education into the first half of the 20th century. When the Social Democratic party (SAP), with a manifesto pledge to abolish the state church and harbouring strong anti-religious factions (Gustafsson 2003: 53), rose to power in the 1920s, state-church tensions could have been expected. Yet once in power, SAP leadership toned down the party's anti-clerical stance to avoid alienating potential voters, and instead struck a compromise: the Swedish state church remained and even received increased autonomy regarding state funds; in return, it was to limit its activities to spiritual matters only (Gustafsson 2003; Naumann 2006).

The separation of state and church regarding welfare provision was, however, initially not as clearcut as the case of childcare services demonstrates: childcare policy had low priority on SAP's policy agenda and was left to whoever was willing to deliver these services. In the early 1940s, only 7 per cent of childcare services were provided by municipalities, the rest was delivered by the parishes and private, often religiously inspired, charities (Antman 1996: 122). Towards the end of the 1950s, however, against the backdrop of widespread secularization and a rapidly expanding Social Democratic welfare state, the Swedish Left grew increasingly hostile towards faith-based and private solutions. Private childcare providers were gradually municipalized and 'crowded out', albeit slowly, by public childcare expansion, though provision remained very scarce (Lundström and Wijkström 1997).

During the inter-war years, the Social Democratic government initiated a series of 'prophylactic' social policy measures geared at improving the well-being of individual family members, particularly mothers and children, such as free maternal and infant health care. Childcare services were not part of this new policy-orientation. The Swedish Social Democratic 'people's home' was firmly built on the male breadwinner norm, and attempts by the influential Social Democratic policy-expert Alva Myrdal to promote childcare provision as 'prophylactic' or 'active' social policy (improving families economy via mothers' employment and childrearing via professional daycare; see Myrdal 1945) were rebuked universally; the consensus remained that active support of female employment was undesirable (Naumann 2006). The introduction of such measures as tax splitting in 1952 underscored this orientation further. Nonetheless, attitudes towards female employment gradually softened in subsequent decades.

During the 1950s and early 1960s, Swedish industry was booming, resulting in labour shortages. Two solutions were debated: demand could either be met by migrant workers or the labour reserve of married women (Hinnfors 1992). Fearing that an influx of unorganized migrant workers could weaken their position in the newly established solidaristic wage bargaining between trade unions and employers, the blue-collar union LO (*Landsorganisationen*), pushed by their own women's organization, became one of the first and strongest proponents of childcare service expansion in Swedish politics (LO 1962; Naumann 2006). The employer's organization SAF also supported claims for employment-oriented childcare policy, and in 1951, LO and SAF formed the Labour Market Women's Committee (*Arbetsmarknadens Kvinnonämnd*) with the main remit of encouraging married women to take up jobs in Swedish factories (Hirdman 1998).

Swedish women did not have to be coaxed into entering the labour market: female employment rates rose steeply in the post-war decades, from 44 per cent in 1950 to 74.1 per cent in 1980 (AMS 1980). Employment rates of mothers with dependent children increased even faster, from 32 per cent in 1960 to 80 per cent in 1980 (Hinnfors 1992: 43). However, women's labour market integration took place not in the industrial sector—which, contrary to economic forecasts, contracted in the 1960s—but in the growing service economy. In the early 1960s, a public debate on gender roles and gender equality unfolded—considerably earlier than in many other European countries. Central to the new ideology was the notion that men and women should share all societal roles, be they employment, childcare, social, or

167

political activities; reconciliation policies such as public childcare provision were crucial to achieving this vision of equality (Baude 1992).

When political parties began responding to these socio-economic changes, new political dynamics created space for ideas and claims around employment-oriented childcare policy to take hold. In 1958, the old red-green alliance between SAP and the farmers' party had broken down over SAP's push for a new contribution pillar of the pension system (ATP) strategically aimed at integrating the new middle-classes into the welfare state compromise. By garnering support from the growing ranks of white-collar employees, SAP had strayed into the electoral territory of the Liberals. The Liberals, hitherto second strongest party in Sweden but weakened through the ATP struggle, were in turn looking for new constituencies and issues to campaign around. In 1961, the Liberals entered the election campaign with the slogan 'justice for women' alongside a gender equality agenda including equal wages, abolition of joint taxation and expansion of childcare services (Drangel 1984), thus moving into core Social Democratic ideological ground. SAP's leadership hastened to catch up by including gender equality promises in their social programmes and manifestos.

Pressure on government to initiate policy change in line with new gender equality demands mounted during the 1960s: gender equality activists forged cross-party political, public and economic alliances, beginning to effectively lobby the Swedish corporatist system (Baude 1992); more radical feminists rallied on the streets of Swedish cities (Naumann 2005). Demand for public childcare was not only triggered by new gender ideologies, however, but also by sheer need: by the late 1960s, public daycare was available for only around 3 per cent of preschool children, while another 6 per cent of children were cared for by private childminders (Hinnfors 1992: 49). However, SAP was also put under increasing pressure from its traditional core constituency, blue-collar workers, to renew its class equality promises in the wake of lay-offs, rising unemployment and wage pressure caused by de-industrialization.

In 1968, a commission of Social Democrats and trade union representatives, chaired by Alva Myrdal, was tasked with developing a programme that could respond to the new economic and political challenges. The ensuing report presented a new concept of 'radical equality' that spanned economic and family life (SAP/LO 1969). In economic terms, greater equality was to be achieved by giving workers greater control over the market via 'workers' funds' (a concept that never really took off); and in people's private lives by promoting the dual-earner family supported by public childcare services. This new model would introduce greater income equality between families and prevent poverty; it would grant children from all backgrounds equal educational opportunities;

and it would create equality between men and women. The first 'social invest-ment' document had been created.

The new Social Democratic party leader Olof Palme was quick in adopting the new family model, and in 1970 announced the government's plan to abolish joint taxation for married couples. To break with the male breadwin-ner tradition and to pursue a dual-earner family vision was a top-down deci-sion that met with strong opposition from both the labour movement's base and the Swedish public (Leijon 1991). The Prime Minister was publicly accused of 'chasing housewives'—who in 1970 still constituted 40 per cent of women—and within weeks 10,000 protest letters from 'furious housewives' landed on Palme's desk (Dagens Nyheter, 18.02.1970). Despite internal party conflict, the Social Democratic leadership maintained course and pushed through further employment-oriented family policies in swift order: a Pre-school Act (1973) and Childcare Act (1975) that obliged municipalities to provide a childcare place for every child below the age of 7 whose parents were in gainful employment or education, and a generous parental leave Act (1974) that replaced previous maternity leave legislation (Antman 1996).

Palme's commitment to gender equality may have been real, but it was also wedded to economic and political interests: in order to fulfil the equality promises the government had made to various social groups, welfare state generosity had to be increased. Women's demand for labour market integra-tion thus fitted the government's need for increased employment rates and tax revenue to finance expensive welfare state expansion. The extensive child-care programmes SAP launched did not cease after recession hit the Swedish economy in 1973. On the contrary, the Swedish government used public sector expansion, including childcare services, as part of its anti-cyclical Keynesian economic policy and as a means to ride out the financial crisis: increasing childcare and other social services created public sector jobs—mostly taken up by women—and maintained productivity and consumption. In addition, competition for women's votes between SAP and the Liberals kept the new employment-oriented family policies on the agenda: opinion polls in the early 1970s showed that young working women saw in the Liberals as the more 'woman-friendly' party (Hinnfors 1992); the Social Democratic party, on the other hand had started to lose electoral support during the early 1970s and was trying hard to win women's trust.

Due to the Liberal party's strong support, the new policy direction was not reversed in 1976 when a conservative coalition government gained power even though considerable ideological differences existed with respect to family and gender issues between the Liberals on the one hand, and the Moderates and Centre party on the other (Drangel 1984). Ideological conflict so weakened the conservative block that the Moderates left the government after only a few years, while the Liberals, strongly focused on pushing the dual-earner family model, remained in government.

Once the policy route of childcare service expansion was taken, it set off 'positive feedback' effects that compelled successive governments to continuously invest greater sums into the daycare system. As women poured into the labour market, demand for childcare services grew exponentially; female employment also created demand for other household-oriented services in turn increasing demand for (female) labour in the expanding social service sector. Employment-oriented childcare policy remained highly popular among young parents, thus political parties did not dare depart from the new direction. By the 1980s, the vast majority of Swedish families had abandoned the male breadwinner model, and were relying on two incomes (albeit with women tending to work part-time). From the end of the 1960s to 1979, public childcare services expanded from a coverage rate of 3 per cent to 28 per cent, rising still further to 49 per cent in 1989 (Hinnfors 1992: 49). Investment in childcare services as a proportion of public expenditure grew in this period from 0.26 per cent to 2.75 per cent; however, it was not until the end of the 1990s that sufficient coverage prompted government legislation imposing an obligation on municipalities to provide a childcare place for every child from the age of 1.

Germany

As in Germany, in Sweden the nature of the state-church relation also shaped the institutional formation of formal childcare provision. During the 19th century Catholic, Protestant, and (secular) Fröbel organizations began to organize collective childcare in the German Reich, soon expanding their activities in competition with each other. When the state engaged with childcare provision in the late 19th century as a response to the Social Question, religious/secular competition was interlaced with a public/private conflict. In the Weimar Republic, the Social Democratic and Liberal parties strongly favoured public welfare services, including childcare, but the Catholic Centre party (*Zentrumspartei*) successfully represented the interests of the independent welfare organizations. In 1922, the Youth Welfare Act was passed, establishing the principle of subsidiarity in childcare provision with independent—and in the main, religious—welfare organizations taking priority in the delivery of childcare services, but with the state taking on substantial financial responsibility. In 1928, 70 per cent of childcare services were provided by independent, mostly faith-based welfare associations, and 30 per cent by the municipalities (Erning 1987: 20). This public/private mix of service provision was replaced with a unified state childcare system during the Nazi regime, which in turn was abolished after World War II (Reyer 1987: 77ff).

The childcare arrangements of the Weimar Republic were reinstated more or less unchanged in the FRG in 1953, reflecting both historic policy legacy and, perhaps more significantly, the endurance of religious influence in welfare politics.

After World War II, the newly formed Christian Democratic party (CDU) became the strongest political force, convincing voters that their concept of social market-economy (*soziale Marktwirtschaft*) and Christian family image were the best defence against both right and left totalitarian tendencies in a democratic society (Moeller 1993). In particular, social Catholic doctrine, with its strong emphasis on the married-couple family based on traditional gender roles, became influential in the shaping of social policy and family law during the CDU's first lengthy term in power (1949–1969) (Bösch 2002). In line with these normative orientations, the CDU was strongly opposed to both maternal employment and state-intervention into private family life.

In light of the conservative atmosphere in post-war West Germany, it is perhaps unsurprising that, when socio-economic changes similar to those in Sweden began to evolve in the 1950s and 1960s, these were noted with great concern. Women's increased labour market orientation was not welcomed as a remedy for the labour shortage facing German industries, but perceived as a 'crisis of the family' (Kolbe 1999). Wage-earning women were publicly vilified by conservative politicians, paediatricians, and the media as 'greedy double earners' who inflicted life-long damage through maternal deprivation on their children (Naumann 2006). However, the hostility to women's employment was not due to normative orientations alone, but also to economic considerations: supporting women's wage-earning capacity and the 'dual-earner family' would increase families' spending-power and consumption and could thus interfere with the anti-inflationary economic policy on which West German economic and political actors agreed in the post-war period. Hiring foreign 'guest workers' in response to labour shortage was perceived as economically more beneficial (Naumann 2006).

Notably, the Social Democratic party (SPD) also did little during its period in power (1966–1985) to support women in combining family and work. The SPD's reluctance to modernize West German family policy can, on one hand, be explained by Cold War politics: West German Social Democrats were eager to distance themselves from their Socialist East German brothers and sisters, and family policy was well suited to demonstrate their allegiance to the West, as the West German SPD could emphasize that in their 'free' Germany, mothers were not forced to go and work but were allowed to stay with their children (Moeller 1993). Second, there was little pressure on the SPD from other leftwing actors to implement employment-oriented family and care policies: neither the blue-collar trade union DGB (*Deutscher Gewerkschaftsbund*) nor the feminist movement had expansion of childcare services and parental leave high on their agenda (Naumann 2005). As for the trade unions, their historic ambivalence towards women's employment was reinforced by the presence of a strong Catholic wing in the labour movement. The absence of mainstream political actors promoting gender equality arguably pushed the feminist movement towards more radical positions—the aim for women to 'free' themselves from family life altogether—and made them uninterested in questions regarding the reconciliation of work and family life (Naumann 2005).

In 1969, a window of opportunity seemed to open for a re-orientation in family policy, as the newly elected Social Democratic party leader and chancellor, Willy Brandt, signalled his support for women's claims for a right to work and promised to expand childcare services. However, in the early 1970s, when the SPD family minister Katharina Focke presented a proposal for employment-oriented childcare policy, it was shelved before it could go before parliament. The economic crisis ended the budding support for female labour market participation and for any related costly social programmes. While Sweden pursued an anti-cyclical economic strategy during this time, Germany opted for budgetary constraint and inflation control, hence women's demands for labour market integration were perceived as a burden rather than opportunity (Naumann 2006).

During the 1970s and 1980s, initiatives advocating employment-oriented childcare policy were continuously blocked by the strong Christian-conservative alliance comprising the CDU, welfare organizations, and the Catholic Church; meanwhile, such issues were met by a lack of interest from the SPD and the liberal FDP. Nevertheless, a slow modernization of West German family policy took place: the introduction of policies such as the three-year parental leave, aimed at a *successive* compatibility model, enabled mothers to interrupt or reduce employment for childcare, rather than the simultaneous reconciliation of work and family. Then, in 1991, new legislation suddenly came into force guaranteeing every child from the age of 3 a right to a preschool place, and stipulating municipal responsibility to provide childcare for the under-3s, according to need (Struck and Wiesner 1992).

This Act of 1991 was passed under a Conservative government with much grumbling from within Christian-democratic ranks. It was not so much the result of new consensus about the desirability of maternal employment, but the by-product of a tenuous compromise over abortion law. During the unification process, conflict between conservative West German politicians promoting very restrictive abortion legislation and East German politicians accustomed to liberal abortion regulations was resolved by designing a series of 'preventive' policy measures (intended to convince women not to seek abortions, the so-called 'Pregnant Women and Family Services Act'—*Schwangeren- und Familienhilfegesetz*). One of these was the expansion of formal childcare to help mothers combine work and family life (Struck & Wiesner

1992: 454; Meyer 1996: 66). In practice, the new childcare policy had little effect as an employment-oriented measure: in East Germany, universal day-care provision already existed; in West Germany, however, many municipa-lities responded to the new law by cutting back on daycare provision to expand part-time kindergarten places for 3- to 6-year-olds, thus meeting the legal requirements (DJI 1998). Nevertheless, the 1991 Act signalled important tectonic shifts in German post-unification politics: most East Germans held gender norms that differed considerably from the West German conservative family image and were more in line with the adult-worker model. For East Germans, women's right to work whether they had children or not, and wrap-around childcare services to make this possible, were a matter of course. In addition, East Germans, insofar as they were religiously affiliated, were mainly Lutherans. The resultant change in the denominational balance within political parties and constituencies proved consequential, particularly for the family policy-orientation of the CDU.

The first move in this new direction, however, was made by the red-green coalition that entered into government in 1998. Both the SPD and the Green party had promised radical changes, including gender equality reforms, in their election campaigns, and both parties received strong support from young female voters (Die Grünen 1998; SPD 1998; Hartenstein and Müller-Hilmer 2002). Yet the expansion of formal childcare did not figure promi-nently on their agendas: the two parties followed a West German tradition of feminist claims that focused on such issues as women's political representa-tion, violence against women and women's equal career opportunities, but that did not emphasize the reconciliation of family and work. Also, with respect to labour market and social policy, the red-green government at first followed a more traditional leftwing orientation by focusing on demand-side measures and state intervention into the market. However, at the beginning of the 2000s, the economic situation deteriorated, unemployment figures soared and pressure mounted for the government to initiate more radical changes.

The red-green coalition went into the next general election in 2002 with a new set of supply-side oriented 'activating' labour market policies inspired by 'Third Way' thinking (Clasen and Clegg 2004). Part of their proposals was also a new type of family policy, in which the expansion of childcare services was 'the most pressing task' (SPD 2002. 47): as a means to enhance children's educational achievements; to support the reconciliation of family and work; to prevent poverty in families; and to encourage an increase in fertility rates. Both parties also promised to radically reform parental leave policy into a one-year leave with income-replacement in line with the 'Swedish Model' (Die Grünen 2002: 46). Central architect of this new type of family policy was the leader of the Bavarian SPD, Renate Schmidt, who had lobbied for women's right to work and the expansion of childcare provision for decades. Schmidt strategically placed childcare at the centre of the debate about welfare state sustainability, presenting it as an economic rather than a gender equality issue. She pointed out how employment-oriented childcare measures would have positive effects on the economy and on demographic trends, particularly as they would encourage well-educated women to have more children (Schmidt 2002; BMFSFJ 2003). When the red-green government was re-elected, Schmidt became family minister and, coining the term 'sustainable family policy' (*Nachhaltige Familienpolitik*), she had by 2003 fully appropriated this formerly conservative policy field for a left 'Third Way' strategy. Schmidt's policy plans received strong backing from the left political leadership as well as from employers' associations.

In 2004, the Childcare Expansion Act (*Tageseinrichtungsausbaugesetz, TAG*) was enacted, commencing a steady growth in daycare places for preschool children from the age of one (BMFSFJ 2006). Notably, the TAG law passed parliament with support from the CDU. By 2004, the red-green coalition had lost majority in the *Bundesrat*, thus depending on votes from conservative *Länder* governments. However, the CDU also continued to support the new direction towards an adult-worker model after it came into power in 2005. In fact, it was the Christian-Democratic family minister, Ursula von der Leyen, who set new, more ambitious targets for the expansion of childcare services (a coverage rate of 35 per cent for under-3s by 2013). She prepared and pushed through the Parental Leave Act (2007) and the new Children's Support Act (*Kinderförderungsgesetz, KiföG* 2008b); and she wrested financial agreement from central government to cover a third of the estimated costs of new child-care places until 2013 (BMFSJF 2008a; DJI 2008).

Two factors are important when considering the CDU's radical change of direction with respect to family policy: the emergence of a new gender cleavage cutting across political parties and creating electoral competition for women's votes; and the economic framing of the childcare issue. Von der Leyen shared the policy goals of her Social Democratic predecessor Schmidt, but also enjoyed firm support from the new CDU chancellor Angela Merkel—a support she urgently needed, as her advancement of 'sustainable' family policy programmes met with strong opposition within CDU ranks. Merkel was certainly not a feminist in the West German understanding of the word (Langguth 2007). Yet she was strongly in favour of female employment and respective support measures, not least because they fit with the new 'activating', thus more market-oriented, social policy direction she backed as part of the Grand Coalition government.

Merkel and von der Leyen represented a new breed of political leader for the CDU: both women, both academics, both Protestants, and both promoting a swift modernization of the German family model, while the CDU's membership base predominantly consisted of male, conservative, Catholic workers or small-scale businessmen (Walter 2004). Yet this constituency was dwindling, not least due to age: the majority of CDU supporters were over the age of 60 (Namislo et al. 2006). Even more striking were changes in female voting behaviour: historically, women had been the most loyal supporters of the CDU (Bösch 2002). This support, however, was fading: in the 1998 election, young women favoured the left over the conservative parties, most likely reflecting increased employment-orientation within this generation of women; and by 2002, the CDU had also lost support among older women (Hartenstein and Müller-Hilmer 2002). Electoral evaluations also indicated that women were more likely to vote for the large centre parties SPD and CDU, while men tended to vote for more radical, smaller parties on the left and right (Schorn and Gisart 2010)—as a commentator poignantly summarized: 'the centre is female' (von Billerbeck in *Die ZEIT* September 2002). Consequently, both CDU and SPD have in recent years begun to woo women, particularly young, well-educated, and career-oriented women, by promoting employment-oriented family policies with a clear middle-class bias (see also Ostner 2010; Fleckenstein and Seeleib-Kaiser 2011).

Whereas party competition spurred German governments into action to finally modernize social policies, the strategic reframing of childcare as an economic, rather than a gender equality issue, was important to create broad support for the new childcare policy. The framing of childcare as an issue of economic necessity allowed the CDU to virtually make a u-turn in their position on family policy without 'losing face' and to jump on a policy bandwagon that was highly popular with the electorate. Economic framing provided a symbolic bridge to forge political consensus without drawing to light ideological differences around family and gender issues that still exist in German society, and that had foiled any development in this policy field for decades. The success of employment-oriented childcare policy, however, came at a price: the loss of an equality focus, both with respect to gender and class.

Conclusion

The narrative accounts provided above show that, despite variations in institutional design and political constellations of the two welfare states along differing timelines, a mixture of similar factors paved the way for postindustrial childcare policy in both countries. In Sweden in the 1970s, and Germany in the early 2000s, a reorientation towards the adult-worker model in family policy was initiated by Social Democratic and red-green coalition governments respectively, suggesting greater affinity of this family model with preferences and ideological positions of left-wing actors than conservatives.

But notably, path-departure was consolidated by conservative coalition governments. In both cases, new childcare policy was implemented through top-down decisions by political leaders without being anchored in the respective party base or core constituency. Instead, they responded to changing voter alignments that created party competition for women's votes (in Sweden between SAP and the Liberal party, in Germany between the SPD and the CDU).

The new gendered cleavage line that cut across the left-right political spectrum also created new intra- and inter-party alliances between 'femocrats'. These political actors successfully lobbied the political leadership for the expansion of childcare provision by strategically framing the issue to fit within broader economic goals. It is these twin political pressures, from within political parties and from the electorate, that created opportunities for the historically neglected issue of childcare to move onto governments' policy agendas in both countries. An important factor for governments to promote, and for other influential actors to support, the new family policy direction was, however, the economic framing of childcare and other family policies and their 'fit' with the dominant economic paradigm of the respective country and time.

The similarity between the two stories helps us to identify the factors responsible for bringing childcare onto the political agenda. However, we can also gain additional insights by focusing on the main difference between the two stories, namely the timing of the transition to employment-oriented childcare policy—three decades earlier in Sweden than in Germany. Here, a number of factors stand out. First, the absence of a religious cleavage in Swedish post-war politics, that might have impeded such policy development on normative grounds, facilitated political alliances over gender issues that cut across the class cleavage. Importantly, the ideologically moderate but cohesive women's movement was able to exert pressure on political parties of the left and right, both from within and outside the political system. Second, the institutional design of the Social Democratic welfare state, with its more individualistic social rights-orientation and focus on full employment, facilitated the integration of the demands of a new generation of gender equality- and work-oriented women.

In post-war Germany, on the other hand, organized religion was successful via the cross-denominational Christian Democratic party in re-establishing and defending the traditional male breadwinner/female housewife family in policy and law. In particular, social Catholicism became influential. Postindustrial economic, individualistic and employment-oriented childcare policy was clearly at odds with the Christian view of the family as the organic unit. In addition, no alliances developed between the autonomous feminist movement and more moderate 'femocrats' around childcare as a policy issue. It took the long-term mounting of pressures such as increasing female employment rates, decreasing fertility rates and general concerns over welfare state sustainability, combined with changing voter alignments, to bring employment-oriented childcare policy onto political parties' agendas. Not least, a contingent event—German unification—had effects on political cleavages by decreasing the influence of Catholicism within Christian Democracy and introducing new gender norms into the conservative party. Last, the key to understanding the delayed transition to postindustrial childcare policy in Germany is its misfit with the dominant economic paradigm in the post-war decades: in Sweden, women's entry into the labour market and related expansion of social services could be integrated in and even supported the country's anti-cyclical Keynesian economic strategy; but the anti-inflationary policy orientation in Germany impeded both.

This chapter has aimed to illustrate how intersecting cleavages delineate the range of politically feasible policy solutions at any given time, on one hand by creating historic policy trajectories, and on the other by structuring interest constellations and normative orientations. The chapter has also shown that a multidimensional approach to welfare reform politics is necessary: the development of a 'new' postindustrial childcare policy cannot be understood by focusing on class divisions alone, but has been centrally shaped by the weakening or absence of religious cleavages, and the intensifying of cross-cutting gender conflict. This is not to say that 'class' would not matter: in Sweden, 'working class strength' in the form of a dominant Social Democratic party gave postindustrial childcare policy a specific 'Social Democratic' imprint as it was integrated into a new narrative combining economic productivity, redistribution and gender equality objectives. Childcare policy became the 'flagship' of this new Social Democratic orientation, and since the 1970s, there has been legitimatory pressure on this policy to deliver with respect to both class and gender equality.

In Germany, it was also Social Democracy that first promoted employment-oriented childcare policy, but it was a transformed Social Democracy that had re-oriented itself to a new 'Third Way' ideology, apart from traditional socialist goals. In the German case, postindustrial childcare policy was designed not as redistributive, but as market-oriented 'activation' strategy. The Hartz IV laws and other policy reforms signal a decline in welfare state generosity and a diminished concern with growing inequalities. There is also considerably less focus on gender equality as a policy goal than in Sweden. In fact, it appears that the omission of a discussion on gender equality in the economically oriented concept of 'sustainable family policy' made a broader consensus around 'new' childcare policy possible, as it avoided touching upon the strong tensions and differences around family and gender norms that still exist in German society today.

Notes

1. In Sweden, virtually all children aged 6 attend so-called 'preschool-classes' before they start compulsory school at the age of 7.
2. Gender regime theory highlights how national welfare state arrangements are grounded in family and gender norms (Lewis 1992), but conceptualizes gender on the level of norms and institutions, not on the level of agency; it remains unclear whether gender regime theory accepts Esping-Andersen's argument that class conflict is the most important factor in welfare state development. On the other hand, a wide range of feminist case studies has emphasized the positive impact of women's political mobilization on the development of employment-oriented family policy, but without engaging with general welfare state theories (see e.g. Tyyskä 1995; Naumann 2005; Kremer 2006).
3. High divorce rates and incidents of domestic abuse suggest, however, that gender conflict can become quite intense on the individual household level.

Bibliography

Antman, P. (1996) *Barn och äldreomsorg i Tyskland och Sverige. Sverigedelen*, Skriftserien Fakta-kunskaper 5, Stockholm.

Arbetsmarknadsstyrelsen (AMS) (1980) *Equality in the Labour Market; Statistics*, Stockholm, AMS.

Bahle, T. (1995) *Familienpolitik in Westeuropa. Ursprünge und Wandel im internationalen Vergleich*, Frankfurt a.M., Campus.

Bahle, T. (2009) Public Child Care in Europe: Historical Trajectories and New Directions. In Scheiwe, K. & Willekens, H. (Eds.) *Child Care and Preschool Development in Europe. Institutional Perspectives*. Basingstoke, Palgrave Macmillan, 23–42.

Bartolini, S. & Mair, P. (1990) *Identity, Competition, and Electoral Availability: The Stabilisation of the European Electorates 1885–1985*, Cambridge, Cambridge University Press.

Baude, A. (1992) *Visionen om jämställdhet*, Kristianstad, SNS förlag.

Bergqvist, C. (1994) *Mäns makt och kvinnors intressen*, Uppsala, Uppsala Universitet.

Bonoli, G. & Reber, F. (2010) The Political Economy of Childcare in OECD Countries: Explaining Cross-national Variation in Spending and Coverage Rates. *European Journal of Political Research*, 49, 97–118.

Bösch, F. (2002) *Macht und Machtverlust. Die Geschichte der CDU*, Stuttgart, Deutsche Verlagsanstalt.

Bundesministerium für Familie, Senioren, Frauen und Jugend (BMFSFJ) (2003) *Nachhaltige Familienpolitik im Interesse einer aktiven Bevölkerungsentwicklung*, Berlin, Gutachten von Professor Bert Rürup und Sandra Grusescu.

Bundesministerium für Familie, Senioren, Frauen und Jugend (BMFSFJ) (2006) *Kinderbetreuung für Kinder unter drei Jahren. Bericht der Bundesregierung über den Stand des*

Ausbaus für ein bedarfsgerechtes Angebot an Kindertagesbetreuung für Kinder unter drei Jahren, Berlin, BMFSFJ.

Bundesministerium für Familie, Senioren, Frauen und Jugend (BMFSFJ) (2008a) *Dossier: Ausbau der Kinderbetreung. Kosten—Nutzen—Finanzierung*, Berlin, BMFSFJ.

Bundesministerium für Familie, Senioren, Frauen und Jugend (BMFSFJ) (2008b) *Gesetz zur Förderung von Kindern unter drei Jahren in Tageseinrichtungen und in Kindertagespflege (Kinderförderungsgesetz—KiföG)*, Bundesgesetzblatt Nr. 57, Bonn, BMFSFJ, 2403–9.

Bündnis 90/Die Grünen (1998) *Grün ist der Wechsel. Programm zur Bundestagswahl 98.*

Bündnis 90/Die Grünen (2002) *Grün wirkt! Unser Wahlprogramm 2002–2006.*

Clasen, J. & Clegg, D. (2004) Does the Third Way Work? The Left and Labour Market Policy Reform in Britain, France, and Germany. In Lewis, J. & Surender, R. (Eds.) *Welfare State Change. Towards a Third Way?* Oxford, Oxford University Press, 89–110.

Curtin, J. (1999) *Women and Trade Unions: a Comparative Perspective*, Aldershot, Ashgate.

Daly, Mary (2011) What Adult Worker Model? A Critical Look at Recent Social Policy Reform in Europe from a Gender and Family Perspective. *Social Politics*, 18, 1–23.

Deutsches Jugendinstitut (DJI) (1998) *Zahlenspiegel. Tageseinrichtungen für Kinder. Pluralisierung von Angeboten*, Munich, DJI.

Deutsches Jugendinstitut (DJI) (2008) *Zahlenspiegel. Daten zu Tageseinrichtungen für Kinder*, Munich, DJI.

Drangel, L. (1984) Folkpartiet och jämställdhetsfrågan. In *Liberal ideologi och politik 1934–1984*. Falköping, AB Folk & Samhälle, 342–425.

Erning, G. (1987) Quantitative Entwicklung der Angebote öffentlicher Kleinkindererziehung. In Erning, G., Neumann, K. & Reyer, J. (Eds.). *Geschichte des Kindergartens*, Vol. 2, Freiburg i.B., Lambertus, 29–39.

Esping-Andersen, G. (1990) *The Three Worlds of Welfare Capitalism*, Cambridge, Polity Press.

Esping-Andersen, G. (1999) *Social Foundations of Postindustrial Economies*, Oxford, Oxford University Press.

Fleckenstein, T. & Seeleib-Kaiser, M. (2011) Business, Skills and the Welfare State: The Political Economy of Employment-oriented Family Policy in Britain and Germany. *Journal of European Social Policy*, 21, 136–49.

Gustafsson, G. (2003) Church–State Separation Swedish-style. *West European Politics*, 26, 52–72.

Hartenstein, W. & Müller-Hilmer, R. (2002) Die Bundestagswahl 2002. Neue Themen—neue Allianzen, *Aus Politik und Zeitgeschichte*, B49–50, 18–26.

Hinnfors, J. (1992) Familjepolitik. Samhällsförändringar och partistrategier, 1960–1990, No. 26, Göteborg Studies in Politics, Stockholm.

Hirdman, Y. (1998) *Med kluven tunga. LO och genusordningen*, Uddevalla, Media Print.

Huber, E. & Stephens, J. D. (2000) Partisan Governance, Women's Employment, and the Social Democratic Service State. *American Sociological Review*, 65, 323–42.

Kaspersen, L. B. & Lindvall, J. (2008) Why No Religious Politics? The Secularization of Poor Relief and Primary Education in Denmark and Sweden. Archive européen sociologique, XLIX, 119–43.

Kolbe, W. (1999) Gender and Parenthood in West German Family Politics from the 1960s to the 1980s. In Torstendahl, R. (Ed.) *State Policy and Gender System in the Two*

German States and Sweden 1945–1989. Uppsala, Opuscula Historica Upsaliensia 22, 133–68.

Korpi, W. (1983) *The Democratic Class Struggle,* London, Routledge & Kegan Paul.

Kremer, M. (2006) The Politics of Ideals of Care: Danish and Flemish Child Care Policy Compared. *Social Politics,* 13, 261–85.

Kriesi, H. (2011) Restructuration of Partisan Politics and the Emergence of a New Cleavage Based on Values. In Enyedi, Z. & Deegan-Krause, K. (Eds.) *The Structure of Political Competition in Western Europe,* London, Routledge, 259–71.

Kulawik, T. (1999) *Wohlfahrtsstaat und Mutterschaft. Schweden und Deutschland 1870–1912,* Frankfurt a.M., Campus.

Landsorganisationen (LO) (1962) Daghemsfrågan—ett arbetsmarknadsproblem, by Gustav Persson, Stockholm.

Langguth, Gerd (2007) *Angela Merkel. Aufstieg zur Macht, Biografie,* München, dtv.

Leijon, Anna-Greta (1991) *Alla rosor ska inte tuktas!* Stockholm, MånPocket.

Lewis, Jane (1992) Gender and the Development of Welfare Regimes. *Journal of European Social Policy,* 2, 159–73.

Lundström, T. & Wijkström, F. (1997) *The Nonprofit Sector in Sweden,* Manchester, Manchester University Press.

Manow, P. & van Kersbergen, K. (2009) Religion and the Western Welfare State—The Theoretical Context. In van Kersbergen, K. & Manow, P. (Eds.) *Religion, Class Coalitions and Welfare State Regimes,* Cambridge, Cambridge University Press, 1–38.

Markkola, P. (2001) Lutheranism and the Nordic Welfare States in a Gender Perspective. *Kvinder, Koen och Forskning,* 2, 10–19.

Meyer, T. (1996) Ausgerechnet jetzt. Über die Einführung des Rechtsanspruches auf einen Kindergartenplatz in der Krise des Sozialstaates. *DISKURS,* 2, 62–7.

Moeller, R. (1993) *Protecting Motherhood. Women and the Family in the Politics of Post-War West Germany,* Berkley, University of California Press.

Morgan, K. J. (2002) Forging the Frontiers Between State, Church, and Family. *Politics & Society,* 30, 113–48.

Morgan, K. J. (2006) *Working Mothers and the Welfare State. Religion and the Politics of Work-Family Policies in Western Europe and the United States,* Stanford, Stanford University Press.

Myrdal, A. (1945) *Nation and Family: The Swedish Experiment in Democratic Family and Population Policy,* Cambridge, MA, MIT Press.

Namislo, D., Schorn, K. & von Schwartzenberg, M. (2006) Wählerverhalten bei der Bundestagswahl 2005 nach Geschlecht und Alter. Ergebnisse der Repräsentativen Wahlstatistik. *Wirtschaft und Statistik,* 3, 220–37.

Naumann, I. (2005) Child Care and Feminism in West Germany and Sweden in the 1960s and 1970s. *Journal of European Social Policy,* 15, 63–79.

Naumann, I. (2006) Childcare Politics in the West German and Swedish Welfare States from the 1950s to the 1970s, PhD thesis, European University Institute, Florence.

Ostner, I. (2010) Farewell to the Family as We Know it: Family Policy Change in Germany. *German Policy Studies,* 6, 211–44.

Reyer, J. (1987) Geschichte der öffentlichen Kleinkindererziehung im Deutschen Kaiserreich, in der Weimarer Republik und in der Zeit des Nationalsozialismus. In

Erning, G., Neumann K. & Reyer, J. (Eds.) *Geschichte des Kindergartens*. Vol. 1. Freiburg i.B., Lambertus, 43–82.

Rölli-Alkemper, L. (2000) *Familie im Wiederaufbau. Katholizismus und bürgerliches Familienideal in der Bundesrepublik Deutschland, 1945–1965*, Paderborn, Ferdinand Schöningh.

Schmidt, R. (2002) *S.O.S. Familie. Ohne Kinder sehen wir alt aus*, Berlin, rowohlt.

Schorn K. & Gisart, B. (2010) Wahlverhalten bei der Bundestagswahl 2009 nach Geschlecht und Alter. Ergebnisse der repräsentativen Wahlstatistik. *Wirtschaft und Statistik*, 3, 219–36.

Sozialdemokratische Partei Deutschlands (SPD) (1998) Arbeit, Innovation und Gerechtigkeit. Das SPD Programm für die Bundestagswahl 1998.

Sozialdemokratische Partei Deutschlands (SPD) (2002) Erneuerung und Zusammenhalt. Regierungsprogramm 2002–2006.

Statistiska Centralbyrån (SCB) (2009) *Förskola i siffror*, Sveriges officiella statistik, Stockholm, SCB.

Struck, J. & Wiesner, R. (1992) Der Rechtsanspruch auf einen Kindergartenplatz. Wirkungen und Nebenwirkungen einer Entscheidung des Gesetzgebers. *Zeitschrift für Rechtspolitik*, 12, 452–6.

Sveriges Arbetarparti/Landsorganisationen (SAP/LO) (1969) *Jämlikhet. Första rapport från SAP-LOs arbetsgrupp för jämlikhetsfrågor*, Båros, Sjuhärdadsbugdens Tryckeri.

Taylor-Gooby, P. (2008) The New Welfare Settlement in Europe. *European Societies*, 10, 3–24.

Tyyskä, V. (1995) *The Politics of Caring and the Welfare State. The Impact of the Women's Movement on Child Care Policy in Canada and Finland, 1960–1990*, Helsinki, Academica Scientiarum Fennica.

Von Billerbeck, L. (2002) Die Mitte is weiblich, *DIE ZEIT*, September, <http://www.zeit.de/2002/09/Die_Mitte_ist_weiblich>, 2010 accessed 2 September.

Walter, F. (2004) Zurück zum alten Bürgertum: CDU-CSU und FDP. *Aus Politik und Zeitgeschichte*, B 40, 32–8.

9

Europe's Transformations Towards a Renewed Pension System

Bernhard Ebbinghaus

Introduction

Social protection for the elderly and people with disabilities has been, and continues to be, the largest part of welfare state activity. Not least due to demographic ageing, age-related social expenditure is expected to increase further. Social insurance against income losses due to old age and disability represents a major pillar in the more than hundred year old Bismarckian welfare systems in Continental Europe, but also the postwar Beveridge reforms in Anglophone or Nordic countries extended means-tested to universal basic pensions to all residents. The postwar 'welfare system for the elderly'[1] has been relying on the intergenerational contract between past and current cohorts, between current and future generations. The commonly shared expectation has been that the working population pays for the retired because they had previously paid into the system during their working lives and have therefore earned their retirement. However, the old welfare system for the elderly has come under severe economic, fiscal, and demographic pressures. European welfare states face multiple problems due to persistent unemployment, fiscal restrictions on public spending, and the challenges of an ageing society. Will these challenges lead to new 'leaner' welfare systems for the elderly across Europe? Will people have to provide more for themselves, work longer, and retire later, while being at greater risk of poverty in old age?

Some observers have claimed that the welfare system for the elderly is difficult to change because of the intergenerational contract. The 'new politics' of the welfare state perspective, prominently advanced by Paul Pierson (2001b), used pension policy as the prime case of path-dependent inertia and policy feedback. In the case of pay-as-you-go pensions, rewriting the intergenerational contract would be difficult due to the double-payer problem, the fact that those who pay contributions, which are used for current pensioners' acquired rights, would additionally need to save for their own future pension (Myles and Pierson 2001). Given 'blame avoidance' strategies (Weaver 1986), vote-seeking politicians would be unwilling to opt for radical reforms in order not to upset the growing older population as well as those working people who have already paid into the system and who expect to receive their promised pensions when retiring (see Bonoli, Chapter 5, for a discussion on the notion of blame avoidance). Moreover, trade unions and senior citizen groups mobilize against and use their channels of political influence to oppose such systemic reforms. Given these powerful status quo interests, there does not seem to be much opportunity for a 'new' welfare system in the entrenched policy area of pensions to arise. Yet haven't we nevertheless seen major long-term changes in recent years?

Demographic and economic pressures cannot be ignored forever, and these have led to some pension policy changes over the last three decades. Indeed, there have been ongoing transformations that will alter the welfare system for the elderly as we know it towards a more privatized, partly funded, more delayed and less sufficient income support in old age. These changes have not always been the result of high politics, some happened through 'policy drift' largely unnoticed as the consequence of (un)intended (non)action by non-state actors such as employers, financial institutions, trade unions, and individuals. Pension policy thus provides an interesting—seemingly 'least likely'—case to discover policy change in a welfare system known for its inertia. As will be shown, the welfare system for the elderly did not stand still over the last two decades.

The analysis of the transformation from the old pension system to a converted one needs to take into account the historically derived cross-national diversity in the public-private mix of Europe's pension systems (Ebbinghaus 2011). The analysis will include countries with dominantly public pensions following the Bismarckian tradition in Continental Europe (Austria, Belgium, France, and Germany) and Southern Europe (Greece, Italy, Portugal, and Spain), these provide earnings-related state pensions for most occupational groups but leave rather limited space for private funded pension development. Furthermore, the Nordic countries (Denmark, Finland, Sweden, and Norway) represent different variations of the Beveridge-tradition with basic income security but also different public or private solutions for earnings-related supplementary pensions. Moreover, we consider mature multipillar pension systems (Britain, Ireland, the Netherlands, and Switzerland) with basic pension provisions for all and rather developed private pensions, in particular (quasi-)mandatory occupational pensions. Finally, the analysis will also cover the development in some of the new EU-members in Central and Eastern Europe (Czech Republic, Estonia, Hungary, Poland, Slovakia, and Slovenia), which reformed their public pension systems with more market-oriented complements over the last two decades.

This chapter will discuss four transformative changes in pension systems across Europe that considerably alter the welfare system for the elderly. First, the pension architecture has been changing toward a multipillar system, with increased shifts from first pillar public to second pillar occupational and third pillar private personal pensions. Second, as part of the transformation toward private pensions, but also in some cases as an integral part of public provision, pre-funded pensions increase in scope as they are seen as a solution to the demographic challenge. However, the recent financial crisis has revealed some potential problems with relying mainly on funded pensions. Third, a paradigm shift also occurred through attempts to reverse the trend towards early retirement and postponed exit from work through changes in old age and disability pensions, long-term unemployment insurance, and other benefits systems. Fourth, the increased reliance on employment-related or defined-contribution benefits will increase the risk of poverty and increase inequality in old age, particularly for those new social risk groups with precarious employment. Flexible employment, low female labour force participation, and long-term unemployment together with other social inequalities will lead to lower income protection in old age. The comparative analysis thus maps four major challenges for the renewed welfare system for the elderly.

The Retreat of the State from Old Age Income Protection

Old age and disability pensions are a key pillar of modern welfare state architecture and a cornerstone of the 'European social model' (Natali 2008: 220). Thanks to public pensions, older people are able to withdraw from their working lives at a societally granted retirement age or even earlier when they fulfil special conditions. Since the 1970s, retiring around age 65 or even earlier has become the social norm for the 'Third Age' in all European welfare states (Kohli et al. 1991). Combined with societal ageing, this led to the paradox trend that people live longer, while retiring earlier and for a longer period than ever before. This has been questioned since European welfare states have grown to their limits (Flora 1986) as a consequence of rising mass unemployment, increased early retirement and inflationary pressures following the first oil crisis in 1973. Pension expenditure (about 12 per cent of GDP in the EU-27) represents the largest social protection programme in European welfare states (about 45 per cent of social expenditure that represent 7 per cent of GDP in EU-27). As a consequence of the on-going ageing of societies, the demographic dependency ratio, the share of older people (65 and older) in relation to the working age population (15 to 64 years of age), will double for the European Union to over 50 per cent until 2050, thus two working people support one elderly. Parallel to such demographic developments, global economic challenges have placed considerable constraints on welfare states in times of 'permanent austerity' (Pierson 2001a).

These economic and demographic problems challenge the financial sustainability of public pensions, particularly in pay-as-you-go (PAYG) systems that use incoming contributions for current pensioners. International organizations such as the World Bank and OECD, but also national policymakers and their economic advisers, have long advocated for a shift away from PAYG-financed public pensions towards mainly prefunded private pensions (World Bank 1994; OECD 1998). This is largely motivated by an economic logic of financial *sustainability* in ageing societies under fiscal austerity, though a secondary aim is often also to boost financial capital markets in order to foster economic growth. The transformation from public to private pension was introduced rather gradually since the 1980s, as radical approaches to reshape pension systems were constrained by the specific institutional structure already in place, thus, for instance, the Thatcher government's effort to abolish the state second pension largely failed (Pierson 1994). Nevertheless, there have been considerable sequences of changes even in Bismarckian welfare systems of Continental Europe (Bonoli and Palier 2007; Palier 2010) that have led to a restructuring of the welfare system for the elderly.

The new pressures and challenges translated into different problems depending on the existing arrangements and governance institutions. Pension systems vary in the historically evolved public-private mix, following either a more Bismarckian tradition of maintaining income through earnings-related state pensions or a Beveridge-model of combining public basic pensions and (mainly private) supplementary pensions. We can distinguish different public-private configurations with specific problem loads (Ebbinghaus and Gronwald 2011): Continental dominant public pension systems are late in developing a multipillar system, Nordic pension systems with hybrid privatization tendencies, and mature mulitpillar systems (Britain, the Netherlands and Switzerland). Countries with an expensive PAYG-financed Bismarckian public pension in Continental Europe engaged in introducing new pillars of occupational and/or personal pensions, while simultaneously cutting back public pensions. The Nordic countries combine universal public pensions with specific second-tier pensions, though adopting very hybrid multipillar solutions. Countries with developed multipillar systems were mainly concerned with the improvement of the regulatory framework for private pensions under the new economic conditions. Since the 1990s, the transformation of socialist to market-oriented systems in new EU member states in Central and Eastern Europe (CEE) led to the introduction of private funded pensions in addition to rather meagre public old age pension insurance (Orenstein 2008a).

The cross-national variation in public-private mix can be seen in public, mandatory private and voluntary private pension expenditures (see Figure 9.1). The Bismarckian pension systems of Continental Europe (Austria, Belgium, Germany, France, and Italy) spent since the 1980s a substantial share of resources (more than 12 per cent of GDP) on old age and disability pensions, largely through public pay-as-you-go schemes (only Belgium has a significant share of voluntary expenditure). Also Spain, Portugal, and Greece have expanded their pension expenditure since their democratization and EU membership in the mid-1980s, but they still have not reached the expensive level of the Italian 'pensioner state' (Ferrera 2000). The new EU members from Central and Eastern Europe provide largely public pensions, varying from a very low level in Estonia and Slovakia, to a medium level in the Czech Republic, to a rather high 'Bismarckian' level in Hungary, Slovenia, and Poland. The newly introduced private-funded pensions are not yet mature; instead, the public pay-as-you-go systems still determine current retirees' income. Among the Beveridge multipillar systems with basic public security,

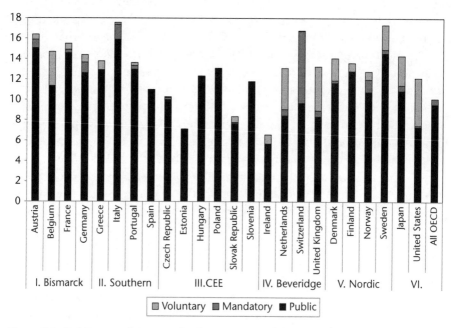

Figure 9.1. Public, mandatory, and voluntary expenditures on old age, survivor, and disability pensions (%GDP) in 2007

Source: OECD Social Expenditure Database 1980–2007, Paris, OECD <www.sourceOECD.org>, 2011.

Ireland spends a relatively low level due to its young population, while the Netherlands, the United Kingdom, and Switzerland spend a medium level (around 10 per cent) via public pensions and a substantial share of funded private pensions. Among the Nordic countries, a high share of expenditure is still provided by public pensions, but mandatory personal and negotiated occupational pensions have grown in recent years. Thus, Europe's public pensions are more in line with Japan than with the liberal United States, with the exception of a few low spenders (Estonia, Slovakia and Ireland).

The recent transformation of the public-private pension mix varies across Europe (Natali 2008; Ebbinghaus 2011). Some of these changes have been relatively slow in retrenching the public pillar, in particular the more generous pensions, and by introducing measures in reaction to the increased need to regulate occupational and personal pensions. Yet there were also important path 'departures' in the public pillar, most notably the pension reforms in Sweden and Italy in the mid-1990s. These reforms introduced 'notional' defined contributions (NDC) which make public benefits dependent on individual working life contributions and the macroeconomic-demographic development. Elsewhere, demographic adjustment factors were also introduced to make PAYG-systems more sustainable in ageing societies. For instance, a 'sustainability' factor was introduced in Germany as of 2005. Also notable were the introduction of funded personal pensions in public first pillars (an important component of the Swedish reform) and the emergence of voluntary personal pensions, for instance, in Germany, Finland, and France. Most notable for a shift toward funded systems was their introduction in CEE countries in the late 1990s or early 2000s, in particular Estonia, Hungary, Poland, and Slovakia (Müller 2001; Orenstein 2008a).

Institutional change often occurred as twin processes in public and private pensions: reduction of the former increased the push for expansion of the latter. These new private pension arrangements add a new layer to the multipillar, multitier retirement income system. They bring about transformative change without completely altering the public pillar, though there is a long-term conversion from the status maintenance to a basic income function in the Bismarckian systems. These reform steps indicate a gradual path departure moderated by institutional layering, conversion or displacement (Streeck and Thelen 2005), depending on institutional capacities and preconditions. In the long-run, these institutional changes may be the first steps towards a more substantial change in the public-private mix of the future. While the state partially retreated from its responsibilities to finance adequate state pensions, the scope for public regulation and control of private pensions increased, at least potentially. The need for regulation and the political relevance of pensions has increased due to privatization, in particular with the shift towards funded pensions (Leisering 2006). In respect to their social outcome, these transformations of the welfare system for the elderly have made pension benefits far more dependent on individual labour market performance. This is the case through NDC or point systems in earnings-related public pensions systems as well as through firm-sponsored DB or personal DC contributions in privately funded pensions. The future pension system will thus be more detrimental to those with atypical or lacking employment due to family care responsibilities, unemployment and low employability.

Financialization and Pension Fund Capitalism

Following the advice from international organizations and national economic policy advisors, privately funded pension systems have gained importance in Europe and across the World (Brooks 2005; Orenstein 2008b). While PAYG-systems are seen as unsustainable given the ageing of societies and public finance constraints, the claim is that funded systems will rely on savings for old age retirement independent of demographic developments. Moreover, funded pensions also foster capital markets, thereby at least partly increasing also domestic economic growth. Although some countries have a long tradition in pension fund capitalism, other European countries have only recently decided to change from predominantly public to multipillar pension schemes (Ebbinghaus and Wiß 2011). The Anglophone 'Liberal Market Economies' (LME), the United Kingdom and Ireland, have extended pension fund assets given the rather limited basic pensions and long tradition of occupational pensions. However, there are also two Continental European countries that have developed considerable funded occupational pensions on top of first tier public pensions: the Netherlands with negotiated supplementary pensions, and Switzerland with mandatory occupational pensions. In addition, there is wide variation with respect to Nordic pension systems, including funded elements as part of mandatory public pensions (Sweden), mandated occupational pensions (Finland), and negotiated occupational pensions (Denmark). The Continental European countries with a Bismarck public pension tradition were late in developing funded pensions, though recent reforms might be able to alter this in the future. Finally, following the introduction of market economies, major reforms in pension systems of Central and Eastern Europe have growing privately funded pensions, particularly in Hungary (until 2010), Poland, and the Baltic countries (Müller 2001; Müller 2008; Orenstein 2008a).

The difference in the scope of pension fund development depends on the timing and degree of state or collective regulation, as well as on the need and incentives to save. In addition, general tax incentives or special subsidies for low income groups also provide possibilities for fostering the development of private pension savings, a rather 'hidden side' (Howard 1997) of welfare state

activity. Thus direct intervention (mandatory membership by law), interme-
diary action (extension of collective agreements) or indirect means (tax
incentives), together with self-regulatory collective agreements, are crucial in
extending the scope of funded private pension systems. In addition, the long-
term cut backs in PAYG-systems will lower future public benefits, thereby
increase the pension gap to maintain living standards and thus increase the
pressure towards private savings. We would expect the reversed effect of past
'crowding-out' when public pensions are scaled back, thus the retreat of the
state from old age income maintenance would be fostering the growth of
funded private pensions. However, this is dependent on additional factors,
not least the willingness of the social partners, the employers or individuals to
save for old age.

In contrast to the current private pension expenditure already discussed, the
scope of current pension fund assets (see Figure 9.2) provides a more significant indicator of the potential impact of private pension on old age income
(OECD 2011), though it is more difficult to evaluate its future scope. In Iceland, the Netherlands, and Switzerland, autonomous pension funds have
invested more than the annual economic activity, followed by the United
Kingdom and Finland (around 50 per cent), as well as Ireland and Denmark
(40 per cent of GDP). In addition, personal pensions via life or group insurance
contracts also play an important role in the Nordic countries, in particular
Denmark. In contrast, Continental Bismarckian systems, and all Central and

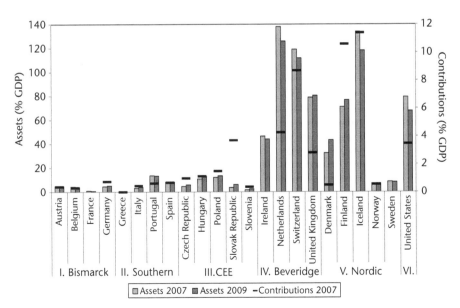

Figure 9.2. Assets and contributions to private pension funds (%GDP) in 2007/2009
Source: OECD Pension Database, Paris, OECD <www.sourceOECD.org>, 2011.

Eastern European countries still have underdeveloped pension funds (less than 15 per cent of GDP). Except for Portugal, Poland, and Hungary, all other countries have thus far developed rather unimportant pension funds (less than 10 per cent of GDP in 2009). Also with respect to contributions (OECD 2011), these are relatively unimportant (below 1 per cent of GDP), except in Slovakia, Poland, and Hungary. Given the rather low accumulated savings, these recently introduced funded private pensions are not paying out much in benefits thus far (less than 1 per cent of GDP), though this will change in the future. Hungary even rolled back its funded pensions in 2011.

The financial crisis hit capital markets considerably in late 2008, immediately impacting on pension funds. Within a year, assets declined by more than 25 per cent in the United States, Iceland, and Ireland, while most other European pension funds had a nominal decline by more than 10 per cent, but less than 20 per cent, with few exceptions (OECD 2010; Pino and Yermo 2010). Given the partial recovery thereafter, the assets have recuperated, but not necessarily made up for the losses by 2010 (and it will be unlikely in 2011). The differential losses are largely determined by the investment portfolio, in particular risky stock market investments (equities, currencies, hedge funds, commodity trading) vis-à-vis more conservative investments (in particular, public bonds, non-risky loans, and domestic real estate). Regulation with explicit portfolio standards can be crucial in limiting the exposure to risky investment: the particularly high losses in Ireland are due to the large exposure to foreign risky investment, while the exceptionally unbuttered Danish pensions are a result of their investment in bonds. Besides regulation, the governance of pension funds, that is, who decides and who controls pension investments, is also crucial (Ebbinghaus and Wiß 2011). Privately funded pensions thus depend on a set of regulations by the state and other collective actors, as well as many decisions by employers, social partners, and individuals.

The immediate consequences of the financial market crash for current and future pensioners are very different depending on the scope and maturity of funded pensions. In already mature multipillar systems, the current financial crises had direct effects for all those close to or already on retirement if they had not yet transferred their savings into life annuities. Lower than expected pension returns, and therefore delaying retirement, would be the most likely consequence. In the Netherlands, Switzerland, and the United Kingdom, funded private pensions are already contributing to more than 40 per cent of pension income for more than half of the elderly population (Ebbinghaus and Neugschwender 2011). Any decline in private pensions will make maintaining living standards more difficult, but whether it affects poverty depends on the minimum income protection through basic public pensions or means-tested assistance (Bahle et al. 2011). In the countries in which privately funded pensions are still developing, the current crisis has led to a blow in public expectations and could affect future savings behaviour in voluntary systems. In the CEE countries, there have been attempts to revisit the funded pension strategy and refocus on public pay-as-you-go systems that would provide less financial market risks; most notable is Hungary's turn-around in nationalizing prefunded pensions (Orenstein 2011).

There are also further consequences of the financial crisis on the financing mechanism of funded pensions, revealing the particular problem of who will be responsible of liabilities and who owns surpluses. The crisis put particular pressure on defined benefit (DB) systems, where employers or a collective fund promises retirement benefits in return for contributions. In fact, DB systems are threatened by the underfunding of their liabilities, thus requiring an increase in contributions, and/or a cut in benefits, though it depends on the regulations in place (for instance, in the Netherlands the underfunding ratio was made less strict, see Anderson 2011). Also in defined contribution (DC) with a guaranteed minimum rate of return, similar problems can arise (for example in Switzerland, the minimum rate was lowered by the Federal government, see Bonoli and Häusermann 2011). In general, pressures on companies to withdraw from DB schemes will be further propelled, thereby increasing even more the tendency to individualize the financial risks on individuals. While employers had used DB schemes for binding skilled workers to their firm and using surpluses in pension funds to finance early exits in order to restructure their workforce, a further shift toward DC schemes will enhance transportability but also individualize financial risks, while employers no longer take any particular responsibility for old age income.

Privately funded pensions are not new to European welfare systems, but they have grown in importance or changed their character where they already existed for a longer time. They were set-up to provide more economically sustainable protection against income insecurity in old age in ageing societies. However, from the two financial crises of the 2000s, we learn a lesson already taught by the Great Depression of the late 1920s that prefunded pensions may entail considerable uncertainty about the risk of short-term financial crisis and unfounded expectations of long-term rates of return. We face a double paradox: the more policies will seek to lower the financial risks of prefunded pensions, the less these will be able to offer higher benefits than pay-as-you-go systems, while the more financial market risks are allowed, the more we will be uncertain about whether the risk of old age income security can be fully insured. The increased privatization and financialization of pensions thus entails considerable insecurity, in addition to the social differences entailed by different employment and income prospects across social groups.

Reversing Early Exit from Work and Active Ageing

Since the 1970s, early exit from work before the age of 65 has become a widespread social practice in most advanced welfare states for adjusting to social and economic pressure in a socially acceptable way (Kohli et al. 1991; Ebbinghaus 2006; Hofäcker 2010). As a consequence, the transition from work to retirement was no longer exclusively regulated by the statutory old age pension, but depended on the personal and social situation of older workers as well as general economic and firm-related conditions. Both the availability of preretirement benefits (the 'pull' factor) and an economic environment leading to labour shedding (the 'push' factor) led to massive early retirement in many European economies. Variations across welfare regimes, however, were significant (Ebbinghaus 2006): Continental European social insurance systems facilitated massive early retirement, whereas the Scandinavian welfare states aimed at maintaining old-age employment levels and Anglophone liberal market economies induced shorter waves of early exit during economic downturns. In the 1990s, fewer than every third man aged 60–64 was still working in Continental European welfare states and in most of Central and Eastern European new transition economies, whereas about every second in the Nordic welfare states and the Anglophone liberal economies. Since the OECD's 1994 Job Study and EU's Lisbon Strategy since 1999, international and national policymakers called for reducing disincentives to work and increasing employment rates. A paradigm shift has occurred in both pension and employment policies, instead of early retirement as a passive labour market policy, the aim today is to retain older workers longer in working life and postpone retirement (OECD 2000). This will not only reduce expenditure, but also increase social or tax contributions and lead to higher economic growth.

Reversing early exit from work has proven difficult as the trend towards early retirement has been common in European welfare states, particularly in those providing multiple 'pathways' to early exit from work (Kohli et al. 1991). Focusing on the pull effect of welfare benefits, economists seek to explain early retirement as a worker's individual choice. According to this labour supply model, early exit from work pays off when the wealth accrual from preretirement benefits exceeds the net wage earnings from continued work; therefore, economists recommend an increase in retirement age and defined contribution schemes to eliminate disincentives to work (Gruber and Wise 1999). This incentive model neither explains why some welfare states facilitate early retirement more than others, nor why older workers have a higher risk of dismissal and unemployment. Comparative studies have shown that there are considerable regime-induced variations in the availability of 'pathways' to early exit, both public programmes and firm-sponsored plans (Kohli et al. 1991).

Old age pensions provide an exit pathway, though this often represented an unintended consequence of socially motivated policies. Due to paternalist concerns, women were granted an earlier statutory pension age in some countries (e.g. Britain and Italy), though these rules are being phased out, partly because of EU law on gender equality and fiscal concerns. In addition, flexible pensions allow earlier drawing of benefits, sometimes without or with only a small reduction in benefits, though again financial penalties have become more common across systems. Where flexible pensions are unavailable (e.g. British or Dutch basic pensions), occupational plans by firms may top up or replace public benefits, albeit the move from DB to DC occupational pensions makes this less attractive. Taking into account long working lives, some Continental European countries granted workers under 65 early statutory pensions or special seniority rules, though most of these programmes have been gradually closed since the 1990s. Largely motivated as labour reduction policies, unemployment benefits and special preretirement schemes are additional pathways. Given their higher risk of joblessness, older workers could draw on long-term unemployment benefits without active job-search, except in liberal welfare regimes. In addition, governments or the social partners set up preretirement schemes, some of which required replacement by a job-seeker, but already during the 1980s, several of these schemes were reduced or closed due to their high costs and limited employment effects. Disability pensions for workers with age-related health impairments are a further pathway. While Britain pays meagre benefits and only applies medical considerations, most Continental and Scandinavian disability schemes provide generous benefits, grant 'partial incapacity' benefits, and consider the labour market situation. Again, there have been reforms limiting the take-up of disability pensions, most notably in the Netherlands in the 1990s.

In addition, economic 'push' factors are at work (Ebbinghaus 2006). In the face of increased deindustrialization, mass unemployment, and international competition, the available exit pathways provide opportunities for labour shedding. Early retirement can facilitate downsizing or restructuring of a firm's workforce in a consensual way. It also allows circumventing employment protection law, union-imposed seniority rules ('last in, first out'), and age-related wage scales. Politicians, unionists and workplace representatives initially embraced 'early exit' as a way to reduce labour supply and open up positions for job-seekers. In Continental Europe, the externalization of adaptation costs onto publicly financed schemes was often facilitated by self-administration delegated to the social partners. Scandinavian governments have been more committed to active labour market policies and subsidies of partial pensions, at least until the unprecedented unemployment in the early 1990s. Given limited public pathways, large British companies use firm-sponsored plans to induce early retirement, but risks are increasingly shifted to individuals. In general, ageism in hiring, work organization, training and firing contributes greatly to older workers' labour market problems. Thus, early exit is also a consequence of firms' production strategies and 'human resource management' (Naschold and de Vroom 1994).

Massive use of early retirement, particularly in Continental Europe since the 1970s and CEE countries since the 1990s, has been driving up social expenditure and labour costs, reinforcing—not alleviating—unemployment problems. The OECD recommends that 'public pension systems, taxation systems and social transfer programmes should be reformed to remove financial incentives to early retirement, and financial incentives to later retirement' (OECD 2000: 8). Employability of older workers and continued training ('lifelong learning') are other areas for action, particularly promoted by the European Employment Strategy (Jespen et al. 2002). Nevertheless, welfare state reforms affecting exit from work still occurs in the national arena in response to the particular problem load, institutional capacities and political reform coalitions. Retrenchment occurred mainly on the incentive side, motivated by fiscal considerations, bringing social expenditure under control and making transfer systems sustainable. Although past practices provide major obstacles for reform as actors at various levels have grown accustomed to early retirement, recent reform efforts have led to a slow change. Some countries have accelerated their way out of the impasse, most notably the Netherlands, Denmark, and more recently Germany, while some still remain stuck in an undecided switch of direction. A major reason for this difficulty in reversing early exit is the institutionalization of early retirement practices in welfare state and production systems, as well as the interest of coalitions of workers and employers supporting these.

As part of its Lisbon Strategy, the European Council in Stockholm, 2001, set a target employment rate of 50 per cent among women and men aged 55 to 64 by 2010 (see Figure 9.3). The Continental European countries have had a long history of relatively low employment. Even by the target year 2010, the old age employment rate is below the EU-target in the Bismarckian Continental welfare states (Austria, Belgium, and France) as well as in southern Europe (Italy, Greece, and Spain), with the notable exception of Germany and Portugal with recent turnarounds. Not only early retirement among older men, but also relatively early retirement and low levels of employment among older women has led to the low employment levels in Continental Europe. Similarly, the transition economies experienced massive early exit and low levels of old age employment, though Estonia is an exception among CEE countries. The Anglophone liberal welfare states, but also after recent turnarounds the Netherlands, Denmark, and Finland, exceed the EU target, while Switzerland has always had a high level of activation, similar to the level achieved in

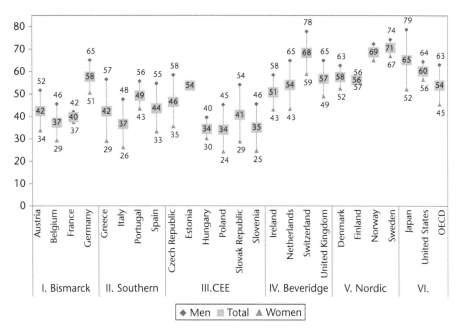

Figure 9.3. Employment rate of older people (age 55–64) in 2010
Source: OECD Labour Force Statistics 1960–2010, Paris: OECD (www.sourceOECD.org), 2011.

Norway and Sweden. While there are still notable gender differences, these are particularly small in some of the Nordic countries (and Estonia).

In order to lower early retirement and postpone exit from work, some of the following measures have been embraced over the last two decades (Ebbinghaus 2006): raising the pension age (ending special rules for women or long-term contributors); reducing disincentives to work (shifting to actuarially fair flexible pensions and defined contribution benefits); closing special schemes (or tightening replacement conditions); limiting unemployment pathways (benefit retrenchment, introducing active job search and training); tightening disability conditions (restricting labour market consideration, reforming implementation). However, interventions in one pathway often simply lead to substitution with the second-best alternative, merely shifting costs between public programmes, unless privatization transfers the burden to firms or workers. Given the social partners' interest in early exit and its overall popularity, retrenchment attempts met considerable political resistance. Thus, some governments have engaged in social dialogue, negotiating phased-in reforms and delegating some issues to collective bargaining. Some of the recent phased-in reforms to extend retirement age in the future have been widely discussed. Most notably, Greece and Spain, hit by the financial market and sovereign debt crisis, but also France with a long early retirement tradition, have introduced recent pension reform efforts that met wide public outcry. Also, in the future, the renewed welfare systems across European countries will continue the substantial push towards delayed exit from work and higher activation rates among older workers. The main concern will be whether those unable to find suitable work will meet long periods of old age unemployment and suffer from low pension income.

As long as the underlying push factors remain potent, welfare cut backs will not be very effective or even counterproductive. There is also a need to adapt working conditions to prevent impairments and to better suit older workers' needs, all areas for improvement at the workplace level. Partial pensions, pioneered in Sweden, could smooth the transition from work to retirement, and help retain experienced workers, but its success depends on employers' offering part-time jobs. Laws and information campaigns against discrimination are means to combat ageism in hiring, training, and firing. Also, public labour market policies need to embrace activation and training measures for older unemployed workers, while the social partners should reconsider age-related bargaining policies that intensify the early-exit push (Jespen et al. 2002). Given early retirement's complexity as a social practice and the large cross-national variations, no one solution can reverse the early-exit trend and provide a solution for all. We need sound policies to promote active ageing and sustainable pension policies to meet the new exigencies, otherwise unemployment and poverty may further increase for older people.

The Return of Old Age Poverty

Pension reforms over the last two decades cut back public pension benefits, gradually extended the official retirement age, and fostered privately funded pensions, although many of these changes will be more visible in the future. While the sustainability endeavour was driving much of these pension reforms, the *adequacy* of retirement income has often been neglected from current public debates, partly because poverty in old age seems to be no longer such a pressing concern in Europe's advanced welfare states. Poverty and income inequality varies across pension systems in Europe; they are also on the rise, due to the continued retreat of public pensions and the larger reliance on voluntary prefunded private pensions. The shift towards more occupational and personal pensions has had, and will have, major repercussions for the income situation of older people today and in the future. While public insurance provides more universal and redistributive social benefits by mandating wide coverage and by pooling risks, private pensions tend to reproduce, if not amplify, market-income inequalities existent during working life in the period after retirement. Unless mandated by law or enforced by collective

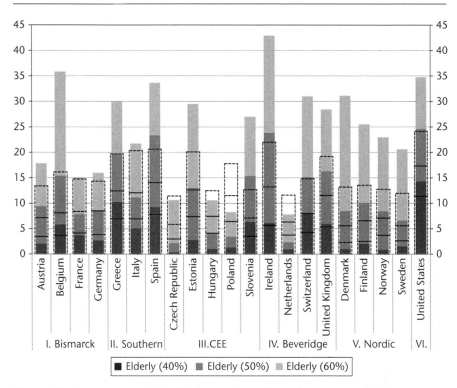

Figure 9.4. Poverty rates of the elderly vs. the total population around 2005

Note: Household adjusted poverty rates at 40%, 50%, and 60% median income; elderly (shades of grey): age 65 and older; population (broken lines): poverty figure for total population; 2005 except Belgium: 2000.
Source: Luxembourg Income Study, Key Indicators, Luxembourg, LIS <www.lisdatacenter.org>, 2011.

agreements, voluntary private pensions are less widespread and provide non-redistributive benefits that depend solely on contributions. Furthermore, private pensions are increasingly based not on defined benefits (DB), but rather on defined contributions (DC) that are fully funded and dependent on cumulative returns of capital. This shifts financial risks onto individuals. Quite clearly, the financial and economic crises around 2001/2002 and 2008/2009 indicated the sometimes substantial risk of funded pensions: in countries with high-risk investment strategies, invested assets declined substantially.

Cross-national comparison shows considerable variation across Europe (Ebbinghaus and Neugschwender 2011) when we analyse poverty rates measured at 40, 50, or 60 per cent of median income (see Figure 9.4). An analysis of severe and conventional poverty rates in old age (measured at 40 per cent and 50 per cent of median income) reveals that Beveridge basic security is not always capable of effectively reducing poverty despite the explicit purpose to do so, while some contributory Bismarckian systems are better suited to reduce poverty, despite focusing on status maintenance. The lowest poverty rates are found in the case of the relatively generous Dutch basic pension, as well at the Danish basic pension (and tested supplement). Before recent reforms, Finland and Sweden showed very low poverty rates for the universal basic and earnings-related pensions (Kangas and Palme 1996), and the new system with transfer-tested pension guarantees fares very well. In contrast, Ireland, the United Kingdom, and Switzerland with basic security and Belgium, Greece, Italy, and Spain as well as Slovenia with social insurance pensions have the highest severe and conventional poverty rates, particularly Ireland, Spain, and Greece come close to US levels. Considering the at-risk-of-poverty rate (at 60 per cent-level), the elderly population is more at risk than the working population with the exception of the social insurance systems of France, Germany, Czech Republic, Hungary, and Poland as well as the Dutch multipillar system. In the other countries, whether Beveridge multipillar systems (Britain, Ireland, Switzerland), mixed systems of all Nordic countries or pure Bismarckian systems (Belgium, Greece, Italy, and Spain), the contributory earnings-related elements of public or private pensions lead to significant levels of at-risk-of-poverty for more than every fifth elderly person.

The impact of multipillar systems, in comparison to dominantly public pension systems, on poverty and inequality in old age is rather mixed, suggesting that the effect of privatization depends not merely on the public-private mix as such, but much more on its design (Rein and Turner 2004). To reduce severe poverty among those of retirement age, minimum income security via first-tier pension arrangements, in particular sufficient basic, guaranteed, or minimum pensions are important. This will become even more crucial given the interrupted and non-standard employment careers of the current and future workforce. In addition, the earnings-related pensions are essential for maintaining living standards for the majority of those who expect more than a minimum provision. While Bismarckian systems traditionally provide such earnings-related public pensions, the Beveridge basic pension systems rely on second-tier state pensions or on private occupational and personal pensions. While state pensions provide some redistributive features, in particular social credits, for instance for child-caring activities, private pensions rarely achieve social goals, unless tax subsidies, state regulation, or collective agreements intervene. Among current pensioners, most multipillar systems achieve lower poverty and inequality than the Bismarckian earnings-related pensions, though Britain and Ireland perform badly on both. Since pension benefits are the major income source for the majority of retirees, inequalities in old age derive largely from the design of the public-private pension mix.

Access conditions, contribution records, and benefit regulations are all crucial factors affecting the impact of private pensions on old age income inequality. Mandatory supplementary pensions (as in Finland, France, and Switzerland) as well as wide-spread collective agreements (as in Denmark, Netherlands, and Sweden and, more recently in Belgium, Germany, and Italy) are important to increase coverage among current workers. The British 'contracting out' of private pensions and the German tax incentives for personal pensions are also means to increase coverage, but at the cost of tax expenditures. Today's rate of recipients depends on past efforts, thus only the mature multipillar systems have achieved a high and more equal distribution of private pensions with respect to gender, household type, and income group. Among current recipients, the public pillar still dominates in Belgium and Italy, while Germany and Denmark have assumed medium levels and the other multipillar systems already have widespread second and third pillar pensions, although some vulnerable groups may be underrepresented.

There are significant disparities with respect to gender, household, and income group: women, single pensioners, and low income households rely much more on public pensions than do the other social groups (Ebbinghaus and Neugschwender 2011). In multipillar pension systems (such as Britain, Denmark, Netherlands, and Switzerland), the highest income group profits most from supplementing their public retirement income via funded pensions. As a consequence, in these countries private pensions have become a major cause of the reproduction of market income inequalities in old age—at least above the level of public basic security. The Bismarckian systems, designed to maintain status, have effectively reproduced inequalities from their early days. Although these countries have increasingly introduced socially redistributive elements such as child rearing credits, the recent reforms will again reduce public pension benefits, which will provide room for market-induced inequalities through voluntary private pensions, unless state or collective regulation succeeds in increasing coverage and socially redistributive elements.

Although public pensions, particularly in multipillar systems, have reduced the risk of poverty and the degree of inequality in old age, the different combinations of public-private mix still entail a relatively similar overall reproduction of social inequalities found prior to retirement (Ebbinghaus and Neugschwender 2011). Individual pension income and inequalities in resources in old age derive from particular features of the pension system design: in the Bismarckian predominantly public pension systems via their general equivalence principle, in the mature and emerging multipillar systems via the major importance of earnings-related pensions for the income of the broad majority in the future, and in the hybrid systems via their mixed structure, which also links current labour market integration to later benefits. Recent policy reforms will have major effects, many of which will only become visible in the coming decades. The increased emphasis on occupational and personal pensions results from attempts to offset the costs of public insurance in ageing societies and under fiscal austerity. However, public pensions that provide universal minimum income in old age will become even more important in the future. Moreover, as European welfare states have been challenged by the financial and economic crises of the 2000s, individuals relying on funded pensions have also faced increased financial risks, and these may continue to grow as the reliance on the performance of privately funded pensions. Only broad-based public policies and collectively negotiated self-regulation can pool risks and redistribute social benefits to effectively counteract social inequalities in the lengthening phase of life after retirement. In the future, the on-going trend of privatization may lead to a gradual convergence of countries as their pension systems become multi-pillar. As shown for the selected European pension systems, the shift toward increasing privatization amplifies the already existing level of social inequality in these ageing societies.

Conclusion

The transformation of the welfare systems for the elderly across Europe has been happening, and will continue, mostly in slow motion. These changes occurred partly through some major systemic reforms, but more often through multiple smaller public policy interventions, sometimes through non-decisions by public actors, and by subterranean adaptations by non-state actors such as employers, unions, and individuals. The main features of the renewed welfare state for the elderly have taken shape at least in its contours. The state no longer guarantees the same living standard maintained through public pensions for its current, and in particular future retirees, as it did for former retiring generations. This chapter explored four transformations of pension policy and its impact on the new welfare system in Europe, discussing the differences across still mainly Bismarckian public systems and the Beveridge-type mulitipillar systems.

The *first* major transformation changed the goals of *public* policy for old age. After many more or less important reform steps, the public PAYG-pension systems in Europe will provide leaner benefits due to the freezing of contribution rates, economic and demographic automatic stabilizers, and the larger reliance on contributory benefits over the entire working life. The new welfare system for the elderly is one where the state assumes more limited responsibility for providing minimum social protection, and often retracts from guaranteeing achieved living standards. This retreat of the state, however, will not end but downscale its commitment of significant public resources as it provides, on average, lower benefits for ever more pensioners due to its financial constraints. This may lead to a shift from broad pension policy for all to more targeted social measures, preventing poverty and compensating for some disadvantages, while leaving the maintenance of living standards to the market actors: employers, unions, and individuals.

The *second*, parallel transformation has been the increased *privatization* of pension provision across Europe, in particular we witness a shift towards funded pensions with more individual responsibility and risk-bearing. The long-term conversion of the public pension systems is supposed to be compensated by privately funded pensions through public mandate, collective agreements, employer benevolence, or foresighted individual savings. However, it remains questionable whether this will be the case for all and whether these supplementary pensions suffice; this largely depends on the governance and regulation of these private pensions. Although all European countries move toward a multipillar system, pension fund capitalism first developed in the Anglophone, partly Nordic, and some Continental European countries (the Netherlands and Switzerland). The current financial crisis has a significant impact on current and expected future returns of funded pensions, requiring immediate responses and long-term regulatory adaptation. The more funded pensions rely on risky investments, and the more benefits are based on defined contributions, the more these financial risks will become individualized. In the countries with developing private pensions, particularly in Eastern and Southern Europe, the current crisis may have a dampening effect on future development, and some calls for a reversal have been voiced. Although the state may have retreated from direct commitments, through its tax treatment and regulation it indirectly supports and steers funded pensions. Also, non-state actors, the employers, unions, and the financial sector play a varying role in self-regulating funded pensions—this is the other hidden side of the 'new' welfare system. Governance matters for pensions: decisions by many corporate and individual actors about savings need to be adopting an appropriate savings strategy for old age income.

The *third* transformation is the reversal of early exit from work, in order to lower the number of those drawing pensions prematurely and increasing the share of those contributing through gainful work to pension financing. This policy change has been paradigmatic: it follows not only from policies to cut cost pressures, but also from a new concept of 'active ageing' and employment growth, replacing earlier policies of labour shedding and redistributing work from the old to the young. Not only does public pension policy have to be adapted to lower the disincentives to continue working for older workers, but also the rules of disability benefits, long-term unemployment, and special preretirement programmes have to be altered. These interdependencies require coordination across several social policy fields. Yet pull-oriented social policy changes, though more steerable by government, do not suffice in order to achieve the policy goal of active ageing. Economic push-factors also need to be addressed, that is, the pressures of seniority wages, outdated skills, and restructuring needs. This requires concerted action of many actors from firm to workplace representatives and older workers: ending ageist personnel policies of firms, investing in life-long continuing vocational training, adapting work environments and active labour market policies for older workers. If these accompanying policies fail and social protection has become more lean or unavailable, older workers may not only face long-term unemployment, but also poverty.

Finally, the *fourth* transformation, a potential increase in old age poverty for social risk groups, may result from the previously mentioned developments: the cutting back of public pensions, the insecurities of funded pensions, and potential threat of unemployment among older workers. The public pension system (including social assistance) remains to be the main protector against old age poverty. Both well-developed Beveridge basic pension systems, and relatively well-developed Bismarckian systems have been able to lower old age poverty thus far. However, old age poverty may indeed increase in the future, increasing political pressures to raise basic pension levels or provide guaranteed minimum income in earnings-related systems. The increased tightening of benefits to the employment relationship and contribution record in both public and private pensions will further lead to inequalities between those that have had advantageous employment, and those with precarious jobs and new social risks. The retreat of the state from its old age protection goal may ironically increase the political pressures for its increased role in securing and regulating old age income provision in old age. The transformed welfare system for the elderly may thus require further adaptations by policymakers and non-state actors.

Notes

1. Since old age pensions are provided by a variety of actors (public agencies, employers, pension funds, private insurances) the term 'welfare system' is used instead of 'welfare state'.

Bibliography

Anderson, K. (2011) The Netherlands: Adopting a Multipillar Pension System to Demographic and Economic Change. In Ebbinghaus, B. (Ed.) *The Varieties of Pension Governance: Pension Privatization in Europe*, Oxford, Oxford University Press, 292–317.

Bahle, T. Hubl, V. & Pfeiffer, M. (2011) *The Last Safety Net: A Handbook of Minimum Income Protection in Europe*, Bristol, Policy Press.

Bonoli, G. & Häusermann, S. (2011) Switzerland: Regulating a Public-Private Heritage of Multipillar Pension Governance. In Ebbinghaus, B. (Ed.) *The Varieties of Pension Governance: Pension Privatization in Europe*, Oxford, Oxford University Press, 318–47.

Bonoli, G. & Palier, B. (2007) When Past Reforms Open New Opportunities: Comparing Old-Age Insurance Reforms in Bismarckian Welfare Systems. *Social Policy & Administration*, 41, 21–39.

Brooks, S. (2005) Interdependent and Domestic Foundations of Policy Change: The Diffusion of Pension Privatization Around the World. *International Studies Quarterly*, 49, 273–94.

Ebbinghaus, B. (2006) *Reforming Early Retirement in Europe, Japan and the USA*, Oxford, Oxford University Press.

Ebbinghaus, B. (Ed.) (2011) *The Varieties of Pension Governance: Pension Privatization in Europe*, Oxford, Oxford University Press.

Ebbinghaus, B. & Gronwald, M. (2011) The Changing Public-Private Pension Mix in Europe: From Path Dependence to Path Departure. In Ebbinghaus, B. (Ed.) *The Varieties of Pension Governance: Pension Privatization in Europe*, Oxford, Oxford University Press, 23–53.

Ebbinghaus, B. & Neugschwender, J. (2011) The Public–Private Pension Mix and Old Age Income Inequality in Europe. In Ebbinghaus, B. (Ed.) *The Varieties of Pension Governance: Pension Privatization in Europe*, Oxford, Oxford University Press, 384–422.

Ebbinghaus, B. & Wiß, T. (2011) The Governance and Regulation of Private Pensions in Europe. In Ebbinghaus, B. (Ed.) *The Varieties of Pension Governance: Pension Privatization in Europe*, Oxford, Oxford University Press, 351–83.

Ferrera, M. (2000) Reconstructing the Welfare State in Southern Europe. In Kuhnle, S. (Ed.) *Survival of the European Welfare State*, London, Routledge, 166–81.

Flora, P. (1986) Introduction. In Flora, P. (Ed.) *Growth to Limits: The Western European Welfare States Since World War II*, Berlin, de Gruyter, XII–XXXVI.

Gruber, J. & Wise, D. A. (Eds.) (1999) *Social Security and Retirement around the World*, Chicago, University of Chicago Press.

Hofäcker, D. (2010) *Older Workers in a Globalizing World. An International Comparison of Retirement and Late-Career Patterns in Western Industrialized Societies*, Cheltenham, Edward Elgar.

Howard, C. (1997) *The Hidden Welfare State: Tax Expenditures and Social Policy in the United States*, Princeton, Princeton University Press.

Jespen, M., Foden, D. & Hutsebaut, M. (Eds.) (2002) *Active Strategies for Older Workers*, Brussels, ETUI.

Kangas, O. & Palme, J. (1996) The Development of Occupational Pensions in Finland and Sweden: Class Politics and Institutional Feedbacks. In Shalev, M. (Ed.) *The Privatization of Social Policy? Occupational Welfare and the Welfare State in America, Scandinavia and Japan*, London, Macmillan, 211–40.

Kohli, M., Rein, M., Guillemard, A.-M. & van Gunsteren, H. (Eds.) (1991) *Time for Retirement: Comparative Studies on Early Exit from the Labor Force*, New York, Cambridge University Press.

Leisering, L. (2006) 'From Redistribution to Regulation: Regulating Private Old-Age Pensions as a New Challenge in Ageing Societies. In Sigg, R. & Cantillon, B. (Eds.) *Social Security in a Long-Life Society*, Geneva, ISSA.

Müller, K. (2001) The Political Economy of Pension Reform in Eastern Europe. *International Social Security Review*, 54, 57–79.

Müller, K. (2008) The politics and outcome of three-pillar pension reforms in Central and Eastern Europe. In Arza, C. & Kohli, M. (Eds.) *Pension Reform in Europe: Politics, Policies and Outcomes*, London, Routledge, 87–106.

Myles, J. & Pierson, P. (2001) The Comparative Political Economy of Pension Reform. In Pierson, P. (Ed.) *The New Politics of the Welfare State*, New York, Oxford University Press, 305–33.

Naschold, F. & de Vroom, B. (Eds.) (1994) *Regulating Employment and Welfare: Company and National Policies of Labour Force Participation at the End of Worklife in Industrial Countries*, Berlin, W. de Gruyter.

Natali, D. (2008) *Pensions in Europe, European Pensions: The Evolution of Pension Policy at National and Supranational Level*, Brussels, P.I.E. Peter Lang.

OECD (1998) *Maintaining Prosperity in an Ageing Society*, Paris, OECD.

OECD (2000) *Reforms for an Ageing Society*, Paris, OECD.

OECD (2010) Pension fund assets struggle to return to pre-crisis levels, *Pension Market Focus*, 7, 1–2.

OECD (2011) *Pensions at a Glance 2011. Retirement-income systems in OECD and G20 countries*, Paris, OECD.

Orenstein, M. A. (2008a) Out-liberalizing the EU: Pension Privatization in Central and Eastern Europe. *Journal of European Public Policy*, 15, 899–917

Orenstein, M. A. (2008b) *Privatizing Pensions. The Transnational Compaign for Social Security Reform*, Princeton, Princeton University Press.

Orenstein, M. A. (2011) Pension Privatization in Crisis: Death or Rebirth of a Global Policy Trend? *International Social Security Review*, 64, 65–80.

Palier, B. (Ed.) (2010) *A Goodbye to Bismarck? The Politics of Welfare Reforms in Continental Europe*, Amsterdam, Amsterdam University Press.

Pierson, P. (1994) *Dismantling the Welfare State? Reagan, Thatcher, and the Politics of Retrenchment*, New York, Cambridge University Press.

Pierson, P. (2001a) Coping with Permanent Austerity: Welfare State Restructuring in Affluent Democracies. In Pierson, P. (Ed.) *The New Politics of the Welfare State*. New York, Oxford University Press, 410–56.

Pierson, P. (Ed.) (2001b) *The New Politics of the Welfare State*, New York, Oxford University Press.

Pino, A. & Yermo, J. (2010) The Impact of the 2007–2009 Crisis on Social Security and Private Pension Funds: A Threat to Their Financial Soundness? *International Social Security Review*, 63, 5–30.

Rein, M. & Turner, J. (2004) How Societies Mix Public and Private Spheres in their Pension Systems. In Rein, M. & Schmähl, W. (Eds.) *Rethinking the Welfare State. The Political Economy of Pension Reform*, Cheltenham, Edward Elgar, 251–93.

Streeck, W. & Thelen, K. (2005) Introduction: Institutional Change in Advanced Political Economies. In Streeck, W. & Thelen, K. (Eds.) *Beyond Continuity. Institutional Change in Advanced Political Economies*, Oxford, Oxford University Press, 1–39.

Weaver, K. R. (1986) The Politics of Blame Avoidance. *Journal of Public Policy*, 6, 371–98.

World Bank (1994) *Averting the Old Age Crisis: Policies to Protect the Old and Promote Growth*, Oxford, Oxford University Press.

10

Insider-Outsider Dynamics and the Reform of Job Security Legislation

Johan B. Davidsson and Patrick Emmenegger

Introduction[1]

There is a constant tension between the flux and uncertainty inherent in economic activity and labour's desire for security (Piore 1980). Employers are interested in flexibility in order to cope with macroeconomic shocks, while employees value security. One of the most important forms of flexibility is related to the job security of workers. Job security refers to the managerial capacity to dismiss[2] employees to allow for downsizing or to use new forms of employment—such as fixed-term contracts—when hiring new workers (Regini 2000: 16). In this context, flexibility denotes the employers' ability to hire and fire, while security denotes the employees' protection from being fired or from being hired on a fixed-term contract only.

If the employers' need for flexibility is accepted as a given, we face the question whether only some labour market participants bear the brunt of economic adjustment. Are all labour market participants equally affected by the employers' need for flexibility, or are some labour market participants enjoying the benefits of stable employment relationships and high wages, while others provide all the flexibility, but do not get any security in return? Following Piore (1980: 24), we can speak of a dualism within the labour market, when portions of the labour force are insulated from uncertainty and variability in demand. These labour market participants can be referred to as labour market insiders. In contrast, labour market outsiders are those employees that provide the much-needed flexibility, either in the form of atypical employment or unemployment.

Unions play a crucial role in determining this distributional outcome. As defenders of their members' interests, unions are said to have an interest in protecting their members against employer demands, while ignoring the interests of non-members (cf. Lindbeck and Snower 1988). Given the over-representation of labour market insiders among the union rank and file, unions are expected to assent to reforms that increase labour market flexibility at the expense of labour market outsiders, while opposing reforms that disadvantage labour market insiders (cf. Rueda 2007). Thus, in this interpretation, the unions' membership composition is decisive in determining the unions' reaction to employer demands for more flexibility.

In this chapter, we disagree with this interpretation. We argue, rather, that the unions' organizational interests are the crucial variable explaining union behaviour. As we show below, unions in countries characterized by rigid job security legislation often have a strong interest in retaining high levels of protection for workers with permanent contracts because some institutional features of the existing policies are crucial for their long-term positions of power. At the same time, though, unions have an interest in participating in the deliberation of labour market policies. This participation allows them to influence the direction of reform. However, it also forces them to enter negotiations with employers and the government, and it presupposes some basic willingness to compromise.

In difficult economic times, when unions are asked to make concessions, they will assent to labour market reforms, but only those reforms that do not fundamentally threaten to undermine their organizational interests. In the context of job security legislation, this means that unions defend the interests of labour market insiders by protecting permanent contracts, while they compromise on the regulation of temporary employment. This solution allows them to protect their organizational interests both by retaining their institutional role in the administration of lay-offs, and by living up to their institutional role as one of the organizations responsible for the direction of labour market policy reform. We thus argue that the main reason why unions defend insider interests is that unions' own organizational interests are at stake.

We demonstrate our argument using two case studies of France and Sweden. The case selection is based on two criteria. First, we have selected most dissimilar cases. According to Ebbinghaus (2006: 128, 130), French unions organize few workers. The typical union member is old, employed and works for the public sector. In contrast, Swedish unions organize around 80 per cent of all labour market participants. The unemployed and the young are only slightly under-represented, while union density among women is even higher than among men.[3] Sweden is thus often considered to be a prime example of encompassing unionism, while French unions are described as weak and riddled by insider-outsider divides (cf. Obinger et al. 2012; Palier and Thelen 2012).

Second, we rely on a least likely case design. Both countries are for some reason unlikely to suffer from the aforementioned insider-outsider dynamics. Sweden, for example, with its encompassing unionism, is particularly unlikely to suffer from insider-outsider dynamics if representational interests are the main driving force behind these dynamics because typical outsider groups are well represented (cf. Obinger et al. 2012). France, by contrast, is an even less likely case because French unions are said to be weak and industrial relations to be dominated by the state (Crouch 1993). Thus, French unions are least likely to have a voice in political reforms and to have any organizational interests to defend.

We proceed as follows: In section 2, we discuss the relationship between flexibility and security. In section 3, we present our argument about the organizational interests of unions and how this relates to insider-outsider dynamics. In section 4, we provide empirical evidence on labour market policy reforms in France and Sweden. A final section concludes.

Economic Pressure and Political Reactions

In recent decades, labour markets have come under pressure. Developed economies have reacted differently to these new challenges. Countries characterized by flexible labour markets and low social wages have further liberalized their labour markets and are thus experiencing an increase in wage inequality. As a result, low-skill employment has remained high because remuneration continues to correspond to the relatively low productivity levels. In contrast, in countries characterized by rigid labour markets and high social wages, macro-economic shocks have led to the emergence of two-tier labour markets consisting of a core of labour market insiders in standard employment relationships and a periphery of labour market outsiders that provide the needed flexibility (Emmenegger et al. 2012). Temporary employment is particularly important to this end.

As argued by DiPrete et al. (2006), the labour markets of all advanced economies have become more flexible in recent years. However, this flexibilization was achieved through different means. While in some countries skill-based wage inequality has increased (e.g. the US), in other countries (e.g. France) institutional change 'has produced an upward trend in the density of insecure jobs and an increased concentration of low-skill workers in insecure jobs' (Di Prete et al. 2006: 311). Wage inequality and temporary employment are thus two different ways to achieve the same goal: the flexibilization of labour markets in advanced economies.

Table 10.1 shows the relationship between temporary employment (for all age groups and for those aged 15 to 24) in 2008[4] and wage inequality[5] in

Table 10.1. Determinants of temporary employment in 2008

Dependent variable:	Temporary employment (all age groups)	Temporary employment among ages 15 to 24
Wage inequality	-81.13^{**}	-289.22^{**}
	(-3.26)	(-4.08)
Unemployment rate	2.15^{**}	5.39^{**}
	(4.47)	(3.93)
Adj. R-squared	0.55	0.55
N	18	18

Note: ** $p < 0.01$,* $p < 0.05$; t-values in parentheses.

advanced economies, while controlling for the unemployment rate in 2008. The OLS regressions show that wage inequality is a highly significant predictor of temporary employment. Decreasing wage inequality from US levels (Gini of 0.312) to Swedish levels (Gini of 0.237) increases the share of temporary employment by 6.1 percentage points among all age groups and 21.7 percentage points among those aged 15 to 24. Thus, temporary employment seems to compensate for low levels of wage inequality.

Temporary employment has considerably increased in recent years, in particular in countries characterized by otherwise rigid labour markets. For instance, in France temporary employment increased from 4.7 per cent in 1985 to 13.5 per cent in 2009. In Sweden, temporary employment has increased from 11.9 per cent in 1987 to 15.1 per cent in 2004. According to the OECD (2003: 49), temporary work was responsible for 50 per cent of the overall employment growth in France and for 17 per cent in Sweden in the period 1991 to 2001. Temporary work is particularly important in the case of young labour market participants. Among those aged 15 to 24 in 2009, we observe shares of temporary employment of 51.2 per cent in France, and 53.4 per cent in Sweden.

These developments were made possible by the deregulation of temporary employment, which led to an increase in temporary employment, except in those countries that already had high levels of temporary employment at the beginning of the period under investigation (most notably Greece and Spain). The bivariate correlation between changes in temporary employment and in the regulation of temporary employment amounts to $r = -0.37$ if Greece and Spain are omitted from the sample.[6] Greece and Spain are special cases because temporary employment was widespread (at some points in time above 20 (Greece) and 30 (Spain) per cent of total employment), even though the usage of temporary employment has been highly regulated. Most likely, this indicates that the rules governing temporary employment have not always been enforced in Greece and Spain.

However, the usage of temporary employment has not been deregulated everywhere. In countries characterized by a low level of regulation of permanent contracts, temporary employment is a less important source of labour market flexibility. As a consequence, temporary employment has not been deregulated in the English-speaking countries. In contrast, in countries where permanent contracts are highly regulated, temporary employment was deregulated in order to increase labour market flexibility (Booth et al. 2002). Davidsson and Naczyk (2009: 22) report that fixed-term contracts play a particularly important economic role in countries that are otherwise characterized by long job tenures. In contrast, countries with a high share of regular employees with short tenures feature low levels of temporary employment.

In sum, temporary employment has proven to be an important source of labour market flexibility in otherwise rather rigid labour markets. This development has been made possible by first the creation and more recently the deregulation of temporary employment. In the next section, we discuss the politics behind these labour market reforms. Inspired by the insider-outsider theory of employment and unemployment, power-resources theory and the literature on corporatism, we argue that organizational interests have led unions to fight reforms that would have threatened insider interests with regard to the regulation of permanent contracts. In contrast, unions were (more) willing to compromise on reforms that deregulated temporary employment.

Unions Playing Defence

Unions play a particularly important role in the area of labour market policy. With the exception of the British unions, who were excluded from the political arena during the first Thatcher government,[7] it is in this area that unions in Western Europe have retained their influence (see Table 10.2). The existing

Table 10.2. Policy-area coverage of unions' political influence

Austria	Social policy, fiscal policy, monetary policy, investment policy, industrial policy, social welfare, labour law, job creation and training, employment, EU issues
Ireland	Overall macro-economic strategy, social welfare, government spending in general, employment policy including active labour market policy, regional policy
Italy	Taxation, expenditure (especially pensions), labour law
Netherlands	Social security, employment policy
Sweden	Many sectors until 1992, then restricted to labour market policy and pensions
Germany	Social insurance, labour law, health, reconstruction of the East
Spain	Employment law and social security
France	Employment law and social security
UK	None

Source: Compston (2003).

explanations for the insider-outsider dynamics that we can observe in labour market reforms have put their focus on the membership composition of unions (Lindbeck and Snower 1988) and the vote-maximizing strategies of political parties (Saint-Paul 1996; Rueda 2007). In contrast to these explanations, we argue that dualist reforms take place when unions make use of their political influence in order to defend organizational interests.

Since the 1980s, unions have been on the back foot in the context of retrenchment and deregulation. The political inclusion of unions in the area of labour market policy has forced them, on the one hand, to accept reforms in order to justify their position in the policymaking process, and on the other hand, to focus their efforts on the defence of those issues most fundamental to their long-term position of power, their organizational interests. In the following, we explore this argument further by introducing the concept of 'institutional power resources' and by discussing what mechanisms are at play in the reform of job security legislation.

The concept of 'institutional power resources' (IPRs) finds its origin in power-resources theory and the literature on corporatism (Davidsson 2011). It draws on the former's focus on power relationships and the latter's interest in the institutions and structures of union (and employer) participation in the political process. There is a tendency in the literature to concentrate on corporatism as a structure, or an institution, rather than as a policymaking process (Molina and Rhodes 2002: 320). The same structural bias has been prevalent in power-resources theory (e.g. Olsen and O'Connor 1998). In order to understand how institutions are linked to outcomes, however, we need to look more closely at the political negotiations that have taken place and how they have evolved over time. As we shall see, in the period of retrenchment and deregulation, unions' preference for protecting their organizational interest in the negotiations over reforms has been accentuated.

Two aspects of power are contained in the concept of IPRs (Davidsson 2011). First, the institutionalized political participation of unions (and employers) is a power resource in itself.[8] Such political participation cannot be reduced to any other measure of union power. In France, for example, the membership rates of unions are lower than in most other European countries, including the UK, but unions still play a significant part in labour market reform through their participation in the deliberation and administration of policy. Second, some institutional features of existing policies are crucial for the actors' long-term positions of power and can thus also be regarded as a power resource. In Sweden, for example, legislation has given unions a bargaining role in dismissals, in particular in determining which workers have to be dismissed, the so-called 'last in, first out' principle. Employers are only allowed to deviate from this principle if unions agree. This gives unions the opportunity to negotiate for improvements and concessions in return for their agreement. The concept of 'institutional power resources' can thus be defined as the power resources that become the property of unions (and employers) as a result of their ability to hold on to these *two types of institutions*.

In the post-war era, unions were in a strong position and could argue for maximalist solutions, i.e. increased protection of all types of workers. As Emmenegger (2011) has shown, virtually all European countries strengthened job security legislation in the 1970s. In the harder times that followed, unions have been put on the back foot as a result of new economic conditions and rising levels of unemployment. In this new context, unions have had to opt for second-best solutions, prioritizing the defence of policies that are most important for their long-term position of power.

Golden (1997) argues that in times of work-force reductions, unions are not primarily concerned about preventing job loss, but about preserving the union organization. Analogously, in the reforms of job security legislation, we argue that unions have assented to reforms, but only to such reforms that have not fundamentally threatened to undermine their organizational interest.[9]

In both France and Sweden, public legislation awards unions with an important role in the administration of lay-offs, which allows unions to defend the compensation of workers in the form of redundancy pay and training measures, and to protect union delegates against dismissals. For example, in France, union delegates have the right to be informed and consulted by the employers, including the establishment of social plans in the case of collective dismissals for economic reasons. With regard to the latter, unions have the right to question the social plan by inviting an external accountant. The public administration (DIRECCTE) then forms its decision regarding the social plan on the basis of all existing information. The unions also have the right to represent workers in legal proceedings and to take employers to court for not having followed regulations contained in the relevant legislation or collective agreements. Union delegates also have special protection in the legislation: the dismissal of a delegate has to be approved by the labour inspector (civil servant).

In Sweden, the 'last in, first out' principle contained in the job security legislation is optional in the sense that derogations to the principle can be negotiated between the unions and the employers. This confers on unions the opportunity to bargain for compensation, often in the form of increased redundancy pay or training measures. The position of unions as a bargaining partner also makes it possible for them to protect union delegates against dismissals.

Unions' organizational interest is also linked to the power accorded to unions in the workplace and in wage bargaining by the existence of high levels of job security. If workers are more secure in their employment position, they are more likely to be involved in union activities at the level of the workplace, and strong job security creates a wage penalty for the unemployed, which help insulate unions from competition in wage bargaining.

In sum, we argue that rather than their membership compositions, unions' organizational interests are the decisive variable explaining union behaviour in labour market policy reform. This view implies that French and Swedish unions should show a similar inclination to compromise on dualist reforms that protect the interests of insiders, but sacrifice outsiders' interests when facing employers' demands for flexibility, even though French unions are dominated by labour market insiders, while Swedish unions organize both insiders and outsiders.

The Case Studies

In this section, we present two case studies: France and Sweden. We take the arrival of high and persistent unemployment as our starting point. This event represents a turning point between two periods. In the former, there was a trend towards increased job security legislation because unions could press for maximalist solutions. In the latter, there was a trend towards labour market flexibility where unions had to prioritize their organizational interests. In France, the level of unemployment began to rise from the mid-1970s onwards. First it was believed to be a short-term effect of the business cycle, but later it was accepted as a more structural phenomenon by the Conservative Barre government in 1977 and by the Socialist Fabius government in 1984. In Sweden, the economy was sheltered from rising unemployment by successive currency devaluations during the 1970s and 1980s. The increase in unemployment, therefore, came later and as an effect of the switch to fixed-currency regime and the financial crisis in the early 1990s. The Conservative Bildt government opted for a structural reform in the early 1990s, whereas the shift in focus in the Social-Democratic Party came with the Persson government in 1996.

In most countries, it was the realization that unemployment had stuck and that old solutions no longer seemed to work that made governments take on board a new perspective that emphasized the importance of labour market flexibility. Given the change in economic conditions and in the beliefs of policymakers, we should expect a general deregulation of job security legislation. However, the reforms introduced in these two countries have been directed at deregulating only those parts of public legislation that concern temporary employment. Below, we show that the dual nature of these reforms can be explained by the correspondence between job security legislation for regular employment and union's efforts to protect their organizational interest.

France

This section tracks the reforms of job security legislation in France from its creation in the 1970s until today. We focus on two key periods: the negotiation over labour market flexibility in the mid-1980s and the recent flexicurity negotiations.

France has often been characterized as a country with an omnipotent state that dominates civil society. This so-called Jacobin tradition of a strong and centralized state has been the common understanding of French politics since the publication of Tocqueville's *L'Ancien régime et la révolution*. However, unions and employers became part of the running of the social-insurance system already after the Second World War and were later also involved in the establishment and the reforms of job security legislation.

The signing of the Grenelle Accords by the government, the unions and the employers' association was a response to the events of May 1968 and the sponsoring of the New Society by Prime Minister Jacques Chaban-Delmas. Both aimed at the modernization of social relations and the inclusion of unions and employers in the deliberation of labour market policy reform. This was the starting point for the establishment of a tradition in which the unions and employers began to be perceived as legitimate partners in the area of labour market policy reform; new legislation was from that moment onwards often pre-negotiated by the unions and the employers.

The Grenelle Accords contained provisions committing unions and employers to future national-level collective negotiations. The first accord (1969, amended in 1974) dealt with the issue of job security. It contained provisions concerning the information and consultation of unions and the requirement of companies considering lay-offs to first explore alternative solutions, and if none were to be found, to develop a social plan which entitled the dismissed workers to financial compensation. Companies also had to justify the economic reasons for lay-offs. These provisions created a need for introducing some form of administrative control over the procedure of lay-offs (Duprilot 1975). Two new laws were introduced. The 13 July 1973 Law introduced a judicial procedure for individual dismissals, in which the Labour Court evaluated the motivation of the employer, while the 3 January 1975 Law introduced the administrative authorization of all individual and collective lay-offs made on economic grounds (Duprilot 1975). One of the consequences of these two laws was that when the administrative authorization was repealed in 1986, the judicial protection remained in place and came to be also applicable to collective lay-offs. The 3 January 1979 Law for the first time also introduced restrictions on the use of fixed-term contracts.

The new laws considerably strengthened the position of the unions in the process of dismissals. The unions were now entitled to be informed and consulted (but not to bargain), and the union delegates could represent the workers in legal proceedings and take employers to court for failing to inform them or for failing to submit a social plan. Union delegates were especially protected against dismissals (requiring authorization from the labour inspector).

When the Socialist government came into power in 1981, its first concern was to introduce further restrictions on temporary employment. As Howell (1992: 197) writes: 'The PS [Socialist Party] came to power deeply concerned about the growth of 'precarious' forms of work. The fear was that the growth of such types of work would not only create a more precarious and vulnerable existence for workers but would also lead to a fragmented, dualistic labor force.' These concerns translated into the 5 February 1982 Law that introduced further restrictions on the use of fixed-term contracts and limited their duration to six months.

However, the failure of the expansive macroeconomic policies of the government's first years and the continued rise in unemployment forced a fundamental rethinking within the party that shifted the focus to labour market policy. An acceptance for the need of labour market flexibility grew within the PS. Its origin can be found in the change in industrial policy under Laurent Fabius and the departure of the Communist Party (PCF) from the government in the summer of 1984. One senior official in the Ministry of Labour described the new thinking on industrial policy as follows: 'it was [now] more important to promote the creation of new jobs, and mobility, than it was to defend [existing] jobs ... and this was in the interest of the worker.'[10]

Negotiations on the issue began in July 1984 in response to initiatives by the employers and the unions, and with the support of the government. The employers had announced the idea of ENCAs (*emplois nouveaux à contraintes allégés*), which sought to introduce exceptions to the job security legislation for new hires, including the abolition of the need for administrative authorization for lay-offs. The leader of the major employers' organization (CNPF), Yvon Gattaz, promised that such a reform would create 500,000 new jobs (*Le Figaro*, 23 January 1984). The government's position rested on two legs: the need for more labour market flexibility, and the inclusion of the unions in labour market governance. The ideal sought by policymakers, according to a senior official, was something akin to the Swedish model of tripartism, which required strong unions.[11]

The unions were, apart from the more radical CGT, ready to enter negotiations. According to one of the CFDT negotiators, the reason was their desire to create a larger space for the social partners in the area of labour market reform.[12] The idea was to institutionalize co-operation both on the political level and on the level of the workplace, jointly managing the necessary structural transformation of the economy. The employers were, however, more radical. They sought the deregulation of job security legislation and a reduction of union representation in firms. The big controversy was the employers' proposal of the ENCAs. The unions refused to make any compromise on this issue. The breakthrough came first in early December when the employers decided to drop their demands with regard to the ENCAs (*Le Figaro*, 4 December 1984).

The other demands of the employers—focusing on reduced union representation and the deregulation of fixed-term contracts—were also difficult for the unions to accept. Nonetheless, the unions, except the CGT, signed a draft agreement containing a compromise on the first issue regarding threshold levels for union representation and an acceptance of an increase in the duration of fixed-term contracts to 18 months. Unions were, thus, willing to compromise on the issue of temporary employment.

At the same time, the union rank-and-file were building a momentum for the refusal of the agreement. After the negotiators had consulted with their member organizations, three out of four refused to sign the agreement. There were several reasons for this, union representation, temporary contracts, etc., but in general there was a sense that the agreement was slanted towards the employers.[13] Since the unions and the employers could not reach an agreement, the government stepped in. However, to a large extent, it did so following the content of the draft agreement and union preferences. The 25 July 1985 Law, softened the regulation on temporary work: more grounds were admissible for the use of fixed-term contracts and the maximum duration was extended to 24 months (with administrative authorization).

The return of a Conservative government in 1986 represented a temporary break with the inclusion of unions in labour market reform; the government deregulated the job security legislation for regular as well as temporary workers. The 30 December 1986 Law repealed the administrative authorization for lay-offs, and the 11 August 1986 Law further softened the regulation of temporary work: it was no longer necessary to justify the use of fixed-term contracts and the duration of fixed-term contracts was set to 12 months (two renewals). The repeal of the authorization for lay-offs was according to a senior official in the Ministry of Labour during the Conservative government primarily driven by ideology:[14] the idea that the state through the office of the labour inspector (a civil servant) had the power to decide over the economic decisions of firms was controversial, if not offensive, to the employers. To hand over the control to a judge, the existing alternative as a result of the 1973 and 1975 laws, seemed the better option since the office of the judge was considered to be more neutral. Hence, the deregulation had little effect and in fact strengthened the unions' position since their role was larger in the juridical than in the administrative process.

Table 10.3. Job protection legislation reforms in France (R = enacted by a right government; L = enacted by a left government)

		Insider policies: regular contracts		Outsider policies: fixed-term contracts
Period 1:				
1973	+ (R)	Increased protection for individual dismissals (motive, procedure: jur.)		
1975	+ (R)	Increased protection for collective dismissals (motive, procedure: adm.)		
1979			+ (R)	First regulation in law.
1982			+ (L)	6/12 months. Grounds for use of FTCs (3). 1 renewal. 5% severance pay
Period 2:				
1985			– (L)	6/12 months (24 months with administrative authorization). 1 renewal. Grounds (5 + 2)
1986	– (R)	Abolishment of the administrative procedure for collective dismissals*	– (R)	12 months. 2 renewals. No longer need to motivate use of FTCs.
1989	+ (L)	Requirement of a social plan for those laid off		
1990			+ (L)	18 months (24 certain cases). Grounds (3).
2002	+ (L)	Stricter conditions for the social plan**	+ (L)	Severance pay raised to 10%
2008			– (R)	New special temporary contract for engineers and managers. 36 months.

Note: * This did not in any real sense reduce employment protection for regular workers. Rather, it was a change from an administrative to a judiciary process (see main text). ** The Raffarin (R) Government eased the procedural requirements after they won the election in 2002.

After 1986, France witnessed the strengthening of job security for regular workers and a limited re-regulation of job security for temporary workers. The requirements of a social plan for employees in case of collective dismissals were strengthened by the 2 August 1989 Law, the 27 January 1993 Law, and the 17 January 2002 Law. With regard to temporary work, the 12 July 1990 Law reduced the maximum duration of fixed-term contracts to 18 months (24 months in certain cases) and restricted the grounds for resorting to temporary employment, but did not go back to the situation before 1985. In the 17 January 2002 Law, severance pay for fixed-term contracts was increased from five to ten per cent. The job security for regular workers has remained strong throughout the period, although in a different shape and form than before 1986. The regulation of temporary contracts has oscillated to some degree, but has on the whole been liberalized during the period (Glaymann 2005: 59).

After a period of non-activism of the social partners in labour market reform, due to the fall out of the employers as a result of the 1997 legislation work time reduction, the Conservative government decided in 2005 to introduce the *contrat nouvelle embauche* (CNE), which extended the trial period to two years for permanent contracts, during which the employer would not have to justify a dismissal, and in 2006 the *contrat première embauche* (CPE), which did the same for young people. Both proposals ran into problems.[15] This in turn led to two things. First, discussions, framed in terms of flexicurity, started between the employers and the unions over the 'modernization of the labour market' in 2006. Second, the government introduced the 31 January 2007 Law on the modernization of social dialogue, which mandates that before legislating in the area of labour law, a proposal to negotiate has to be issued to the unions and the employers, and if the negotiations result in an agreement, that this agreement has to be reflected in the new legislation.

In 2007, during his election campaign, Nicolas Sarkozy had been advocating a new contract that would remove the distinction between regular and temporary workers, the *contrat de travail unique* (Le Monde, 08.09.08). However, both employers and unions rejected the idea, which had not been part of their discussions after 2006. The unions' rejection of the *contrat unique* is straightforward; they were not prepared to accept any changes to the job security legislation concerning regular employment. The FO, for example, refused all changes to the Labour Code.[16] The employers feared that the flexibility they had in using temporary employment might be threatened since one contract would expand the courts' influence to all workers.[17] In order to avoid the government imposing a law, which they could do if no agreement was reached, the parties proposed to create the possibility of dismissal by mutual consent, a rather toothless reform (Cahuc and Zylberberg 2009).

The real initiative in the direction of deregulation of job security for regular workers was the proposal by the employers for an extended trial period of up to two years, which in practice would be the equivalent of the CNE, but which would avoid the possibility of a legal process. The employers also wanted to create a new type of fixed-term contract that would allow for a duration of 36 instead of 18 months. The unions were critical of the extended trial periods. They were more open to negotiate on the issue of temporary work, although with reservations. The CFDT held as condition for the approval of the new type of fixed-term contract that it should be introduced at the sector level, following collective negotiations (*Le Monde*, 16 January 2008). In the negotiations, unions asked for higher compensatory damages for unfair dismissals and increased transferability of rights and benefits (*Le Monde*, 8 September 2008).

The final agreement was hailed as a success and the first step towards flexicurity by the signatories. In reality, however, not much progress had been made, neither with regard to flexibility (Cahuc and Zylberberg 2009) nor with regard to security (Fabre et al. 2008). The unions were able to preserve the legal protection for regular employment and the distinction between permanent and temporary contracts with the rejection of the *contract unique* (Freyssinet 2007). The agreement contained an extension of the allowed duration of the trial period, but only to a maximum of two, three or four months depending on profession (the period could be doubled in length by sector-level collective agreements). It also contained a new fixed-term contract allowing for a duration of up to 36 months, but which was limited with regard to its applicability: it only concerns engineers and higher level white-collar workers. On the other side of the bargain, the agreement contained higher compensatory damages for unfair dismissals and the partial preservation of certain rights during unemployment, for example health insurance. The 2008 reform thus followed the pattern of marginal reforms that had been estab-lished in the mid-1980s where unions protected the job security legislation for regular workers, but compromised on temporary employment.

Sweden

This section tracks the reforms of job security legislation in Sweden, from its creation in the 1970s until today. We focus on two key periods: the negotiation over labour market flexibility in the mid-1990s, and the recent negotiations on a new principal agreement (huvudavtal).

In the Swedish post-war economic model, unions and employers jointly regulated the labour market, a tradition that goes back to the principal agree-ment signed in Saltsjöbaden in 1938. The model was based on a high rate of structural transformation, which was to some extent facilitated by the system of central regulation and wage bargaining. In the 1970s, this model came under pressure as the focus shifted to the negative consequences of high levels of structural transformation, in particular for older workers (SOU 1973; Hellberg and Vrethem 1983). These discussions originated in demands made by the unions and led to reform proposals by the Liberal and the Social-Democratic Party (Nycander 2008; Emmenegger 2010; Hamskär and Gustafsson 2010). The result of these initiatives was the introduction of job security legislation in 1971 and 1974.

One crucial element of Swedish job security legislation is the criteria for the selection of the dismissed workers—the 'last in, first out' principle. This has given unions increased bargaining power in collective dismissal procedures where they can trade the possibility for employers to make exceptions to the principle in turn for, most commonly, increased redundancy payments. In addition, as in France, this procedure has made it possible for the unions to exclude their own delegates from dismissals.

The first shift in the area of labour market policy came with the Conservative government, which was in power during the first years of the financial and economic crisis. A government report presented radical proposals for reform (SOU 1993: 32), *inter alia* challenging the 'first in, last out' principle. The bill that the government finally presented to parliament included more moderate changes. The 'last in, first out' principle was kept intact, but the employer won the right to exempt two employees from the formal procedures. Additionally, the maximum duration for temporary employment was extended from 6 to 12 months (Prop. 1993/1994: 67). Both the employers' organization and the Conservative Party had wanted to go further, but—according to a senior official[18] who worked in the Ministry of Labour between 1988 and 2007—chose in the end a more modest proposal for two reasons. First, the Minister of Labour, Börje Hörnlund, represented the Centre Party which was at the time more moderate with regard to labour market policy and which sought primarily changes that would benefit its constituency of small firms, hence the exemption of two employees. Second, the government was afraid of the unions' reaction if they attacked the 'last in, first out' principle.

The reactions from the unions and the Social-Democratic Party (SAP) to the proposal of the Conservative government were strongly critical, and after the SAP returned to power in 1994 they repealed the legislation. The question is, however, whether this repeal represented the opinion of leading figures within the SAP. Anne Wibble, who was Finance Minister for the Conservative government, writes in her memoirs that 'Göran Persson [then Finance Minister of the SAP government] had only a few months earlier said that the proposed changes in reality were quite reasonable...but Göran Persson changed his mind after having been told off by the LO' (Wibble 1994: 64).

Not much later, the continually rising levels of unemployment forced the SAP to reconsider its position. During the 1980s and the early 1990s, the SAP had changed its view on macroeconomic policy towards economic liberalism after failures to contain inflation (Blyth 2002; Lindvall 2004). In relation to labour market policy, it was the arrival of high and persistent unemployment, shocking to Swedish policymakers, which made the party open to new ideas. According to a senior official in the Ministry of Labour there were, at the time, constant discussions and deliberations to find solutions to the problem of unemployment and in those discussions the employers pushed strongly for labour market flexibility.[19]

In 1995, the government appointed a commission, including representatives of both unions and employers, with the aim of arriving at a new common agreement on labour market reform. The directive stated *inter alia* that the goal was to promote increased flexibility and to find a new balance between the security of workers and the needs of the business sectors (Dir. 1995: 30). During the negotiations, there was a considerable distance between the positions of the unions and employers and neither showed much willingness to compromise. The main employers' organization (SAF) sought a deregulation of job security for regular workers. Their main priority was to remove the 'last in, first out' principle and to extend the trial period for employment. The LO was strongly critical of any changes to the 'last in, first out' principle and wanted for their part a right to leaves of absence to try out a new job and increased protection for workers on part-time contracts (*Dagens nyheter*, 24 January 1996). For the unions, defending the existing legislation was first and foremost a question of power. Hans Karlsson, negotiator for the LO, wrote in a press article during the discussions between the employers and the unions and with reference to their proposals that "[it] would be unforgivable if the high rates of unemployment made us give up in fundamental questions of power" (*Dagens nyheter*, 30 March 1996). This focus on the 'last in, first out' principle by both unions and employers explains the failure of the negotiations (Nycander 2008). During the spring of 1996 the commission was dissolved.

After the failure of the negotiations, the Minister of Employment, Ulrica Messing (SAP), announced that the government would now turn to legislation. At the same time, she opened up for a discussion about also making changes to the 'last in, first out' principle (*Dagens nyheter*, 30 May 1996).[20] The announcement created strong tensions within the Social-Democratic Party and between the party and the LO. Many MPs from the SAP have a close relationship to the LO and sometimes still hold positions within the union organization. Before the social-democratic group in parliament was scheduled to discuss the proposal by the government, the LO used every possible means at their disposal to influence the outcome. For the first time they arranged demonstrations directly aimed at the SAP. They also threatened to withdraw 20 million SEK from their contributions to the SAP (*Dagens nyheter*, 7 September 1996). Finally, they made clear that the MPs who held positions within the union organization, and who often elected chairmen at the local level, might lose the support of the central organization when seeking re-election (*Dagens nyheter*, 5 September 1996).

The proposed legislation was only accepted when it satisfied union demands. One of the MPs, who had up to this point been one of the most critical voices, explained his decision to vote yes in the following manner: '[t]he "last in, first out" principle, which is the foundation of the labour law, is being retained and with that I believe that I can say that we have got a good compromise' (*Dagens nyheter*, 6 September 1996). The bill submitted to parliament (Prop. 1996/1997: 16) made no changes to the 'last in, first out' principle.[21] However, it increased the maximum duration of temporary employment to 12 months (limited to 5 employees per company) and 18 months for first-time hires. Additionally, the new law made it possible for collective agreements concluded at the local level to derogate from the legislation on temporary employment. Earlier, such derogation was only possible with the consent of the parties at the national level. With regard to temporary employment, the bill thus went, with the consent of the unions, beyond the reform of the Conservative government in 1993.

After the reform in 1997, no additional changes were made to job security legislation before the election victory of the Conservative coalition in 2006. The Conservative coalition declared early on, to the disappointment of the employers' organization, that they had no intentions of introducing any changes to job security legislation concerning regular workers, i.e. 'last in, first out' principle. This was a promise made in the election campaign.[22] They did, however, increase the maximum duration of temporary employment to 24 months and removed the requirement for the employer to justify the need of such work (Prop. 2006/2007: 111).

When the employers realized that the government would not legislate, they approached the unions with a proposal to enter negotiations over a new principal agreement. The employers put forward two demands: First, they wanted to remove the 'last in, first out' principle, i.e. giving them the right to decide the order of selection, which was to be based on competence. Second, they wanted to introduce restrictions to the unions' right to sympathy action. They argued that sympathy action against firms that had signed a collective agreement was unreasonable in a modern labour market (*Dagens industri*, 22 September 2007). The LO was open to discussion with regard to the second point, changes in the rules governing industrial action (*Svenska dagbladet*, 16 September 2007). PTK, which was negotiating on behalf of the unions of professional employees, was open to changes in both areas. The demands from the unions included more security for workers in their transition between jobs. For instance, they requested increased redundancy payments, longer periods of notice and more funds for vocational training. More

Table 10.4. Major job security legislation reforms in Sweden (R = enacted by a right government; L = enacted by a left government)

	Insider policies: regular contracts			Outsider policies: fixed-term contracts	
Period 1:					
1971	+ (L)	Protection for older workers			
1974	+ (L)	Introduction of employment protection legislation			
Period 2:					
1993	– (R)	2 exceptions to "last in, first out"	– (R)	Duration increased from 6 to 12 months	
1994	+ (L)	Repeal	+ (L)	Repeal	
1997			– (L)	Duration 12 months (18 for first time hires), CB could derogate.	
2001	– (R)*	2 exceptions to "last in, first out"			
2006			– (R)	Duration 24 months. No restrictions	

Note: * The SAP was in minority government, but the reform was taken in parliament by the conservative coalition and the Green Party.

importantly, the base for an agreement should be a shared commitment to the collective-agreement model with a view to expand its coverage and to establish a new climate of mutual trust between the unions and the employers (LO press conference, 11 March 2009). The unions also wanted to find a common response to the decision of the European Court of Justice in the *Laval Case*, which had ruled that EU firms that posted workers in Sweden did not have to follow the Swedish collective agreements.

The more formal negotiations began in the fall of 2008, and it soon became evident that the main point of discord again was the 'last in, first out' principle. In their proposal for an agreement, the employers offered increased support for laid-off workers and the commitment to negotiations on the *Laval* issue. In return, they wanted progress to be made on both of their two key demands (SN Press release, 11 March 2009). The unions put forward a proposal in which they agreed to a 'delay mechanism' for sympathy action, but rejected any significant changes to the 'last in, first out' principle. This was not enough for the employers, and they withdrew from the negotiations and called for the government to make legislative changes. The government, however, has not responded to the employer's demands yet. The failure of these negotiations taken together with the government's deregulation of the use of temporary employment means a continuation with the dualist pattern of the earlier reforms in Sweden.

Conclusions

In both France and Sweden, we observe a dualist reform pattern. Job security for regular workers has remained in place, while the protection for temporary workers has been deregulated. The two cases thus lend support to our argument: countries characterized by rigid labour markets and high social wages have adjusted to economic pressures by introducing flexibility at the margin. We have also shown that this has been the intention of policymakers. Both social-democratic and conservative parties, and to some extent unions, have accepted the need for increased labour market flexibility. But why have we not seen a general deregulation of job security legislation?

We have argued that dualist reforms take place when unions make use of their political influence to defend policies that correspond to their organizational interest. In both cases, we have seen the crucial role that unions have played in the area of labour market reform. The introduction of job security legislation in the 1970s gave the unions an important role in the administration of lay-offs. In France, the legislation has given the unions the role of guarantors: they protect worker's interests in dismissal procedures. In Sweden, the legislation has given the unions a bargaining role. Moreover, in both cases, we have seen how unions have protected the rights of dismissed workers, for instance, by forcing employers to provide higher redundancy payments. In France, where redundancy payments are decided by law, unions have continually pushed for higher financial compensation.

Job security legislation performs two additional functions that are in the organizational interest of unions. First, legislation ensures (France) or facilitates (Sweden) the exemption of union delegates from collective dismissals. In France, the labour inspector has to authorize such dismissals and in Sweden the unions can protect their delegates in the bargaining process. Lacking such legislation, union delegates would have no other option than to file for discrimination. Second, the existence of substantial job security facilitates the involvement of workers in union activities at the workplace and insulates them in wage bargaining from the competition of the unemployed. During the reforms described in the case studies, unions have thus been willing to participate in negotiations to protect their inclusion in policymaking, and in the negotiations, have protected those policies that correspond to their organizational interest. When under pressure, unions have opted for the second-best solution of com-promising on the regulation of temporary employment because this does not threaten their organizational interests.

Alternative explanations—focusing on vote-maximizing strategies of political parties and representational interests of unions—are put into question by the evidence presented in the case studies. First, even though union density in Sweden is considerably higher than in France and union structure more encompassing, similar insider-outsider dynamics can be observed. When under pressure, Swedish unions have compromised on temporary employment. Second, it is not only under social-democratic governments that we can observe dualist reforms. Conservative governments were in charge during the 2008 reforms in France and the 1993 and 2006 reforms in Sweden. Moreover, the social-democratic parties' decision to introduce dualist reforms was not a reflection of demands from its core constituency. Both the 1985 reform in France and the 1997 reform in Sweden were a result of the political parties having decided to limit themselves to dualist reforms either in order to ensure the unions' position of power, or as a result of union influence within the party. In both cases, the new legislation was in line with union preferences. Finally, Conservative governments have wanted to introduce more general reforms but have been unable to do so with the exception of the 1986 reform in France, often because of union resistance.

To what extent can we generalize our argument? The study simultaneously relies on a least likely and a most dissimilar case design. Thus, it should be possible to make contingent generalizations. The scope conditions of the generalization are determined by our theoretical argument. In countries where unions have established 'institutional power resources' we are likely to observe a dualist reform pattern. Note that the concept of 'institutional power resources' includes two types of institutions: unions have to be included in the policymaking process, and to consider some institutional feature of existing policies as crucial for their long-term organizational interests, in this case job security legislation for regular workers. Thus, our argument is relevant for cases only if they satisfy two necessary conditions: unions' political influence, and the existence of institutional features such as job security legislation. In contrast, in countries in which such political influence and such policies were never established, we are likely to observe different reform patterns.

Notes

1. A previous version of this chapter was presented at conferences in Boston (CES), Lisbon (ECPR) and Lucerne (SPSA). We thank all participants and in particular Alexandre Afonso, Silja Häusermann, Johannes Lindvall, George Ross, B. Rothstein and Sven Steinmo for helpful comments. P. E. would like to acknowledge the financial support of the Danish Agency for Science, Technology and Innovation for the project 'The Politics of Job Security Regulations in Industrialized Western Democracies'.
2. The terms 'lay-off' and 'dismissal' are used interchangeably.
3. Ebbinghaus (2006: 128, 130) provides the following ratios. Male/female: France (0.84), Sweden (1.03); <34/35–54 years old: France (0,45), Sweden (0,88); state/private employees: France (3.28), Sweden (1.15); unemployed/employed: France (0,11), Sweden (0,84).
4. Data if not otherwise indicated are from OECD Labour Force Statistics <http://www.oecd.org/>, accessed 20 September 2010.
5. Wage inequality is measured using the latest available Gini coefficient from the Luxembourg Income Study Key Figures <http://www.lisproject.org/keyfigures.htm>, accessed 20 September 2010.
6. The period of investigation is a function of data availability and varies between 9 and 14 years.
7. However, they retained their influence within the Labour Party (Rueda 2007).
8. Traxler et al. (2001) have called the institutionalized participation of unions in the deliberation of labour market policy reforms a 'secondary power resource'.
9. This feature is not exclusively belonging to unions. In Sweden, for example, the debate over wage-earner funds, which threatened the firms' right to manage, triggered a radicalization of the employers (Stråth 1998).
10. Interview.
11. Interview with senior official, Ministry of Labour.
12. Interview with CFDT negotiator.
13. Interview with negotiator CFDT.
14. Interview.

15. The CPE proposal was retracted as a result of popular protests. The CNE was introduced, but even though it afforded employers the right to dismiss workers on a new regular contract during the first two years without having to justify the action, the Courts made use of Convention no. 158 (1982) of the ILO to reinstate a demand for 'valid reason' (Gaudu 2008).
16. Interview with negotiator CFDT.
17. Interviews with negotiators for CFDT and Medef (former CNPF).
18. Interview.
19. Interview.
20. The Centre Party, which supported the minority government, also put pressure on the SAP over this issue.
21. The Conservative group in parliament together with the Green Party re-introduced the two exemptions to the 'last in, first out' principle in 2001 against the will of the social-democratic minority government.
22. This promise was made again in the 2010 election campaign.

Bibliography

Blyth, M. (2002) *Great Transformations: Economic Ideas and Institutional Change in the Twentieth Century*, Cambridge, Cambridge University Press.

Booth, A. L., Dolado, J. J. & Frank, J. (2002) Symposium on Temporary Work: Introduction. *Economic Journal*, 112, 181–8.

Cahuc, P. & Zylberberg, A. (2009) *Les réformes ratées du Président Sarkozy*, Paris, Flammarion.

Compston, H. (2003) Beyond Corporatism: A Configurational Theory of Policy Concertation. *European Journal of Political Research*, 42, 787–809.

Crouch, C. (1993) *Industrial Relations and European State Traditions*, Oxford, Oxford University Press.

Davidsson, J. B. (2011) Unions in Hard Times: Labour Market Policies in Western Europe: Two Patterns of Reform, PhD dissertation, European University Institute, Florence.

Davidsson, J. B. & Naczyk, M. (2009) The Ins and Outs of Dualisation: A Literature Review, RECWOWE Working Paper No. 02/2009.

DiPrete, T. A., Goux, D., Maurin, E. & Quesnel-Vallee, A. (2006) Work and Pay in Flexible and Regulated Labor Markets: A Generalized Perspective on Institutional Evolution and Inequality Trends in Europe and the US. *Research in Social Stratification and Mobility*, 24, 311–32.

Dir. (1995:30) *Kommission om den svenska arbetsrätten*.

Duprilot, J. P. (1975) Le contrôle administratif des licenciements. *Droit social*, 6, 53–72.

Ebbinghaus, B. (2006) Trade Union Movements in Post-Industrial Welfare States. In Armingeon, K. & Bonoli, G. (Eds.) *The Politics of Post-Industrial Welfare States: Adapting Post-War Social Policies to New Social Risks*, London, Routledge, 123–42.

Emmenegger, P. (2010) The Long Road to Flexicurity: The Development of Job Security Regulations in Denmark and Sweden. *Scandinavian Political Studies*, 33, 271–94.

Emmenegger, P. (2011) Job Security Regulations in Western Europe: A Fuzzy Set Analysis. *European Journal of Political Research*, 50, 336–64.

Emmenegger, P., Häusermann, S., Palier, B. & Seeleib-Kaiser, M. (2012) *The Age of Dualization: The Changing Face of Inequality in Deindustrializing Societies*, New York, Oxford University Press.

Fabre, A., Lefresne, F. & Tuchszirer, C. (2008) L'Accord du 11 Janvier sur la modernisation du marché du travail. *Revue de l'OFCE*, 4, 5–28.

Freyssinet, J. (2007) L'Accord du 11 Janvier 2008 sur la modernisation du marché du travail: Un avenir incertain. *Revue de l'IRES*, 54.

Gaudu, F. (2008) La réform du contrat de travail dans la loi du 25 Juin 2008. In *Regards sur l'actualité. Dossier: La modernisation du marché du travail*, Paris, La Documentation Francaise.

Glaymann, D. (2005) *La Vie en intérim*, Paris, Fayard.

Golden, M. A. (1997) *Heroic Defeats: The Politics of Job Loss*, Cambridge, Cambridge University Press.

Hamskär, I. & Gustafsson, S. (2010) Framtidens arbetsrätt bör byggas på fakta, *Lag & avtal*, 27 August.

Hellberg, I. & Vrethem, M. (1983) *Lagen om anställningsskydd: Tillkomst och tillämpning*, Sociologiska institutionen, Gothenburg, Gothenburg University.

Howell, C. (1992) *Regulating Labor: The State and Industrial Relations Reform in Postwar France*, Princeton, Princeton University Press.

Lindbeck, A. & Snower, D. J. (1988) *The Insider-Outsider Theory of Employment and Unemployment*, Cambridge, MA, MIT Press.

Lindvall, J. (2004) The Politics of Purpose: Swedish Macroeconomic Policy after the Golden Age, Doctoral dissertation, Department of Political Science, Gothenburg, Gothenburg University.

Molina, O. & Rhodes, M. (2002) Corporatism: The Past, Present, and Future of a Concept. *Annual Review of Political Science*, 5, 305–31.

Nycander, S. (2008) *Makten över arbetsmarknaden*, Stockholm, SNS Förlag.

Obinger, H., Starke, P. & Kaasch, A. (2012) Responses to Labor Market Dualization in Small States since the 1990s. In Emmenegger, P., Häusermann, S., Palier, B. & Seeleib-Kaiser, M. (Eds.) *The Age of Dualization: The Changing Face of Inequality in Deindustrializing Societies*, New York, Oxford University Press, 176–200.

Olsen, G. M. & O'Connor, J. S. (1998) *Power Resources Theory and the Welfare State: A Critical Approach*, Toronto, University of Toronto Press.

Palier, B. & Thelen, K. (2012) Dualization and Institutional Complementarities: Industrial Relations, Labor Market and Welfare State Changes in France and Germany. In Emmenegger, P., Häusermann, S., Palier, B. and Seeleib-Kaiser, M. (Eds.) *The Age of Dualization: The Changing Face of Inequality in Deindustrializing Societies*, New York, Oxford University Press, 201–5.

Piore, M. J. (1980) Dualism as a Response to Flux and Uncertainty. In Berger, S. & Piore, M. J. (Eds.) *Dualism and Discontinuity in Industrial Societies*, Cambridge, Cambridge University Press, 23–45.

Prop. (1993/1994:67) *Om ändringar i lagen om anställningsskydd och i lagen om medbestämmande i arbetslivet*.

Prop. (1996/1997:16) *En arbetsrätt för ökad tillväxt.*

Prop. (2006/07:111) *Bättre möjligheter till tidsbegränsad anställning, M.M.*

Regini, M. (2000) The Dilemmas of Labour Market Regulation. In Esping-Andersen, G. & Regini, M. (Eds.) *Why Deregulate Labour Markets?* New York, Oxford University Press, 11–29.

Rueda, D. (2007) *Social Democracy Inside Out: Partisanship & Labor Market Policy in Industrialized Democracies,* Oxford, Oxford University Press.

Saint-Paul, G. (1996) Exploring the Political Economy of Labour Market Institutions. *Economic Policy,* 11, 263–300.

SOU (1973:7) *Trygghet i anställningen: Anställningsskydd och vissa anställningsfrämjande åtgärder.*

SOU (1993:32) *Ny anställningsskyddslag.*

Traxler, F., Blaschke, S. & Kittel, B. (2001) *National Labour Relations in Internationlized Markets: A Comparative Study of Institutions, Change, and Performance,* Oxford, Oxford University Press.

Wibble, A. (1994) *Två cigg och en kopp kaffe,* Stockholm, Ekerlids förlag.

Part IV
Continent-wide Perspectives

11

Turning Vice Into Vice

How Bismarckian Welfare States have Gone from Unsustainability to Dualization[1]

Bruno Palier

Continental European welfare systems have, for a long time, been portrayed as the least adaptable. In the mid-1990s, Gøsta Esping-Andersen emphasized the rigidity of the continental welfare state arrangements, speaking of a 'frozen continental landscape' 'immune to change' (Esping-Andersen 1996: 66–7). Fritz Scharpf and Vivien Schmidt (2000) similarly argued that even though all welfare states are, in various ways, vulnerable to increasingly open economies, 'Christian Democratic' welfare systems based on social insurance not only face the greatest difficulties of all, but are also the most difficult to reform. Paul Pierson (2001) also observed that significant welfare state reform has been rarest and most problematic in Continental Europe.

Since the advent of the new millennium, however, major changes have become highly visible in the welfare arrangements of continental European countries. During the 2000s, as a comparison of national reform trajectories (Palier 2010a), as well as reforms in different social insurance fields (old age, unemployment, health insurance; Palier and Martin 2007) has shown, all continental European countries have implemented important structural re-forms that have altered their welfare systems. Employment policies and unemployment insurance systems have changed, shifting away from a 'labour shedding' strategy and towards the development of activation policies (Clegg 2007). Austria, France, Germany, Italy, and Spain have each gone through several waves of pension reform, introducing innovations such as voluntary private pension funds and emphasizing increasing employment rates among the elderly (Bonoli and Palier 2007). In health care, reforms grafted two new logics onto the traditional insurance approach: a logic of universalization through state intervention, and a market logic based on regulated competition (Hassenteufel and Palier 2007). Furthermore, countries well known for their ingrained familialism and traditional approach to the gender division of labour have radically changed their child- and elder-care policies. Since the late 1990s, they have developed formal caring facilities and parental leave schemes, facilitating the combination of work and family life for women—and the creation of 'low end' jobs in the personal service sector (Morel 2007).

What have been the politics of these unexpected changes? Among the few researchers who identified possibilities for change in Continental European welfare states, some have argued that partisan politics is central. Levy (1999), in particular, argued that left parties are in a position to be able to turn 'vice into virtue' and to render Bismarckian welfare systems both more economically efficient and socially just. When he analysed the few changes he identified in Italy, the Netherlands, and Germany at the end of the 1990s, Paul Pierson tended to view the reform path for these countries as one requiring 'careful negotiation among all, or at least most, major political actors', based on the construction of a 'new middle' coalition, that would be able to combine cost containment and modernizing recalibration on the basis of elite negotiation and mutual legitimation (Pierson 2001: 451).

A decade after these seminal publications, it is possible to test these hypotheses on the politics and orientation of welfare reforms in Continental Europe. If Jonah Levy was right, one should see welfare systems mainly reformed by progressive coalitions or through social pacts, and these reforms should have the virtue of rendering the systems more economically viable and more socially just. However, recent collective research (Palier and Martin 2007; Palier 2010a) shows that if both Jonah Levy and Paul Pierson were right in emphasizing the possibility of negotiated solution to overcome the apparent dilemma posed by the twin pressures of cost containment and popular support, they wrongly assumed that negotiated reforms would be able to modernize welfare systems (i.e. to provide better protection to women, youth, migrants or low-skilled workers). On the contrary, except in a few (Dutch, Swiss or Austrian) cases, most of the negotiations have been based on the acceptance of reforms by the main trade unions (who overly represent male industrial workers in Continental Europe) as long as most of their cost would be passed on to labour market outsiders and/or future generations.

In this chapter, I will first trace back the main and common characteristics of the reform trajectory that are followed by Continental European welfare systems. This trajectory can be divided into four main sequences, that I will analyse in turn, with a specific focus on their politics. I will then analyse what

Bismarckian welfare systems have become. Continental Europe witnessed the development of dual welfare systems, with a sharper line being drawn between contributory benefits and occupational insurance for core workers and a new but growing world of assistance and in-work/non-contributory benefits for 'atypical' workers and labour market outsiders. This dualization of welfare is to be associated with transformations on labour market and developments in employment policies (see Davidsson and Emmenegger, Chapter 10), but they also have to be attributed to the specificities of the politics of reforms in Bismarckian welfare systems. Negotiations between elite and representatives of core workers have indeed allowed reforms formerly conceived as unlikely, but the compromises have most often been made at the expense of outsiders.

How Did Continental European Welfare System Change? The Commonalities and Politics of the Typical 'Bismarckian' Reform Trajectory

The expansion of Bismarckian welfare systems was based on a specific post-war compromise. In Continental Europe, where Christian Democrats either dominated governments or played a pivotal role, post-war reforms built on existing institutions, and utilized 'Bismarckian means' to reach Beveridgean objectives, i.e. to protect all individuals against all social risks (Palier 2005). Governments progressively extended pre-existing social insurances to cover all the risks of all dependent workers and the self-employed (and their relatives), supposing that mainly men would be in the workforce while women would stay at home and care for the children and/or dependent elderly (Lewis 1992). This dependence by families on the income and social privileges of male family heads resulted in greater importance being given to job security and to guarantees of employment status (the seniority principle, regulation of hiring practices, and employment termination) than to the development of employment for all (Esping-Andersen 1996).

It is precisely the assumption of 'full male employment' that has been undermined by the changes in the economic and social context since the 1970s. These changes (increasing capital mobility, intensified competition between economies, de-industrialization, mass and structural unemployment, population ageing, rising female labour market participation) have increasingly challenged the functioning of the Bismarckian welfare systems and called for adaptation and reforms. Despite what many scholars predicted, all continental European countries implemented important structural reforms of their welfare systems (a shift to multipillar pension systems, activation, competition in health insurance, and care policies outside the family). Even though the changes only became fully apparent over the past decade, they must be understood as the culmination of a longer reform trajectory.

Starting from an initial reaction to the 1970s employment crisis that was highly determined by the institutional logic of the Bismarckian system itself (labour shedding and increase in social contributions), the orientation of reforms has changed only progressively, by a succession of measures that build on the consequences of the preceding ones. The transformation of welfare systems have happened through an incremental process, in which the adoption of given measures facilitated the acceptance and growth of certain policy options—that would otherwise have been extremely difficult, if not impossible, politically—and undermines others. Individuals and collective political actors exploited the new opportunities that apparently marginal earlier reforms opened up, and through their actions came to change the whole system. Therefore, if we want to understand the general process through which Continental European welfare systems have been transformed, we cannot analyse any one (big or small) reform in isolation from the whole reform process. This reform process we refer to as the 'reform trajectory'. The 'reform trajectory' is made up of different phases, with each characterized by a predominant type of policy change or reform. One can distinguish four main phases in the typical Bismarckian welfare reform trajectory. In what follows, I will analyse the main characteristics of these four phases.

Save the industry!

For most of the Continental European countries, what was really at stake in the late 1970s and early 1980s was to save their (industrial) economic and social system. De-industrialization particularly hit old industrial countries (or regions) like Germany, France, Belgium, Northern Italy, Austria, and their associated social model. Confronted with an increase in international competition, especially in manufacturing, most continental countries did not want to give up on industry in favour of high and low skill services (as, essentially, the UK seems to have, at least in its macro-economic policies), nor promote and invest in innovation and new industries (like California or the Nordic countries did); they decided instead to defend and preserve as much as possible their traditional industries by increasing protection and productivity of the core industrial workers, laying off older and less productive workers and outsourcing many activities (mainly low skilled services) which previously provided relatively well paid and protected jobs within the industrial firms themselves (Palier and Thelen 2010). The main focus was to preserve the most productive male breadwinner's job and social protection by removing all his potential competitors from the labour market. This strategy meant more employment protection for the core workers (Rueda 2007), but also more spending for those removed from the labour market who were receiving compensation (Esping-Andersen 1996). Unemployment insurances, invalidity allowances, and early pension have been expanded dramatically in order to support this strategy and provide income to the 'removed' people.

This first reaction was extremely consensual: all the main actors (among them the social partners, where unions and employers from manufacturing industry were dominant—see Ebbinghaus and Visser 2000) agreed that the best way to respond to the crisis was to protect the jobs and social protection of the most productive employees, and to remove the least productive ones (who were anyway not well represented in the political and social systems of Continental Europe). This strategy of course had a price—numerous and generous allowances had to be financed—but apparently almost everybody was ready to pay this, especially since it was not the state budget and therefore the tax-payers who would have to shoulder this burden, but instead the social insurance schemes and social contributions. Indeed, an often neglected but crucial feature of the Bismarckian welfare reform trajectory is that it was social insurances that had to foot the bill for the labour shedding strategy. 'Loading' the social insurances system in this way was a low-risk political strategy for governments in the short-term, as they had neither to impose cuts nor to increase taxes. They could thus claim credit for helping the victims of the crisis, while justifying increases in social contribution rates as necessary to guarantee the viability of the highly popular social insurance schemes.

As a consequence, for social insurances, the main problems created both by the economic slowdown and by the first reaction to it have been low employment rates and deficits in the social budgets. In order to balance the accounts of social insurance schemes, governments mainly raised the level of social contributions. In the beginning of the 1990s, this strategy appeared more and more unsuccessful and particularly in contradiction with the main policy orientations at the European level. First negotiated retrenchments started to spread in Continental Europe.

Save the welfare systems! The first wave of retrenchment, in the early 1990s

In the early 1990s, for France, Italy, Spain, Belgium, and for accessing countries like Austria and later the Visegraad countries, the 'European constraints' have been instrumental in stopping the previous social policy response to economic and social difficulties. Even for the countries for which the Maastricht criteria were not so new (like Germany and other countries attached to the D-Mark), the fact that they had also previously increased their level of social contributions (for their consolidation measure, and in the case of Germany, to finance unification) meant a problem in the context of globalization and single European market. What triggered a reversal in the reforms, from expanding social benefits (and increasing social contributions) in order to buffer the impact of the crisis and industrial restructuration, towards attempt at cost control, was the perception that the level of social contributions was growing to unbearable economic limits.

However, what is striking in the discourses justifying most of the reforms of this period is that, even if the level of social contributions is under criticism, the whole system of social insurances is not (yet). On the contrary, it is most often presented as itself victim of the continuing crisis, for unemployment and slow growth increase deficits and prevent revenues to be high enough. Most of the time when a government presented a reform during the 1990s, the announced goal was to save the system, even if it was to implement retrenchment.

Either in old age pension, or for unemployment or invalidity benefits, in all the cases, the main technique used for reducing social insurance benefits was to strengthen the link between the amount and duration of contributions and the volume of the benefits. This, of course, relied on the already existing logic of the schemes (the right to social benefits derives from paying social contributions). Typically, unemployed (or invalid) were asked to have contributed during a longer period before inactivity to be entitled to the full allowance; the number of years for being entitled to full pension was increased, or deduction for pensions claimed before the standard age of retirement was introduced. Benefits were thus reduced mainly for those who could not have a long, full-time career, but preserved for the 'typical' workers. In order to relieve social insurance deficits, decisions were also made to remove the financing of 'non-contributory benefits' from the social insurance budgets.

At the turn of the 1990s, projects of reforms often triggered considerable opposition, and had to be negotiated with the social partners to gain acceptance. As mentioned, during the preceding period, the cost of new social expenditure aimed at buffering the consequences of the crisis, and especially the cost of labour shedding (and of German unification) has been put on social insurances shoulders. The social partners have for long complained to governments about this, claiming that the cost of the non-contributory benefits was explaining a lot of the financial difficulties met by social insurances. In almost all Continental countries, social partners have asked the State to take its responsibility, and to finance with taxes (and not with social contributions) the non-contributory benefits.

During the 1990s, only negotiated reforms could be passed in Continental Europe. Reforms that passed were those which were accompanied by a

238

'clarification of responsibility', the government proposing that the social partners were to assume the financing of non-contributory benefits (flat rate social minima for the elderly, the handicapped, the long-term unemployed; credit of contributions for period out of work because of unemployment, child rearing, etc.) in exchange for their acceptance of cost containment measures in social insurance benefits. In the eyes of the social partners, this guaranteed the financial viability of social insurances.

Reforms have thus been implemented and negotiated so that they would preserve and save social insurances. However, in the meantime they progressively changed their scope. What these reforms have changed is the capacity of social insurances to be 'quasi-universal', as they were supposed to be since the 1960s–1970s. By reducing the replacement rates in unemployment benefits or pension, they no longer insure full income guarantee. By removing more and more people (with atypical profiles) from social insurances, they do not cover the whole population. Since the coverage of social insurance is shrinking through these reforms (fewer people covered, less generous benefits), more and more space is created for the development of new benefits, either complementary at the top of compulsory social insurance (voluntary private pensions for instance), or at the bottom, for those who lost (or never gained) their rights to social insurance.

Through the way they have been negotiated, these first reforms have sown seeds of dualization within the welfare systems themselves. In the negotiations, the trade unions have managed to guarantee the position of current 'insiders' through a long phasing-in period for reforms in pension rights (Bonoli and Palier 2007) and a dual recalibration of unemployment insurance benefits, with greater benefits for those who worked full-time previously and less for those with more precarious careers (Clegg 2007). In order to 'relieve' social insurances from covering the long-term unemployed and the non-standard workers, the counterpart to these reforms started to institutionalize a new world of welfare for 'atypical' workers, through the development of tax-financed, non-contributory, income-tested benefits.

However, these reforms have progressively underlined structural problems linked with Bismarckian social insurances: they are unable (and unwilling) to cover those who cannot fully contribute to the system (the socially excluded, precarious workers, and atypical profiles); their main source of financing (social contributions) seem to hinder job creation and competitiveness; moreover, the traditional 'spokesmen' of social insurances (the social partners and especially unions) are able to block important reforms. From victim, the welfare systems progressively appeared as major causes of the Continental European difficulties, leading to (incremental) institutional reforms that afterwards enabled structural reforms.

Reforming welfare institutions

The political difficulties raised by these attempts at retrenchment and their relative failures (social expenditure continued to increase, unemployment to be high), led governments to learn that the institutional setting of the system were partly explaining their problems. Two main institutional characteristics of Bismarckian welfare systems have been of crucial importance to shape problems and solutions: financing by social contributions and the (formal and/or informal) involvement of the social partners in the governance of the welfare systems. These two institutional traits are strongly differentiating Bismarckian social protection systems from statist or market ones. They have generated many of the economic and political problems faced by welfare systems in Continental Europe. The high level of social contributions appeared detrimental from an economic point of view. It also appeared politically detrimental, since this mode of financing highlighted the link of Bismarckian social protection to the realm of employment and work, and thus to the representatives of this world, who claimed to have a say in the reforms. Social partners, especially Unions, have often been able to block reforms.

Learning how much these institutional traits were explaining their difficulties in the reforms they sought to implement, governments concentrated more and more on institutional 'meta-policy reforms' (Clegg 2007), aimed at transforming the very bases of these welfare systems: changes in financing mechanisms (toward less social contributions and more taxes) as well as in governance arrangements (weakening of the social partners, privatization or 'étatisation').

Three main mechanisms have been driving the movement from contribution to tax financing: first, the role of tax financing has been increased in the cases of (negotiated) retrenchment reform when government committed to pay for non contributory benefits that social insurances were paying for beforehand; second, in the framework of employment policies, many continental European governments have decided to exempt employers from paying some social contributions in order to lower the cost of unskilled labour—in these cases, governments have either given tax subsidies to the employers, or compensated the social insurance funds with tax money for the loss of social contribution due to these exemptions, thus again switching from social contribution to taxes; finally, and more rarely, genuine new taxes have been created either to substitute for social contribution, or to finance new types of social expenditure (Like the *Contribution sociale généralisée* in France and the *Ökosteuer* in Germany) (Manow 2010).

As a consequence of these changes, the weight of social contribution in Continental European countries has decreased between 1995 and 2006 (while it was stabilized or even increased in all other European countries). Social contribution as a percentage of total taxation has diminished by -1.5 points of percentage in Austria, -2.3 in Belgium, -6.2 in France, -1.8 in Germany, -1.4 in Italy, -3.5 in the Netherlands, and -2.7 in Spain.[2] Even if social contributions are still playing the biggest role in the financing of Continental Welfare systems, the relative share of other taxes has increased.

Changes in financing introduced or increased the role of new instruments usually linked to a different logic of welfare (taxation). One could conclude for a case of 'hybridization' and a more mixed type of welfare system. On the contrary, our analysis shows that the changes in financing are contributing to a clearer separation between two worlds of welfare, the contributory social insurances on the one hand, and the realm of non contributory benefits on the other. In this second world of welfare, one can find the various basic safety nets. These new sources of finance may also be used to finance new or developing services, more clearly separated from insurances than before, such as health care, and services for labour market (job placement, training, etc.) and care policies.

Mechanisms that weakened the influence of the social partners have also been varied. One has been removing the social partners as a 'natural' consequence of the change in financing: when the state finances (through taxation) it also wants to make the decisions; another way has been to by-pass the social partners, by excluding them (informally or formally) from the consulation/concertation games. In many cases this occurred through a shift in power from the social partners to the parliament, the social partners losing their traditional role in the social policymaking through procedural changes; administrative reforms have also contributed to weakening the role of the social partners by changing the governance structure of some important social insurance bodies. Finally, liberalization or privatization (complete or partial) of former funds/agencies held by the social partners has also contributed to weaken the traditional roles of the social partners (Ebbinghaus 2010).

The traditional role of the social partners in compulsory social insurances has been weakened, government have progressively gained more political capacities to impose their reforms, as will be shown in the next section. One should not, however, conclude that there is a general weakening of the social partners in labour market and social policies, since employers remain quite influential in the most recent reforms, and collective negotiation may undergo a revival in complementary social protection (especially in pension) and within the decentralized labour market policies.

At least, with these institutional transformations, governments have gained more control on the financing and the decision-making in basic social protection. They have acquired new political capacities to take the tough decisions, and some financing capacities for new types of benefits aimed at either targeting the most needy, and/or covering new social risks. These changes weakened the traditional pillars of the Bismarckian welfare systems, thus allowing for more structural changes, which occurred in the early 2000s. These 'meta-policy reforms' indeed appear to be a pre-condition for further changes (Clegg 2007: 77). They enabled further retrenchments to be imposed, and they paved the way for the deeper structural changes that became visible during the 2000s.

Restructuring Bismarckian welfare systems

In the late 1990s, despite a decade of difficult economic and social policy reforms, Continental European countries still faced considerable economic and social problems. If the level of unemployment was on the decrease everywhere in Europe in the end of the decade, the rates of employment in continental Europe were still very low. If deficits have been contained to meet Maastricht criteria, some countries still had a huge debt (Belgium, Italy especially); and deficits were higher here than in many other European countries. Apart for some exceptions (like the Netherlands or Spain), economic growth rates on the continent were lower than in the other European countries (and lower than in the US or Canada). From the outside, 'Old Europe' was stigmatized for its poor economic performances compared to the capacity of other models (Anglo-saxon or Nordic) to overcome their own difficulties.

Moreover, in the late 1990s, the negative impacts of social and demographic changes became more visible. While the inactivity rate of the older worker was on the increase, the baby boomers were about to leave on pension during the coming decade. The demographic dependency ratio (inactive/active) was the most unfavourable in Continental Europe. While women willingly entered the labour market in most European countries, their difficulties to combine work and family life in most conservative welfare systems became more evident, and the idea that this could be detrimental to fertility started to be discussed. Finally, if unemployment was fluctuating, long-term unemployment and social exclusion was increasing, especially among the low-skilled workers. In the European continent, there was an increasing awareness of the emergence of new social risks (such as precarious employment, long-term unemployment, being a member of the working poor, single parenthood, or inability to reconcile work and family life; Bonoli 2005) and of the incapacity of the traditional welfare systems to protect people against them.

Faced by continuous difficulties and failures of their past attempts to address them, Continental European governments got convinced that to solve their structural difficulties, structural changes of their welfare systems were necessary, including the adoption of a new social policy agenda. For the first time, reforms were explicitly aimed at changing and restructuring the welfare systems. Since the early 1990s, new social policy paradigms, and new social programmes were spreading around, from outside Continental Europe (see Jenson, Chapter 2). These new ideas and experiences constituted a credible alternative to the typical Continental answers (i.e. 'passive' income compensation, labour shedding), and seemed adapted to the new economic context (globalization, single market and increased competition) and new economic policy orientation that goes with the Maastricht criteria (a sound public budget, limited debt, low inflation rate). Moreover, they were also addressing the new social risks, and seemed to have been implemented successfully in some European countries (UK, but also, in their own fashion, Nordic countries).

Adopting this new agenda meant for Continental Europe to radically re-orient their main strategies (labour shedding). In that sense, it meant to implement a paradigmatic change in the policies adopted (from labour shedding to activation) without necessarily implying that the whole system would be changed. Since the early 2000s, a new wave of reforms has been developing. These reforms testify a new will to overcome the 'welfare without work' trap. Activation of the unemployed, limitation of early exit, measures for increasing the participation of women, older workers and unskilled workers are amongst the biggest innovations. Important pension reforms have also been adopted, aimed at further reducing the cost of public pensions and at favouring the development of a private fully funded complement. In health care, in the countries having a health insurance system, more regulatory power is given to the State, and more competition between heath insurances is being introduced. Since further retrenchments are adopted, minimum income protection is generalized, to protect the weakest from the general retreat of social insurances. This has gone through the structural transformation of traditional social insurances (see Table 11.1). Finally, reforms (in a more limited number of countries) also include attempts at 'modernizing' Bismarckian welfare systems in order to provide a better protection against new social risks through the (more or less timid) development of new social policies.

Of specific importance for the Continental European countries are the attempts at increasing the employment rate of the elderly (meaning a shift away from the early exit strategy) and the attempt at supporting women's entry (and stay) on the labour market. Since the latter goal cannot be met only with social insurances, and since other new social risks have emerged, in addition to these structural reforms in traditional social insurance schemes, new social policies (marked by both new goals and new instruments) are emerging: minimum income guarantees, leave and care policies.

Confronted with long-term unemployment, more volatility on the labour market, precarious jobs, social exclusion and above all, the shrinking coverage of social insurances, all countries but Italy have either expanded and generalized, or created minimum income guarantees, either as a general safety net,[3] or as specific minimum income in different policy fields.[4] Italy got stuck

Table 11.1. The structural reforms in traditional social insurance schemes

- In Germany, the 2001 Riester pension reform planned further restrictions of the level of public pension, but also created the possibility for complementary future pension rights through personal or occupational pension plans. The pension replacement rate was further reduced in 2004, and the postponement of the legal retirement age to 67 is planned; during the early 2000s, the four so-called Hartz reforms deeply transformed German labour market and unemployment insurance, introducing activation and expanding low-cost jobs; between 2003 and 2007, increased healthcare co-payment for patients, increased competition amongst health insurance providers and new tax financing arrangements were implemented (Hinrichs 2010).

- In France, the 2001 unemployment reform generalized activation to most of the unemployed, while more and more in-work benefits have been developed (*Prime pour l'emploi, revenu de solidarité active*). The 2003 pension reforms expanded the scope of retrenchment to public sector workers, but also created pension saving plans, both individual and occupational. Throughout the 2000s, co-payments have been increased in the ambulatory healthcare sector giving private insurance an increasing role in the system, while the 2004 and 2008 health reforms increased the control of national and regional public authorities over the rest the system (control of patients in general, and over the hospital sector) (Palier 2010b).

- In Austria, the various pension acts of the first half of the 2000s closed early exit options, harmonized the system by integrating federal civil servants into the general scheme, diminished the level of Pay As You Go benefits and progressively introduced a supplementary private pillar (financed through the conversion of the previous severance payments). Employment policies have also been characterized by tighter eligibility conditions for unemployment benefits, a stronger reliance on activation policies and increased efforts to create employment opportunities for the unskilled. In healthcare, due to ever-increasing co-payments, the share of private health expenditure as a percentage of total health expenditure has increased continuously and new funding principles apply (diminishing employers' contributions), while new state agencies have been created to better control the system (Obinger and Tálos 2010).

- In Belgium, after the reform of unemployment insurance to focus it more on minimum income protection, some timid activation measures were adopted between 1999 and 2005, as well as a 'generation pact', aimed at diminishing early retirement (but without great success); public pensions, as provided through social security, have become so low that average to high earners have come to rely on occupational and private schemes to obtain a pension commensurate with their past earnings. The 2003 Law Vandenbroucke on supplementary pensions aimed to generalize access to such private provision (Hemerijck and Marx 2010).

- In the Netherlands, activation policies date back to the mid-1990s, with the so-called 'Melkert jobs' for low-skilled workers, women, younger workers, foreign nationals, and the long-term unemployed; activation was pushed further with the introduction in 1997 of cuts in employers' social security contributions for hiring the long term unemployed and low paid workers, and with the Jobseekers Employment Act (WIW) in 1998, which imposed an individualized assessment interview on each new unemployment benefit. Competition between health insurance schemes became effective in 2005. Since a majority of pensions were already fully funded, there have not been such big changes in this area as in the other cases, but strong incentives have been created to reduce early exit (Hemerijck and Marx 2010).

- In Italy, structural pension reforms date back to 1995, the Dini reforms having introduced a public notional defined contribution system, to be implemented through a long transition process that would preserve the unions' core constituencies; in the 2000s, supplementary defined contribution schemes have been highly favoured through the automatic conversion of severance payments (TFR) into pension saving plans; the flexibilization of the Italian labour market as well as active labour market policies (mainly targeted at the most disadvantage groups) were developed in the late 1990s. However, blockages could not be overcome to promote adequate unemployment insurance and a real minimum income safety net (Jessoula and Alti 2010).

- In Spain, despite the absence of such visible pension reforms as in the German, Italian or French cases, private pensions introduced in the late 1980s have grown steadily. The labour market has also been flexibilized (through the massive use of temporary work contracts), and active labour market policies have also been introduced (Guillen 2010).

- In Switzerland, fully funded pensions already existed, and private health insurances were already in competition. Changes towards including some 'outsiders' within the scope of insurance schemes have been adopted. The turn to activation is also very visible, starting in 1995 with more access to training, followed in the 2000s with a strengthened commitment to the re-integration of disabled and changes in family policies to improve the capacity to combine work and family life (Häusermann 2010).

Source: Palier (2010a).

244

into experimentation of minimum income, without being able to overcome institutional and political obstacles to generalize its minimum insertion income.

This development of assistance schemes shows that instead of a temporary cyclical change on the labour market, the increasing number of atypical workers, the development of long-term unemployment, the raising numbers of outsiders was perceived as durable and necessitating a permanent answer. This development (or rediscovery) of assistance schemes was also implied by the politics of retrenchment, by which social insurances were shrinking and not able to protect the most 'atypical' ones anymore. This could be interpreted as a return to old Bismarck, when the policy for the worker (*Arbeiterpolitik*) was clearly distinguished from the policies for the poor (*Armenpolitik*, see Leibfried and Tennstedt 1985); but this should in fact be interpreted as a rupture with the post-war compromise, when Bismarckian institutions were supposed to reach Beveridgean goals and cover the whole population, and as an institutionalization of dualism within social protection. However, one should note that in some countries, if a basic safety net was developed for the poorest, some reforms have also tried to re-integrate some workers within social insurance schemes (mainly part time workers) previously left out by overly strict eligibility criteria of the social insurance schemes, especially in the Netherlands, Spain, Switzerland, or Austria (See Häusermann, Chapter 6).

Other innovations have been introduced, since the late 1990s, to cope with the new social risks. The first one concerns long-term care, with Germany expanding its social insurance system in 1995 by creating a specific regime to cover this new risk. Apart from the fact that employers were actually compensated for their social contribution to this new scheme (thus breaking the golden German rule of *Parität* in the financing of compulsory social insurance schemes), no important innovation was introduced with the *Pflegeverischerung*. More innovative was the later adopted tax financed scheme in Austria (*Pflegegeld*), and the new benefit for the dependent people in France (*Allocation personnalisée à l'autonomie*).

What appears to be really innovative for some conservative Bismarckian systems are the measures aimed at investing in children's development, (re)conciling work and family life and, the preoccupation with gender equality. Some of the most conservative welfare systems started to adapt to the demise of the male breadwinner model by providing more formal care facilities for children, by reforming their parental leave so that it would not definitely break women's careers and by favouring a better share of care work between mothers and fathers, and by better protecting single mothers. The change and the announced plans are quite radical in Germany; in Spain, Switzerland, and the Netherlands, governments are trying to modernize their welfare systems, rendering them less conservative. This 'revolution' is, however, quite ambiguous, since the goals have been as much about improving women's condition as (and perhaps more) about supporting higher fertility (Henninger et al. 2008), and creating lower paid jobs (for women) in the service sectors (Morel 2007).

Meanwhile, some other countries have remained quite conservative, mainly because conservative parties oppose these changes in Italy, Austria, and most of the Visegraad countries. France and Belgium are somehow regressing, and some of the traits that made them distinctive from the typical male breadwinner model are being currently weakened, such as the availability of early childcare facilities (fiscal constraints in France are causing *écoles maternelles* to close down some classes for the youngest children).

The politics of innovative welfare reforms in Bismarckian welfare systems

Most of the structural reforms implemented in traditional social insurance schemes have been conflictual, usually raising a high amount of discontent (as well as triggering impressive strikes and demonstration in Austria—against the pension reform, or in Germany—against the Hartz IV reform). Governments appeared no more cautious in their way of presenting the negative roles of social protection structures. According to their explicit discourses, the systems needed to be changed, reduced, activated, and modernized. However, not all the Unions opposed the reforms, and governments have often tried to play the division, giving concession to the modernizers (such as Ver.di—the German Union of the service sector, or CFDT in France) against more traditional opposing Unions (such as IG Metall in Germany or FO and CGT in France). These reforms have been implemented though social pacts in Spain and in The Netherlands, although this procedure did not prevent political and social conflicts. Partly because they gained more political capacities through the institutional reforms reviewed above, and partly because of a 'divisive' strategy, governments have been able to impose their reforms despite opposition and discontent. Some concession has, however, often been made to unions and their core constituencies (long phasing in pension reform, targeting of activation).

The new social policies were more consensual among the social partners, probably because they did not touch core social insurance schemes, but added new layers to the existing social insurance system. The development of assistance in the form of minimum income benefits was welcome by most of the social and political actors, because it was addressing a pressing social issue, and relieving social insurance schemes from an 'undue' burden. Difficulties were not absent though, especially for the new policies concerning families and women. The Parliament had to by-pass the social partners in Switzerland; the Spanish Catholics strongly opposed Zapatero; and in Italy or

Austria, the modernizing project of the social democrats were buried by the conservatives when they came to power.

Towards Dualized Neo-Bismarckian Welfare Systems

Taken together, all the reforms have contributed to a reorganization of the entire welfare system: they have lost their encompassing capacities, partly turned to activation and employment-friendliness, and weakened the strongest elements of their male breadwinner bias. Instead of the emergence of new hybrid welfare systems, we see that Continental Europe witnessed the development of dual welfare systems that differentiate between the protection of the core workers and the conditional assistance of the 'atypical' (low skilled) ones.

A long goodbye to encompassing social insurances

A first key change is that the compulsory social insurance schemes are no longer able to guarantee income maintenance, to cover the whole population, and to protect against all the main social risks. The main goal of social protection in Bismarckian systems was initially to provide income security to workers and their families. This goal was broadened in the late 1960s, and social insurance systems were then supposed to cover the whole population, all social risks and guarantee near-total income maintenance. Even if they did not in reality cover the whole population in the past, at least in the late 1960s and the 1970s (and sooner for Germany, see the 1957 pension reform), covering the whole population was clearly the objective—directly through social insurance for male workers or indirectly for their spouse and children through the 'family wage' (Esping-Andersen 1996). The explicit goal was to include the whole population in the social insurance schemes and for social assistance to be consigned to history.

The various waves of retrenchments have increased the 'contributivity' of benefits and the 'equivalence' principle, leading coverage and replacement rates to decline. In most of the cases, fewer people are covered than before and a lower proportion of past wages are replaced in both old age insurance and unemployment insurance. Though some recent reforms have endeavoured to include part-time workers within the systems (in the Netherlands, Switzerland, Spain, and partly Austria, France, and Germany), social insurance can no longer be considered as 'quasi-universal' (Leisering 2009). The goal of securing the previously achieved standards of living has also vanished. In most of the cases, replacement rates have been lowered in pensions, so that people need a private complement to maintain their standard of living during old age.

In some cases, the equivalence principle itself has disappeared (in Belgian unemployment insurance, where it did not exist for long, but more importantly, in German, Austrian, Belgian, and Italian compulsory old age insurance), to be replaced by a relatively generous minimal pension guarantee. Income maintenance does not seem to be an achievable goal for Bismarckian welfare systems any more, and is being progressively replaced by *minimum income maintenance*. More and more assistance schemes have been developed to cover the uninsured and to guarantee a basic safety net, thus adding a new goal to the system: *preventing poverty*. Traditional Bismarckian welfare systems were also not easily able to cope with new social risks, and needed to add new social policies to address them. Hence, it can also be said that the typical Bismarckian institutions are no longer able to cover all social risks, and need other types of policies (new services and targeted benefits).

If the Bismarckian welfare systems are less fragmented in various social insurance funds than before (there have been mergers, concentration and reduction of the number of schemes and funds in many countries), they are now simultaneously more fragmented into a greater diversity of social policies, the core of social insurance no longer being able to suffice.

The Bismarckian welfare systems have also tried to adapt to changes in society, notably the demise of the male breadwinner model. It certainly cannot be said that in Continental Europe social policies have driven the entry of women into the labour market, but they have belatedly tried to adjust to this trend by offering more scope for women to combine work and family life. However, this has been done in quite a 'conservative' way, since in the name of 'free choice', low-skilled women are still given incentives to stay at home to take care of the kids, while more-skilled women are offered more (but still very expensive) possibilities to have their children cared for (Morel 2007).

Progressively, at least in the reforms, the former goal of supposedly 'passive' income maintenance has been replaced by a new one, *activation*, in all fields: unemployment, active ageing, and supporting women's participation in the labour market. This activation turn has been relatively successful in terms of employment rate, but not in terms of job quality and associated social protection (Emmenegger et al. 2012). Next to these new goals and principles, there has also been a modification in the policy instruments deployed.

Dual welfare systems

The multiplication of policies and the diversification of goals and principles might lead us to conclude that the Continental European welfare systems have become more hybrid, where traits of the two other 'worlds of welfare' can be found today. Instead of a blurred and incoherent mix of policies, however, I would instead argue that the new welfare systems of Continental

Europe are, in fact, characterized by a dualized structure, comprised of (less and less) social insurance on the one hand (for the 'insiders'), and more developed targeted assistance and activation schemes (for the 'outsiders') on the other.

In most of the Continental European countries, *entitlements* to old age pension, unemployment insurance, invalidity and work accident insurance are still based on work records and status. However, as a result of retrenchment policies, the amount of contribution paid is more central to the calculation of the benefits than before, thus increasing the 'actuarial' principles in the eligibility criteria. Next to the traditional social insurances, access to other benefits is now based on different criteria: more and more, citizenship is defining entitlement to health care, family benefits, and access to services such as child care, while need, poverty, and citizenship conditions are often combined into what some authors call a 'selective universalism' (Ferrera 2006) that defines access to minimum income assistance schemes.

There has been a clear diversification of the *types of benefits* in recent decades. Though contributory cash benefits still play the most important role, they are now less proportional to former wages than calibrated on 'real' amounts and durations of contributions paid. One can even see a certain residualization of benefits in some cases (old age pension in Germany, Austria, Italy, and Belgium; unemployment benefit in Belgium), where formerly proportional earnings related benefits are becoming more and more like minimum income guarantees. For those who can no longer access contributory benefits, income- and sometimes means-tested benefits have been either expanded or created in all countries. In-work benefits have been added to assistance ones. Bismarckian welfare systems still lack social services, despite plans to increase child and elderly care. In many cases, instead of these new services being directly provided, cash benefits (often income-tested) are used to pay for these services whose growth in the market sphere is being encouraged by either subsidies or social contribution exemptions. Next to public welfare, private protection is also playing an increasing role, especially in pensions and health care. Complementary private pension funds are voluntary, and can take two main forms, either collective (thus being funded jointly by employees and employers, with state subsidies), or individual (with the state subsidizing individuals or households).

The modes of *financing* have also changed, drifting from social contributions to taxes in order to make the welfare system's financing more 'employment friendly'. After a sharp increase in social contributions up to the mid-1990s, a reversal has subsequently been implemented, and the share of social contributions has since been decreasing (from 17 per cent to less than 15 per cent of GDP on average in Austria, Belgium, France, Germany, the Netherlands, and

Italy—Manow, 2010). Social contributions are far lower than before, when they were the main means of financing social benefits in Continental Europe, even though they still play the biggest role (on average, they got closer to 60 per cent of all resources, compared to the earlier average of 70 per cent). Once again, this is not so much suggestive of a blurring of the system, since in many countries reforms have strictly distinguished between the uses of social contributions (to pay for contributory benefits in social insurance), and the use of other forms of taxation, to be allocated to non-contributory (either universal or targeted) benefits.

Due to other institutional reforms, *social policymaking* has also greatly changed in Continental Europe. In most countries, the social partners can no longer be considered as veto players, at least for compulsory social insurances. Because of *étatisation* or privatization, and sometimes both together, they have increasingly been by-passed in reform events. Even if the status of social insurance funds has rarely been changed (with the notable exception of health insurance in the Netherlands, Germany, and France), those who decide on and manage them are closer to the state (national or local public authorities) than they were previously. Moreover, private companies play a much more important role, whether in employment policies and job placement, pensions (new facultative funded pension plans) or health care (*mutuelles complémentaires* in France, health insurances for glasses and dental care in Germany).

The interpretation of these shifts is not easy. We can, in fact, consider that these new goals and new instruments reflect the adoption of the new economic orthodoxy in social policy: we are all supply-siders now! This adoption does not, however, mean a total absorption and radical transformation of Continental welfare systems. As much as Hall (1989) detected different variants of Keynesianism, we see here the emergence of a Continental European *variant* of supply-side social policies. The new supply-side orientations have been adapted to Bismarckian ways of thinking and doing. Though one can see some liberal dynamics in the residualization of public pensions, the increasing role of private ones, and the development of assistance schemes, one should notice that many private pensions are based on collective agreements, and thus keep a corporatist flavour. Furthermore, when assistance schemes have been activated, this targeted only the outsiders, while shielding most of the former insiders. What is most striking is the dualization of welfare, which makes most of the Continental European countries switch to what can be called a neo-conservative, neo-corporatist welfare system. Only a few 'post-Bismarckian' social policy fields have emerged: universal health care in some countries, development of childcare facilities in many.

Conclusion: Dualization More Than Modernization

How to assess the recent transformation of Continental European welfare systems? As mentioned in the previous analysis, there has been some modernizing reforms in Continental Europe. And, as might be expected by previous literature (Levy 1999), most of the 'modernization' reforms, aimed at improving the condition of part-time workers and especially of women, have been implemented either by social democratic governments or by coalitions including parties of the left. The Italian pension reforms, which depended on the support of the left, were explicitly aimed at reducing the inherent inequalities of a pension system that paid extremely generous pensions to civil servants and rather poor pension to the self-employed and others. Schröder's 2001 pension reform in Germany created minimum benefits for the elderly and partly improved the pension calculation rules for women. More recently, modernizing changes in social insurance, pushed by the new left, the Greens and womens' organizations, have allowed a better integration of part-time work and an improvement of womens' situation in Switzerland, while simultaneously reducing the level of benefits for core insiders. In Spain, the socialist government of Zapatero has greatly contributed to an improvement in the situation of labour market outsiders, and especially women. What is at stake here is whether the new social risk bearers can lever some representation within the parties that are or can be in government (Häusermann 2010).

However, the implementation of such reforms has not, in fact, been the monopoly of the centre-left. In Austria, it was the Grand Coalition that introduced new measures to cope with poverty and new social risks; in France, the right-wing Fillon government introduced slightly better calculation rules for part-time work in its pension reform; and in Germany, the Grand Coalition has pushed forward work-life balance policies that the previous red-green coalition could not implement (such as a Swedish-style parental leave, see Naumann, Chapter 8).

In fact, few clear examples can be found of explicit 'vice-into-virtue' bargains, where those representing insiders make some concession to allow improved protection of the usual losers of Bismarckian systems (atypical workers, labour market outsiders, women, unskilled workers, etc.). We should even underline that, in the recent structural reforms as in earlier ones, material concessions have been made to core insiders above all. Almost all pension reforms have included long phasing in periods, so that the current core constituencies of trade unions will not be immediately hit by the reforms (Bonoli and Palier 2007). Activation has not been imposed on all the unemployed, but mainly targeted on the margins of the labour market. While core workers have continued to benefit from early exit and still relatively generous unemployment benefits (including part-time benefits during the crisis, such as the

German *Kurzarbeit*), the long term unemployed and beneficiaries of the new or expanded minimum incomes have progressively been put under activation pressures (Clegg 2007). Care policies have not attempted to alter the gendered division of household labour, and have tended to reproduce the patterns of stratification specific to Bismarckian welfare systems, with lower-income women particularly encouraged to use long, low-paid care schemes that result in their withdrawal from the labour market (Morel 2007).

The reforms of the last decades that we have analysed have resulted in multiple dualizations: the development of two worlds of welfare within the public system; the addition of a private component to the public system; and the division of the population between insured insiders and assisted and/or activated outsiders. The shrinking of social insurance has left space both above (for private voluntary components, i.e. private pension funds and private health insurances) and underneath (for covering the poorest with minimum incomes) the public system. Besides the remaining—but more individualized and partly privatized—social insurance schemes, a secondary world of work and welfare is developing for outsiders, made up of secondary 'atypical' jobs, activation policies and income-tested targeted benefits. This is a new architecture for the Bismarckian welfare systems, with social insurance still central but no longer hegemonic. This new architecture has created new forms of vertical dualism in society and generates more social inequalities (Emmenegger et al. 2012).

The population itself seems to be increasingly divided into, on the one hand, those who can rely on rather generous social insurance programmes and continue to have access—thanks to their employers or their own wealth—to private complements, and on the other hand, those who have fallen out of that system and are dependent on minimum benefits. To the latter group, one should probably add those being activated into atypical contracts under which they benefit from second-rank jobs and social protection (Clegg 2007). Social protection reforms have thus contributed to increased inequalities and has divided society between insiders and outsiders.

In many countries (especially Italy, Belgium, Germany, and Austria), public pensions provided through social security will become so low that average-to-high earners will have to rely on occupational and private schemes to obtain a pension commensurate with their past earnings. A division has emerged between people with access to such schemes and those without (Jessoula and Alti 2010). Even if some governments (as in Germany) have planned a progressive state subsidy (taking the income and number of children into account), the development of complementary pension funds will induce broader inequalities among pensioners, again entrenching divides between insiders (having good income and employed in large firms, where they enjoy good collectively bargained benefits) and outsiders, whose employers are too small to afford pension plans, and who themselves do not have the means to put extra money aside.

In countries where private complementary health insurances are playing a growing role (France, but also Germany, the Netherlands, or Switzerland, in their own fashion), the same trends can also be observed in the health care sector (Hassenteufel and Palier 2007).

What is also striking is the social impact of the dualization of welfare itself. It may be that in Germany, the trend towards dualization is most visible and consequential. With the Hartz IV reforms, the unemployed who are not entitled to the standard insurance benefits must now rely on a flat rate benefit set at the social assistance level, known as ALG II, which also covers the working poor. Increasing poverty in Germany can be traced to the implementation of this dualizing reform. Hinrichs underlines the increased number of poor children in Germany. 'Unemployment of their parents and single parenthood are the primary reasons. In January 2008, three years after the implementation of the *Hartz IV* act, about 1.9 million children below the age of 15 lived in households of *ALG II* recipients (*Bedarfsgemeinschaften*), i.e. every sixth child received means-tested benefits' (Hinrichs 2010).

In France, the minimum income (RMI: *Revenu Minimum d'Insertion*) receipt has continuously increased over the 1990s, reaching 1.2 million in 2007, about 3.5 per cent of the population (family members of the recipients are included). About 10 per cent of the population depends on a minimum income, and more and more of the poorest are 'activated' into mostly low paid jobs.

If the dual route to welfare and labour market reform is the typical 'conservative- corporatist' way of adapting to the new economic and social environment, this segmented pathway will be quite robust and will shape the future of Continental Europe. Even if the situation was already fragmented and inegalitarian before, certainly in Germany, France, Italy, and Austria, but also partly so in most of the rest of Continental Europe too, recent trends will deepen divisions and lead to the consolidation of a more cleaved world: dual labour markets, dual welfare systems and a society divided between insiders and outsiders.

Notes

1. This chapter relies on collective research previously published in Palier (2010a).
2. Eurostat, *Taxation trends in the European Union*, table A.3_T, p. 255.
3. Like the Belgian Minimex, the French RMI thereafter RSA, the Spanish regional assistance benefits or the basic safety nets implemented in the Visegraad countries.
4. Such as the assistance income for the long term unemployed (ALG II) or the minimum income for the elderly created in Germany, the many minimum protection schemes developed in Switzerland in various fields (supplementary means-tested pension benefits, subsidies for low-incomes earners), Austria, or the Netherlands.

Bibliography

Bonoli, G. (2005) The Politics of New Social Policies. Providing coverage against new social risks in mature welfare states. *Policy and Politics*, 33, 431–49.

Bonoli, G. & Palier, B. (2007) When Past Reforms Open New Opportunities: Comparing Old Age Insurance Reforms in Bismarckian Welfare Systems. *Social Policy and Administration*, 41, 555–73.

Clegg, D. (2007) Continental Drift: On Unemployment Policy Shift in Bismarckian Welfare Systems. *Social Policy and Administration*, 41, 597–617.

Ebbinghaus, B. (2010) Reforming Bismarckian Corporatism: The Changing Role of Social Partnership in Continental Europe. In Palier, B. (Ed.) *A Long Goodbye to Bismarck? The Politics of Welfare Reform in Continental Europe*, Amsterdam, Amsterdam University Press, 255–78.

Ebbinghaus, B. & Visser, J. (2000) *Trade Unions in Western Europe since 1945 (Handbook and CD-ROM)*, London, Palgrave Macmillan.

Emmenegger, P., Häusermann, S., Palier, B. & Seeleib-Kaiser, M. (2012) *The Age of Dualization*, Oxford, Oxford University Press.

Esping-Andersen, G. (1996) Welfare States without Work: The Impasse of Labour Shedding and Familialism in Continental European Social Policy. In Esping-Andersen, G. (Ed.) *Welfare States in Transition: National Adaptations in Global Economies*, London, Sage.

Ferrera, M. (2006) *Le politiche sociali. L'Italia in prospettiva comparata,* Bologna, Il Mulino.

Guillen, A. (2010) Defrosting the Spanish Welfare State: The Weight of Conservative Components. In Palier, B. (Ed.) *A Long Goodbye to Bismarck? The Politics of Welfare Reform in Continental Europe*, Amsterdam, Amsterdam University Press, 183–206.

Hall, P. A. (Ed.) (1989) *The Political Power of Economic Ideas*, Princeton, Princeton University Press.

Hassenteufel, P. & Palier, B. (2007) Comparing Health Insurance Reforms in Bismarckian Countries: Towards Neo-Bismarckian Health Care States? *Social Policy and Administration*, 41, 574–96.

Häusermann, S. (2010) Reform Opportunities in a Bismarckian Latecomer: Restructuring the Swiss Welfare State. In Palier, B. (Ed.) *A Long Goodbye to Bismarck? The Politics of Welfare Reform in Continental Europe*, Amsterdam, Amsterdam University Press, 207–32.

Hemerijck, A. & Marx, I. (2010) Continental Welfare at a Crossroads: The Choice between Activation and Minimum Income Protection in Belgium and the Netherlands. In Palier, B. (Ed.) *A Long Goodbye to Bismarck? The Politics of Welfare Reform in Continental Europe*, Amsterdam, Amsterdam University Press, 129–56.

Henninger, A., Wimbauer, C. & Dombrowski, R. (2008) Demography as a Push toward Gender Equality? Current Reforms of German Family Policy. *Social Politics*, 15, 287–314.

Hinrichs, K. (2010) A Social Insurance State Withers Away. Welfare State Reforms in Germany—Or: Attempts to Turn Around in a Cul-de-Sac). In Palier, B. (Ed.) *A Long Goodbye to Bismarck? The Politics of Welfare Reform in Continental Europe*, Amsterdam, Amsterdam University Press, 45–72.

Jessoula, M. & Alti, T. (2010) Italy: An Incomplete Departure from Bismarck. In Palier, B. (Ed.) *A Long Goodbye to Bismarck? The Politics of Welfare Reform in Continental Europe*, Amsterdam, Amsterdam University Press, 157–82.

Leibfried, S. & Tennstedt, F. (1985) Armenpolitik und Arbeiterpolitik. In Leibfried, S. & Tennstedt, F. (Eds.) *Politik der Armut und die Spaltung des Sozialstaats*, Frankfurt, Suhrkamp, 64–93.

Leisering, L. (2009) Germany: A Centrist Welfare State at the Crossroads. In Alcock, P. & Craig, G. (Eds.) *International Social Policy. Welfare Regimes in the Developed World*, 2nd edition, Basingstoke, Palgrave, 148–70.

Levy, J. (1999) Vice into Virtue? Progressive Politics and Welfare Reform in Continental Europe. *Politics & Society*, 27, 239–73.

Lewis, J. (1992) Gender and the Development of Welfare Regimes. *Journal of European Social Policy*, 2, 159–73.

Manow, P. (2010) Trajectories of Fiscal Adjustment in Bismarckian Welfare Systems. In Palier, B. (Ed.) *A Long Goodbye to Bismarck? The Politics of Welfare Reform in Continental Europe*, Amsterdam, Amsterdam University Press, 279–300.

Morel, N. (2007) From Subsidiarity to 'Free Choice': Child- and Elder-care Policy Reforms in France, Belgium, Germany and the Netherlands. *Social Policy and Administration*, 41, 618–37.

Obinger, H. & Tálos, E. (2010) Janus-Faced Developments in a Prototypical Bismarckian Welfare State: Welfare Reforms in Austria since the 1970s. In Palier, B. (Ed.) *A Long Goodbye to Bismarck? The Politics of Welfare Reform in Continental Europe*, Amsterdam, Amsterdam University Press, 101–28.

Palier, B. (2005) *Gouverner la sécurité sociale: Les réformes du système français de protection sociale depuis 1945*, 2nd edition, Paris, PUF.

Palier, B. (Ed.) (2010a) *A long Goodbye to Bismarck? The Politics of Welfare Reforms in Continental Europe*, Amsterdam, Amsterdam University Press.

Palier, B. (2010b) The Dualizations of the French Welfare System. In Palier, B. (Ed.) *A Long Goodbye to Bismarck? The Politics of Welfare Reform in Continental Europe*. Amsterdam, Amsterdam University Press, 73–100.

Palier, B. & Martin, C. (Eds.) (2007) Reforming the Bismarckian Welfare Systems, *Social Policy and Administration*, 41, special issue.

Palier, B. & Thelen, K. (2010) Institutionalizing Dualism, Complementarities and Changes in FraXnce and Germany. *Politics and Society*, 38, 119–48.

Pierson, P. (2001) Coping with Permanent Austerity: Welfare State Restructuring in Affluent Democracies. In Pierson, P. (Ed.) *The New Politics of the Welfare State*, Oxford, Oxford University Press.

Rueda, D. (2007) *Social Democracy Inside Out: Government Partisanship, Insiders, and Outsiders in Industrialized Democracies*, Oxford, Oxford University Press.

Scharpf, F.W. & Schmidt, V.A. (Eds.) (2000) *Welfare and Work in the Open Economy*, 2 Volumes, Oxford, Oxford University Press.

12

The New Spatial Politics of Welfare in the EU

Maurizio Ferrera

Introduction

The policy developments examined in this book are occurring in a macro-institutional framework that is evolving over time. This is particularly the case for the member states of the European Union, which operate in a context where social sovereignty is increasingly limited by various aspects of the process of European integration, often in a rather unpredictable way. The direct impact of EU institutions on social policies is admittedly limited, but some rules may prove to be formidable constraints on member states' ability to define key aspects of social policy, such as who is covered. This is an essential aspect of the process of welfare state transformation and discussions of the new welfare settlement that is emerging in Europe must take it into account.

In recent years the literature on the (new) politics of EU social policy has followed three main strands of theoretical and empirical investigation. The first has focused on the 'Europeanization' of national systems, in the wake of both greater integration and increasingly similar socio-economic challenges. This literature has addressed issues of convergence/divergence, has explored the role of various social, institutional and political actors as well as the relative weight of ideas, interests and institutions in shaping both the top-down and the bottom-up dynamics of Europeanization, in a multi-level governance perspective.[1] A great deal of attention has been dedicated to the OMC as a novel instrument to promote change and innovation through 'soft' incentives and new forms of experimental governance.[2] The second strand of literature has focused more specifically on legal frameworks and decision-making rules, and issues of institutional (in)compatibility between market integration, on the one hand, and domestic redistribution on the other.[3] Scholars working within this strand have tried to identify the specific points of friction between the EU as a 'regulatory state'[4] and domestic redistributive orders, and to highlight the (mainly) destabilizing effects of the former on the latter, in particular on domestic welfare regimes. From this second perspective, the new politics of social policy in the EU is essentially a contest between market-making and market-correcting logics, supported by distinct actor coalitions and governed by asymmetric decision rules (negative vs positive integration).[5] Many scholars have stressed the high salience—for this type of new politics—of judicial arenas and actors, in particular of the European Court Justice serving as 'market police'.[6] A third and more recent strand has finally tried to bring the process of European integration under the umbrella of the classic 'state-building' school, aimed at analysing the historical formation of nation-states.[7] According to this third perspective, EU integration can be seen as a new phase in the long term development of the European state system, characterized by a gradual weakening of spatial boundaries and an overall re-structuring of socio-political and institutional configurations. The welfare state was (and still largely is) a key component of the nation-state. The integration process has been posing increasing challenges to its institutional foundations, originating a 'sovereignty contest' over the bounding rules that govern social sharing practices and thus defining 'who has access to what forms of protection'.

Building on the third strand, this chapter has two objectives. The first is to offer a brief descriptive reconstruction of the contested process that has produced an increasing EU harmonization—over the last 50 years—of the rules of access into domestic sharing spaces on the side of 'outsiders'. The second objective is that of interpreting this process in terms of 'spatial politics', i.e. a conflict between (essentially) national governments, that is, guardians of distinct arrangements reserved to their citizens, and EU institutions programmatically interested in cross-border economic integration and, more generally, in regulative standardization based on non-discrimination principles. The first section of the chapter will specify the analytical framework. The second and third sections will discuss the process of spatial standardization (including its politics) in respect to two sets of outsiders: nationals of other EU member states and third country nationals. The conclusion will offer a summary assessment of the current boundary configuration of social protection within the EU, and highlight some open questions of both analytical and substantive (mainly political) nature.

The Welfare State as a Spatial Organization

Social sharing builds on 'closure'.[8] It presupposes the existence of a clearly demarcated and cohesive community, whose members feel that they belong to the same whole and that they are linked by reciprocity ties vis-à-vis common risks and similar needs. Since the 19th century (and in some countries, since much earlier) the nation-state has provided the closure conditions for the development of sharing dispositions and practices within its own territory. European integration, on the contrary, rests on 'opening': on weakening or tearing apart those spatial demarcations and closure practices that nation-states have built to protect themselves. Free movement, free ('undistorted') competition and non-discrimination have been the driving principles of the integration process. Through the promotion of these principles, the EU has greatly contributed to the expansion of individual options and choices, but often at the price of challenging those closure conditions that sustain social solidarity. When the integration project was launched in the 1950s, the idea was that the European Communities would concentrate on economic opening, while the member states would keep for themselves the sphere of solidarity and welfare. The compromise, however, was inherently fragile and precarious. Starting from the 1980s, the division of labour has become increasingly untenable: advancements in economic integration (and in particular the completion of the single market and the establishment of EMU) have prompted the introduction of direct or indirect constraints also in the sphere of domestic sharing arrangements, gradually destabilizing some of its constitutive pillars.

The problematic relationship between the opening pressures linked to European integration and the closure foundations of the nation-based welfare state can be framed, analytically, through the concept of *boundary*. Boundaries are sets of norms and rules that define the type and level of closure of a given collectivity vis-à-vis the exterior, gating the access to the resources and opportunities of both the in-space and the out-space, and facilitating bonding dynamics among insiders. Historically, the formation of the nation-state consisted in a multidimensional process of boundary-building around given portions of the European territory. The establishment of social sharing schemes (typically, through compulsory public insurance) between the end of the 19th and the beginning of the 20th century was an important dimension/step in this process. In its turn, European integration can be read as a large scale operation of boundary re-drawing: the re-definition or removal of state-national boundaries within the EU space in respect of an increasing number of functional spheres and institutionalized practices, including social sharing. In the wake of free movement and competition rules, the nation-state is no longer the sole and ultimate arbiter of inclusion and exclusion into its own redistributive spaces. Given the salience of social sharing for material life chances, cultural identities and legitimation dynamics, reshuffling the national boundaries means affecting the basic architecture of Europe's societies and political systems.

Addressing the relationship between European integration and national welfare states through the concept of boundary has some implications. The first is that the attention is immediately drawn towards an elementary, yet fundamental mechanism through which social solidarity is typically generated: a mechanism which we can term 'internal bonding through external bounding'. As mentioned above, solidarity builds on reciprocity expectations: if a space of interaction is confined by boundaries vis-à-vis the exterior (that is, if insiders cannot easily escape from it and outsiders are not easily admitted), reciprocity expectations can consolidate, stabilize and generalize over time. The role played by boundaries for group formation and political production is an old theme of classical sociology. The bounding/bonding nexus has not attracted the interest it deserves, however, in the welfare state literature. One obvious reason is that most of this literature has concentrated on intranational developments in the second half of the 20th century, that is, developments taking place within relatively constant boundary configurations. The 'foundational' role of such configurations for bonding dynamics and their politics has thus remained largely in the shadows.

Another implication has to do with the analytical toolkit. Framing our theme in terms of closure and opening, bounding and de-bounding, requires the elaboration of a vocabulary and conceptual map that are adequate for exploring the spatial dimension of social sharing and its 'new' politics in the EU. The welfare state must be reconceptualized as a spatial organization, delimited by boundaries which were traditionally under the exclusive control of national authorities and are now under challenge on the side of an external authority structure. This situation produces a new type of politics, which revolves around spatial positioning and behaviours ('entries', 'exits', 'staying in', 'staying out', 'letting in', 'pushing out', 'keeping in', 'keeping out', etc.) that were not pertinent or relevant in earlier, pre-integration phases.[9]

In line with the classical state-building approach, we can distinguish between two types of boundaries: territorial and membership boundaries. Social rights are about access to material resources and opportunities, granted by the state to (certain categories) of persons. As the other two sets of right that constitute modern citizenship (civic and political), social rights presuppose, however, a more fundamental right, i.e. the 'right to have rights' within the territory of the state. As has been noted (Heater 1990; Brubaker 1992), modern citizenship is a 'territorial filing' device, i.e. it allocates persons to states; and, in so doing, it is also a powerful filtering device, an instrument of closure. From this perspective, the welfare state is, at its base, a geographical space, with a recognizable territorial scope demarcated by administrative borders and filing rules. Historically, the territorial boundaries of the welfare state were virtually coterminous with state borders; the sharing community coincided with the national community. European integration has gradually altered this situation, challenging the territorial closure of welfare arrangements. The new spatial politics of welfare in the EU thus connotes, in the first place, a novel type of contention which revolves around 'locality' rights and prerogatives, i.e. rules and rule-making on territorial positioning and movements.

Along the membership dimension, in its turn, the welfare state can be seen as a space of social interaction in which territorial insiders share some common traits and/or are subject to a common set of norms and rules. More precisely, the welfare state can be seen as a bundle of membership spaces: it consists of different functional schemes (for pensions, health care, unemployment, social assistance and so on), different 'layers', 'tiers', and 'pillars' of provision (e.g. basic vs. supplementary insurance), characterized by their own regulations and surrounded by codified membership boundaries that mark insiders and pit them against outsiders. Seen in this light, the welfare state has always had a spatial politics, i.e. conflicts on inclusion and exclusion rules, and on the relative positioning of different social groups within the bundle of sharing arrangements. The insider-outsider cleavage that lies at the heart of the current labour market literature (discussed by other chapters of this volume), focuses largely on the stratification of the labour force based on membership within occupational and social protection spaces characterized by different norms and rules. However, this traditional spatial politics rests on a stable territorial basis whose boundaries are given and uncontested, and it unfolds in the shadow of a single, ultimate hierarchy, that of the nation state and its key rule-making institutions. European integration has changed the situation, not only by gradually weakening the welfare state's territorial closure, but also by posing new direct and indirect constraints on its internal membership boundaries, thus casting a new shadow of supranational hierarchy on domestic political interactions. The impact of integration on the membership boundaries of the welfare state is a relatively recent phenomenon. Its visibility is still low also because this impact is not uniform across the various risk-specific schemes, tiers and pillars of provision. Nevertheless, it has already prompted dynamics of interest articulation and aggregation at various levels of the Euro-polity. The conflict around entries into and exits from membership spaces (as distinct from territorial spaces per se) is the second face of spatial politics.

The new spatial politics of welfare in the EU involves a great number of actors, public and private. Its main and original protagonists are, however, national governments and the supranational institutions of the EU, in particular, the Commission and the ECJ. In the following sections of this paper we will thus focus on such actors, illustrating some of their 'spatial games' around the territorial and membership boundaries of domestic social protection regimes. We will reconstruct development separately for EU nationals and Third Country nationals. Even though EU 'space-building' in the sphere of welfare has affected all schemes and tiers of provision, we will focus our attention on non-contributory social assistance. This membership space can be considered in many respects to be the *sancta sanctorum* of sharing practices: it provides help under the form of subsidies and services merely based on need considerations and thus rests on the purest form of solidarity, almost devoid of reciprocity expectations; it is financed through general revenues, i.e. the common pool of resources of a given political community; it is often anchored to sub-national levels of government, characterized by closer proximity to citizens/voters and greater attention to local identities and traditions (and, correspondingly, greater suspicions against outsiders). Even more than other schemes or tiers of welfare provision, social assistance is thus particularly sensitive to external interferences and lends itself well to illustrating some emblematic dynamics of the new spatial politics.

Contentious Boundaries: National vs. EU Citizens of Other Member States

Europe has a long tradition of cross-border migrations, stretching back to the late 19th century. Until the First World War, migrant workers could enter national spaces (especially labour markets) without difficulty and subject to very little control (Strikwerda 1997). It was only after the war that state frontiers started to be policed and that passports, visas, and work permits were introduced. In the inter-war period, citizenship begun to be used as an instrument of closure and as a filter to separate insiders from outsiders, and distinct national immigration policies made their first appearance. These policies had an external side, primarily linked to territorial movements (border controls, exit and entry authorizations, deportation rules, and so on) and an internal side, linked to domestic membership spaces (the rights and duties of legal immigrants vis-à-vis the labour market, the welfare state, and so on).[10] The nation state remained the sole sovereign and rule-maker on both fronts. In many respects it can be said that the 1950s marked the apex of national closure. This situation started to rapidly change, however, after the adoption of the Rome Treaty in 1958.

With the famous Van Gend (1963) and Costa (1964) rulings, the ECJ was able to affirm the principles of the direct effect of EC law and its supremacy over national laws (Weiler 1994). By conferring justiciable rights on individuals, the constitutionalization of the EC order also started to gradually encroach on the sphere of citizenship. Tuned as they were towards the creation of a common market, the Treaties essentially provided an economic constitution. Modern markets, however, rest on a basket of basic rights: in order to exchange goods and services, one has to have a right to belong to that marketplace to begin with; secondly, one has to have a right to options, that is, the freedom to exercise choices based on opportunities and preferences. A market citizen is a 'thin' citizen (Caporaso and Tarrow 2009), not necessarily protected by a bill of fundamental rights. Yet she is still a citizen, bearer of at least a modicum of civil rights.

One of the most fundamental civil rights in the market sphere is the freedom of work: the right to follow the occupation of one's choice in the place of one's choice (Marshall 1950: 10). Article 48 of the Rome Treaty recognized this right, prohibiting all forms of discrimination by the member states regarding employment, starting, of course, with discrimination based on nationality. This article became directly applicable, and already in 1965 the Court found that the free movement of labour was a fundamental pillar of the EC and was to be implemented as fully as possible from a legal point of view.[11] By 1961, all intra-European visas had been eliminated and in 1968 Regulation 1612/68[12] and Directive 360/68[13] struck down all remaining restrictions to territorial 'entries' and 'exits'. In 1970, Regulation 1251[14] specified that a worker could also rightfully reside (i.e. 'stay in', in our spatial language) within the member state in which she had worked also after retirement. Between 1960 and 1968, migration flows within the Six grew on average 4.7 per cent each year: in 1968, about 830,000 EC workers were living in a member state other than their own.[15] The establishment of an EC-wide freedom to work and of a common labour market with no internal territorial borders was a revolutionary achievement, especially in view of the highly restrictive regime that had been put in place in most European countries after the First World War.

What about the social rights of migrant workers, i.e. the 'membership' dimension of free movement? This was certainly not a trivial question. When freedom of work was first established in Europe's national labour markets, typically during the 19th century, there were as yet no social rights. The insecurity implications of such freedom did trigger off a demand for social protection, which led to the first wave of public insurance schemes between the 1880s and the 1920s. However, the creation of the EC common labour market during the 1960s took place in a social rights-thick environment. Despite the pledge of the Treaties to keep EC hands off national sovereignty in this realm, the issue of introducing at least some form of coordination between the various national sets of rules could not be avoided in order to solve conflicts of laws. The abolishment of territorial demarcations around the national labour market was undermining a fundamental tenet of social legislation, i.e. the territoriality principle (rights are inseparably linked to territory) (Cornelissen 1996).

As a matter of fact, the problem had already arisen in the wake of the Paris Treaty (1951): more than 200,000 migrant workers were active in the steel and coal sectors of the original Six (Lyon Caen and Lyon Caen 1993). In the early 1950s, social entitlements were still not very developed: but the issue of protecting migrant workers (and their family members) through a common supranational regime, rather than by multiple and heterogeneous bilateral agreements appeared on the political agenda, also in the wake of a parallel initiative by the Council of Europe. In 1957, a European Convention on the Social Security of Migrant Workers was signed in Rome. Article 51 of the Rome Treaty clearly recognized that migrant workers should not be penalized in terms of social protection, and in 1958 a regulation, largely inspired by the Convention, was issued (3/1958)[16] establishing the four basic principles of coordination: (*a*) non-discrimination and equality of treatment; (*b*) aggregation of all periods of insurance, in whatever country; (*c*) benefit exportability from one member state to another; and (*d*) applicability of a single law, the *lex loci laboris* (that is, the laws of the country of work).

At the time when they were first introduced, these provisions did not seem at odds with the institutional separation between the economic and social spheres, and the division of labour between supranational and national authorities. Coordination did not involve any regulatory standardization (in any case subject to unanimity). It was considered a natural corollary of the freedom of work, and protecting migrant workers was seen as a positive goal by socially minded policymakers in the national capitals and in Brussels. The 1958 regulation explicitly upheld the territoriality principle by recognizing the primacy of the legal rules of the country of work. And in any case, EC provisions only affected relations between states. The constitutionalization of EC law, however, changed the picture and from the mid-1960s, litigation also began to take place in this delicate field.

The first wave of litigation, between the mid-1960s and the early 1970s, comprised only a handful of cases, originating in disputes over interpretation: but they put down some important landmarks and immediately set the tone for future developments. The first landmark was established with the *Unger* judgment in 1964[17] which, not surprisingly, concerned the *territorial* closure of national systems. The Dutch authorities were refusing to reimburse medical expenses incurred in Germany by a person who was no longer working, but nevertheless, was voluntarily insured in a public scheme of the Netherlands. The Court found that this was discriminatory, ruled in favour of *Unger*, and proposed a common definition of 'employed person' (see *infra*). The lesson was that member states could not keep their social gates closed by manipulating legal definitions, since the ECJ would standardize them in order to uphold free circulation. Another case in 1965 confirmed the principles of direct applicability and EC law supremacy in the specific field of social protection. Thus, in *van der Veen*[18] the Dutch government, again, was forced to grant benefits to a worker returning from France, a request rejected based on laws passed after 1958. Member states could not invoke the principle of *lex posterior* to reaffirm their sovereignty.

Two other landmarks laid down in 1966 and 1969 concerned the *membership* dimension of closure: when does a domestic scheme—a collectivity of redistribution—fall within the material scope of EC coordination rules?[19] In the *Vaassen Gobbels* case of 1966[20] the Court found that even non-public social schemes (that is, schemes that were not run by the state) were to be considered social security as long as they were statutory. Almost paradoxically, if a national scheme is compulsory, if it 'locks in' a given group—regardless of management and/or its public or private law status—then it should allow for entries and exits based on EC law provisions. In the *Torreken* case of 1969,[21] on the other hand, the ECJ held that a 'residual', means-tested pension scheme such as the Belgian *révenu garanti d'existence* could be considered part of social security too, and thus must be open to non-nationals. This was a direct and explicit challenge to domestic 'marking' rules regarding need-based redistribution.

In order to clarify legal ambiguities and take into account the new interpretative jurisprudence of the ECJ, a new regulation on social security coordination was issued in 1971 (Reg. 1408).[22] This text reaffirmed the four basic principles listed above: (*a*) non-discrimination and equality of treatment; (*b*) aggregation of all periods of insurance, in whatever country; (*c*) benefit exportability from one member state to another; and (*d*) applicability of a single law, that of the country of work. Regulation 1408 also offered standardized definitions of the core notions ('worker', 'benefit', and so on) so as to avoid manipulative games on the part of state authorities. The most important move on this front, following *Unger*, was the shift from 'employed persons' to 'insured persons' as the axial concept to define the personal scope of the regulation. While still leaving intact national prerogatives on insurance rules (that is, boundary setting along the membership dimension), the new approach preempted manipulative games based on labour market status. The regulation basically endorsed in this way the expansionist views of the ECJ, regarding not only the direct and permanent effect of EC coordination rules, but also the desirability of wide territorial entry/exit gates linked to domestic sharing spaces.

Despite *Torrekens*, Article 4 of the 1971 regulation excluded 'social assistance' from the material scope of the coordination regime. The rationale behind such provision was that the free movement of workers required the portability of work-related entitlements, but not necessarily the neutralization of the territoriality principle for social rights unrelated to work (and contributions). Not surprisingly, member states wanted to reserve these rights to their own citizens. As mentioned above, the sphere of asymmetrical solidarity (that is, public support based purely on need considerations) in fact presupposes those ties of 'we-ness' that typically bind the members of a national community—and only them. As a matter of fact, the 'guest worker' regimes that operated in the 1950s and 1960s (most typically in Germany) envisaged some sort of reverse solidarity: legal immigrants were required to pay taxes on their earnings, and thus to partly contribute to the financing of national assistance programmes; but in case of economic need they had no entitlements and actually faced the risk of expulsion.[23] Besides financial (and symbolic) worries, member states also faced administrative complications regarding free movement in this field of social protection, given the presence of means-testing and conditionality requirements, and given the sensitivity of benefit levels to national (and even regional) living standards.

Since the 1971 regulation did not provide a clear-cut definition of social assistance, responsibility for drawing distinctions fell to the ECJ, which from the very beginning adopted an expansionary orientation aimed at subsuming most of the controversial cases under the notion of social security (as opposed to social assistance), and thus within the scope of coordination. The landmark ruling on this front was the *Frilli* case[24] in 1972, in which the Court ruled that, whenever the claimant had a legally defined position which gave him or her an enforceable right to the benefit—with no discretionary powers on the part of the granting administration—the benefit could not be treated as social assistance by national authorities. This ruling gave non-nationals access to most of those 'social minima' linked to citizenship (typically social pensions) mentioned above. Other rulings in the 1980s went even further by making these benefits exportable from the country of payment to the country of (new) residence. The *Piscitello* case[25] of 1983 dealt with the refusal of the Italian authorities to pay a social pension to a poor elderly person who had moved to Belgium. The *Giletti et al.* case[26] of 1987 dealt with the refusal of French authorities to pay a means-tested pension to Italian migrants who had returned home. In both cases the ECJ upheld the exportability of benefits. The second case made more impact, since in its wake French taxpayers were de facto subsidizing some poor elderly people in Italy's Mezzogiorno.

Again, the ECJ's activism in striking down national boundaries in such a delicate area provoked member-state reactions, especially regarding the link between residence and eligibility: a typical spatial issue affecting both the territorial and membership dimension. France refused to implement the Court rulings on exportability, and the Commission opened an infringement procedure against it (Van der Mei 2003: 154 ff). Fearful of having to subsidize foreign elderly people leaving its territory, Germany abandoned a planned establishment of a minimum old-age pension, distinct from its social-assistance guaranteed income (Leibfried and Pierson 2000; Conant 2001). At the same time, the Commission drafted a proposal to amend the 1971 regulation in this respect. Supranational agreement was eventually reached—despite the joint-decision trap caused by the unanimity requirement—in order to regain some national control over territorial boundaries. In 1992, Regulation no. 1247 was adopted,[27] which inserted a specific coordination mechanism for non-contributory 'mixed' cash benefits into Regulation no. 1408/71. The two main novelties were: (*a*) the principle that such benefits, though regarded as social security benefits, shall be granted exclusively in the territory of the member state in which the beneficiary resides; and (*b*) the inclusion of a positive list (amendable) of benefits for each country as a prerequisite for imposing residence requirements. In other words, nationals of other EU member states can claim the social assistance subsidies included in the list, but they must be legal residents in the host state in the first place; and second, they must 'consume' the benefit in the latter's territory, abiding by the conditionality requirements attached to such benefits (such as work availability). The 1992 regulation made no reference to in-kind benefits. However, when Germany tried to disguise a new benefit for long-term care introduced in 1994 as a benefit in kind, the ECJ promptly intervened to block any manipulatory attempts at legal pre-emption.[28]

In this new regulatory framework, the line of defence by national systems thus shifted to control over rules of residence, regarding who can 'stay in' after entry, and at what conditions. While the various European treaties are based on the principle of free circulation of *workers*, member states had maintained some important prerogatives in deciding which *non-workers* can legally reside in their territory. Family members do have residence (and benefit) rights, and so do persons looking for a job, but only if the latter are in receipt of an unemployment benefit from the country of last employment, and only for up to three months if they move to a different country. Residence eligibility for all other kinds of non-workers (for example, students, pensioners, and unsubsidized unemployed) remained highly contentious until the early 1990s. Already in the 1970s, the ECJ started to uphold the free movement of persons based on freedom of service, protected by the EC treaty. In 1979, the Commission presented to the Council a directive proposal for establishing a general right of residence, even though conditional upon proof of sufficient resources. This proposal provoked a veritable avalanche of objections by the member states (Martinsen 2004). In 1984, however, the ECJ offered a clear and systematic formulation of the doctrine of passive freedom of service in *Luisi Carbone* (1984).[29] According to the Luxembourg judges, all EC nationals have a right to travel with a view to receiving (and not only providing) services. In 1990, three directives (90/364, 90/365, and 90/336)[30] established the right of residence for students, pensioners, and all 'other' non-economically active persons; but the preamble of all three directives clearly states that claimants must not represent an 'unreasonable burden' on the public finances of the member states. These texts thus allow national authorities to apply a sort of 'affluence test': would-be residents must give evidence that they have resources in excess of the income thresholds for social assistance benefits, thereby discouraging social tourism in search of benefits.

As it did for the notion of 'employment', the ECJ took steps towards defining a Community concept of residence, directly linked to the Treaties and to the principles of EU citizenship (Mabbet and Bolderson 2000). In the *Swaddling* case,[31] for example, the Court said that the meaning of residence could not be adapted to suit the unilateral and uncoordinated preferences of the various national systems, while in the *Martinez Sala* case,[32] the Court went very close to recognizing the right of a Spanish citizen to the German child allowance based purely on her status as an EU citizen. In the *Grzelczyk* case (2001)[33] the ECJ took two further steps. In the first place, it found that the Treaties offered a sufficient basis for prohibiting member states from denying any social assistance benefits to lawfully resident EU nationals; the only power they had was that of performing the 'affluence test' prior to immigration or not to renew the residence card when it expired. This went definitely beyond the 1971 and 1992 regulations to the extent that it recognized social assistance entitlements directly based on Treaty provisions: free circulation is not only about territorial movements, but also about admission into national membership spaces, including non-contributory benefits. Second, the *Grzelczyk* ruling interpreted the 1990 directives as if they had established a certain degree of financial solidarity between nationals of a host member state and nationals of other member states. If the financial burdens are 'reasonable'—one could argue, following the Court—a single member state has no right to deny help to a needy EU citizen: quite a long way from the old-fashioned guest-worker regimes.[34]

Also in the wake of ECJ jurisprudence, in April 2004 a new directive (n. 38) was adopted 'on the right of citizens of the Union and their family members to move and reside freely within the territory of the Member States'.[35] Making explicit reference to the Charter of Fundamental Rights (adopted in 2001), this directive treats free movement and free residence as a primary and individual right conferred by Union citizenship and as a fundamental freedom of the internal market. The regime introduced by the directive can be summarized as follows:

- Union citizens have an unconditional right of residence in a host member state for an initial period of three months;

- after this initial period, conditions may be imposed in order to prevent persons exercising their right of residence becoming an unreasonable burden on the social assistance system of the host country; however,

- an expulsion measure should not be the automatic consequence of recourse to the social assistance system. The host member state should examine whether it is only a matter of temporary difficulties, should take into account the duration of residence and the amount of aid granted;

- expulsion remains possible on grounds of public policy, public security or public health;

- after a continuous period of five years without expulsion, an unconditional right of residence should be granted.

As far as access to social rights is concerned, in the wake of directive 38/2004 and Regulation 883/2004 (which amended the 1971 Regulation), a two-track system has been established:

- EU citizens who are or have been covered by social security legislation of one of the members states and who reside in another member state (at the conditions laid down by directive 38/2004) enjoy the same benefits of the nationals of the latter state. The only territorial limitation is with regards to non-contributory benefits included in a list, which can be 'consumed' only in the territory of the granting state.[36]

- EU citizens who are not, or have not, been covered by social security legislation can obtain social assistance benefits, but under certain limitations, in the new country of residence. After five years, upon obtaining permanent residence, they acquire full entitlement to social assistance benefits on a par with nationals, with the above mentioned territorial limitation.

The implementation of the residence directive was aimed at strongly circumscribing the social sovereignty of the member states along both the territorial and membership dimensions, including the very delicate field of needs-based assistance. The directive constrained not only the legal autonomy of member states in delimiting the sphere of social assistance, but also the actual exercise of this autonomy, through the 'proportionality' qualifications for expulsion measures justified in financial terms. Transposition was to be completed by April 2006, although by that date, only a minority of member states had complied.[37] In order to step up the process, the Commission started infringement proceedings against the remaining 19 states. By the end of 2008 the process of transposition formally ended, but with very disappointing results: 'Not one member state has transposed the directive effectively and correctly in its entirety. Not one article of the directive has been transposed effectively and correctly by all member states' (EC 2008: 3). Not surprisingly, member states have tried to water down those articles of the directive which jeopardized or neutralized their ultimate right to decide who to admit ('let in') into their needs-based membership space and who to expel ('push out') from the national territory in case of 'unreasonable burdens' or unlawful behaviours.

Barriers have been maintained for family members of EU citizens who are Third Country nationals; for non-nationals the status of resident has been decoupled from the status of worker, in order to make expulsions easier; the requisite of 'sufficient resources' has been defined in very restrictive ways, without regard to personal circumstances; a number of countries have maintained to prerogative of automatic expulsion for lack of resources or the periodic verification of the economic conditions. In general, member states have tried to keep large discretion in determining those 'grounds of public policy, public security or public health' that can justify expulsion. A new round of the 'spatial game' between domestic and supranational authorities has thus started. The 2006 infringement proceedings for failed communication were terminated, but in 2008 the Commission opened five new proceedings for incorrect applications. An increasing number of complaints have been addressed to the Commission and the ECJ has already ruled against some of the closure provisions contained in transposed legislation.[38] As a reaction to this ruling, a number of Member States have launched a political initiative aimed at narrowing down the scope of Directive 2004/38. Their goal is to insert 'extra-safeguards' under the justification that the rights conferred by EU law, and as interpreted by the ECJ, leave room for 'abuses' and 'misuses' of the freedom to move (Carrera and Faure Atger 2009). The issue got highly politicized in the Summer of 2010 when the French government attempted a 'deportation' of several thousand Roma people—a move that was immediately condemned by the Commission, but that emblematically illustrates the tension that has been building up around this question.

With the incorporation of the Charter of Fundamental Rights and a clear reformulation of the meaning and content of EU citizenship, the Lisbon Treaty entered into force in 2009 has, given to existing EU laws on free movement, residence and access to social protection, a constitutional status that is likely to skew the spatial game in favour of the supranational level, promoting a more balanced 'nesting' of national sharing spaces within the EU architecture. It should be noted, however, that the Treaty includes an 'abortion' clause (Verschueren forthcoming) that puts some gating powers back into the hands of national governments, at least in respect of future legislation. Article 48 of the TFEU recognizes the right of each member state to suspend the adoption of a legislative proposal related to the social entitlements of migrant persons if its implications are considered to negatively affect 'important aspects of its social security system, including cost, scope, financial balance or structure'. If a member state requests the suspension, the matter is referred to the European Council where the proposal can be blocked.[39] Under the pre-Lisbon status quo, member states did have the possibility of ultimately blocking a proposal in this delicate sphere: the co-decision procedure that regulates legislation on the social security rights of migrants envisaged unanimity for Council decisions. However, a blockage that can be exerted (or threatened) at the very beginning of a legislative process—as in the new Article 48 procedure—is likely to be much more effective than a blockage that is attempted at the very end, possibly after a lengthy and controversial conciliation process between Parliament and Council. Article 48 was inserted in the Treaty after the French and Dutch referenda. In euro-parlance it is also known as the 'social security emergency brake': an expression that clearly signals the wish of member states to keep options open.

Contentious Boundaries: EU Citizens Vis-à-vis the *Extra-comunitari*

During the 1950s and 1960s, immigration of foreign workers was encouraged by many countries (such as Germany, France, and Belgium) to fill gaps in their labour markets. Some of these migrant workers came from countries inside the EC (Italy in particular), but many were 'third country nationals'—TCNs, a novel marker of outsiderhood evoking an entitlement differential anchored to a supranational bounded space (the EC) rather than a national one. The big waves of immigration of the 1950s and 1960s took place in a social and institutional context that essentially considered foreign workers to be guests admitted into the labour market and into employment-related social schemes, but on a temporary and reversible basis. In this phase, the entitlement differential between EU and non-EU migrants was not very significant; access rules depended on national authorities, applied to all foreigners, and varied across countries. As we have seen, the common labour market started to fully operate only after 1968, and full social security entitlements were only guaranteed to migrant workers of the EC member states with the 1971 Regulation. In 1963, the Association Agreement with Turkey[40] envisaged some special privileges for workers migrating from this country into Europe, introducing the 'mixed' category of a TCN protected by an Association Agreement. Such privileges, however, only became operative in the 1980s.

The economic crisis of the 1970s marked a watershed. European countries suddenly stopped welcoming immigrant workers, especially from third countries (Italian emigration had spontaneously ended in the meantime). The general expectation was that most migrants would return to their country of origin. But this did not happen. Many foreign workers had been joined by their families and were interested in permanent settlement. In the wake of national (but also supranational, especially on the part of Turkish citizens) litigation (Guiraudon 2000), large numbers of TCNs acquired 'denizenship' status, that is, the right to legally reside, work, and 'share' in the country of immigration; some even obtained naturalization. In 1976, the Cooperation

Agreements with the Maghreb countries (Morocco, Algeria, and Tunisia)[41] created a second category of special TCNs. Their privileges were inferior to those envisaged for Turks, but included equal treatment in work and remuneration conditions within domestic labour markets. All TCNs, however, remained excluded from the 1971 regulation on social security coordination. Thus, their welfare rights were entirely dependent on national rules—which obviously reflected strong national preferences on the issue—and cross-border movements were discouraged.

Given the frustration of their re-emigration expectations and objectives, during this second phase (the 1970s and 1980s) European countries started to rein in their immigration rules, but discovered that the EC legal order was imposing unexpected constraints along both the territorial and membership dimensions. The ECJ considered the Association and Cooperation Agreements as part of this order, with direct effect and supremacy over national provisions. Some articles of the Rome Treaty itself (such as Article 7a) could be interpreted as an obligation to create a common market for all persons, regardless of nationality, and thus extended to the *extra-comunitari*. And in the mid-1970s, this expansionary interpretation started to be voiced by the Commission (later backed by the European Parliament), which proposed including all migrants within the scope of its ambitious Social Action Plan of 1975. Thus, the 1980s witnessed the emergence of another stream of spatial games between national governments—strenuously affirming their prerogatives on citizenship and denizenship vis-à-vis TCNs and their policies of differential treatment—and supranational institutions (Commission, Parliament, and ECJ)—typically pushing for equal treatment and the expansion of rights, including in the sphere of social protection (Conant 2001).

Despite the restrictive turn of national policies, the 1980s and the 1990s witnessed continuing—and, indeed, for some countries, increasing—flows of migration. New legal entries especially included family members, but also asylum seekers and refugees. Moreover, mounting numbers of illegal migrants started to 'sneak in' (another spatial concept connoting covert entries into a space different from one's own) across the Union's border, especially from the Mediterranean Sea, and to 'hide inside' (*ditto*) the underground economy. Once a major source of emigration, the south European member states in the 1980s and 1990s rapidly turned into receiving countries (Venturini 2004). During the 1990s, positive net migration became the largest component of population change in the EU, fluctuating around a total of 850,000 immigrants per year. In 2000, TCNs represented around 4 per cent of men and women living inside the EU.

Given the 'jobless growth' syndrome and indeed rising unemployment levels, the member states tried to respond to this upsurge of new migration with a policy of closure, accompanied by stricter enforcement rules and more closely linked to security policy in general (Bommes and Geddes 2000; Conant 2001). Migration suddenly became a contentious issue in national politics, with some old and new parties voicing against undesired entries as well as calling for the preservation of domestic public order (and often for protection of domestic labour markets and sharing arrangements as well). Thus, during the 1990s, virtually all member states legislated for major restrictive changes to their migration regimes (EC 2003). They also engaged, however, in joint policy efforts, aware that the challenge of migration required at least some common responses to be more effective, especially within the framework of the new single market and of weakening internal frontiers. How to reconcile the implementation of common measures with the maintenance of national sovereignty on citizenship and denizenship (on 'filing' and 'marking' rules)? The solution was found in keeping this area of cooperation strictly outside the EC institutional order. The Schengen Agreement of 1985 was an intergovernmental treaty. The Maastricht Treaty established a separate third pillar, for justice and home affairs (covering also immigration, visa, and asylum policies), wholly outside the Community framework and thus immune from ECJ interference. The new EU citizenship remained strictly complementary to member state citizenship, despite proposals from the Commission to also grant it to TCNs after five years of legal residence. And with the countries of the former Soviet bloc, the new Association Agreements of the 1990s were carefully worded so as to exclude direct legal effects (Conant 2001).

This phase of 'thin Europeanization' (Geddes 2000) came to an end with the Amsterdam Treaty of 1997. The emergence of a transnational advocacy coalition for the rights of third country nationals, and the activism of supranational actors such as the Commission and Parliament, prepared the ground for a new phase of gradual communitarization of immigration and asylum policy, driven by a discourse promoting the goals of social inclusion, non-discrimination and access to rights on the side of legal immigrants, coupled with the establishment of more vigorous policies to control the external border of the Union. The new Treaty brought virtually all issues concerning immigration and asylum within the first pillar. Article 61 of the Amsterdam Treaty formulated the goal of progressively establishing an area of freedom, security, and justice within the EU; and Article 62 explicitly recognized that this should apply to all persons, including the nationals of third countries. In the wake of the new Treaty, the Tampere European Council of 1999 requested a more effective integration policy, aimed at granting legally resident TCNs rights and obligations comparable to those of EU citizens. In their turn, most of the provisions of the Charter of Fundamental Rights proclaimed at Nice in 2000 were applicable to all persons, irrespective of their nationality. This 'inclusive' phase did lead to two important provisions: Regulation 859/2003, extending the provisions of the old 1971 Regulation to TCNs; and Directive

109/2003, regulating the long-term residence of TCNs inside member states. However, during the negotiations for these measures, the climate around immigration issues suddenly changed, in the wake of the terrorist attacks of '9/11' and the subsequent economic crisis, as well as increasing fears about the implications of the forthcoming Eastern enlargements. Member states went back to a more restrictive approach and engaged themselves in a new spatial game vis-à-vis supranational authorities in order to defend their bounding prerogatives in respect of TCNs.

Until 2003, the EU coordination Regulation 1408/71 applied to EU nationals, but only to limited categories of TCNs, such as members of the family of EU nationals, stateless persons and refugees. There was no instrument of social security coordination that dealt with the position of all TCNs in cross-border situations. Regulation 859/2003 extended the scope of Regulation 1408/71 to TCNs moving within the EU.[42] It was a brief but significant legal instrument, bringing TCNs within the personal scope of the old coordination rules, without affecting the rules themselves. To be covered by the Regulation, two important conditions have to be fulfilled: (1) being legally resident in a member state; and (2) showing intra-EU movement (some sort of cross border element). Member states succeeded to remain the ultimate filters for both conditions.

The so-called Long-Term Residence Directive (109/2003), created in its turn a single status of long term resident (LTR) for all TCNs living in the member states. The LTR status must be recognised after five years of continuous legal residence, on condition that TCNs prove that they have stable resources sufficient to live, without recourse to the social assistance system of the member state concerned, and sickness insurance, also for family members. LTRs acquire equal treatment as nationals with regard to access to employment, education and vocational training, social protection and social assistance (with some limitations), free access to the entire territory of the state. Moreover, they enjoy enhanced protection against expulsion (which is limited to cases of serious threat to public policy or security).

The 2003 Regulation and the LTR Directive did not confer to TCNs full free movement rights on par with EU citizens. They have, however, created a new set of spatial rights, called 'mobility rights' or 'right to secondary movements': once they have legally entered into a member state (the 'first movement'), TCNs can move to another member state for short periods of up to three months and they can access a sort of fast track for residence in the second state beyond the three months, under conditions partly regulated by EU law. When in the second member state, TCNs enjoy the same social security rights as nationals, as established by the 2003 Regulation. Separate directives have regulated between 2004 and 2009 family reunions of TCNs, and have further facilitated secondary movements for students, researchers and highly qualified workers.

While it cannot be denied that the wave of immigration directives of the 2000s have significantly improved the position of TCNs and correspondingly curbed domestic discretion over their territorial and membership inclusions, it must be noted that member states were able to manoeuvre small wedges into the legal text that de facto still allow them to exercise ultimate sovereignty over who is admitted to long-term residence and social sharing schemes. The most effective wedge is constituted by the 'civic integration' clauses contained in both the LTR directive and the family reunion directive. Such clauses allow the member states to subordinate the concession of the status of LTR to integration conditions (e.g. participation to integration programmes, language acquisition, civic education courses, etc.) Though originally linked to the 'inclusion' discourse, integration clauses have gradually become a key element of a new restrictive approach aimed at containing and controlling migration flows on the part of national governments. It is interesting to note that the spatial politics that have accompanied the regulative steps of the 2000s has pitted against each other not only the national vs. the supranational level, but also different actors within each of the levels. The insertion of civic integration derogatory clauses (as well as a weak definition of mobility rights for TCNs) was the result of combined pressures of some member states (most notably Germany, Austria, France, the Netherlands) which did not trust the filtering capacity of other member states (especially the Southern and Eastern European states). At the supranational level, Parliament and Council have often argued with each other on rights and rules.

The Lisbon Treaty has not introduced significant changes with respect to the status quo resulting from the 2000 directives. It has indeed given a common definition of the constitutive elements of immigration policy (defined as: 1. the conditions of entry and residence, and standards on the issue by Member States of long-term visas and residence permits, including those for the purpose of family reunification; 2. the definition of the rights of third-country nationals residing legally in a Member State, including the conditions governing freedom of movement and of residence in other Member States); it has brought this policy under the ordinary legislative procedure of the EU, involving co-decision between Parliament and Council. But it has also confirmed the legitimacy of integration conditions and has excluded the harmonization of national measures on the issue. Moreover, the Treaty explicitly leaves in the hands of the member states the right to determine the volume of TCNs coming from third countries to their own territory. While for EU nationals the Union has become a quasi-unitary territory with 27 'open' and coordinated welfare systems, for TCNs the EU remains a fragmented territory with limited mobility gates and conditional access to social protection.[43]

Conclusion

Since the 1970s, the EU has undertaken a slow but incisive process of 'space-building' in the social sphere, aimed at creating a community of equals in terms of access to benefits. With regard to EU nationals, the territorial boundaries of national welfare states have been almost entirely removed and membership boundaries greatly weakened. With regard to Third Country nationals, space-building on the side of the EU has made less progress, but some significantly bounding prerogatives have been subtracted from the member states, especially in the case of long term residence (itself subject to harmonized EU rules).

The encounter between closed nation-based welfare states and European integration has generated a new 'spatial politics', defined by new *objects* of contention (spatial positionings and movements) and new *modes* of contention (voice for/against entries or exits). In the new spatial politics, actors define their interests based on their position in arenas crossed by boundaries that confer (different) rights, and impose (different) obligations to the membership or territorial spaces created by them. Being 'in' or 'out', being able to enter or exit from these spaces makes a substantial difference for actors and their life chances. Spatial positioning per se, thus becomes a salient goal and a distinct object of voice activities. The multi-level character of the EU polity (and especially the EC institutional order as a new 'law for exit-and-voice') offers, in its turn, a rich repertoire of strategies for actors pursuing their novel spatial interests.

This chapter has focused exclusively on the moves of national governments and supranational institutions (the European Commission and European Court of Justice). This is, however, only the tip of the iceberg: the new spatial politics of welfare in the EU has already started to involve a great number of other actors: sub-national governments, national courts, interest groups, political parties. The analysis of case law gives the impression that this type of politics is mere 'litigation', taking place in judicial arenas removed from the more visible and contentious ordinary arenas of the political system. Yet this is only partly the case. In fact, litigation around entries and exits has always been accompanied by social and political mobilization; the last decade in particular has witnessed an increasing organization and mobilization of Third Country nationals voicing for acquiring and expanding their rights. Although legal disputes typically involve single individuals, their outcomes can provoke (as has been the case in the field covered by this chapter) institutional changes that affect much larger constituencies. We must keep in mind that, in the sphere of immigration, the size of the potentially affected constituencies is now huge within the EU. The total stock of legal non-nationals (i.e. persons who are not citizens of the country in which they reside) in 2009 was 31.8 million people, of which 19.9 million were Third Country nationals. In 2008, 3.8 millions immigrated into one of the EU member states, with peaks in Spain (726,000), Germany (682,000), the UK (590,000), and Italy (535,000). These numbers attest that the spatial politics has all the potential for rapidly spilling over not only from the judicial into the civic and the legislative arenas, but also into the wider and much more contentious electoral arena.

If our diagnosis is correct, two big questions loom over the EU's institutional and political future. The first question is: How coherent, how institutionally viable is the new social sharing order put in place by the EU, based on territorial 'fusion' and membership coordination rules across member states/ spaces? One worry is that the acceleration of cross-border movements may destabilize the financial and organizational equilibriums of national schemes, originating problems of social efficiency: current institutional rules tend to create asymmetries between private costs and benefits, on the one hand, and social costs and benefits, on the other hand (Höpner and Schäfer 2010). The emergency brake put in place by the Lisbon Treaty can help to maintain the balance between openness and closure of national systems, but only by allowing the member states to prevent the adoption of new measures in the future. A fine-tuning of the current status quo may prove necessary, in a wider process of a more coherent 'nesting' of Economic and Social Europe (Ferrera 2009). The Monti Report on the re-launch of the internal market addresses some of the issues originated by the free movement of workers/persons and even envisages the possible creation of a single post-national membership space for mobile workers (the so-called '28th scheme', for pensions and health care) (Monti 2010).

The second question is more delicate: How politically sustainable is the new sharing order? The spatial politics framework outlined in this chapter can be used not only for analytical, but also for theoretical purposes, i.e. to generate hypotheses about the political implications of opening. Historically, state formation implied a gradual foreclosure of exit options, which encouraged voice structuring and the transformation of local/ethnic/cultural cleavages into functional cleavages (mainly the class cleavage). By contrast, European integration implies a gradual re-opening of exit options for insiders, but especially the creation of novel entry options for outsiders. As mentioned, outsiders have started to associate and mobilize, but the most salient development has been the mobilization of insiders and the politicization of *insider-hood* as such. European countries have been witnessing the emergence and expansion of increasingly strong political formations voicing against entry and even asking their government to adopt severe 'push-out' measures. Right wing, ethno-populist parties do not focus exclusively on immigration and even when they do, they raise broad cultural questions and not only redistributive issues (Berezin 2009). Yet all such formations ask for restrictions to the free movement and mobility provisions associated with European integration targeting Third Country nationals but also EU nationals, especially in the wake of the Eastern enlargement: this is especially visible in countries such as the Netherlands, Sweden, Italy, and France. If right-wing populist parties strategically target 'Brussels' as the culprit for opening dynamics, this might rapidly activate a spiral of 'negative politicization' of the whole integration process, with disastrous consequences for the overall architecture of the Union and its functioning.

Will the old national cleavage configurations mainly based on functional alignments be able to 'absorb' the new spatial conflicts? Scholarly opinions range from moderate optimism (Kriesi et al. 2006; Burgoon 2011) to outright pessimism (Fliegstein 2008; Höpner and Schäfer 2010). National and EU institutions will have to walk on a tight rope in the future to maintain a sustainable political balance between opening and closure: and the state of the health of the EU and global economy (combined with the social consequences of the new Growth and Stability Pact) will certainly play a crucial role.

Notes

1. For a discussion of the main voices of this strand of literature, see especially Falkner (2007, 2010).
2. Cf. Zeitlin and Heidenreich (2009). Recent reviews of the literature on the OMC are offered by Kroeger (2009) and Vanhercke (2010).
3. The standard reference here are Leibfried and Pierson (1995, 2000). For a recent restatement of this debate, cf. Caporaso and Tarrow (2009) and Höpner and Schäfer (2010).
4. Cf. Majone (1996).
5. The most influential analyses in this vein have been offered by Fritz Scharpf since the early 1990s. An updated reformulation of his perspective is contained in Scharpf (2010).
6. For a recent review and discussion of the ECJ, see especially Martinsen (2011); Martinsen and Falkner (2010).
7. Cf. especially Flora (1993, 2000); and Bartolini (2005); Ferrera (2005).
8. This section builds on Ferrera (2005, in particular, ch. 1).
9. The pioneers of the spatial analysis of politics were Hirschman (1970) and Rokkan (1974). On Rokkan's theory and the Rokkan-Hirschman model, see Flora et al. (1999).
10. The literature on migration in Europe and its relationship with European integration has been burgeoning over the last decade. See especially Bommes and Geddes (2000); Geddes (2000); Guiraudon and Joppke (2001); Faist and Ettee (2007).
11. Case 44/65, *Hessische Knappschaft v Maison Singer and sons* [1965] ECR 965.

12. Regulation (EEC) No 1612/68 of the Council of 15 October 1968 on freedom of movement for workers within the Community, *Official Journal L 257 19/10/1968 p. 0002–0012, English special edition: Series I Chapter 1968 (II) p. 0475.*

13. Council Directive 68/360/EEC of 15 October 1968 on the abolition of restrictions on movement and residence within the Community for workers of Member States and their families, *Official Journal L 257 19/10/1968 p. 0013–0016, English special edition: Series I Chapter 1968(II) p. 0485.*

14. Regulation (EEC) No 1251/70 of the Commission of 29 June 1970 on the right of workers to remain in the territory of a Member State after having been employed in that State, *Official Journal L 142, 30/06/1970, p. 0024–002;, English special edition: Series I, Chapter 1970(II), p. 0402.*

15. Cf. Straubhaar (1988). This figure includes only workers in possession of official work permits and is therefore an underestimation.

16. Règlement n° 3 concernant la sécurité sociale des travailleurs migrants, *Official Journal B 030, 16/12/1958, p. 0561.*

17. Case 75/63, *Mrs M.K.H. Hoekstra (née Unger) v Bestuur der Bedrijfsvereniging voor Detailhandel en Ambachten (Administration of the Industrial Board for Retail Trades and Businesses)* [1964] ECR 177.

18. Case 100/63, *J.G. van der Veen, widow of J. Kalsbeek v Bestuur der Sociale Verzekeringsbank and nine other cases* [1964] ECR 565.

19. The expression 'material scope' refers to the range of benefits—and thus indirectly the range of schemes—to which coordination rules apply; the expression 'personal scope' (used *infra*) refers to the range of social groups or categories.

20. Case 61/65, *G. Vaassen-Göbbels (a widow) v Management of the Beambtenfonds voor het Mijnbedrijf* [1966] ECR 261.

21. Case 28/68, *Caisse régionale de sécurité sociale du nord de la France v Achille Torrekens,* [1969] ECR 125.

22. Regulation (EEC) No 1408/71 of the Council of 14 June 1971 on the application of social security schemes to employed persons and their families moving within the Community, *Official Journal L 149, 05/07/197, p. 0002–005; English special edition: Series I, Chapter 1971(II), p. 0416.* A second regulation spelled out the administrative rules for implementing the provisions of the 1971 regulation: Regulation (EEC) No 574/72 of the Council of 21 March 1972 fixing the procedure for implementing Regulation (EEC) No 1408/71 on the application of social security schemes to employed persons and their families moving within the Community, *Official Journal L 074, 27/03/197, p. 0001–0083; English special edition: Series I, Chapter 1972(I), p. 0159.*

23. Under a 1953 European Convention on social and medical assistance, guest workers could be eligible for medical benefits and also for assistance subsidies—the latter, however, only after a minimum of five years of residence (ten for those above 55 years of age) and only as long as they had a valid residence permit, which was always temporary.

24. Case 1-72, *Rita Frilli* v. *Belgian State* [1972] ECR 457.

25. Case 139/82, *Paola Piscitello* v. *Istituto nazionale della previdenza sociale (INPS)* [1983] ECR 1427.

26. Joined cases 379, 380, 381/85, and 93/86, *Caisse régionale d'assurance maladie Rhône-Alpes* v. *Anna Giletti, Directeur régional des affaires sanitaires et sociales de Lorraine* v. *Domenico Giardini, Caisse régionale d'assurance maladie du Nord-Est* v. *Feliciano Tampan*, and *Severino Severini* v. *Caisse primaire centrale d'assurance maladie* [1987] ECR 955.

27. Council Regulation (EEC) No 1247/92 of 30 April 1992 amending Regulation (EEC) No 1408/71 on the application of social security schemes to employed persons, to self-employed persons and to members of their families moving within the Community, Official Journal L 136, 19/05/1992 p. 0001–0006.

28. Case C-160/96, *Manfred Molenaar and Barbara Fath-Molenaar* v. *Allgemeine Ortskran-kenkasse Baden-Württemberg* [1998] ECR I-00843. The Court confirmed this doctrine in the subsequent *Jauch* case (Case C-215/99, *Friedrich Jauch* v. *Pensionsversicher-ungsanstalt der Arbeiter* [2001] ECR I-01901), concerning the Austrian long-term care allowance. In this latter case (as well as in *Leclere*: Case C-43/99, *Ghislain Leclere and Alina Deaconescu* v. *Caisse nationale des prestations familiales* [2001] ECR I-04265) the Court has also started to question the criteria used by member states for including special non-contributory benefits in the Regulation Appendix (see Sindbjerg Martinsen 2004 for a more detailed discussion).

29. Joined cases 286/82 and 26/83, *Graziana Luisi and Giuseppe Carbone* v. *Ministero del Tesoro* [1984] ECR 377.

30. Council Directive 90/364/EEC of 28 June 1990 on the right of residence; *Official Journal* L 180, 13/07/1990 p. 0026–0027. Council Directive 90/365/EEC of 28 June 1990 on the right of residence for employees and self-employed persons who have ceased their occupational activity, Official Journal L 180, 13/07/1990 p. 0028–0029. Council Directive 90/366/EEC of 28 June 1990 on the right of residence for students, Official Journal L 180, 13/07/1990 p. 0030–0031.

31. Case C-90/97, *Robin Swaddling* v. *Adjudication Officer* [1999] ECR I-01075.

32. Case C-85/96, *María Martínez Sala* v. *Freistaat Bayern* [1998] ECR I-02691.

33. Case C-184/99, *Rudy Grzelczyk* v. *Centre public d'aide sociale d'Ottignies-Louvain-la-Neuve* [2001] ECR I-06193.

34. In the recent *Collins* case (C-138-02 Case C-138/02, *Brian Francis Collins* v. *Secretary of State for Work and Pensions* [2004] ECR-I-02703 the ECJ has again invited member states to implement the residence requirement for means-tested benefits in a 'proportional' way, that is, only to the extent that it is based on objective con-siderations that are independent on the applicants' nationality and proportionate to the legitimate aims of the national provision.

35. Directive 2004/38/EC of the European Parliament and of the Council of 29 April 2004 on the right of citizens of the Union and their family members to move and reside freely within the territory of the Member States amending Regulation (EEC) No 1612/68 and repealing Directives 64/221/EEC, 68/360/EEC, 72/194/EEC, 73/148/EEC, 75/34/EEC, 75/35/EEC, 90/364/EEC, 90/365/EEC, and 93/96/EEC (Text with EEA relevance), *Official Journal* L 158, 30/04/2004 p. 0077–0123.

36. The 1992 list was updated by Regulation 833/2004, with some technical amendments in 2009.

37. Denmark, Ireland, the Netherlands, Austria, Slovenia, Slovakia, Bulgaria, and Romania.
38. The most controversial regarded the rights of TCN spouses of EU nationals: see ECJ, Case C-127/08, *Metock* [2008].
39. The European Council has four months for either referring back the draft legislative proposal to the Council (in which case the ordinary legislative procedure will continue) or requesting the Commission to submit a new proposal (in which case the act originally proposed will be considered as non adopted). There is also a simpler solution for the European Council: 'taking no action', which means that the proposed act falls without the need for further initiatives. This simpler option was not envisaged by the Constitutional Treaty and has been inserted during the Lisbon negotiations. A declaration agreed by all member states specifies that the European Council shall decide 'by consensus' in the procedure envisaged by Article 48.
40. Agreement establishing an Association between the European Economic Community and Turkey, Official Journal P 217, 29/12/1964 p. 3687–8.
41. Cooperation Agreement between the European Economic Community and the Kingdom of Morocco, *Official Journal* L 264, 27/09/1978 p. 0002–0118; Cooperation Agreement between the European Economic Community and the People's Democratic Republic of Algeria, *Official Journal* L 263, 27/09/1978 p. 0002–0118; Cooperation Agreement between the European Economic Community and the Republic of Tunisia, *Official Journal* L 265, 27/09/1978, pp. 0002–0118.
42. Council Regulation (EC) No 859/2003 of 14 May 2003 extending the provisions of Regulation (EEC) No 1408/71 and Regulation (EEC) No 574/72 to nationals of third countries who are not already covered by those provisions solely on the ground of their nationality, *Official Journal* L 124, 20/05/2003, pp. 0001–0003.
43. We do not address in this chapter the issue of irregular TCNs, which has become an increasingly hotter object of contention between members states (e.g. Italy and France, especially after the sudden inflows of immigrants from Libya in 2011, in the wake of the war) as well as between member states and the EU.

Bibliography

Bartolini, S. (2005) *Restructuring Europe*, Oxford, Oxford University Press.

Berezin, M. (2009) *Illiberal Politics in Neoliberal Times: Culture, Security and Populism in the New Europe*, Cambridge, Cambridge University Press.

Bommes, M. & Geddes, A. (2000) (Eds.) *Immigration and Welfare*, London, Routledge.

Brubaker, R. (1992) *Citizenship and Nationhood in France and Germany*, Cambridge, MA, Harvard University Press.

Burgoon, B. (2011) Immigration, Integration and Support for Redistribution in Europe, Working Paper 2011/260, Madrid, Juan March Institute.

Caporaso, J.A. & Tarrow, S. (2009) Polanyi in Brussels: Supranational Institutions and the Transnational Embedding of Markets. *International Organization*, 63, 593–620.

Carrera, S. & Faure Atger, A. (2009) Implementation of Directive 2004/38 in the Context of Enlargement, Special Report/April 2009, Brussels, Ceps.

Conant, L. (2001) Contested Boundaries, Citizens, States and Supranational Belonging in the European Union, Working Paper RSC no. 2001/27, Florence: European University Institute.

Cornelissen, V.R. (1996) The principle of Territoriality and the Community Regulations on Social Security. *Common Market Law Review*, 33, 13–41.

European Commission (2003) *Commission Communication on Immigration, Integration and Employment*, Brussels, COM (2003) 336 final.

European Commission (2008) *Report from the Commission to the European Parliament and the Council on the Application of Directive 2004/38/EC on the Right of Citizens of the Union and their Family Members to Move and Reside Freely Within the Territory of the Member States*, Brussels, COM (2008) 840 final.

Faist, T. & Ettee, T. (2007) (Eds.) *The Europeanisation of National Policies and Politics of Immigration*, Houndmills, Palgrave Macmillan.

Falkner, G. (2007) Europeanization and Social Policy. In Graziano, P. & Vinck, M. (Eds.) *Europeanization: New Research Agendas*, Basinstoke, Palgrave Macmillan, 253–65.

Falkner, G. (2010) European Union. In Castles, F., Leibfried, S., Lewis, J., Obinger, H. & Pierson, C. (Eds.) *The Oxford Handbook of the Welfare State*, Oxford, Oxford University Press, 292–305.

Ferrera, M. (2005) *The Boundaries of Welfare*, Oxford, Oxford University Press.

Ferrera, M. (2009) The JCMS Annual Lecture: National Welfare States and European Integration: In Search of a 'Virtuous Nesting'. *Journal of Common Market Studies*, 47, 219–33.

Fliegstein, N. (2008) *Euroclash: The EU, European Identity and the Future of Europe*, Oxford, Oxford University Press.

Flora, P. (1993) The National Welfare State and European Integration. In Moreno, L. (Ed.) *Social Exchange and Welfare Development*, Madrid, Consejo Superior de Investigaciones Scientifica, 58–74.

Flora, P. (2000) Externe Grenzbildung und Interne Strukturierung. Europa und Seine Nationen. *Berliner Journal für Soziologie*, 10, 157–66.

Flora, P., Kuhnle, S. & Urwin, D. (1999) (Eds.) *State Formation, Nation Building and Mass Politics in Europe. The Theory of Stein Rokkan*, New York, Oxford University Press.

Geddes, A. (2000) *Immigration and European Integration: Towards Fortress Europe?* Manchester, Manchester University Press.

Guiraudon, V. (2000) *Les Politiques d'immigration en Europe*, Paris, L'Harmattan.

Guiraudon, V & Joppke, C. (2001) (Eds.) *Controlling a New Migration World*, London, Routledge.

Heater, D. (1990) *Citizenship: The Civic Ideal in World History, Politics and Education*, London, Longman.

Hirschman, A. O. (1970) *Exit, Voice and Loyalty*, Cambridge, MA, Harvard University Press.

Höpner, M. & Schäfer, A. (2010) Polanyi in Brussels? Embeddedness and the Three Dimensions of European Economic Integration, MPIfG Discussion Paper 10/8, Cologne, Max Planck Institute for the Study of Societies.

Kriesi, H., Grande, E., Lachat, R., Dolezai, M., Bornschier, S. & Frey, T. (2006) Globalization and the Transformation of the National Political Space: Six European Countries Compared. *European Journal of Political Research*, 45, 921–56.

Kroeger, S. (2009) (Ed.) What Have We Learnt: Advances, Pitfalls and Remaining Questions in OMC Research, *European Integration Online Papers (EIoP)*, Special Issue 1, vol. 13, art.5.

Leibfried, S. & Pierson, P. (1995) (Eds.) *European Social Policy between Fragmentation and Integration*, Washington, DC, Brookings Institution.

Leibfried, S. & Pierson, P. (2000) *Social Policy*. In Wallace, H. & Wallace, W. (Eds.) *Policy-Making in the European Union*, fourth edition, Oxford, Oxford University Press, 267–91.

Lyon Caen, G. & Lyon Caen, A. (1993) *Droit Social International et Européen*, Paris, Dalloz.

Mabbet, D. & Bolderson H. (2000) Non-discrimination, Free Movement and Social Citizenship in Europe: Contrasting Provisions for the EU Nationals and Asylum-seekers. In Behrendt, C. & Sigg, R. (Eds.) *Social Security in the Global Village*. New Brunswick, Transaction Publishers, 189–210.

Majone, G. (1996) *Regulating Europe*, London, Routledge.

Marshall, T.H. (1950) *Citizenship and Social Class*, Cambridge, Cambridge University Press.

Martinsen D.S. (2004) European Institutionalisation of Social Security Rights: A Two Layered Process of Integration, Ph.D. Dissertation, Florence, European University Institute.

Martinsen, D.S. (2011) Judicial Policy Making and Europeanization: The Proportionality of National Control and Administrative Discretion. *Journal of European Public Policy*, 18, 944–61.

Martinsen, D.S. & Falkner, G. (2010) Social Policy: Problem Solving Gaps, Partial Exits and Court Decision Traps. In Falkner, G. (Ed.) *The EU's Decision Traps: Comparing Policies*, Oxford, Oxford University Press, 128–45.

Monti, M (2010) *A New Strategy for the Single Market*, <http://ec.europa.eu/bepa/pdf/monti_report_final_10_05_2010_en.pdf>.

Rokkan, S. (1974) Entries, Voices, Exits: Towards a Possible Generalization of the Hirschman Model. *Social Sciences Information*, 13, 39–53.

Scharpf, F. (2010) The Asymmetry of European Integration, or Why the EU Cannot be a 'Social Market Economy'. *Socio-Economic Review*, 8, 211–50.

Straubhaar, T. (1988) *On the Economics of International Labour Migration*, Stuttgart, Verlag Paul Haupt.

Strikwerda, C. (1997) Reinterpreting the History of European Integration: Business, Labour and Social Citizenship in Twentieth-Century Europe. In Klausen, J. & Tilly, L. (Eds.) *European Integration in Social and Theoretical Perspective. From 1850 to the Present*, Lanham, Rowman & Littlefield, 51–70.

Van der Mei, P.A. (2003) *Free Movement of Persons Within the European Community*, Oxford-Portland, Hart.

Vanhercke, B. (2010) Delivering the Goods for Europe 2020? The Social OMC Adequacy and Impact Re-assessed. In Marlier, E. & Natali, D. (Eds.) *Europe 2020. Towards a More Social EU?* Brussels, P.I.E. Peter Lang, 115–42.

Venturini, A. (2004) *Post-War Migration in Southern Europe*, Cambridge, Cambridge University Press.

Verschueren, H. (forthcoming). The EU Social Security Coordination System: A Close Interplay Between the EU Legislature and Judiciary. In Syrpis, P. (Ed.) *The Judiciary, the Legislature and the EU Internal Market*. Cambridge, Cambridge University Press.

Weiler, J. (1994) A Quiet Revolution—The European Court of Justice and Its Interlocutors. *Comparative Political Studies,* 26, 510–34.

Zeitlin, J. & Heidenreich, M. (2009) (Eds.) *Changing European Employment and Welfare Regimes: The Influence of the Open Method of Coordination on National Reforms*, London, Routledge.

Conclusion

13

Multidimensional Transformations in the Early 21st Century Welfare States

Giuliano Bonoli and David Natali

Introduction

Some ten years ago, several influential articles and books analysing the process of welfare state transformation were published. They painted a picture of the changing social policy landscape in OECD countries, but above all, they provided us with the theoretical tools needed to study the current period of welfare state development. They took contextual developments seriously, such as globalization or the shift toward postindustrial economies. They emphasized the climate of 'permanent austerity' (Pierson 1998) in which reforms take place. These studies also gave us the intellectual tools needed to explain what we were observing in the late 1990s: resilience and immobility, failed attempts at more radical reform, divergence across welfare regimes.

The chapters contained in this book have shown that, over the last decade, change has been more substantial than in previous years. In this final contribution, we assess the extent to which the theoretical tools developed in the late 1990s and early 2000s need to be adapted so that they are able to account for the observed developments. The main emphasis is on the recognition of the multidimensional character of the process of welfare state transformation. This approach, we argue, allows us to provide a more complete picture of what is going on, but also to better understand the mechanisms that are presiding over social policy change in the early 21st century.

Traditionally, political scientists have understood the process of welfare state development as occurring on a single dimension that makes reference to the 'quantity' of protection provided by welfare institutions. This single dimension can be understood in a narrow sense, and focus for example on the replacement rates of key benefits, or in a broader one, and try to capture the degree of 'welfare effort' made in a country with indicators such as social expenditure as a percentage of GDP. From this perspective, welfare state change can only take one of two directions: expansion or retrenchment. During the postwar years, when affluent democracies built their welfare states, social policymaking was dominated by expansion. Since the mid-1970s, in contrast, retrenchment is the key direction of change, with countries being more or less successful in implementing policies under this rubric.

While the quantitative dimension of social provision captured by the notions of expansion and retrenchment is a crucial one, it clearly does not cover the entirety of relevant welfare state transformations. Over the years, several observers have come to the conclusion that other dimensions of welfare provision need to be considered if we want to have a fair picture of the social policy landscape and of the way it is evolving. In this book we take the view that a multidimensional understanding of social policies is an essential precondition for both describing and accounting for the key developments that have occurred in social policies over the last decade or so. The 1990s and the 2000s have seen more than retrenchment.

Looking at developments that have occurred beyond, or beside, retrenchment is important in at least two respects. First, welfare states are important structures that affect the distribution of resources in a society. They impact on the functioning of the labour market, and more generally on the economy of a country. In this respect, the quantitative dimension plays an important role, but it is clearly not the only one. For example, a costly welfare state may have a very different impact on the labour market depending on the relative proportions of active and passive provision. For this reason, we believe that in order to have a fair understanding of the political economy implications of social policies, one needs to consider how these are shaped, not only how generous or how costly they are. In short, a multidimensional understanding of social policy is essential if we are interested in the impact that welfare states have on the labour market, on the economy and more generally on society. Second, as forcefully argued by Häusermann (2010 and Chapter 6), a multidimensional understanding of social policies is particularly useful in accounting for some of the reforms that have been undertaken in recent years. In many cases, these reforms have impacted on more than one dimension of welfare provision, opening up opportunities for new, sometimes unlikely, coalitions. One example is the coalition between employers and left-wing parties for developing subsidized childcare. The former were interested in strengthening the pro-employment dimension of policy, while the latter were interested in expanding social provision. Häusermann shows that support for a reform may be based on its implication for different dimensions of provision. Considering the various relevant dimensions is thus essential in accounting for the developments we observe.

In this chapter we apply a multidimensional understanding of the process of welfare state transformation. Change takes place on the quantitative dimension, but also on two additional ones: the pro-employment orientation of policy and the extent to which welfare arrangements are encompassing or limited to sections of the population only. These three dimensions, which are discussed in more detail below, may not capture all the complexity of a changing welfare state. They allow us, nonetheless, to summarize the most essential features that are relevant for a country's political economy. However, before developing our own multidimensional understanding of policy change, we first look at the notion of multidimensionality in previous scholarship on the welfare state.

Scholarship on Multidimensional Reforms

To be fair, the multidimensional character of social polices and of the process of welfare state transformation has been recognized before. Esping-Andersen's critique of social expenditure as a proportion of GDP as the only relevant dimension of welfare provision can be seen as an attempt to draw our attention to the fact that spending, or generosity, fail to capture the crucial aspect of who gets protection. In other words, 'all spending does not count equally' (Esping Andersen 1990: 19). Esping-Andersen's solution to this problem was to focus on the notion of 'decommodification' which is based essentially on two crucial dimensions of social protection: the level of benefits and their degree of universality. However, the projection of these two dimensions into a single, decommodification index makes it difficult to see where the differences are.

A multidimensional view of social policymaking is more explicit in the work of Paul Pierson. In his 2001 contribution, he identified three dimensions of reform: cost-containment; re-commodification and recalibration. The first one, cost-containment, reflects actual retrenchment but also measures geared toward limiting future rises in spending. The second dimension of change, re-commodification, makes reference to reforms that 'restrict the alternatives to participation in the labour market, either by tightening eligibility or cutting benefit'. Third, Pierson spoke of recalibration, which he saw as a movement towards adapting welfare states to changed socio-economic circumstances. Recalibration was seen as being of two sorts, either 'rationalization', i.e. getting rid of inefficiencies that had developed over the years, or updating, i.e. responding to new needs and demands (Pierson 2001: 421–3).

While we acknowledge the contribution made by Pierson in developing a multidimensional understanding of the process of welfare state transformation, we find that his approach had some limitations. First, the theoretical contribution made by Pierson, mostly in his earlier work, concerns only the first dimension: cost containment (or retrenchment vs. expansion). Pierson was able to develop a very precise set of expectations with regard to how governments are likely to move when policy change affects this dimension, or when change is about retrenchment. In contrast, we know much less what to expect when the goal of reform is to increase 'recommodification' or to promote 'recalibration'. These two dimensions of change remain undertheorized in Pierson's own work. Second, the three dimensions identified by Pierson are difficult to operationalize. This is particularly true of 'recalibration' and 'recommodification'. How do we assess the extent to which a welfare state has been recalibrated? These two dimensions may also be difficult to separate. For instance, does compulsory participation in a job search assistance scheme for unemployed people count as re-commodification or as recalibration?

The three dimensions identified by Pierson are helpful in pointing out that, in addition to retrenchment, other relevant developments are occurring in social policy. We still lack, however, some indications of the theoretical implications of this multidimensional perspective. How do we explain developments on dimensions other than the expansion-retrenchment axis? Can we expect developments on different dimensions to interact? If so, with what consequences for actual policy outputs?

Theoretically relevant suggestions concerning the multidimensional character of welfare state transformation were made, at least implicitly, in other contributions of the late 1990s/early 2000s. Jonah Levy argued that in some Bismarckian welfare states, expansion in new social policies (such as anti-poverty policy) had been made possible by cuts in (over-)generous income replacement programmes, in a movement that he qualified as 'turning vice into virtue'. Countries like Italy and the Netherlands had very generous invalidity insurance and early retirement schemes. These were reformed, and part of the savings achieved were reinvested in the new policies (Levy 1999). Similarly, Bonoli (2001) showed evidence of successful reforms being characterized by the inclusion in a single package of measures of cost-containment—usually referring to the protection against old risks—and improvements in protection of new social risks.

More recently, Natali and Rhodes (2008) have argued that when pursuing multiple goals, reform may be better able at generating the necessary support. This was the case with the complex packages allowing the reform of social protection programmes. Engaging in a process of political exchange is often decisive for creating sufficient support for reforms. Given a particular economic and financial context, policymakers can enlarge the window for winning agreement to change. Reforms, in successful cases, are the result of deals involving a series of political goals. They aim at increased consensus for reforms, while trying to maintain their control over political and organizational resources, and shape policy decisions. Following Rhodes (2001), we argue that the co-existence of different priorities (which results from the existence of different strains on welfare programmes) can increase the opportunities for innovation, and facilitate the adoption of painful policies, including cutbacks. The more reform dimensions there are, the more opportunities exist for 'trading' them with one another.

This view is at the centre of one of the most elaborate accounts of welfare reform based on a multidimensional perspective: Silja Häusermann's study of pension reform in continental Europe. She claims that the multidimensional quality of social programmes creates opportunities for reform in the current context of permanent austerity. She illustrates her point with a comparison of pension reform in three countries. In many cases, these reforms have simultaneously impacted on more than one of the following dimensions: the generosity of insurance benefits, the guarantee of a minimum pension income, the gender-egalitarian character of the scheme and the extent to which pension provision is funded. This multidimensional quality of pension reform has opened up opportunities for coalition formation that would not have been possible in a one-dimensional policy space. Political actors defending different interests and values were able to obtain the inclusion of at least some of their preferences into complex, multidimensional, reform packages. This was instrumental in securing their adoption (Häusermann 2010). Häusermann's account is helpful in understanding why continental European countries, long considered as incapable of reforming their pension systems, have managed to do so in the 1990s and early 2000s. A multidimensional perspective can be helpful in making sense of individual reforms. However, one can also take a broader view and look at the whole exercise of welfare state restructuring as a multidimensional process. This is the use of the multidimensionality perspective we want to make in this chapter.

These studies show that recognizing the multidimensional character of the process of welfare state transformation has been helpful in accounting for instances of reform that would otherwise have remained puzzling. We can think of multidimensionality as a perspective that can help make sense of welfare reforms. The fact that this perspective has emerged in recent years may be related to the content of welfare reform that has become increasingly multidimensional. This, in turn, may be due to the increasingly tight constraints under which social policymaking takes place. With Häusermann (2010: 81) we can hypothesize that multidimensionality is a product of political actors attempting to get out of the dilemmas and constraints that are typical of social policymaking in the age of permanent austerity.

Three Dimensions of Current Welfare State Change

What dimensions, beside the quantitative one, are relevant in the current phase of welfare state transformation? The chapters included in this book have shown the importance of several developments. Of them, two seem to have played a particularly important role in the reform processes over the last decade: the development of a more active orientation in social policy and the reduction in the encompassing character of coverage of some social programmes, a trend that leads to the dualization phenomena observed by many and discussed in some of this book's chapters. These two trends make reference to dimensions of welfare provision that are not well captured by a simple quantitative understanding of social policy. The first one refers to the pro-employment function of a welfare state, while the second one is linked to its encompassing character.

On this basis, we argue that analysis of current change should be based on a combined focus on three dimensions. First, the traditional quantitative dimension, along which countries can move upwards (expansion) or downwards (retrenchment). Second, the pro-employment orientation of policy, or the relative balance between passive and active provision. Third, we are interested in the extent to which social programmes succeed in providing coverage to the whole resident population of a country (encompassing character of provision). Of course, one can identify other important dimensions of differentiation in social policies, and there are indeed examples of major advances in social policy analysis that have looked at dimensions that are not included here.[1] However, we believe that the three dimensions we focus on in this chapter have been particularly relevant over the last decade in determining the impact that the welfare state has had on the distribution of resources and in shaping the way in which it has interacted with its economic context, most crucially, with the labour market. Next we elaborate on why we believe this to be the case.

Level of protection

The first dimension, the level of protection or quantity of welfare refers to the size of social transfers and has big implications for the economy and for the labour market. Welfare states must be financed by taxation or social insurance contributions. The latter, impact directly on labour cost and as a result on a country's job creation capacity (Scharpf 2000). The size of the welfare state also matters for redistribution. Large, expensive welfare states are more successful in reducing income inequalities (Mitchell 1991; OECD 2008: chapter 4). It is true that the distributional impact of a welfare state does not depend on size alone, but also on coverage and the structure of its benefit system. However, a given level of resources is essential for a redistributive welfare state.

Pro-employment orientation

The second dimension, active versus passive provision is largely responsible for determining how the welfare state will interact with the labour market and with the wider economy. The importance of the passive vs. active provision in the process of welfare state transformation is evident. Active welfare states are likely to interact with the labour market in a more productive way, leading to higher employment. This has distributional consequences, as access to employment remains an important factor in escaping poverty. Indeed, increases in wage inequality in many countries and the emergence of non-standard employment mean that a job is less of a guarantee of a poverty-free existence than in the past. However, the available evidence still suggests that the quantity of work performed in a household remains a powerful determinant of its exposure to the risk of poverty (Cantillon 2010; Crettaz 2011). The passive vs. active dimension is also likely to impact on the functioning of the labour market. A more active welfare state means higher supply of labour and possibly a better matching between supply and demand. As a result, active social policies can be expected to have an overall positive impact on the functioning of the labour market. The shift from passive to active provision may be a crucial factor in improving the viability of European welfare states.

Encompassing character

The third dimension, the extent of coverage, is also a crucial determinant of the distribution of resources in a society, and in particular in relation to the protection against social risks. In the dualized welfare states that are emerging in many continental European countries, such protection tends to be considerably stronger for some social groups, the insiders (Palier, Chapter 11). This development can be seen as a process of *de-universalization* of social protection coverage in countries that relied predominantly on employment-related social insurance for the provision of social protection. The process goes together with the deregulation of non-standard employment, which as a result tends to generate fewer social rights. According the Crouch and Keune (Chapter 3) this development results in the rest of society (the outsiders) to be exposed to considerably higher levels of uncertainty in economic and social matters. Exposure to economic uncertainty may have become a key dimension of social stratification in postindustrial societies where welfare states are reducing their reach.

It is clear in our view that, while many dimensions of social policy may be considered to be important, the three we have decided to focus upon in this concluding chapter are crucial in shaping what we have decided to refer to as 'the new welfare state'. This is for at least three reasons. First, these three dimensions jointly define the impact that a welfare state has on the broader political economy of a country; second, they largely determine the social outcomes of a welfare arrangement; and, third, a combined focus on these three dimensions allows us to identify the political dynamics that have shaped recent reforms. This third reason is explored next.

The Mechanisms of Multidimensional Processes

Our focus on the multidimensional quality of welfare reform processes allows us to identify mechanisms that have facilitated the adoption of theoretically difficult-to-adopt reforms. Some of these mechanisms have been identified in previous studies, but here they are reframed so as to fit in the multidimensional perspective we adopt. Together, they help us understand the changes that have taken place in social policies over the last decade.

Political exchange

The notion of political exchange has been theorized by Pizzorno (1977, 1980) and then defined by Regini (1984) with reference to the interaction between governments and the social partners. For Regini, political exchange is 'a type of relation between the state and labour organizations in which a trade-off of different forms of political power occurs. The state devolves portions of its decision-making authority to trade unions, by allowing them to play a part in policy formation and implementation and [. . .] in return for this, trade unions deliver their indirect political power to the state by guaranteeing consensus' (Regini 1984: 128). In other words, this is the case of the political market, where the government exchanges goods (financial resources, social rights, administrative resources) with the social consensus provided by social partners.

In this chapter, we understand political exchange as a notion referring to 'deals' between political actors, in which at least some of the preferences of each participant are included. The notion differs from that of compromise. A compromise can simply consist of a middle way solution between two more extreme positions. Political exchange, instead, entails that actors accept policy changes that are not in line with their priorities but in return get some of their own requests included into the deal. This aspect is particularly important when the leadership of a political actor needs to 'sell' the deal to their rank and file.

Political exchange in welfare reform may take different forms and occur between different actors. It may combine retrenchment in some part of a given programme with expansion in other ones. This type of political exchange has been observed in some reforms of old age pension schemes and unemployment insurance programmes. Basically, retrenchment has concerned the income protection function of the programme, while expansion has either focused on the active or the coverage dimension. These instances have been termed 'modernizing compromises' and will be discussed in more detail below.

On other occasions, political exchange has been more tightly related to actors' own interests. This is the case with some pension reforms that combine the retrenchment in future benefits with concessions that have implications for the management role that given actors can play in the system. This was the case, for example, in some French reforms in the 1990s. The 1993 French pension reform, for instance, together with benefit level reductions, included the setting up of a new tax-financed fund, meant to pay for the non-contributory elements of the pension scheme. This was in response to a long-standing demand by some trade union federations (Bonoli 2000; Palier 2002). Reforms of employment protection law have also taken the form of political exchange. As shown by Davidsson and Emmenegger (Chapter 10) beside reductions in protection for non-permanent workers, French and Swedish reforms have included reassurances concerning protection for permanent workers and the role that trade unions play in administering this part of the law.

Political exchange is a powerful tool for carrying through potentially unpopular welfare reforms. It does not necessarily require the explicit support of each participant. In some cases, simple acquiescence is what can be expected. It allows avoiding the most radical forms of opposition and protest that, on occasions have led to the withdrawal of legislation.

Modernizing compromises

Modernizing compromises can be seen as a particular variant of political exchange that refer to reforms that combine retrenchment on the protective function of postwar welfare states with expansion either on the active dimension or on the coverage dimension.

Multidimensional reforms have sometimes combined retrenchment in the traditional income protection function of social policies with expansion on other 'newer' functions. These have included activation, gender equality, and improved coverage for marginal social groups. These instances are discussed in several studies (Bonoli 1999, 2001, 2009; Levy 1999; Häusermann 2010, Chapter 6, this volume). They describe a kind of virtuous dynamic in the process of welfare state adaptation, which is characterized by constant adaptation to changing social needs and demands. As socio-economic change produces new problems and demands among the general population, welfare states are adapted to take this into account. Women's entry into labour markets increases the demand for childcare and reduces it for widow's pensions. A modernizing compromise converts welfare institutions that responded to older problems and demands into ones that cater for currents needs.

Instances of 'modernizing compromise' or reforms that 'turn vice into virtue' have been documented, but have tended to be rare events. This may be due to the fact that a number of conditions must be fulfilled for such modernizing compromises to be attractive to policymakers.

First, modernizing compromises may be more likely in countries that have a political system with several veto points and veto players, and a tradition of consensus-based policymaking. Theoretically, we can indeed expect modernizing compromises, as any sort of compromise, to be more likely in political systems that reduce the scope for unilateral decisions making. The literature on modernizing compromises suggests that this theoretical expectation is largely empirically confirmed. It is certainly not by chance that many actual examples of modernizing compromises are taken from reforms adopted in Switzerland, a country known for having a constitutional structure that 'forces' political actors to act consensually (Kriesi 1995). Other countries that have seen the adoption of this type of reform tend to be also characterized by veto point and veto player dense political systems. Häusermann, for example, identifies modernizing compromises in German pension reforms. On some occasions, retrenchment in core social insurance benefits was combined with expansion on other dimensions, such as gender equality and coverage for atypical employees (Häusermann 2010: 164). Levy's analysis of Italian and Dutch reforms also points in this direction. Centripetal pressures for reform may be the result of veto point dense political institutions and/or of the presence in the political arena of actors who can act as de facto veto players, such as the labour movement in Italy in the 1990s.

Second, and perhaps more importantly, the scope for modernizing compromises arguably depends on the configuration of actors that negotiate a given reform. Basically, actors who can act as veto players need to have a stake in the reform for it to succeed. This means that for a modernizing compromise to succeed, actors that oppose retrenchment (say, the trade unions and the political left), must have an interest in gaining better coverage against new emerging needs and demands. A Social democratic party may enter into such compromise if, together with a traditional workers' wing, it also has an expanding component made of individuals who are exposed to new social risks, such as reconciling work and family life, atypical employment or other family-related risks. Under such circumstances, trading cuts in core benefits against improvements in the new policies may make sense. In contrast, trade unions that represent mostly (ageing) industrial workers are less likely to see the attractiveness of a compromise that reduces protection for their members while improving it for individuals who tend not to be.

In other terms, the likelihood of modernizing compromises depends on the internal structure of key political actors, in particular the political left and the labour movement. If old and new left values coexist within a single actor, then we can expect this actor to favour a modernizing compromise. If, instead, old left values prevail, than modernizing compromises will be less likely. Studying the internal composition and politics of key political actors may help gain a clearer view of actors' preferences on social policy issues. It may also help reduce the 'indeterminacy' of welfare reforms highlighted by Häusermann in Chapter 6. It is true that equilibria are difficult to predict in a multidimensional space, but a better specification of complex actors' preference schedules may help reduce this uncertainty.

Institutional legacies and prevailing social problems are also likely to impact on the likelihood of modernizing compromises. In pension policy, for instance, the limited coverage of old risks and the emergence of new social risks has constituted an opportunity for modernizing compromises in otherwise retrenchment oriented reforms. On the one hand, at the end of the postwar years, public retirement programmes had an almost universal coverage, but some groups were still excluded. This was the case with the self-employed that in some European countries had more limited protection against old-age risks (Natali 2007). On the other hand, the emergence of new risks may have led to new gaps in public protection. This was the case with atypical workers (with flexible contracts) with limited public protection until the 1990s. Both limits of public protection allowed policymakers to put together politically attractive reform packages that contained some elements of retrenchment and improvement in the coverage of those less well protected groups. This is the case with reforms introduced in liberal, social-democratic and especially in Continental and Southern European countries (see Bridgen et al. 2007). In Germany, Belgium, France and Italy minimum pensions have been improved. In addition, new forms of redistribution have been introduced: this is the case with contribution credits for periods of time spent out of the labour market for caring, training or education (Natali 2007).

Note that extending the coverage of public pension schemes is not only an element in broader compromise-based reform packages. It is also an option that can be politically attractive in its own right. First, it is a typical measure to improve social rights and protection, and thus reformers may claim credit for that. Second, in the short- and medium-term it increases the system's revenues while it does not increase total spending. The government thereby avoids an average increase in social contributions and/or taxes and the living standard of beneficiaries is maintained. Extending the coverage of public pensions is an example of the type of moderate expansion that is available on the menu of today's social policymakers. Politically, these measures are attractive because they allow credit claiming exercises in spite of the overall context of austerity.

Affordable credit claiming

Modernizing compromises and political exchange are mechanisms that help us to understand reforms that are primarily geared towards improving the financial viability of the programmes inherited from the postwar years. These mechanisms are compatible with the framework put forward by Pierson in the 1990s (Pierson 1994, 2001). In fact, the primary objective of reform is cost containment and selective expansion in some new functions turned out to be instrumental in securing a sufficient level of support for complex reform packages. However, as pointed out in many of this book's chapters, over the last 15 years, we have also seen the expansion of some policy areas independent of retrenchment. Expansion in childcare (Naumann, Chapter 8), in active labour market policy (Clasen and Clegg, Chapter 7), or more generally, policies going under the rubric of social investment (Jenson, Chapter 2), have often expanded autonomously, without being part of otherwise cost-containment oriented packages.

As argued by Bonoli in Chapter 5, such instances of reform are more difficult to reconcile with the blame avoidance/credit claiming framework put forward by Weaver (1986) and Pierson (1994, 2001). The framework is based on an understanding of voters' reactions to policy characterized by a negativity bias. Voters are much more likely to react to a loss with electoral punishment than they are to reward a government because of a gain of the same amount (Weaver 1986). From this perspective, it is difficult to understand why the additional funds that governments have channelled into the new policies have not instead been used to soften retrenchment efforts that were pursued simultaneously in other fields of the welfare state.

Chapter 5 provides an explanation for this apparent puzzle, making reference to the notion of affordable credit claiming. It argues that the policy ideas behind these reforms have provided governments with an opportunity for relatively high visibility credit claiming at a rather low cost for the public purse. Since these policies are new in most countries, assigning additional funds to subsidized childcare or active labour market policies is more likely to generate public attention, and as a result voters' credit, than investments of the same size in the generosity of established social programmes. This, in the field of old age pensions, would mean very minor reductions in the extent of retrenchment. As a result, in terms of credit claiming, the return on investment is arguably higher in the new policies. As a matter of fact, especially in the field of childcare policy, expansion oriented reforms have been clearly used for credit claiming by the governments behind them (Naumann, Chapter 8; Morgan 2010).

Affordable credit claiming consists of expansion on the employment promotion dimension and minor increases in the quantitative dimension. It is particularly attractive in the current context of permanent austerity, because other credit claiming strategies (such as, say, an increase in current old age pension benefits) are off the menu. Employment promotion lends itself particularly well to credit claiming. It is based on widespread normative perceptions that value work. In addition, it promises (to those who think of themselves as being net contributors to the welfare state) to reduce dependency on the social programmes they must finance. These elements help us understand why employment promotion has proven to be so attractive to politicians across OECD countries.

Dualization

The notion of dualization has been used to describe the growing segmentation of labour markets in countries that originally had rigid labour laws and that have deregulated non-permanent employment contracts. This development, which has been very strong in Southern Europe and in some Continental European countries, is increasingly producing strong divisions between the core workers, who still enjoy the benefit of highly protected employment contracts and those who occupy a more marginal position in the labour market, referred to as outsiders. The insider/outsider cleavage in labour market policy and outcomes has been widely documented in several recent studies (Rueda 2007; Palier and Thelen 2010; Emmenegger et al. 2012).

According to this strand of literature, the divisions that create an insider/outsider cleavage originate in labour market regulations, but tend to be replicated by social programmes. In fact, in most of the countries concerned by this development (Southern and Continental European countries) welfare states are based on Bismarckian social insurance programmes, meaning that social rights are strongly tied to stable contribution-paying employment. This view has been put forward by Palier and Thelen (2010) who find that in France and Germany divisions that originate in labour market regulations tend to be replicated in the welfare state, leading to an intensification of the cleavage between insiders and outsiders in those countries. Palier (Chapter 11, this volume) extends this argument to other Bismarckian countries, and argues that dualization is the 'Bismarckian' road to welfare state adaptation.

The replication of the insider/outsider cleavage in social policies takes different routes. First, social rights tend to be less developed for atypical workers.

Those on fixed term contracts, the self-employed, as well as other marginal categories of a country's population, tend to have access to limited protection against unemployment and contribute little towards their old age pensions. This effect is essentially due to the institutional setup of social insurance-based welfare states that, as seen above, ties social rights to labour market participation.

Second, the insider/outsider cleavage has been reinforced by recent reforms. This is clearly the case of some pension reforms that have a long phasing-in period (Bonoli and Palier 2008). In this case, retrenchment will not hit core workers, who will still be able to retire on currently favourable conditions. The key losers will be the younger cohorts, who make up precisely the bulk of the outsider population.

According to Palier (Chapter 11, this volume), reforms in unemployment compensation systems constitute another factor that reinforces the insider/outsider cleavage. In this field, however, the case for dualization is less clear. On the one hand, some countries have adopted activation measures for jobless people who are not covered by unemployment insurance that can be harsher than those targeted on short term unemployed. For example, the definition of suitable work differs between these two groups in most countries. However, it is difficult to see a clear pattern replicating the labour market based on an insider/outsider cleavage. In fact, the trend in many countries is towards more integration with regard to both income compensation and labour market services. As Clasen and Clegg (Chapter 7, this volume) show, countries like the UK and Germany, have moved in the direction of less differentiation among jobless people. The trend is particularly strong in the UK, where the differences between unemployment insurance and social assistance have almost disappeared.

Dualization as a strategy for the reform of the welfare state can be understood in the context of our multidimensional framework. The road taken is above all a reduction in the encompassing character of social protection arrangements. It is a path pursued in countries where the opposition against outright retrenchment has traditionally been very strong, and seems to be more politically feasible. The reduction in coverage essentially concerns younger people who are overrepresented among outsiders. In the case of pension reform, losses are targeted on younger cohorts of voters who are much less likely to mobilize politically for a right they may enjoy in a few decades.

The same logic may have played a role in the labour market reforms that initiated the dualization trend. Rather than reduce the level of protection enjoyed by core workers, countries with rigid labour markets have developed a new and more flexible labour market segment. Insofar as these reforms have probably allowed substantial job creation to take place over the last few years, it is difficult to clearly identify the losers of this process. However, what is certain is that the core workers, who tend to be the most vociferous defenders of their acquired rights, are not among them. Indeed, as argued by Emmenegger and Davidsson, the preference for deregulating labour markets at the margin may also be a result of the trade unions 'organizational interests'. This view, however, reinforces the notion that governments have taken the politically easier route to deal with the problem of excessively rigid labour markets, or the 'path of least resistance' (Bonoli, Chapter 5).

The Face of the New Welfare State

The objective of this book was not to provide an answer to the question of whether or not we can talk of a 'new welfare state', i.e. a qualitatively different set of institutions from what OECD countries developed during the postwar years. This question is largely a matter of subjective judgment. Instead, we wanted to be able to characterize the welfare settlement as it exists in the early 21st century. Our focus on multidimensionality allows us to identify patterns of change in several different sub-fields of the welfare state. Empirically, this book provides clear evidence of the direction taken by social policy over the last decade or so. What is more complicated, however, is to provide an interpretation that makes sense of it all.

In addition, our objective was not to provide a monolithic account of what the new welfare state is. Instead, we wanted this book to reflect the different perceptions and uncertainties that are out there among welfare state experts. This is why the various contributions contained in this book point us in different directions and sometimes disagree. In this final section, we do not want to settle the many issues raised. Instead, we review the main domains of uncertainty and disagreement.

First, active social policy, and more particularly the 'activation turn' that has taken place in a majority of OECD countries since the mid-1995s, have provided much food for controversy. Some see this development as a fundamental improvement of the role played by welfare states in the economy. This was clearly the case among proponents of the Third Way in the late 1990s and early 2000s (Giddens 1998; Blair and Schröder 1999). Others regard activation as an essentially punitive mechanism that has developed in order to push low skilled people into low quality jobs they would otherwise avoid (Peck 2001; Palier and Thelen 2010).

This controversy is only partly solved by distinguishing between different types of active social policy. These distinctions tend to draw a line between the 'good' activation policies, which are about improving human capital, and the 'bad' ones, which use essentially negative incentives to move people from social assistance into employment. Examples of such classifications abound.

One of them is found in Torfing (1999) who distinguishes between 'offensive' and 'defensive' workfare. Offensive workfare relies on improving skills and on empowering jobless people rather than on sanctions and benefit reduction, as is the 'defensive' variant. Taylor-Gooby, makes the same point using instead the terms of 'positive' and 'negative' activation (Taylor-Gooby 2004). In a similar vein, Barbier distinguishes between 'liberal activation', characterized by stronger work incentives, benefit conditionality and the use of sanctions, and 'universalistic activation', which is found in the Nordic countries and continues to rely on extensive investment in human capital essentially through training (Barbier 2004; Barbier and Ludwig-Mayerhofer 2004).

These distinctions have limitations. First, they have a strong value-based bias. They tend to simply reflect subjective notions of good and bad policy. Second, as pointed out by Barbier, some active labour market policies developed in continental European countries, most notably in France, do not fall in either category. French policies promoting *'insertion sociale'* aim at providing an alternative to market employment, not a stepping stone towards it (Barbier 2001). Third, the evaluation literature has shown that the most effective programmes in helping people back to employment are not those that invest in human capital, but more those that reinforce work incentives and improve the job search capacity of unemployed people (meta-analyses of ALMP evaluation studies are found in Martin and Grubb 2001; Kluve 2006; OECD 2006). These limitations suggest that a more complex understanding of active labour market policy is needed, probably making reference to more than simply two types of active social policy (see Bonoli 2010 for an attempt).

However, even a more sophisticated distinction among types of active social polices may be insufficient to provide an assessment of the activation turn in terms of what it means for fundamental social policy objectives such as equality, social cohesion, and the fight against poverty.

It has been argued that the fact that poverty has not declined during the 2000s is proof of the failure of active social policies tried during this period (Cantillon 2010; Emmenegger et al. 2012). This interpretation is nonetheless problematic. The activation turn has taken place in a context of huge socio-economic transformations, with economic internationalization and structural transformation advancing at a sustained pace. Social change, immigration, family instability, have continued to represent formidable challenges to the cohesion of European societies. For the critique against active social policy to be receivable, one would need to demonstrate that in the face of these profound transformations passive welfare states would have performed better in terms of poverty reduction and that they would have been sustainable.

It is impossible to test this hypothesis for want of a 'counterfactual' or control cases. In fact, the activation turn has been pervasive among OECD countries. Still, shifts in poverty rates between the mid-1990s and the mid-2000s vary across countries, but there is no indication that countries that have lead the activation movement have performed worse than those where social policy has remained more passive. The little evidence we have points in the opposite direction. Activation 'leaders' such as Denmark, the Netherlands or the UK have all experienced reductions or below average increases in poverty rates over the mid-1990s to mid-2000s period (OECD 2008: 129).

A second domain of uncertainty concerns the potential of a social investment strategy. The notion of social investment has been used by many authors often with slightly different meanings. In this book, we follow Jane Jenson (Chapter 2) and understand social investment as a highly interventionist social policy strategy that concentrates its effort on the improvement of a country's human capital. It focuses on the whole lifecourse of individuals and emphasizes investment in children. It also allows for redistribution, for example towards families, since poverty in childhood can have a detrimental impact on child development.

The ideas summed up by the notion of social investment have been rather popular in the 2000s up to the financial crisis, which has dramatically changed the outlook on what governments can do in this field of policy. As a result, there are big uncertainties today with regard to the feasibility of a social policy strategy that requires relatively substantial investments. Hemerijck (Chapter 4) recognizes the difficulties that a social investment strategy faces in the current context. Nonetheless, given the multiple challenges welfare states have to deal with, a social investment approach remains the most convincing move, at least in the medium term.

Third, we have difficulties understanding how the very strong inegalitarian pressures that are affecting Western societies will be translated into policies. The chapters by Crouch and Keune (Chapter 3) and work by Palier and colleagues (Chapter 11; Emmenegger et al. 2012) suggest that an insider-outsider cleavage, or dualization, is the most likely development. There are powerful political reasons why we should expect dualization to gain ground as a development. As argued by Emmenegger et al. (2012), politically powerful constituencies of insiders can use their influence to continually protect their status, while new labour market entrants are considerably more exposed to economic and social risks.

Uncertainty concerns how dualization will develop over time. First, insider and outsider status, if defined in terms of type of labour market contract for example, are not static groups. In all countries, there are transitions between groups that can be more or less important. In the medium term, a substantial proportion of the population can move from one status to the other. This distinguishes dualization from other views on social stratification that tend to be considerably less fluid. It is much more likely for outsider status to be a temporary fact in one person's life than, say, working class status. Second, it is unclear what the development of the insider-outsider cleavage will be at the societal level. As older insiders reach retirement age and exit the demographic pyramid, will they be replaced by new insiders who will politically sustain the dualized social model? If so, then the movement from outsider to insider status must be substantial. Alternatively, the model will wither away, as the stock of insiders diminishes over time. It is difficult to forecast the future of the insider-outsider cleavage, but what is clear is that the notion of dualization has a transient quality, either at the individual or at the societal level.

Fourth, there are big uncertainties concerning the medium- to long-term impact of the 2008 financial crisis and its aftershocks. The debt crisis in southern Europe and the fact that the European banking system is not yet on safe ground suggest that the current climate of radical austerity is likely to persist for some time. This argues against a continued process of welfare state modernization, of the sort we have seen between the mid-1990s and 2008. Though oriented towards supporting economic performance, this process has some upfront costs. On the contrary, the direction of social policymaking since 2008, as shown by Hemerijck (Chapter 4) is clearly towards retrenchment.

At the start of the second decade of the 21st century, the welfare state remains a central institution in modern capitalist societies, strongly supported in the countries hit by the crisis. However, it has undergone substantial changes over the last decade or so, in terms of functions and in terms of its capacity to provide an encompassing protection against key social risks. As argued here, profound uncertainties remain about the significance and the stability of some of these nonetheless important developments. What is certain, however, is that terms like 'resilience', and 'immobility', are much less relevant descriptors of social policy developments now than they were ten years ago.

Note

1. Among many examples we can mention Esping-Andersen (1990) on decommodification or Lister's (2000) on defamilialization. Both concepts can be seen as dimensions that differentiate social policies.

Bibliography

Barbier, J.-C. (2001) *Welfare to Work Policies in Europe. The Current Challenges of Activation Policies*, Paris, Centre d'études de l'emploi.

Barbier, J.-C. (2004) Systems of Social Protection in Europe: Two Contrasted Paths to Activation, and Maybe a Third. In Lind, J., Knudsen, H. & Jørgensen, H. (Eds.) *Labour and Employment Regulation in Europe*, Brussels, Peter Lang.

Barbier, J.-C. & Ludwig-Mayerhofer, W. (2004) Introduction: The Many Worlds of Activation. *European Societies,* 6, 424–36.

Blair, T. & Schröder, G. (1999) *The Third Way/Die neue Mitte,* London/Berlin, Labour Party/SPD.

Bonoli, G. (1999) La Réforme de l'Etat social suisse: Constraintes institutionelles et opportunitiés de changement. *Revue suisse de science politique,* 5, 57–77.

Bonoli, G. (2000) *The Politics of Pension Reform. Institutions and Policy Change in Western Europe,* Cambridge, Cambridge University Press.

Bonoli, G. (2001) Political Institutions, Veto Points, and the Process of Welfare State Adaptation. In Pierson, P. (Ed.) *The New Politics of the Welfare State,* Oxford, Oxford University Press.

Bonoli, G. (2009) Pension Politics in the 21st Century: From Class Conflict to Moderniszing Compromise? In Dingeldey, I. & Rothgang, H. (Eds.) *Governance Of Welfare State Reform. A Cross National and Cross Sectoral Comparison of Policy and Politics,* Cheltenham, Edward Elgar.

Bonoli, G. (2010) The Political Economy of Active Labour Market Policies. *Politics & Society,* 38, 435–57.

Bonoli, G. & Palier, B. (2008) When Past Reforms Open New Opportunities: Comparing Old-age Insurance Reforms in Bismarckian Welfare Systems. *Social Policy and Administration,* 41, 21–39.

Bridgen, P., Meyer, T. & Riedmuller, B. (Eds.) (2007) *Private Pensions Versus Social Inclusion?* Cheltenham, Edward Elgar.

Cantillon, B. (2010) Disambiguating Lisbon. Growth, Employment and Social Inclusion in the Investment State, Antwerp, University of Antwerp, Centre for Social Policy, Working Paper No. 10/07.

Crettaz, E. (2011) *Fighting Working Poverty in Postindustrial Economies. Causes, Trade-offs, and Policy Solutions,* Cheltenham, Edward Elgar.

Emmenegger, P., Häusermann, S., Palier, B. & Seelein-Keiser, M. (2012) *The Age of Dualiztion. The Changing Face of Inequality in Deindustrializing Societies,* New York, Oxford University Press.

Esping-Andersen, G. (1990) *The Three Worlds of Welfare Capitalism,* Cambridge, Polity Press.

Giddens, A. (1998) *The Third Way. The Renewal of Social Democracy,* Cambridge, Polity Press.

Häusermann, S. (2010) *The Politics of Welfare State Reform in Continental Europe,* Cambridge, Cambridge University Press.

Kluve, J. (2006) The Effectiveness of European Active Labour Market Policy, Bonn, IZA Discussion paper 2018.

Kriesi, H. (1995) *Le Système politique suisse,* Paris, Economica.

Levy, J. (1999) Vice into Virtue? Progressive Politics and Welfare Reform in Continental Europe. *Politics and Society,* 27, 239–73.

Lister, R. (2000) Dilemmas in Engendering Citizenship. In Hobson, B. (Ed.) *Gender and Citizenship In Transition,* Londin, Macmillan.

Martin, J. & Grubb, D. (2001) What Works and For Whom: A Review of OECD Countries' Experiences with Active Labour Market Policies. *Swedish Economic Policy Review,* 8, 9–56.

Mitchell, D. (1991) *Income Transfers in Ten Welfare States,* Avebury, Gower Publishing.

Morgan, K. J. (2010) The End of the Frozen Welfare State? Innovation in Work-Family Policies in Western Europe, Montreal, Paper prepared for the 17th Annual Conference of Europeanists, 15–17 April.

Natali, D. (2007) *Vincitori e perdenti. Come cambiano le pensioni in Italia e in Europa* Bologna, Il Mulino.

Natali, D. & Rhodes, M. (2008) The New Politics of Pension Reforms in Continental Europe. In Arza, C. & Kohli, M. (Eds.) *The Political Economy of Pensions: Politics, Policy Models and Outcomes in Europe,* London, Routledge.

OECD (2006) General Policies to Improve Employment Opportunities for All. *Employment Outlook,* 47–126.

OECD (2008) *Growing Unequal. Income Distribution and Poverty in OECD Countries,* Paris, OECD.

Palier, B. (2002) *Gouverner la sécurité sociale. Les réformes du système français de protection sociale depuis 1945,* Paris, Presses Universitaires de France.

Palier, B. & Thelen, K. (2010) Institutionalizing Dualism: Complementarities and Change in France and Germany. *Politics & Society,* 38, 119–48.

Peck, J. (2001) *Workfare States,* New York, Guildford Press.

Pierson, P. (1994) *Dismantling the Welfare State? Reagan, Thatcher, and the Politics of Retrenchment,* Cambridge, Cambridge University Press.

Pierson, P. (1998) Irresistible Forces, Immovable Objects: Post-industrial Welfare States Confront Permanent Austerity. *Journal of European Public Policy,* 5, 539–60.

Pierson, P. (2001) Post-Industrial Pressures on the Mature Welfare States. In Pierson, P. (Ed.) *The New Politics of the Welfare State,* Oxford, Oxford University Press.

Pizzorno A. (1977) Scambio politico e identità collettiva nel conflitto di classe. In Crouch C. and Pizzorno, A. (Eds.) *Conflitti in Europa. Lotte di classe sindacati e stato dopo il '68,* Milan, Etas Libri.

Pizzorno A. (1980) *I soggetti del pluralismo. Classi, partiti, sindacati,* Bologna, Il Mulino.

Regini, M. (1984) 'Le condizioni dello scambio politico. Nascita e declino della concertazione in Italia e Gran Bretagna', *Stato e mercato,* 9, 353–84.

Rhodes, M. (2001) The Political Economy of Social Pacts: 'Competitive Corporatism' and European Welfare Reform. In Pierson, P. (Ed.), *The New Politics of the Welfare State,* Oxford, Oxford University Press.

Rueda, D. (2007) *Social Democracy Inside Out. Partisanship and Labour Market Policy in Industralised Democracies,* Oxford, Oxford University Press.

Scharpf, F. W. (2000) Economic Changes, Vulnerabilities, and Institutional Capabilities. In Scharpf, F. W. & Schmidt, V. A. (Eds.) *Welfare and Work in the Open Economy. Volume I. From Vulnerability to Competitiveness,* Oxford, Oxford University Press.

Taylor-Gooby, P. (2004) New Risks and Social Change. In Taylor-Gooby, P. (Ed.) *New Risks, New Welfare?* Oxford, Oxford University Press.

Torfing, J. (1999) Workfare with Welfare: Recent Reforms of the Danish Welfare State. *Journal of European social Policy,* 9, 5–28.

Weaver, K. (1986) The Politics of Blame Avoidance. *Journal of Public Policy,* 6, 371–98.

Index

Printed in the United Kingdom by the MPG Books Group Ltd